Harvard Graphics® 2.3 Made Easy

Harvard Graphics® 2.3 Made Easy

Mary Campbell

Osborne **McGraw-Hill**

Berkeley New York St. Louis San Francisco
Auckland Bogotá Hamburg London Madrid
Mexico City Milan Montreal New Delhi Panama City
Paris São Paulo Singapore Sydney
Tokyo Toronto

Osborne **McGraw-Hill**
2600 Tenth Street
Berkeley, California 94710
U.S.A.

Osborne **McGraw-Hill** offers software for sale. For information on software translations, or book distributors outside of the U.S.A., please write to Osborne **McGraw-Hill** at the above address.

This book is printed on recycled paper.

Harvard Graphics® 2.3 Made Easy

1234567890 DOC 99876543210

ISBN 0-07-881692-0

To my husband Dave

CONTENTS AT A GLANCE

CONTENTS

ACKNOWLEDGMENTS

I would like to thank the following individuals for their contributions to this book:

Gabrielle Lawrence, for her help with all aspects of the book.

Jody Fordham, for checking the keystrokes in all the examples to ensure that they worked correctly and for enduring the frustration of creating the symbols chart in Appendix D.

Liz Fisher, Jill Pisoni, Janis Paris, Kathy Krause, Barbara Conway, and Judy Wohlfrom at Osborne/McGraw-Hill for all of their help.

Cary Fulbright and Joy Ho at Software Publishing Corporation for all their help.

INTRODUCTION

Harvard Graphics is the best-selling graphics presentation package. It supports the creation of both text and analytical charts. Business users find that the features of this package allow them to communicate their goals and ideas in a more persuasive format. The package supports many customization options and allows the automation of charts with macros or templates. The graphs can be output to a printer, plotter, or 35-millimeter film. It is also possible to create a slide show with graph images. New symbols included with the package allow the creation of professional-looking output, custom tailored to your need. The new Draw Partner utility provided with the package allows additional flexibility in chart modification. In addition to freehand drawing, Draw Partner supports circular text, flipping, rotating, and magnifying images.

ABOUT THIS BOOK

Harvard Graphics 2.3 Made Easy is designed to meet the needs of the new Harvard Graphics user. Although this book covers all the new features of Harvard Graphics 2.3, you will also find it useful if you are working with the more limited features of a prior release. You will find everything you need, from simple installation instructions to step-by-step examples, to create all types of charts and more sophisticated features like templates and macros.

The disk at the back of your book contains a demo that you can use to learn Harvard Graphics basic features, even if you do not as yet have the Harvard Graphics software on your system. This disk also contains macros and templates that you can use to explore these more advanced features. The disk contains a file called README that you can display on your screen or print on your printer. Place the disk in drive A or B and use the DOS PRINT or TYPE command to look at README for a complete description of the disk contents.

If you have not installed Harvard Graphics on your machine, start with Appendix A for step-by-step instructions that will ensure your success.

If you have already installed Harvard Graphics on your system, you can start with Chapter 1 to learn about the wide variety of chart types that you can create with Harvard Graphics. After completing the overview chapter, feel free to select whichever chapter will help you complete the task you are working on. If you want to learn about all the features of the product, you can proceed through the chapters from the beginning and add new skills with each chapter you complete. Although the sequential approach ensures that you will learn about all aspects of the product, feel free to jump ahead at any time if you need a feature in a later chapter. If you decide not to proceed sequentially, look though Appendix C for examples of chart types to help you select the appropriate chapter.

If you have already mastered the basics of Harvard Graphics, you will still find this book beneficial. Since most users initially master the features on a trial-and-error basis, there are probably many features that you have not used. You can learn about these additional options by proceeding sequentially through the chapters. You can also use the table of contents to help you select topics you want to add to your basic skills set.

ORGANIZATION OF THIS BOOK

This book is organized into 13 chapters and 4 appendices. The demo disk included at the back of the book provides a tutorial on basic Harvard Graphics features, as well as macro and template examples. Each chapter is structured to be completed in a single session. As you finish each chapter you will have added a new chart-building skill. Each chapter, is self-contained, so you can complete the later chapters without the need for entering the exercises in the early chapters.

Chapter 1 provides a perspective on the features offered by Harvard Graphics. You are shown a variety of analytical and text charts created with the product, and can use these images to help you select a chart type to meet your needs. Unlike the other chapters, it is not designed for hands-on practice.

Chapter 2 introduces the Chart Data form for the entry of information to a bar chart. The various components of a graph, such as the X- and Y-axes, are introduced. The use of different X-axis types and their effect on a graph are also discussed. Other enhancements to the basic bar graph are covered, and a completed graph is saved and printed.

Chapter 3 provides an opportunity to look at three new chart types. In addition to the basic line and area chart types, you create a high/low/close graph.

Chapter 4 teaches you how to create a pie chart that gives a different perspective than the other graph types. Pie charts are ideal for showing the components of a whole, whether it is budget dollars, sales units, or head count. The examples provide an opportunity to create and print a pie graph and to use options such as color, removing a slice, 3D, and linking.

Chapter 5 teaches you how to import data in several formats, including ASCII, Lotus 1-2-3, and Microsoft Excel. These options eliminate the duplicate efforts required to type data into the package.

Chapter 6 allows you to create text charts for slides or transparencies that you can use in your presentations. Title, bullet, table, and free-form chart examples are included. The use of multiple charts with text and graphics is also covered.

Chapter 7 makes it easy to create an organization chart after a reorganization. This chapter provides examples for entry, editing, and printing of an organization chart.

Chapter 8 introduces you to chart galleries. Rather than perform all the steps needed to create a custom chart, you can select an appealing image from a chart gallery and add your own data with the features you will learn in this chapter.

Chapter 9 shows you how to use the draw features, even if you are not an artist. Geometric shapes, arrows, and lines can be added to the screen automatically. The features of the new Draw Partner software included with the package are accessible with Harvard Graphics. In this chapter, you will also learn how to integrate Harvard Graphics' many symbols into your chart.

Chapter 10 shows you how to create a slide show that combines text and analytical charts created in earlier chapters. You can substitute the names of your own charts if you have not created charts in earlier chapters.

Chapter 11 teaches you how to define the defaults for text size and other option settings. You can use a template when similar charts are created repetitively. You will learn how to create a chartbook for storing templates.

Chapter 12 covers basic macro concepts and techniques. Short but productive examples are used to prove what a time-saver a macro can be for repetitive tasks. You will find the macros in this chapter on the disk at the back of the book.

Chapter 13 covers the accessory products that Harvard Graphics supports. These include additional symbols and templates. You can look through this chapter to help you select products that will add to your chart-building options. This chapter is also of interest to users of previous releases who use accessory products.

Appendix A provides the instructions you may need if Harvard Graphics is not already installed on your machine. Appendix B covers output options other than a printer. Devices such as plotters and the Polaroid Color Palette are also supported and are discussed here. Appendix C provides a sampler of different graph types. Each example indicates the changes made to the default settings to achieve the results shown. Appendix D shows you what each symbol in the various symbol files looks like. This appendix is a handy reference when you want to select a symbol and do not know which file it is in.

The demo disk at the back of the book introduces you to Harvard Graphics 2.3 screens and features. It is informative even if you have not as yet installed Harvard Graphics. Everything you need to run the demo is already on this disk, and it also contains macro and template files.

CONVENTIONS USED IN THIS BOOK

Several conventions have been used throughout this book to expedite your mastery of Harvard Graphics and make the learning process as easy as possible.

- Entries that you must make to duplicate examples in this book are shown in boldface within numbered steps.
- The word "select" is used to indicate a choice you must make from a Harvard Graphics menu.
- The word "type" is used to indicate information you must type from the keyboard.
- Uppercase letters are used for all file names, although you may use either upper- or lowercase letters in your entries.

ADDITIONAL HELP FROM OSBORNE/McGRAW-HILL

Osborne/McGraw-Hill provides top-quality books for computer users at every level of computing experience. To help you build your skills, we suggest that you look for the books in the following Osborne series that best address your needs.

The "Teach Yourself" Series is perfect for people who have never used a computer before or who want to gain confidence in using program basics. These books provide a simple, slow-paced introduction to the fundamental uses of popular software packages and programming languages. The "Mastery Skills" format ensures your understanding of concepts thoroughly before you progress to new material. Plenty of examples and exercises (with answers at the back of the book) are used throughout the text.

The "Made Easy" Series is also for beginners or users who may need a refresher on the new features of an upgraded product. These in-depth introductions guide users step-by-step from the program basics to intermediate-level usage. Plenty of hands-on exercises and examples are used in every chapter.

The "Using" Series presents fast-paced guides that cover beginning concepts and quickly move on to intermediate-level techniques and some advanced topics. These books are written for users already familiar with computers and software, who want to get up to speed with a certain product.

The "Advanced" Series assumes that the user has reached at least an intermediate skill level and is ready to learn more sophisticated techniques and refinements.

The "Complete Reference" Series provides handy desktop references for popular software and programming languages that list every command, feature, and function of the product along with brief but detailed descriptions of how they are used. Books are fully indexed and often include tear-out command cards. The "Complete Reference" Series is ideal for both beginners and pros.

The "Pocket Reference" Series is a pocket-sized, shorter version of The "Complete Reference" Series. It provides the essential commands, features, and functions of software and programming languages for users of every level who need a quick reminder.

The "Secrets, Solutions, Shortcuts" Series is written for beginning users who are already somewhat familiar with the software, and for experienced users at intermediate and advanced levels. This series provides clever tips, points out shortcuts for using the software to greater advantage, and indicates traps to avoid.

Osborne/McGraw-Hill also publishes many fine books that are not included in the series described here. If you have questions about which Osborne books are right for you, ask the salesperson at your local bookstore or computer store.

OTHER OSBORNE/MCGRAW-HILL BOOKS OF INTEREST TO YOU

We hope tht *Harvard Graphics 2.3 Made Easy* will assist you in mastering this fine product and will pique your interest in learning more about other ways to better use your computer.

If you're interested in expanding your skills so you can be even more "computer efficient," be sure to take advantage of Osborne/McGraw-Hill's large selection of top-quality computer books that cover all varieties of popular hardware, software, programming languages, and operating systems. While we cannot list every title here that may relate to Harvard Graphics and to your special computing needs, here are just a few books that complement *Harvard Graphics 2.3 Made Easy.*

DOS Made Easy, by Herbert Schildt, provides a thorough, step-by-step introduction to using both PC-DOS and MS-DOS up through version 3.3, the popular operating system for the IBM PC and compatible personal computers. If you are a beginning computer user or want to brush up on your DOS skills, this book provides plenty of exercises and examples that enable you to grow from a beginner into an intermediate DOS user. *DOS 4 Made Easy,* also by Herbert Schildt, provides the same format and covers MS-DOS and PC-DOS version 4.0

If you're looking for an intermediate-level book, see *Using MS-DOS,* by Kris Jamsa, which covers all versions through 3.3. A fast-paced, hands-on guide, this book is organized into 15-minute sessions that quickly cover basics before discussing intermediate techniques and even some advanced topics. If you have DOS version 4.0, see *Using DOS 4,* also by Kris Jamsa.

For all PC-DOS and MS-DOS users (from beginners who are somewhat familiar with the program to veteran users) with any DOS version up to 3.3, see *DOS: The Complete Reference, Second Edition,* by Kris Jamsa. This book provides comprehensive coverage of every DOS command and feature. Whether you need an overview of the disk operating system or a reference for advanced programming and disk management techniques, you'll find it here.

If you're looking for the best way to get started in telecommunications or to get more out ot the on-line servcies available today, see *Dvorak's Guide to PC Telecommunications.* This book/disk package, written by the internationally recognized computer columnist John Dvorak with programming whiz Nick Anis, shows you how to instantly plug into the world of electronic databases, bulletin boards, and on-line services. The package includes an easy-to-read comprehensive guide plus two disks loaded with outstanding free software, and is of value to computer users at every skill-level.

WHY THIS BOOK IS FOR YOU

If you want to create professional-looking presentations with a minimum of effort, Harvard Graphics can provide the solution. You can create all types of charts, from a simple bulleted list of key presentation points to sophisticated bar and pie charts that present results of projections at a glance. Harvard Graphics allows you to create a slide show with a variety of transition effects suitable for creating a demo for a trade show or management meeting. The drawing features of the package allow you to enhance images with both drawings and symbol entries.

With this book, you will learn how to use the features of the package with practical step-by-step examples to create a variety of charts. This no-fail approach to trying the new features offers a quick way to build a set of graphic skills that can be used in all types of presentations. With the sample charts shown in this book, you can create presentations with enough variety to make each one unique.

Once you have mastered the basics, you can continue to use this book to learn more advanced techniques, like templates and macros. These new skills increase your productivity with the package and reduce the time required to complete a presentation. If you want to explore the options offered by the accessory packages, this book can guide you through the essential features of all the accessories, including the new Draw Partner, the symbol accessories, and the template assortments offered by Software Publishing Corporation.

LEARN MORE ABOUT OTHER SOFTWARE YOU CAN USE WITH HARVARD GRAPHICS

Here is an excellent selection of other Osborne/McGraw-Hill books on software you can use with Harvard Garphics that will help you build your skills and maximize your computer power.

All Harvard Graphics users, beginners and pros, will find useful the handy desktop resource *Harvard Graphics: The Complete Reference* by Cary Jensen, Ph.D. and Loy Anderson, Ph.D. This comprehensive volume provides step-by-step explanations of every Harvard Graphics feature, including its enhanced drawing tools and expanded interactive presentation capabilities. It covers all versions through 2.3.

If you are a beginning spreadsheet user with Lotus 1-2-3, look for *1-2-3 Made Easy* (for Release 1A, 2.0, or 2.01), *1-2-3 Release 2.2 Made Easy,* or *1-2-3 Release 3 Made Easy,* all by Mary Campbell.

If you are just beginning to learn WordPerfect and are unfamiliar with other word processors or even with a computer, see *Teach Yourself WordPerfect 5.1,* by Mary Campbell, a simple introduction to WordPerfect essentials with plenty of hands-on exercises.

WordPerfect 5.1: The Complete Reference, by Karen Acerson, is ideal for all users, both beginners who are somewhat familiar with WordPerfect and for pros. This desktop resource lists every WordPerfect 5.1 command, feature, and function along with brief yet complete discussions of how they are used. If you are using WordPerfect 5.0, see *WordPerfect: The Complete Reference, Series 5 Edition*, also by Karen Acerson.

chapter 1

OVERVIEW AND BASIC FEATURES

Package Overview
Working with the Basic Package Features

Business graphics are not new. For years smart managers have realized it is possible to project a professional image and present a better message with the aid of graphs and charts. Studies indicate that people can absorb more information from a graph than an array of numbers, and they can retain it for a longer time.

Realizing the advantages of graphics came at a significant cost as recently as a few years ago. A manager had to contact a graphic artist or an individual in the graphics department internally to arrange for the appropriate presentation materials. Few presentations were constructed in less than several weeks, which often meant that the graphics materials arrived the afternoon before a big presentation. The cost ranged from several hundred to several thousand dollars, depending on the size and complexity of the charts required.

Today graphics still offer the same advantages, but the costs have decreased dramatically for individuals who use Harvard Graphics. In only hours you can create the charts that add emphasis and clarity to your presentations. Once your raw data is recorded on the Harvard Graphics forms, you can make changes in just a few minutes. All the variety you need to create an interesting presentation is present, with all types of analytical and text charts as well as drawing capability. Symbol files provided with the package even allow you to create logos and high-interest additions to your charts without the need for any artistic talent.

Harvard Graphics supports output to all of the popular printer and plotter devices. In addition it also interfaces to many of the popular film recorders to create 35-millimeter film images. The screen can also serve as an effective presentation vehicle if you use the slide show feature provided with the package in combination with a large screen monitor.

In this chapter you will look at the package features from an overview perspective. This allows you to focus on the chapters that provide information on an immediate need you may have to create a specific type of chart. Following the overview is an introduction to the basic features of the package that you need for all applications. This section of the chapter also will help you skip from chapter to chapter as you need new chart types.

PACKAGE OVERVIEW

Harvard Graphics is one of the most popular graphics packages because of its ease of use and wide variety of chart types. Harvard Graphics is easy to use because it uses a straightforward menu system with options selectable from the keyboard or a mouse. Features are selected with function keys or by completing one of the forms used to define a chart. Default selections allow you to create a chart with very little effort, because size and layout options are provided until you decide how you want to customize the chart. This means that your initial focus can be on defining and entering your data.

The variety of charting options makes this package suitable for creating all types of written and visual presentations. All outputs created by the package are referred to as *charts,* although it is common to refer to some of the more analytical options as graphs. Whether you want analytical graphs, word charts, a varied symbol library, or drawing capability, this one package can meet your needs.

Harvard Graphics supports object-oriented graphics to ease transfer between the file formats of other programs. This means the package can be defined as a *vector-based* graphics package, as opposed to a bit-mapped package. Vector-based packages create their images from lines and curves, whereas *bit-mapped* packages are dependent on individual pixels or dots on the screen. A vector-based package offers one advantage over bit-mapped graphics. The vector graphic image is composed of a series of objects—

symbols, boxes, lines, arrows, and text. Any of these objects can be changed without affecting anything else in the chart. It is also much easier to alter the size of a particular object on the screen with vector-based packages.

Analytical Graphs

Analytical graphs display numeric data in a form that is easier to understand than reviewing the detail contained in the numbers. Reading through detailed sales figures for a product can leave your head spinning and gives no clear picture of the success of the product. On the other hand, presenting the information in summary form on a graph shows an upward or downward sales trend at a glance.

GRAPH BASICS Harvard Graphics provides support for analytical graphs of many different sizes and shapes. Regardless of the graph type, values to be shown on a graph are stored in a series, and each value represents one data element to be recorded on the graph. For example, a series can contain the 1990 sales figures by product; each of the data elements within the series represents the sales of one product in 1990.

Tick marks (little lines extending from an axis) can add accuracy to your interpretation of the values shown in the graph. Most of these graphs are prepared using a vertical Y-axis and a horizontal X-axis, as shown in Figure 1-1. The X-axis is used to show products, years, or other groupings for the data being measured. Each entity measured is shown by a point along the X-axis. The Y-axis is used to measure quantity, such as sales amount, head count, number of automobiles, or bushels of wheat produced. Harvard Graphics provides options that control the scale used to label the measurements on the Y-axis.

Titles can be used for the graph axes and at the top of the graph to describe the data presented. Harvard Graphics allows for a title line and two lines of subtitle entries if you need them. Legends distinguish one series from another when multiple series are shown on a graph. Footnotes provide you with an option for crediting the source of a graph.

GRAPH TYPES Although Harvard Graphics provides a wide variety of graph types, your selection depends on the type of data you want to show on the graph. As you gain more experience with the package, you will get better at selecting the best graph type to present your message. The chapters of this book that discuss graphs offer suggestions that can help you make these selections.

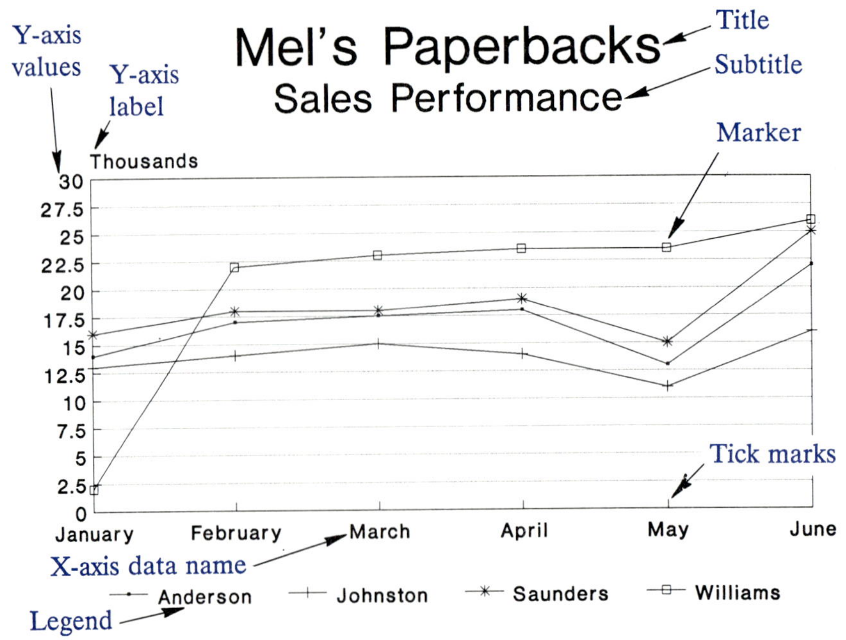

FIGURE 1-1. Graph terminology

Bar charts consist of one or more sets of bars, the height of which is controlled by the data in the series. Bar charts are an excellent choice for presenting data that has changed over time, such as sales volume, the number of customers, or the number of retail outlets. The most basic type of bar graph, which you can create in only a few minutes, is shown in Figure 1-2.

The options and enhancements for bar graphs make this one graph type seem as if it were actually many types. When you want to show data grouped by year, an overlap bar chart can place the value for each series in a given year within the same group. A stack bar chart places the values in each series atop the values from the corresponding previous series. Cumulative bar graphs combine data elements from one series. A cumulative bar graph adds the values from a previous data element to the new data element, making the height of the last bar equivalent to the total of all the values in a series. This type of bar graph can be an excellent way to show total sales of a product during the first six months of the product life. You can use horizontal bars to rank the performance of a number of products. Other enhance-

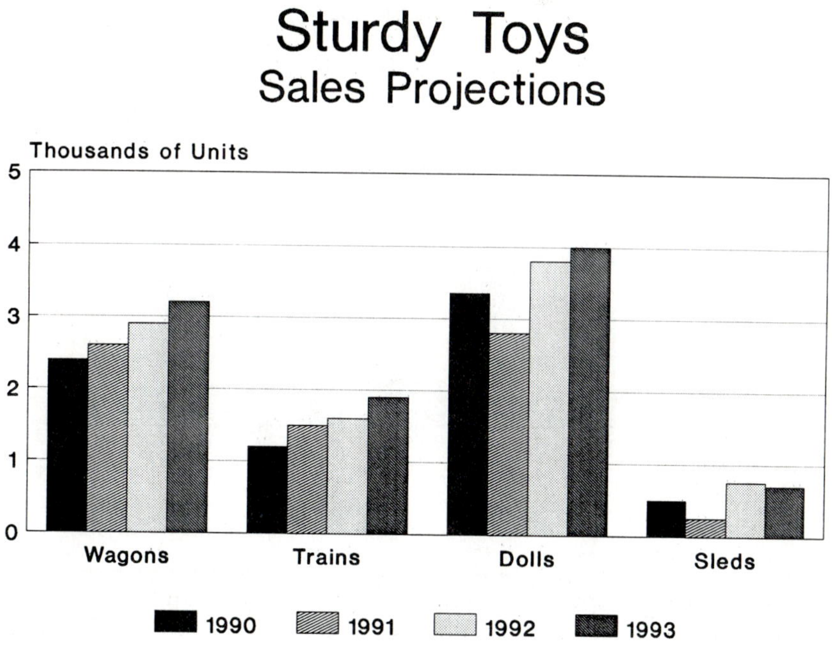

FIGURE 1-2. Plain bar graph

ments, like a 3D effect, can be used to improve aesthetics or to draw attention to product sales increases or decreases. Figure 1-3 adds 3D effects to the graph shown in Figure 1-2.

Pie charts are ideal when you want to communicate what part each series value is of a whole. Although pie charts do not use an X- and Y-axis, it is easy to create a simple pie graph such as the one in Figure 1-4. You can also enhance a pie by adding 3D, exploding a pie slice by pulling it away from the pie, and cutting a pie to link it to a column chart as shown in Figure 1-5.

High/low/close graphs are the perfect way to chart stock and bond prices over time. Actually these charts provide a way to show up to four series of data in one high/low/close chart. At a glance you can see if the opening price of the stock or commodity has held relatively constant, while the high and low values may vary considerably. You will appreciate the ability to change the Y-axis values, because it normally is not possible to show the data effectively if 0 is used as the minimum value shown on the scale. Figure 1-6

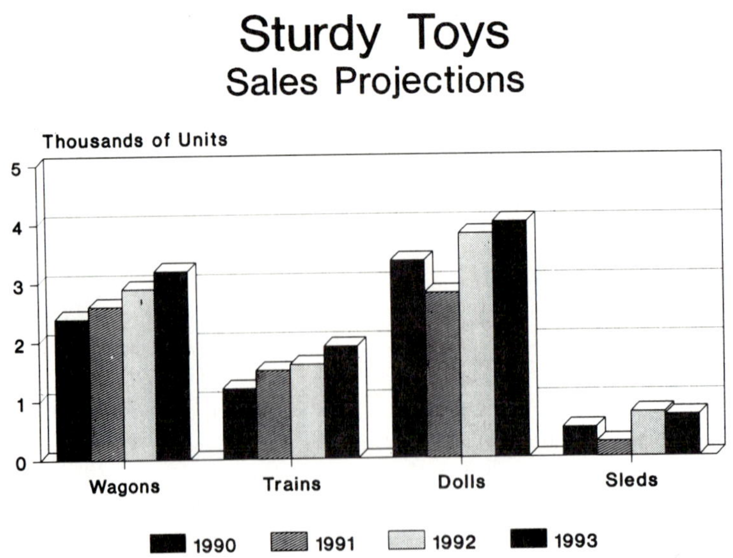

FIGURE 1-3. 3D effect added to bar graph

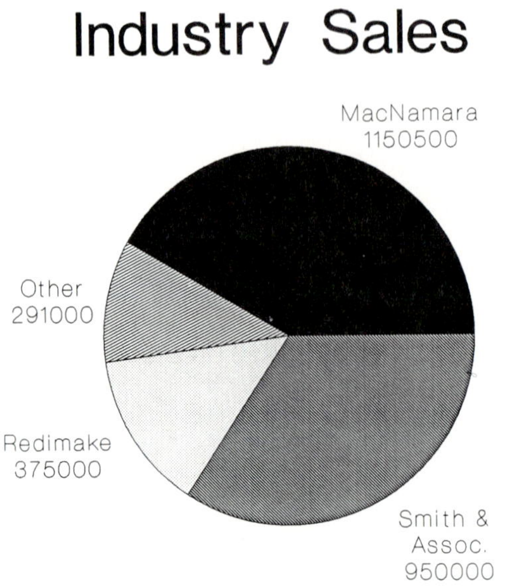

FIGURE 1-4. Pie graph

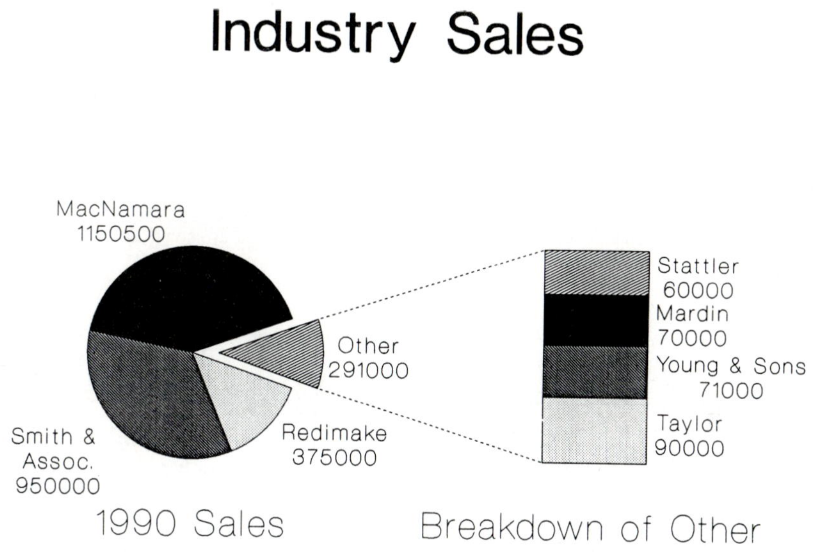

FIGURE 1-5. Linking a pie chart to a column chart

shows the effectiveness of a high/low/close chart and bar chart in presenting market data. This chart also shows how you can include additional series of data such as the bar chart displaying the volume for each day.

Line graphs are another way to show a trend in your data over time. If you have a large number of data points, a line chart can prove to be a better choice then a bar chart, since each data point does not require a bar. Line charts can be smooth, as in a trend line chart. The connection between the points in the line can take on a zigzag appearance if a curve line is not used for the graph. Figure 1-1 showed an example of a line graph.

Area graphs are created in the same way as line graphs except the area underneath the line is filled with a pattern or color. Area charts are striking in appearance and can be used in combination with other graph types, like a line graph. For example, in Figure 1-7 total cost is represented as an area chart and salary costs are shown as a line chart.

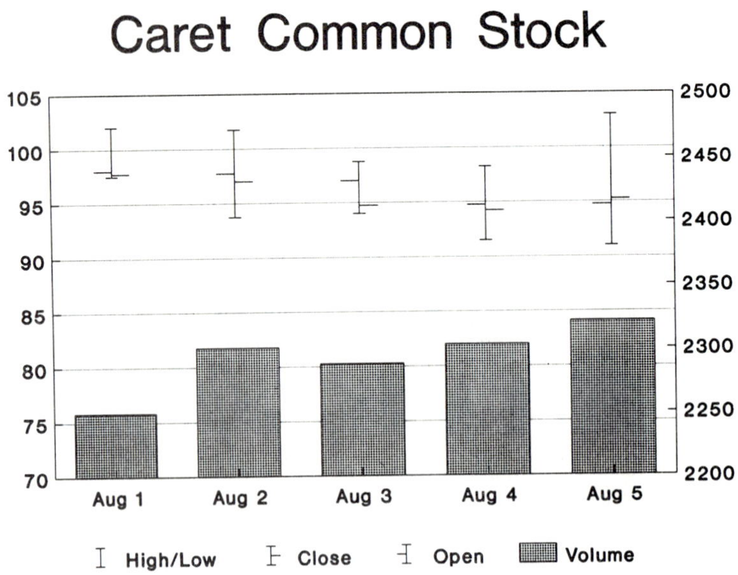

FIGURE 1-6. High/low/close chart

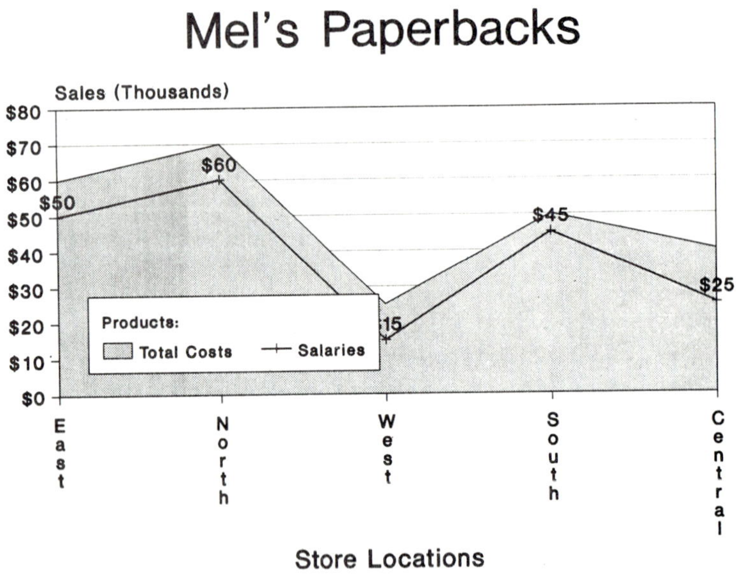

FIGURE 1-7. Area/line combination chart

Staff Meeting
March 12, 1989

- Discuss hiring needs
  - Programmers
  - Clerical staff
- Assign temporary construction parking
  - North lot closed 4/1 to 6/15
  - East lot closed 4/1 to 5/10
  - Shuttle service from Front St.
- Review current projects
- Request volunteers for charity breakfast
- Discuss company picnic

FIGURE 1-8. Bullet chart with two bullets styles

Text Charts

Text charts are word charts. They may be highlights from your presentation, a few important statistics, the names of several good books, or the steps defined to complete a project.

Harvard Graphics provides several types of text charts. Title text charts allow you to create a title page for a report or a title page for a presentation. Simple and bullet lists allow you to enter a series of short items or phrases. If you choose bullets, a special symbol is used to the left of each entry as long as you allow a blank line between each. Figure 1-8 shows a bullet chart with two different styles of bullets. Column charts can have either two or three columns and allow you to place data on the screen in a clean columnar fashion. You might use a column chart to report results by sales person. The name could be placed in the first column and the results in the rows immediately thereafter.

Free-form charts, as the name implies, are entered free-form without regard to rules. You can place any text anywhere on the chart. You can use free-form charts to enter tables with more than three columns. Free-form charts are the best choice when the text you need to enter is longer than usual.

Organization Charts

Organization charts consist of boxes with the names of individuals or organizational units inside each box. A hierarchical structure is normally presented to portray relationships, as in the chart for Mesopotamia Metals found in Figure 1-9.

Chart Galleries

Harvard Graphics 2.3 provides a selection of predefined charts. Similar chart styles are grouped into *galleries.* Rather than selecting a chart type and defining all the options, you can save time by choosing the gallery option that meets your needs. Figure 1-10 shows the selection of galleries available to you.

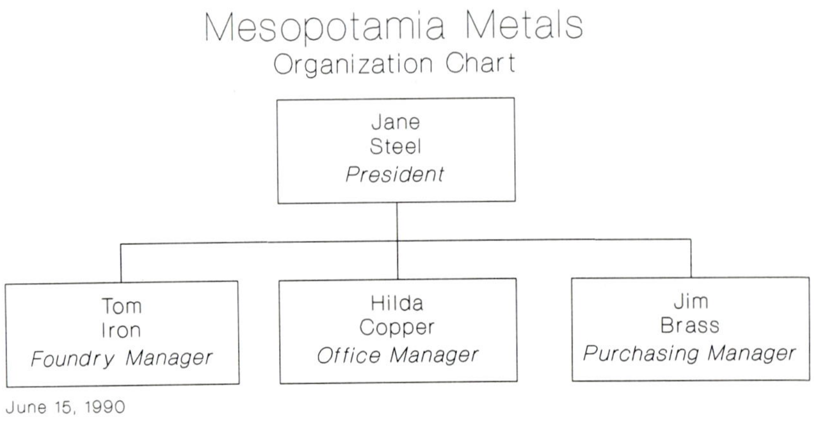

FIGURE 1-9. Organization chart

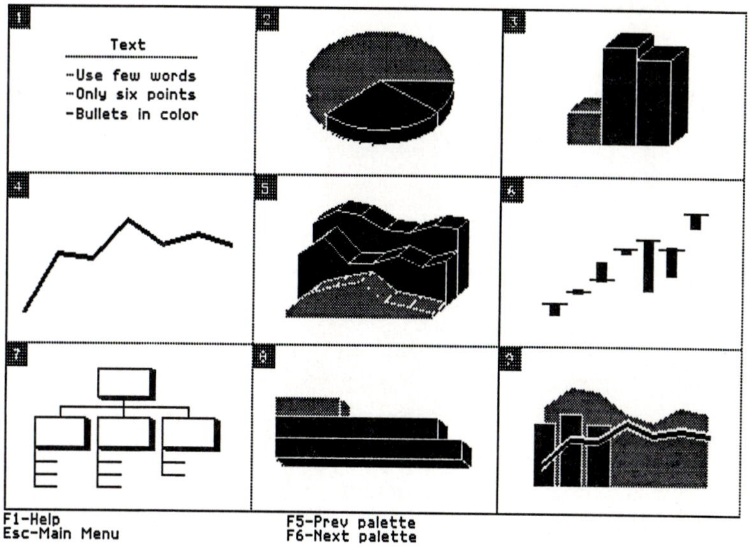

FIGURE 1-10. Initial Gallery screen

Drawing and Symbols

Even if you are not an artist, Harvard Graphics drawing features can improve your presentations. You can use the drawing features to create straight-line charts such as PERT diagrams to assist you with project management activities. PERT (Program Evaluation and Review Techniques) charts diagram a sequence of activities that need to be completed on a project.

The drawing features can add emphasis to a particular line on an existing chart. With just a little artistic talent, you can add a small drawing to a chart. The library of over 500 high-quality symbols from which to select allows you to call up professional-looking symbols and add them to your chart. Features for moving and sizing these symbols make it easy to incorporate them into your charts. Figure 1-11 is a distribution diagram that shows the flow of a product from the source of the raw material to the final delivery of the end product. The symbols on this chart are easier to comprehend than a chart

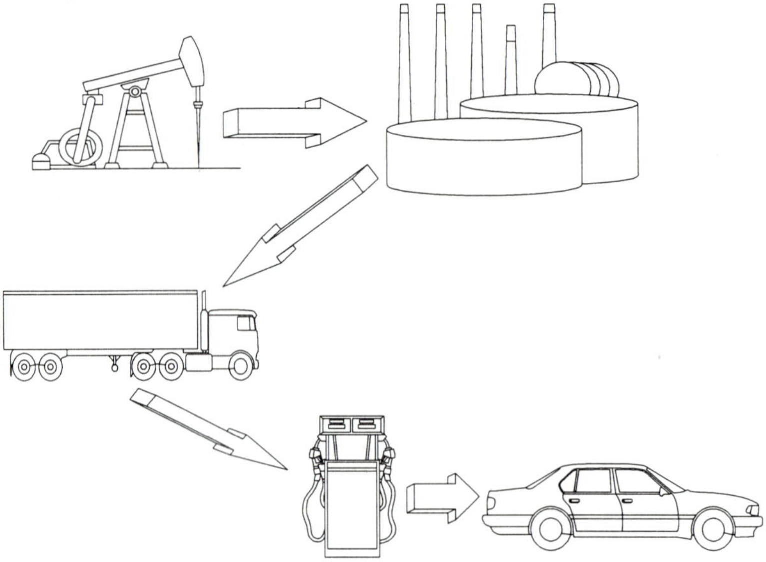

FIGURE 1-11. Distribution diagram

created with words, and it takes less than ten minutes to create because it is composed of symbols from the Harvard Graphics symbol library.

Draw Partner, originally marketed as an accessory product, is now provided with Harvard Graphics 2.3. A preset link to Draw Partner makes it easier for you to use the powerful features of this product. You can use Draw Partner's features to flip, rotate, and magnify charts. New, sophisticated features allow you to include freehand drawings, arcs, and polygons. Since Draw Partner and Harvard Graphics are now combined, you will be able to edit charts in Harvard Graphics after you have made Draw Partner enhancements.

Slide Show

You can create a slide show of charts with Harvard Graphics. A series of sophisticated options allows you to display a ScreenShow on a computer screen. You can add transition effects that control how one screen replaces another and determine the time that slides remain on the screen. The names of transition options such as Rain, Fade, Weave, Blinds, and Iris indicate how the transition from one screen to another can be handled. Shows can be viewed from beginning to end, or you can start anywhere in the middle.

New HyperShow features further enhance a ScreenShow by allowing you to add as many as 20 buttons per chart. You can use these buttons to modify the flow of a presentation. These features allow you to respond to the needs of your audience, altering your presentation while you are making it. New animated slide sequences also allow you to intersperse some sophisticated effects in your presentation.

Other support features include a utility called ShowCopy to copy all the charts in a ScreenShow and practice card capabilities for keeping notes on your presentation.

Templates

A *template* is nothing more than a chart type and a set of options that you define ahead of time. It is useful if you must create many similar charts. You can use your templates every time you create a new chart or just occasionally when you need another version of a popular chart. The name that you use when you save the template determines if it replaces Harvard Graphics defaults for the chart type or if it is just available for your selection.

Chartbooks

Chartbooks are collections of templates that you may want to access on a regular basis. You can store all of your regular chart designs in one or more chartbooks to provide organization and quick access.

Import Features

With Harvard Graphics you can import data from Lotus 1-2-3, Excel, and Symphony. You can even set a default import directory to make it easy to access data from your favorite spreadsheet package. With Harvard Graphics

2.3 you can even use named ranges in your Excel and 1-2-3 files and access these ranges from Harvard Graphics. Once you activate the Import feature you can use F6 to view the named ranges on a worksheet.

Tutorial

Harvard Graphics provides a separate tutorial from the one included on the disk that comes with this book. To use the Harvard Graphics tutorial you must install both your program files and the tutorial files. To start the tutorial once it is installed, you type **hgtutor** with the Harvard Graphics directory active. If you have a monochrome screen you would type **hgtutor mono.**

Support for Other Applications

Harvard Graphics 2.3 allows you to create a link for as many as eight applications that can be accessed through its application menu. Draw Partner and a slide service program (you transmit screens to a service that develops your slides overnight and sends them to you) are linked as applications when you first install Harvard Graphics. You can add applications like DOS if you want to run DOS commands without leaving Harvard Graphics. You can also add accessories like Quick-Charts for quick access to their features. To add an application, all you need to do is supply the name of the application, its memory requirements, and the command needed to start the application from the Harvard Graphics directory. When you exit the other application, you will be back in Harvard Graphics.

Enhancement Products

Although the realm of objects in Harvard Graphics itself will keep you busy with selections for some time to come, Software Publishing also markets a series of enhancement products that expand its capabilities even further. Quick-Charts contains templates for many different chart styles. You can select one of these predefined templates, enter your data, and display a graph in the exact format selected.

The Business Symbols package provides over 300 business symbols suitable for use as logos or chart enhancements, or to liven up your handouts. The Military Symbols package adds a variety of symbols for all branches of the military service.

The U.S. MapMaker product provides a U.S. map with state outlines and city coordinates. You can use these maps to look at regional sales figures or demographics.

Network Version

If you are using Harvard Graphics on a network, you will want to use the special network version. This release of the software allows up to five people to use Harvard Graphics on a network simultaneously. File locking is not part of either the standard or networked version of the package, so it is possible for more than one user to share a file.

WORKING WITH THE BASIC PACKAGE FEATURES

At this point it is assumed that your software package is installed and you are ready to explore the preliminary features of the package that are needed to create a chart of any type. (If you have not as yet installed your package, turn to Appendix A and complete the steps in the simple procedure.) You may feel you do not need to try the new instructions presented in this section, but you will find that you master the package in a shorter period of time if you actually try the examples here.

In this section you will learn how to use either the keyboard or the mouse with the package, how to save a file, and how to change default settings. You will continue to use these skills as you proceed through the book.

Starting Harvard Graphics

If you have not yet installed your package, read Appendix A before proceeding any further since you must install the package as a first step. To start

Harvard Graphics with a hard disk system, activate the drive containing Harvard Graphics. If you have installed the package as directed in Appendix A, this is subdirectory HG. Type **CD\HG** at the C> prompt. You can also copy the batch file from the accompanying disk to the root directory of your C drive and start the package without changing directories by simply typing **HG**.

After you start the package, the title screen briefly displays the Main Menu from which you make your selections. The entries to change the directory and start the program can both be in lowercase if you prefer.

Quitting Harvard Graphics

When you are ready to end your Harvard Graphics session, you can choose Exit from the Main Menu. If the Main Menu is not on your screen you will need to press ESC until the Main Menu appears. The number of times that ESC must be pressed varies depending on your activity at the time you press it. Sometimes pressing ESC once is sufficient, but other times you must press it several times. Since there is no way to escape past the Main Menu, you need not be concerned with pressing it too many times.

Getting Help

The F1 key is known as the Help key and provides information on the features of the package right on your screen. If you are looking at a screen that offers you options, pressing F1 displays a screen that describes each option. If you are looking at a screen that requires entries, the help screen displays information about each of the blank spaces on the screen. This type of help is referred to as *context-sensitive help* because the package attempts to supply exactly the information you need.

Mouse Versus Keyboard

Harvard Graphics supports the use of both the mouse and the keyboard. You do not compromise package features when you select one or the other, because you can access all aspects of the package regardless of which approach you choose. The factors that determine your selection are the availability of a mouse device attached to your machine, and your preference. If your desktop is as messy as mine, you may prefer to use the keyboard rather than attempting to roll your mouse over books, papers, and coffee cups.

KEYBOARD SPECIFICS Many of the keyboard keys are self-defining—you know when you press them the effects they will have. The UP ARROW key, for instance, moves you up one line, and the PGDN key moves you down a page in a multipage screen. If you have used the keyboard to work with other packages, you will find the transition to Harvard Graphics easy. Although some of the keys may have new functions, many have the same function as you find in other programs. Table 1-1 provides a list of the various keys you can use with Harvard Graphics and the function that each key performs. You should scan this list quickly to ensure that there are no surprises.

Key	Function
Arrow keys	Move the cursor one space or line in the indicated direction
TAB	Moves the cursor to the next field or item
SHIFT-TAB	Moves the cursor to the previous field or item
CTRL-RIGHT ARROW	Moves the cursor right one word
CTRL-LEFT ARROW	Moves the cursor left one word
HOME	Moves to the first field or item on the screen
END	Moves to the last field or item on the screen
INSERT	Turns insert mode on and off. When insert is on, anything you type is added in front of the cursor. When insert is off, what you type replaces characters on the screen
BACKSPACE	Moves the cursor to the left one character, deleting the character in its path
DELETE	Deletes the character above the cursor
CTRL-DELETE	Deletes an entire field or line

TABLE 1-1. Special Keyboard Keys

Making a mistake is no problem with Harvard Graphics. If you select the wrong menu item, press ESC and select again. If you type a character incorrectly, press BACKSPACE and then retype your entry. The keys in Table 1-1 provide other options you might want to use to expedite your corrections.

Harvard Graphics has assigned functions to the keys labeled F1 through F10 or F12 located at the left side or the top of the keyboard. Some of these assignments vary from screen to screen. However, the function-key assignments from the Main Menu remain the same; you can always expect the results shown in Table 1-2.

Throughout this book, directions are provided for keyboard entry. If you are using a mouse, refer to the next section for a definition of how you can use a mouse in Harvard Graphics.

Speed Keys

Harvard Graphics 2.3 supports the use of speed keys to activate features quickly. You can use a speed key rather than making a series of menu selections. For example, you can save a chart by selecting Get/Save/Remove

Key	Function
F1	Activates help
F2	Draws the chart that is currently defined. If no chart is defined, your screen is blank
F3	Allows you to access the DOS shell to run one of as many as eight applications
F4	Checks the spelling in your chart
F7	Allows you to change the size and placement of a chart on the page
F8	Allows you to change the default options for the current chart
F10	Selects the current option from the menu

TABLE 1-2. Function-key Assignments from the Main Menu

from the Main Menu and choosing Save chart. To use the speed key option to accomplish the same task, all you need to do is press CTRL-S. Other speed key options are shown in Table 1-3.

MOUSE ACTIONS A mouse is a device that rolls across the desktop to allow you to select objects or commands. The buttons on the top of the mouse are pressed to activate certain features. Harvard Graphics equates the left mouse button to the ENTER key and the right mouse button to the ESC key. This means that you can press the left mouse button to select the current menu option and the right mouse button to back out of the last command you requested.

To use the mouse to select function-key options, you must press both mouse buttons at once. This action toggles on and off the function-key display at the bottom of the screen. Once the display is visible, you can use the mouse to select the desired function key. Of course you can continue to use the function keys or any other key, because the mouse is designed to be used only when you find it more convenient. Table 1-4 provides a summary of these functions for you.

It is important to note that a mouse must be installed before it is operational. The mouse must be plugged in and its software run before you can use it in Harvard Graphics.

Key Sequence	Action
CTRL-D	Activates Draw Partner
CTRL-G	Gets a chart
CTRL-L	Imports Lotus data
CTRL-P	Prints a chart
CTRL-R	Activates Draw/Annotate features
CTRL-S	Saves a chart
CTRL-X	Imports Excel data

TABLE 1-3. Speed Keys

Button or Combination	Action	Keyboard Equivalent
Right button	Removes menu or leaves screen	ESC
Both buttons followed by left button	Selects function key	Function key
Move cursor off page	Displays the next or previous page	PGDN or PGUP
Left button	Select from the menu	ENTER or F10
Left button	Set an option	SPACEBAR

TABLE 1-4. Mouse Features

Menu Selections

The Harvard Graphics Main Menu, shown in Figure 1-12, appears on the screen as soon as you start the package. When you select a menu option, Harvard Graphics takes one of several actions. It may execute your request immediately, although a more likely response is to display a submenu or list of files from which to choose to refine your selection. A list similar to the one in Figure 1-13 displays when Get/Save/Remove and Get Chart is selected to allow you to select the name of the file you want to retrieve. You can use the mouse or UP ARROW and DOWN ARROW to move between the options, and press ENTER when the desired selection is highlighted.

Occasionally Harvard Graphics highlights a menu selection other than the first option. This situation occurs when you have made changes to a chart but have not saved them. When you choose Get/Save/Remove, the submenu automatically has the Save chart option highlighted, since this is the most likely selection.

Sometimes when you make a menu selection, an overlay or form is displayed, as in Figure 1-14. This overlay allows you to specify additional options. You can move from option to option by pressing either TAB or ENTER. The various options frequently are referred to as *fields,* since they contain one piece of important information for the current task. Once you activate a field, you can press the spacebar to cycle through the various

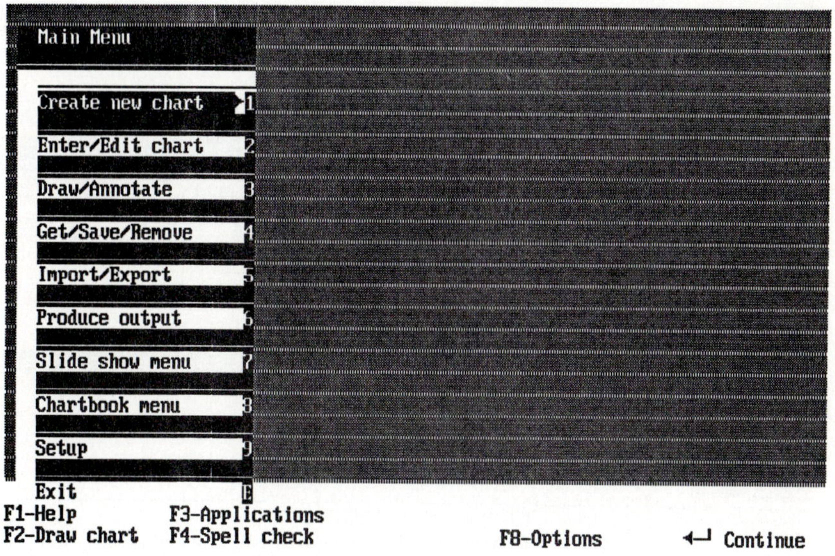

FIGURE 1-12. Main Menu

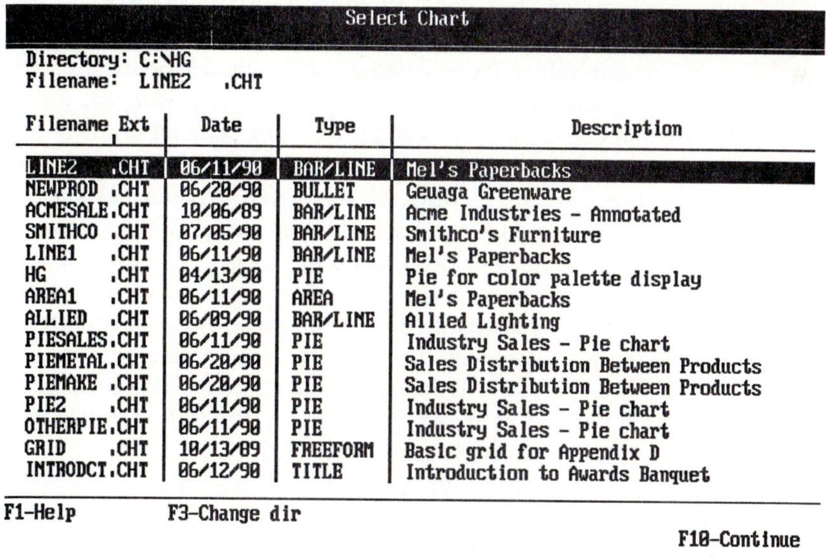

FIGURE 1-13. List of chart files displayed

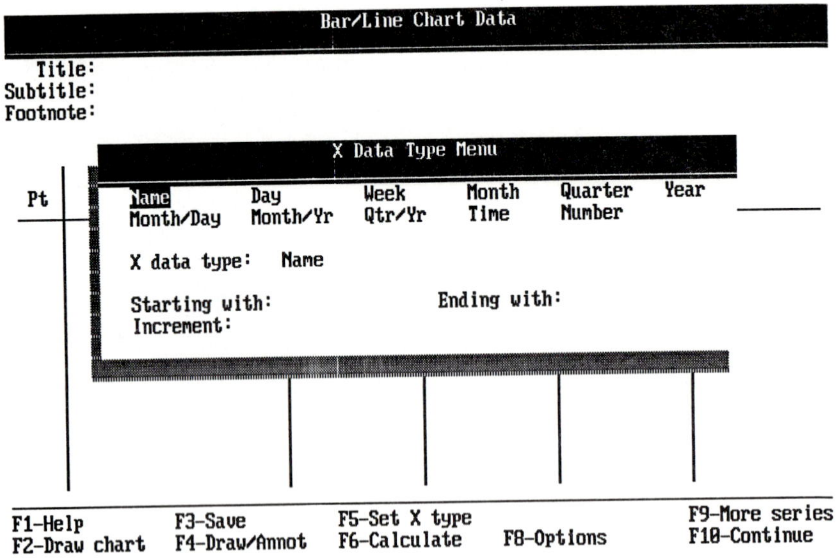

FIGURE 1-14. Data Type Menu overlay

alternatives for that field. In a location where there is no default entry showing, you must type an entry.

You can select menu options with the keyboard by either typing the number to the right of the menu description or using the arrow keys to move to the item and pressing ENTER. Typing the first letter of a menu selection highlights the next selection that starts with that letter, but to actually select it you must press ENTER. If you make a menu selection in error, press ESC and Harvard Graphics returns to the previous screen.

To make menu selections using the mouse, you roll the mouse across the work surface to position the highlight. This can save a significant amount of time on overlay screens with many options since you do not need to proceed sequentially through all the options. The mouse buttons act the same as ENTER and ESC. Once your selection is highlighted you can press the left mouse button to make the selection. Press the right mouse button if you decide you want to back out of the selection.

At any time during the graph definition process, you can switch between the mouse and the keyboard without altering any of the work you are doing. The choice is intended to be a matter of convenience that allows you to mix and match entries and selections.

Output

Harvard Graphics has conveniently organized the creation of all output under the Produce output option in the Main Menu. You use this selection whether or not you print to a printer or draw the chart on a plotter. This same selection is also valid when you use a film recorder for the output image.

Information on the various output devices and definitions of the default setups are found in Appendix B. In this appendix you will learn how to define up to four output devices including a film recorder.

Your monitor is your output device if you create a ScreenShow. The quality of your output depends on the type of monitor and graphics adapter you have. For example, a monochrome monitor cannot display color. You can choose from a wide variety of color monitors and graphics adapters. They vary in the number of pixels or dots per inch that can be used to create the image. For instance, a CGA monitor consists of a pixel grid that is 320 dots by 200 dots and can use 4 colors, whereas a VGA monitor has 640 by 480 pixels and can use 16 colors. Some film recorder devices will only be able to produce output of the same quality level as the monitor.

Saving Files

When you create a chart that you want to save, you can use the Get/Save/Remove option in the Main Menu. You then select Save chart from the submenu. Pressing the CTRL-S speed key is a shortcut that provides the same result as these two menu selections. With either approach, you are presented with the Save Chart form. You must enter a filename in accordance with DOS rules. The name should consist of from one to eight characters with no spaces or special symbols except the underscore. Although my suggestions are even more rigid than the DOS requirement, they help ensure compatibility with subsequent releases of DOS. Unlike most packages, Harvard Graphics allows you to enter up to 40 characters of description in addition to the filename. This descriptive information makes it easy to locate files when you want to retrieve them at a later time. If you do not make an entry, the default is to display the chart title in the Description field.

If you want to save a file in a disk directory other than the current directory, type the entire pathname when you enter the filename. If the current directory is C:\HG and you want to save the current chart as BAR1 in the subdirectory HGCHARTS, you must change the name of the directory in the first field on the form.

Once you save a file, you have a permanent copy of it on disk. You can use the Get/Save/Remove option or the CTRL-G speed key to get a chart at any time. After you specify the name of the file, this command brings the file into memory and allows you to work with it. Files remain in memory until you exit Harvard Graphics, load another file, or tell Harvard Graphics to erase the data after selecting Create new chart from the Main Menu.

Changing Directories

Changing the storage location for one or two charts is a simple process. When you need to change the location for a file, it is easy to make the change on the Save Chart form. If you find yourself changing the location with each file you save, you should change the drive and/or the directory. The directory you use must exist at the time you make the change. If you need to establish a new directory, use the DOS MD command to make the change. You can make this change by following these steps:

1. Select Setup from the Main Menu.
2. Select Defaults from the submenu.
3. Type the new drive and/or directory location and press F10 (Continue).

The screen shown in Figure 1-15 shows the Default Settings screen to change the directory and other chart defaults. The subdirectory you enter in the Data directory field must be created with the DOS MD command before attempting to make the change. All of the files you get or save from this point will default to the new drive or directory that you specify.

Changing Defaults

Figure 1-15 shows that default options other than the chart directory can be changed. You can access these changes at any time with selections from Setup Defaults, using the same screen you used for making the directory change in the previous section. Your changes remain in effect for the current session and subsequent sessions.

```
                              Default Settings

 Data directory:
 Import directory:
 Symbol directory:  D:\HG\symbols

 Gallery directory: D:\HG\gallery
 Gallery filename:  wpick

 Default chartbook:
 Default palette:   hg23

 Orientation: ▸Landscape    Border: ▸None       Font: ▸Executive
               Portrait              Single            Traditional
                                     Double            Square serif
                                     No margin         Roman
                                                       Sans serif
 Menu colors:  Color scheme 1                          Script
               Color scheme 2                          Gothic
               Color scheme 3
              ▸Monochrome
________________________________________________________________________
F1-Help        F3-Intl formats
                                                            F10-Continue
```

FIGURE 1-15. Changing the chart directory and chart defaults

If you want to change the defaults for the current chart, you can use (F8) (Options) from the Main Menu. The changes you make will not be permanent and will only remain until you create a new chart or retrieve another chart from disk.

PERMANENTLY CHANGING DEFAULTS To change defaults permanently, return to the Main Menu and select Setup Defaults. The cursor will be on the Data directory field. To move to other default fields you can use the (TAB) key. Once the field that you want to change is highlighted, you can use the spacebar to change the default entry to one of the other possibilities in the list. For example, to change the Font field from the default of Executive to one of the other entries, select Setup Defaults, press (TAB) nine times to move to the Font field, and then press the spacebar until the font you want to use is highlighted. Other default options can be changed with the same procedure. The change is in effect for all graphs you create in the current session, unless you make additional changes. Other defaults you can change include screen colors, the default drive/directory for files you plan to import, borders around the outside of charts, the default orientation for print output, the symbol and gallery directory, and the default chartbook and palette.

CHANGING DEFAULTS FOR THE CURRENT CHART To change defaults for the current chart, press ESC until the Main Menu is on the screen and press F8 (Options). Your options are more limited than with the Setup command in the menu, and they are temporary rather than permanent. You can still change the font (character style), border style, default print orientation, and the default palette.

chapter 2

LEARNING GRAPH BASICS WITH BAR CHARTS

Getting Started
Adding Information to the Chart
Changing Data
Printing Your Charts
Using Different Types of Bar Graphs
Making Adjusments to Other Graph Features
Changing the Text for Graphs
Checking Your Spelling

Bar charts consist of a series of vertical or horizontal bars that represent your data. The length or height of each bar is determined by the size of each piece of information, so it is easy to make relative comparisons between data values.

Bar charts are one of the most popular forms of analytical charts because they are so versatile. You can use bar charts as a summary visual aid with a verbal presentation, or present them alone in a newsletter, advertising material, or bulletin board summary.

Bar charts allow you to present relationships in data for several time periods and to show several categories of data in one chart. The colors or patterns you use to differentiate the bars can make a dramatic statement to your audience, which will help convey your message. The bold statement made by a bar chart allows your audience to absorb many important pieces of information from the chart with a minimum of discussion.

You might find a bar chart to be a persuasive way to present the increase in sales for your territory over a two-year period. Bar charts are also an excellent means of emphasizing the differences between series of data. If certain products are contributing more to company profits than others, a bar chart that presents profit data for several product offerings over a period of time can make this point clear to your audience.

Bar charts use an X-axis and a Y-axis to create the basic form for the chart. As shown in Figure 2-1, the X-axis is the horizontal axis and is used to show the classifications you establish for your data, if you create a bar chart with the default bar type of vertical. You might use years, months, products, regions, or ages to mark the points along the X-axis. The vertical Y-axis always measures the quantity when bars are shown vertically. This quantity can be expressed in a variety of units, such as dollars, number of units sold,

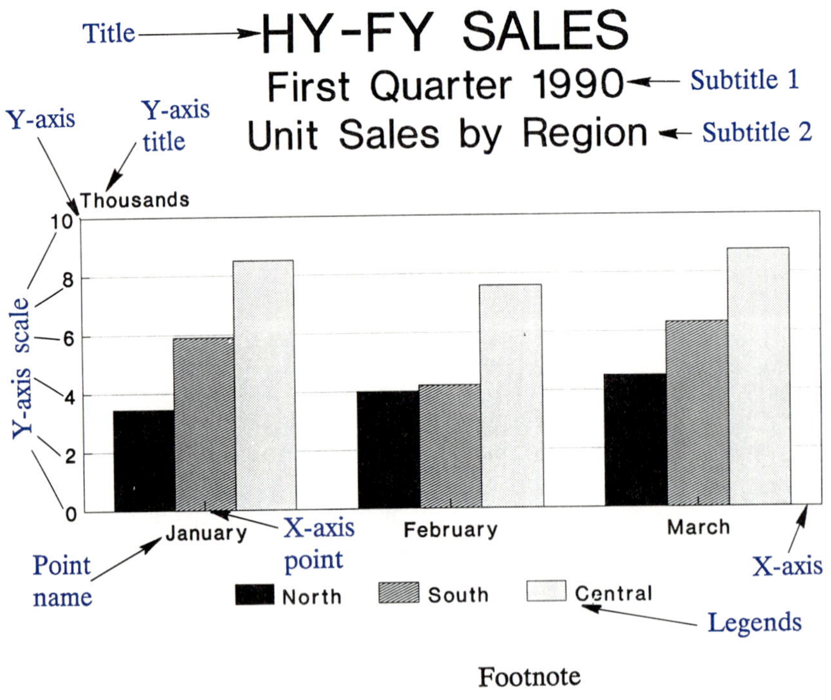

FIGURE 2-1. Bar chart with major components labeled

weight, or number of employees. Adding X- and Y-axis titles will make it clear to anyone looking at your graph what classifications and units of measure you have selected. X-axis data names allow you to mark each point on the X-axis.

In this chapter you will enter data and then create a bar chart in only a few minutes. After completing this basic chart, you will build on its format and create more sophisticated charts. You will have an opportunity to add additional data to the graph as well as try stacked bars, three-dimensional (3D) bars, and other customization options. In Chapter 8, you will learn how to choose bar charts from a gallery for an instant color-coordinated chart design.

GETTING STARTED

Figure 2-2 shows a bar chart that you can create with only a few minutes of work. A title and subtitle appear at the top of the chart. The one series of

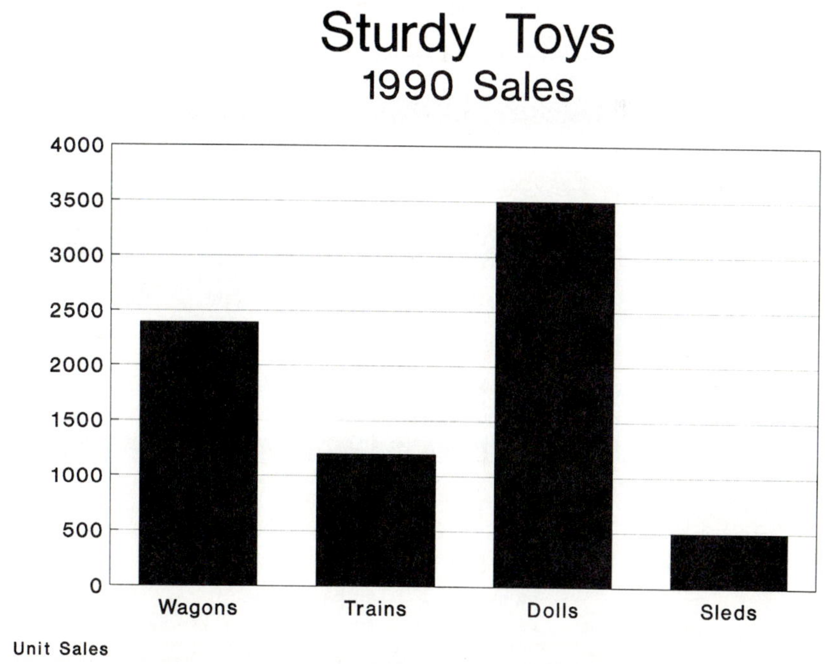

FIGURE 2-2. Quick bar chart for 1990 data

data on the chart represents sales figures for the four top products sold by Sturdy Toys during 1990. The data series has no legend or description since the titles at the top make it clear what the data on the chart represents.

Follow these steps to enter the data and display the chart:

1. Select Create new chart from the Main Menu.
2. Select Bar/Line.

The X Data Type Menu shown in Figure 2-3 is displayed.

3. Press F10 (Continue) to accept the default X data type of Name.

This selection allows you to enter the names of products to represent each of the points on the X-axis. The Bar/Line Chart Data form shown in Figure 2-4 appears on your screen.

4. Type **Sturdy Toys** and press ENTER.

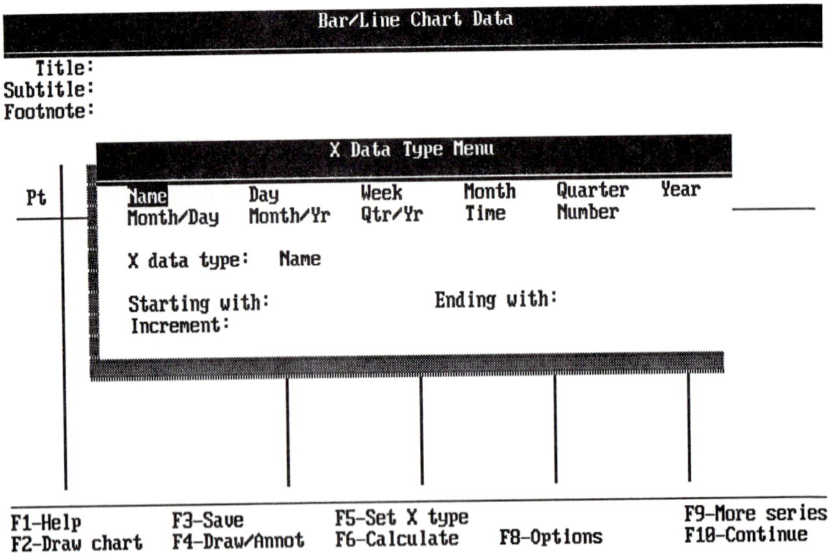

FIGURE 2-3. X Data Type Menu

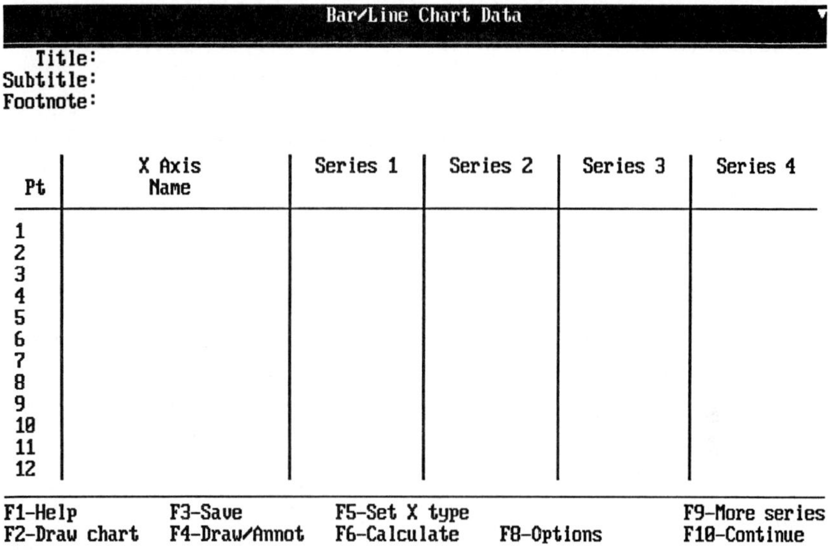

Bar/Line Chart Data

Title:
Subtitle:
Footnote:

Pt	X Axis Name	Series 1	Series 2	Series 3	Series 4
1					
2					
3					
4					
5					
6					
7					
8					
9					
10					
11					
12					

F1-Help F3-Save F5-Set X type F9-More series
F2-Draw chart F4-Draw/Annot F6-Calculate F8-Options F10-Continue

FIGURE 2-4. Bar/Line Chart Data form

5. Type **1990 Sales** and press (ENTER).
6. Type **Unit Sales** and press (ENTER).

The Footnote field is normally used to specify the source for the data presented on the chart, but you can also use it to specify other information about the data shown on the chart. Later you will learn how to enter as many as three footnote lines, although only one is used in this example.

7. Type **Wagons** and press (ENTER).
8. Type **Trains** and press (ENTER).
9. Type **Dolls** and press (ENTER).
10. Type **Sleds** and press (HOME) to move to the first X-axis name.
11. Press (TAB) to move the cursor to the top of the second column.
12. Type **2395** and press (ENTER).
13. Type **1200** and press (ENTER).

14. Type **3500** and press ENTER.
15. Type **500** and press ENTER.

The completed Bar/Line Chart Data form will match Figure 2-5.

16. Press F8 (Options) to display the Titles & Options form.

This form actually contains four pages of options for customizing a bar chart. You can move from page to page in this form with the PGUP and PGDN keys. You will see many of the options later in this chapter. For now, use only one field on this form to remove the legend for Series 1.

17. Press TAB seven times to move to the field for the Legend Title for Series 1.

Pressing TAB always moves you from field to field on the Titles & Options form. If you need to move to a previous field, remember to use SHIFT-TAB. If you are using a mouse, you may simply roll the mouse to the field you want and make your entries. Harvard Graphics will not move off the page boundary of the form unless you use PGUP and PGDN, or press

Bar/Line Chart Data

Title: Sturdy Toys
Subtitle: 1990 Sales
Footnote: Unit Sales

Pt	X Axis Name	Series 1	Series 2	Series 3	Series 4
1	Wagons	2395			
2	Trains	1200			
3	Dolls	3500			
4	Sleds	500			
5					
6					
7					
8					
9					
10					
11					
12					

F1-Help F3-Save F5-Set X type F9-More series
F2-Draw chart F4-Draw/Annot F6-Calculate F8-Options F10-Continue

FIGURE 2-5. Completed Bar/Line Chart Data form

ENTER or F10 (Continue) on the last line. This means that pressing TAB when you are on the last field on a form page takes you to the first field on the page. Likewise, if you are on the first field on a form page, pressing SHIFT-TAB takes you to the last field on the same page.

18. Press CTRL-DELETE to remove the entry Series 1.

Since there is only one data series shown on the chart, there is no need for a legend.

19. Press F2 (Draw chart) to create a graph like Figure 2-2 on your screen.
20. Press ESC twice to return to the Main Menu.
21. Select Get/Save/Remove and then select Save chart.
22. Type **SLS_90** for the filename and press ENTER.

Since you cannot use a space in a filename, you will want to use the underscore character (_) to separate letters in filenames.

23. Type **1990 Sales data for Sturdy Toys** for the file description and press F10 (Continue) to save the file.

Although there were many steps to complete before seeing the graph, most of the steps were needed to enter the data. The actual menu selections needed to create the graph were few. Now that you see how easy it is to represent your data in chart form, you should be ready to enhance your reports and presentations with bar charts. You will find it is just as easy to add more data or use additional options to improve the appearance of a bar graph. Let's look at some of the additional enhancements you can make.

ADDING INFORMATION TO THE CHART

Even though you saved the chart, it is still in memory. You can continue to make changes to it and save the enhanced version under the same or a different filename. You can add some data series and descriptive information, like legends, that describe each series. You can also revise the titles to reflect the addition of the new data.

Showing Additional Data Series

Harvard Graphics allows you to enter as many as eight series of data on one chart. If you use an X data type of Name, you can have as many as 60 sets of values for these series. With other X data types covered later in this chapter, you can use as many as 240 sets of values. In normal circumstances you may find that you cannot create a clear graphic representation of your data if you come close to the limit. With too many bars, the chart becomes difficult to interpret and defeats your initial purpose of presenting a clear picture of your data that does not require a significant level of analysis.

The bar chart was an effective way to present data that represented actual sales, and it is also an effective way to present projections, especially when there are projected increases or decreases in sales volumes. To minimize data entry you can use the data entered for the first chart as a projection of 1990 unit sales and add sales figures for several more years. Follow these steps to revise the bar chart:

1. Press **ESC** to return to the Main Menu.
2. Select Enter/Edit chart to edit the current chart. Note that no legend appears for Series 1 because you deleted it in the previous example.
3. Press **TAB** twice to move to the column for Series 2 so you can add more data.
4. Type the following numbers, pressing **ENTER** after each, to supply sales projections for 1991 for the products listed:

Wagons	**2600**
Trains	**1500**
Dolls	**2800**
Sleds	**250**

5. Press **HOME** and then press **TAB** three times to move where you will make your first entry for Series 3.

6. Type the following numbers, pressing ENTER after each, to supply sales projections for 1992 for the products listed:

Wagons	**2900**
Trains	**1600**
Dolls	**3800**
Sleds	**750**

7. Press HOME and then press TAB four times to move to the first entry for Series 4.
8. Type the following numbers, pressing ENTER after each, to supply sales projections for 1993 for the products listed:

Wagons	**3200**
Trains	**1900**
Dolls	**4000**
Sleds	**700**

Your Bar/Line Chart Data form now matches Figure 2-6.

9. Press F2 (Draw chart) to draw a chart with the three additional series, as shown in Figure 2-7.

Although you can see how the extra data has been added, additional work is still needed to revise the titles and to add legends that allow you to distinguish the contents of each set of bars.

Revising the Titles

When the titles were initially entered, the chart was used to present sales data for the current year. The revised data represents projected sales volume and needs to have the title entries changed to accurately reflect the contents of the chart.

Bar/Line Chart Data

Title: Sturdy Toys
Subtitle: 1990 Sales
Footnote: Unit Sales

Pt	X Axis Name		Series 2	Series 3	Series 4
1	Wagons	2395	2600	2900	3200
2	Trains	1200	1500	1600	1900
3	Dolls	3500	2800	3800	4000
4	Sleds	500	250	750	700
5					
6					
7					
8					
9					
10					
11					
12					

F1-Help F3-Save F5-Set X type F9-More series
F2-Draw chart F4-Draw/Annot F6-Calculate F8-Options F10-Continue

FIGURE 2-6. Adding data to the original bar chart

You also can add titles to the vertical axis, the Y-axis. Later, Harvard Graphics will add a Thousands title for you. You can also add or change Y-axis titles. A chart like the one in Figure 2-7 has only one Y-axis, and you will enter the axis title as the Y1-axis title.

Adding information in fields that you have not used is easy because all you need to do is move to the field and complete your new entry. Revising existing entries requires a little more thought to minimize the work required. To replace an entry you can simply type the new entry if it is longer than the existing one. If the new entry is shorter, you must press DELETE to eliminate each of the remaining characters from the previous entry. Another approach is to press CTRL-DELETE before typing the new entry; this deletes the prior entry with one key sequence. The CTRL-DELETE sequence is also an appropriate choice when you want to eliminate an entry for a field that no longer requires data.

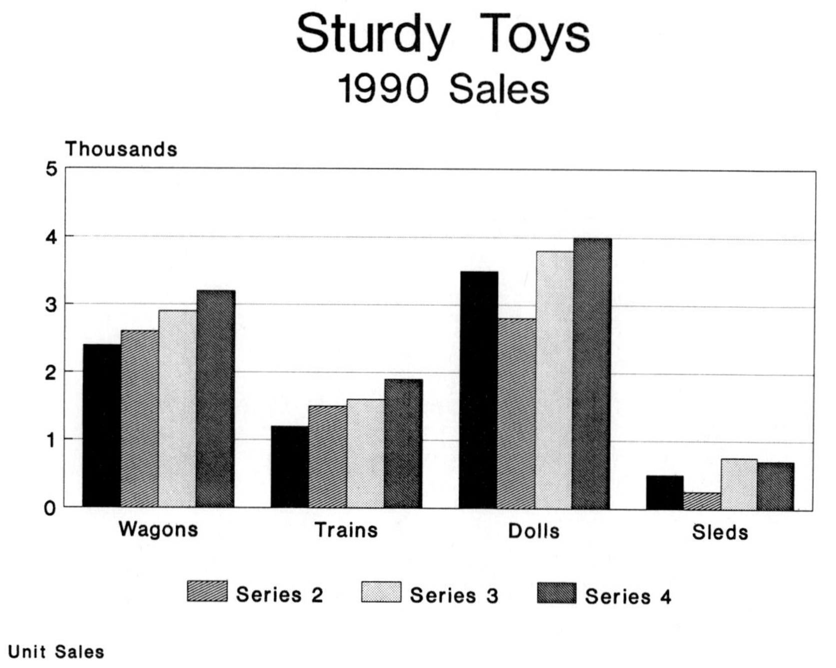

FIGURE 2-7. Chart showing four series

Follow these steps to revise the subtitle and footnote entries on the Titles & Options form:

1. Press ESC to return to the Bar/Line Chart Data form.
2. Press F8 (Options).

The first page of the four-page Titles & Options form will appear.

3. Press TAB to move to the Subtitle field.
4. Type **Sales Projections** and press TAB.

There was no need to press CTRL-DELETE since the new entry was longer than the old entry.

5. Press CTRL-DELETE to eliminate the footnote entry.

You can add a Y-axis label to indicate that the data is shown in units rather than using a footnote to provide this information.

6. Press TAB twice to move to the Y1-axis title.
7. Type **Thousands of Units** and then press F2 (Draw chart) to view the altered chart. Notice the new Y-axis title and subtitle on the chart.

The titles of the chart have been revised to more clearly describe the contents of the chart. You can work with the chart to further refine its appearance by experimenting with different ways of displaying the same information. For instance, the information presented in the Y-axis label could just as easily be displayed in the Subtitle field if the Title field is expanded to include "Sales Projections." After you make these changes, you will notice a little more balance in the distribution of information on the chart.

1. Press ESC to return to the Titles & Options form.

Check to be certain that your cursor is still in the Y1 Axis Title field.

2. Press CTRL-RIGHT ARROW to place the cursor one word to the right after "Thousands."
3. Press DELETE until "of Units" is removed.

You want to leave the word "Thousands" since this text indicates that the values along the Y-axis are thousands, not ones. If you delete the entire Y-axis label, people viewing the graph would not be sure whether values along the Y-axis represent ones, thousands, or millions. Harvard Graphics adds "Thousands" as a scale indicator to the Y-axis title because it intelligently decides that the chart will be scaled in thousands.

4. Press SHIFT-TAB and then type **Leading products** in the X Axis Title field.
5. Press HOME and TAB to move to the Subtitle field.
6. Press INSERT to change the cursor to a box, type **Unit**, and then press the spacebar.

The box indicates that you are in insert mode. The characters you type are added to the existing characters instead of replacing them.

7. Press INSERT again to turn insert mode off.
8. Press F2 (Draw chart).

Adding Legends

Any time you show more than one series of data in a bar graph, you must add legends to describe the data displayed in each series. The chart you have created shows Series 2 through Series 4 in the legend area, but this does not provide any meaningful information about what data is contained in each series. (The legend for Series 1 was deleted in the first chart you created because it was not needed at that time. It does not appear in this chart because the current chart was created through additions to your initial creation.)

You can add legends for each data series through entries on the Titles & Options form. Follow these steps to add the years 1990 through 1993 as legends for the chart data series:

1. Press ESC to return to the Titles & Options form.

The entries you complete in the next few steps will make Page 1 of the Titles & Options form match Figure 2-8.

2. Press TAB until the cursor is in the Legend Title field for Series 1.
3. Type **1990** and press ENTER.
4. Press CTRL-DELETE to remove the legend entry Series 2.
5. Type **1991** and press ENTER.

6. Press CTRL-DELETE to remove the legend entry Series 3.
7. Type **1992** and press ENTER.
8. Press CTRL-DELETE to remove the legend entry Series 4.
9. Type **1993** and press F2 (Draw chart).

Your screen will match Figure 2-9.

10. Press ESC twice.
11. Press CTRL-S to save the chart.

CTRL-S is a speed key. *Speed keys* are key combinations that you can press to quickly perform a routine operation. You can use speed keys to save and get charts, print charts, and perform other operations, which you will learn more about in subsequent chapters. You can use either the speed key or the command to obtain the same results.

12. Type **SLS_PROJ** and press ENTER.
13. Press CTRL-DELETE, type **Sales projections 1990 - 1993** and press F10 (Continue) to save the chart.

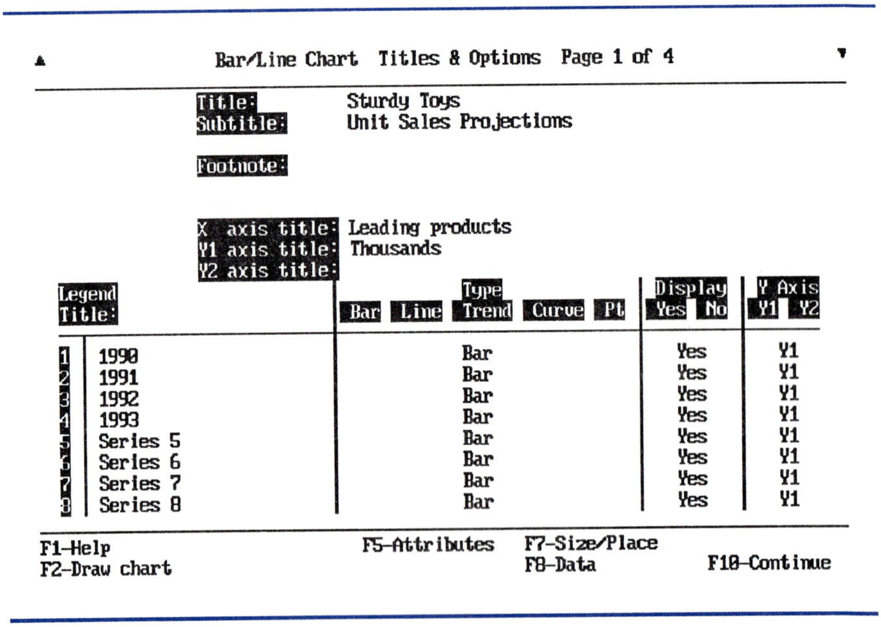

FIGURE 2-8. Adding data for legends

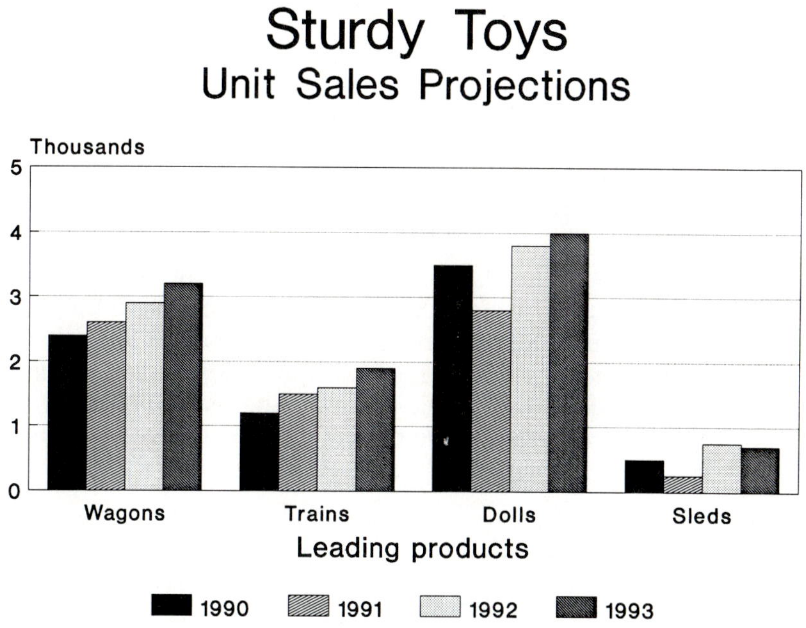

FIGURE 2-9. Graph with legends and titles entered

The data in the chart you just created is ideal for focusing on the growth within each product line because it makes it easy to compare wagon sales for each year. The organization of the data in series by year does not facilitate comparing the total sales for 1990 against the total sales in 1993. To make this comparison you must organize your data differently. In the next section you will look at organizing your data points and series in a different sequence as well as changing the entire data structure to create series by product rather than by year.

CHANGING DATA

Changing data can be as simple as typing a new number. It can also be more complicated if you choose to reorder the points along the X-axis or the order of the series shown on the graph.

Altering Data Values

As you enter new data values, the charts that contain them are updated immediately. As soon as you press F2 (Draw chart), the new value appears in the chart. In effect, this feature provides "what-if" graphics when you are working with a task like projecting headcount or future product sales. Although calculations have not been covered as yet, you will find that you can update calculations to reflect the change in a data value referenced by a formula.

New values that you enter are not saved with the chart data on disk until you specifically request that Harvard Graphics save the data. This means that you can make changes without worrying about losing the original entries that you stored to disk. If you wish to save your new entries, it does mean that you will be responsible for saving the chart to disk.

To see how easy it is to make a change, follow these steps to update the projected sales data for sleds:

1. Select Enter/Edit chart.
2. Press DOWN ARROW three times and TAB twice to move to the 1991 entry for sleds.
3. Type **950**.
4. Press F2 (Draw chart). Notice that the new data is immediately reflected in the height of the bar for sleds in 1991.
5. Press ESC to return to the Bar/Line Chart Data form, and type **250** as the entry for sleds in 1991; this returns the entry to its original value.

You can continue to make changes to as many fields, titles, and legends as you want. The next time you draw the chart on the screen, it will be updated for each of the entries you have made.

Reorganizing Data

You can make some changes to the order of the data shown on your chart. This allows you to correct for an omission in entry, create a more aesthetic graph, or arrange the series or X data entries in alphabetical order.

You can change either the order of the data points on the X-axis or the order of the series. Changing the order of the X-axis data points normally is appropriate only with a data type of Name, as used in the current example. When you begin creating charts with other data types, such as years, months, or days, changing the order of the data point entries is not appropriate unless you accidentally entered them in the wrong order. If this is the case, you can use a special calculate feature to effect the change, which is discussed in Chapter 3, "Creating Line and Area Charts."

The procedure you use depends on whether you want to change the order of the data points or the series. Remember to think of the data points as rows and the series as columns. This makes it easy to keep the two types of changes separate.

CHANGING THE ORDER OF THE X-AXIS DATA POINTS You can use a special key combination to change the presentation order of data points within a bar graph. Use either CTRL-UP ARROW or CTRL-DOWN ARROW, depending on whether you want the data for the current data point to be moved forward or backward in the data point list. When the data point is moved in the list, the data from each series that corresponds to the data point is moved within the table.

After looking at the graph in Figure 2-9 you might decide that the graph would be more visually appealing if you order the X data points from highest to lowest selling product. Although it may be difficult to differentiate between products where sales figures are close, you can still achieve the effect you are striving for if you position them by appearance.

Try these steps to order the graph so that the largest selling product displays first:

1. Move to the row containing the Dolls data point. You can be in any column within the appropriate row.
2. Press CTRL-UP ARROW twice.

The X data point Dolls and the data associated with it now appears in the first row of the Bar/Line Chart Data form.

3. Press F2 (Draw chart) to display the graph.

As shown in Figure 2-10, the data points in the display have been reordered to display the data for dolls first.

4. Press ESC twice to return to the Main Menu.

5. Press CTRL-S to save the chart.
6. Press CTRL-DELETE to remove the old filename since the new filename is shorter.
7. Type **REORDER** for the filename and press ENTER.
8. Press CTRL-DELETE to remove the old description since the new one is shorter.
9. Type **Dolls first** and press ENTER.

It was necessary to save the chart again in order to save a copy of the chart with the X data points in the new sequence. Since a different filename was provided, either set of data can be retrieved later on and displayed as a chart.

CHANGING THE ORDER OF THE SERIES Changing the order of the series in the chart requires a little more work. You must define which series you want to exchange places. After positioning your cursor on the series that

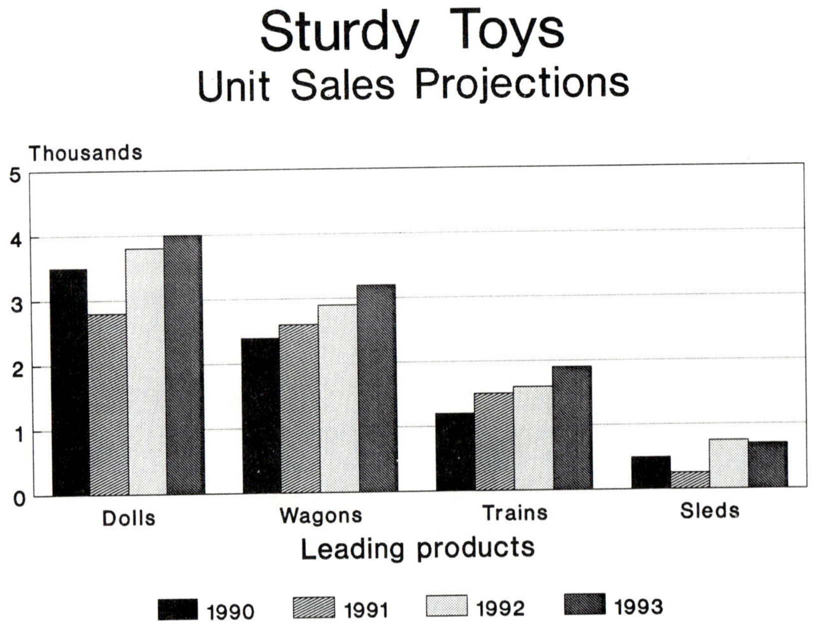

FIGURE 2-10. Changing the order of the data points

you want to relocate, you can press F6 (Calculate). You will need to use a special @ function to define the exchange. Harvard Graphics has 19 @ functions that perform different types of tasks. The format of the function that changes the order of the series is @EXCH(*#n*), where *#n* is the number of the series that you want to exchange locations with the current series. Once this entry is placed in the Calculation field you can press ENTER and view the reorganized series entries.

Although you are more likely to need this type of change when you use products, divisions, or cities as a series, you can use it with the year entries to display them in reverse order, with 1993 shown first and 1990 shown last. To accomplish this change, follow these steps:

1. Select Enter/Edit chart.
2. Press TAB to move to the top of the column containing 1990 data.
3. Press F6 (Calculate).
4. Press TAB to move to the Calculation field.
5. Type **@EXCH(#4)** and press ENTER.

At this point the order of the series is 1993, 1991, 1992, and 1990. One more change between the second and third entries will complete the change.

6. Press TAB to move to the column containing the data for 1991.
7. Press F6 (Calculate).
8. Press TAB.
9. Type @EXCH(#3) and press ENTER.
10. Press F2 (Draw chart) to look at the chart with the series shown in reverse order. Your screen will match Figure 2-11.
11. Press ESC twice.
12. Select Get/Save/Remove.
13. Select Save chart.
14. Press CTRL-DELETE to remove the old filename.
15. Type **SERIES** and press ENTER.
16. Type **Show latest year first** and press ENTER.

There was no need for you to press CTRL-DELETE first since the new entry was longer and completely replaced the older entry.

17. Press ESC to return to the Main Menu.

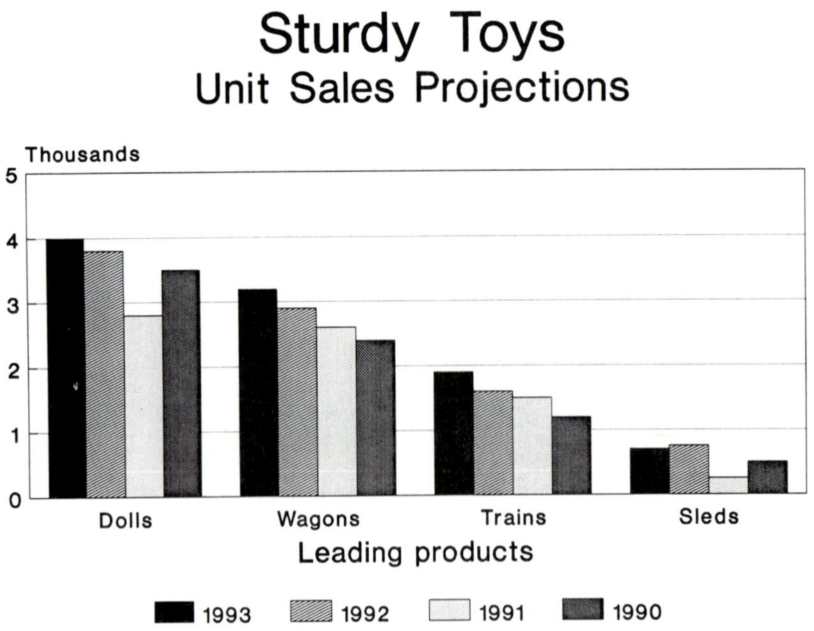

FIGURE 2-11. Changing the order of the series

In Chapter 3 you will take a look at other @ functions you can use with bar charts as well as the line and area charts covered in that chapter.

Creating a Series with a Different Organization

When you created the sales projection chart for 1990 to 1993, you organized the series by year. You can present the same data with a different slant if you organize it so that each product is a series, with the points along the X-axis representing the years 1990 through 1993. Switching to a stacked bar display makes it easy to look at the total sales in a given year. It is important to decide before entering your data which organization structure you want to use, because there is no way to change the data from one structure to the other without reentering it.

If you use the products for the series names, you may want to use a different entry for the X data points, like a time period. You can choose from any of the other options in Table 2-1 when you select your X data type. Selecting one of the new data types will also allow you to specify a starting entry, an ending entry, and an increment. Evenly spaced values can be generated automatically, thus saving you a significant amount of entry time. Table 2-1 also shows some examples of acceptable entries for each of the optional fields and the series of X data values that Harvard Graphics generates.

	Examples			
X Data Type	**Starting**	**Ending**	**Increment**	**Entries**
Name	N/A	N/A	N/A	Boston . . . New York; Computers . . . Monitors
Day	MON	FRI	1	MON, TUE, . . . FRI
	Sunday	Friday	1	Sunday . . . Friday
Week	2	10	2	2, 4, 6, 8, 10
Month	June	December	1	June, July, . . . December
Quarter	First	Fourth	1	First, Second, Third, Fourth
Year	90	95	1	90, 91, 92, 93, 94, 95
	1989	1999	2	1989, 1991, . . . 1999
Month/Day	Sept 1	Sept 29	7	Sept 1, Sept 8, . . . Sept 29
Month/Yr	Jan 90	Jun 90	2	Jan 90, Mar 90, May 90
Qtr/Yr	1/90	4/90	2	1/90, 3/90
Time	9:00 AM	1:30 PM	90	9:00 AM, 10:30 AM, 12:00 AM, 1:30 PM
Number	10	100	10	10, 20, 30, . . . 100
	0	5	.5	0, .5, 1, 1.5, . . . 5

TABLE 2-1. Data Types

The data shown in Figure 2-12 is identical to the data entered in the earlier data form, except it is organized in series by product name. Follow these steps to enter the data for the new chart:

1. Select Create new chart.
2. Select Bar/Line.
3. Press the spacebar until Year appears as the X data type, and then press ENTER.
4. Type **1990** for the Starting with field and press ENTER.
5. Type **1993** for the Ending with field and press ENTER.
6. Type **1** for the increment and press ENTER.

Note the years for the X data points have been entered for you. Although these entries saved a few keystrokes compared with entering each of the X data values directly on the Bar/Line Chart Data form, other X data types, like Day and Month, offer even greater time savings.

7. Type **Sturdy Toys** for the Title field and press ENTER.
8. Type **Sales Projections** and press ENTER.

Bar/Line Chart Data

Title: Sturdy Toys
Subtitle: Sales Projections
Footnote: Management Projections

Pt	X Axis Year	Dolls	Wagons	Trains	Sleds
1	1990	3350	2395	1200	500
2	1991	2800	2600	1500	250
3	1992	3800	2900	1600	750
4	1993	4000	3200	1900	700
5					
6					
7					
8					
9					
10					
11					
12					

F1-Help F3-Save F5-Set X type F9-More series
F2-Draw chart F4-Draw/Annot F6-Calculate F8-Options F10-Continue

FIGURE 2-12. Data organized by product

9. Type **Management Projections** and press TAB twice.

10. Enter the following data as the entries for Series 1 for doll sales:

    3350
    2800
    3800
    4000

    Press ENTER after each entry to move to the next row on the form.

11. Press HOME and then press TAB twice to move to the column for Series 2 entries for wagon sales.

12. Complete the following entries, pressing ENTER after each:

    2395
    2600
    2900
    3200

13. Press HOME and then press TAB three times to move to the column for Series 3 data, train sales.

14. Complete the following entries, pressing ENTER after each:

    1200
    1500
    1600
    1900

15. Press HOME and then press TAB four times to move to the Series 4 column for sled sales.

16. Type the following, pressing ENTER after each entry except the last:

    500
    250
    750
    700

17. Press F8 (Options) to display the Titles & Options form.

18. Press TAB twice to put the cursor in the Footnote field, and then press DOWN ARROW to move to the second line of footnote entries. The Titles & Options form allows you to enter a second line of subtitle data and as many as three lines of footnote data.

19. Type **Based on average industry growth** and press (ENTER).
20. Press (TAB) until the cursor is in the Legend Title field for Series 1.
21. Enter the following legends, pressing (CTRL-DELETE) before each entry and (ENTER) after each, except the last entry.

    Dolls
    Wagons
    Trains
    Sleds

22. Press (F2) (Draw chart) to display the graph shown in Figure 2-13.
23. Press (ESC) until the Main Menu appears.
24. Press (CTRL-S) to save the chart.
25. Type **PRODUCTS** and press (ENTER).

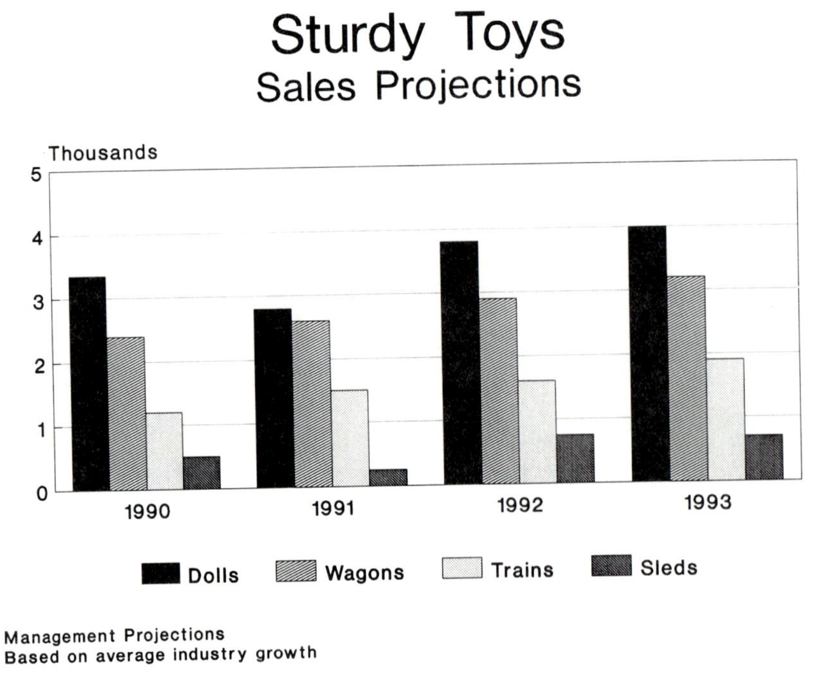

FIGURE 2-13. Graph from new data entries

26. Type **Series stored by product** for the Description field and press (ENTER).

PRINTING YOUR CHARTS

Although charts make an impressive display on the screen, there are times when you want to print them and incorporate them into reports and other printed material. Once you have created the chart you want, press (ESC) to return to the Main Menu. Select Produce output, make a few selections, and if your printer is attached you will have output quickly. Although you may only need to change a few print settings, let's look at all of them to explore this new type of output. To print the current graph follow these next steps:

1. Select Produce output.
2. Select Printer.

The Print Chart Options form shown in Figure 2-14 is added to the screen. If the arrow cursor marks each of the correct settings, and if your printer is

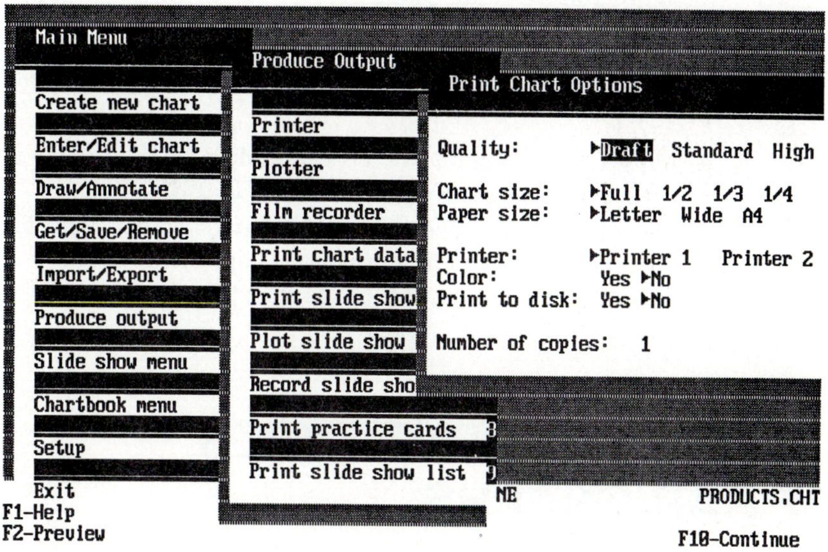

FIGURE 2-14. Print Chart Options form

attached and on, press F10 (Continue) to print the current chart. You should look at each option before printing for the first time.

3. Press the spacebar until the desired entry in the Quality field is marked with the arrow cursor.

The options available depend on your printer. High quality is the best but requires the most time for printing. Draft quality is the quickest output method, but provides the poorest quality of the three selections. With printers such as Hewlett Packard LaserJet and other non-Postscript printers, additional memory may be needed to store the image of the chart as it prints it.

4. Press TAB to move to the Chart size field. Again press the spacebar until the desired size is highlighted.
5. Press TAB to move to the Paper size field. Press the spacebar if you want to alter the setting.
6. Press TAB to move to the Printer field, and then press the spacebar if you need to make a change.

You can install two different printers to work with Harvard Graphics. Details on installation are found in Appendix A, if you are not certain of your selections.

7. Press TAB to move to the Color field. Press the spacebar if your output device is not color.

Harvard Graphics knows from the printer selected if the printer can print colors. If your printer cannot print colors, Harvard Graphics automatically prints the chart in black and white.

8. Press TAB to move to the Print to disk field. Press the spacebar if you want the output sent to a file called HG.PRN.
9. Press TAB to move to the Number of copies field, and type a new number if you need more than one copy of the chart.
10. Press F10 (Continue) to print the chart.

USING DIFFERENT TYPES OF BAR GRAPHS

You can enhance the bar graphs you have created in many different ways. Harvard Graphics provides six basic styles that form the basis of any bar chart. A number of enhancements do not change the bar style but add extra information to the display. The combination of styles and enhancements provides a wide range of options that allow you to create graphs with enough visual variation to maintain your audience's interest. Experiment with your entries to create the most attractive graphs possible.

Using Different Graph Styles

The default graph style for a Harvard Graphics bar chart is a *cluster bar* chart, which groups the corresponding values from each series around each of the appropriate data points. The *overlap bar* style allows you to overlap the bars in the series and even to vary the amount of overlap that is used. A *stack bar* chart places the values from each series on top of each other in order to have the total height of the bar at each data point represent the total of all series entries with the specified value. A *100% bar* style draws the bars so that the total height of each bar equals 100%, and the bar is divided so that each value represents a percentage of that total. The *Step bar* style is similar to a histogram that shows each value as a bar with no spacing between the bars. A *paired bar* style is the most sophisticated bar option. It allows you to display data on a chart with two different sets of values for the Y-axis. For example, you might show two different types of related data for branch offices. You can show sales data by office on the right and headcount numbers on the left. The sales data shown at the right can be measured on the Y2-axis, and the headcount numbers can be shown on the left on the Y1-axis.

Try a few variations of bar styles, using the Sturdy Toys data and the steps given in the next five sections. To see the step and paired bar styles used effectively, you must enter new chart data.

CREATING AN OVERLAP BAR CHART Changing a bar chart to an overlap style is easy and can, along with the cluster bar chart, lend variety to your charts. Follow these steps to make the change:

1. Select Enter/Edit chart.
2. Press F8 (Options).
3. Press PGDN to move to Page 2 of the Titles & Options form, as shown in Figure 2-15.

4. Press the spacebar to move the arrow cursor in the Bar style field to Overlap.

5. Press F2 (Draw chart) to view the graph as shown in Figure 2-16.

The default for the amount of overlap on the bars is 50%. If you want to alter the amount of overlap, press TAB to move to the Bar overlap field, and increase or decrease the overlap percentage by typing a higher or lower number, respectively.

CREATING A STACKED BAR CHART A stacked bar style is effective when you want to know the total for all the series at each X data point. Each series represents total sales for a product. You can determine the total sales for all products by the total height of the stacked bar, because it is built by entering the value of each series one atop the other. This chart type is also effective for graphing data in several series that represent the headcount for

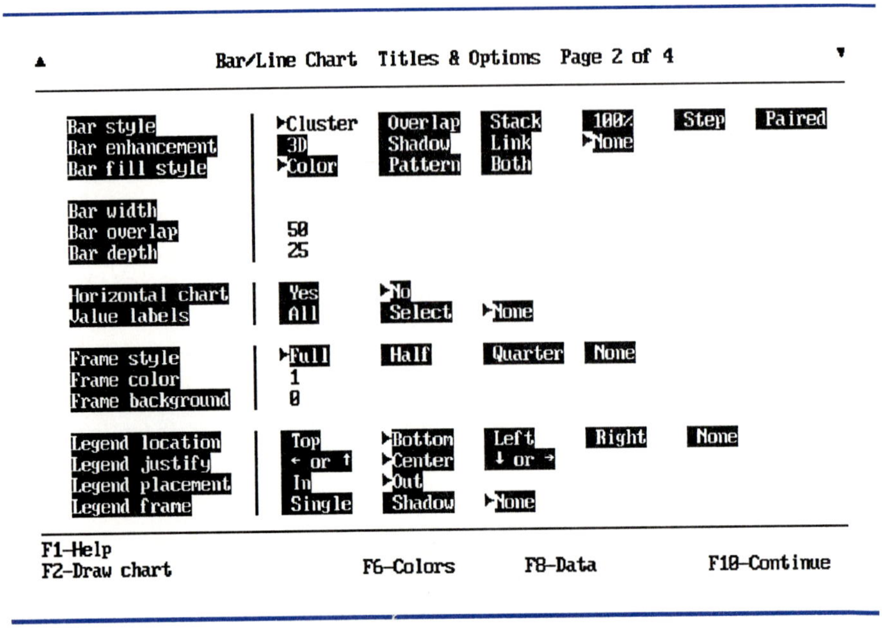

FIGURE 2-15. Page 2 of the Titles & Options form

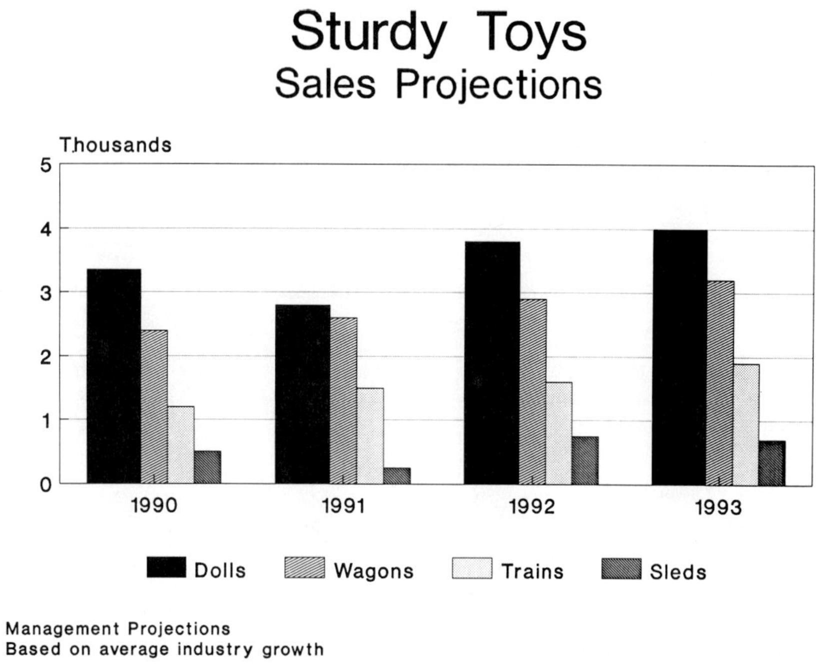

FIGURE 2-16. Overlay chart

several company divisions. The total height of the stacked bar represents the total company headcount.

To change the graph style to stacked bar, follow these steps:

1. Press (ESC) to return to the Titles & Options form.
2. Press the spacebar to change the Bar style field to Stack.
3. Press (F2) (Draw chart). Your chart will look like Figure 2-17.

If you are working with a color monitor, you will see a bar for each X data point, with each component from the various series shown in a different color. If your display is monochrome, each component will display in a different pattern.

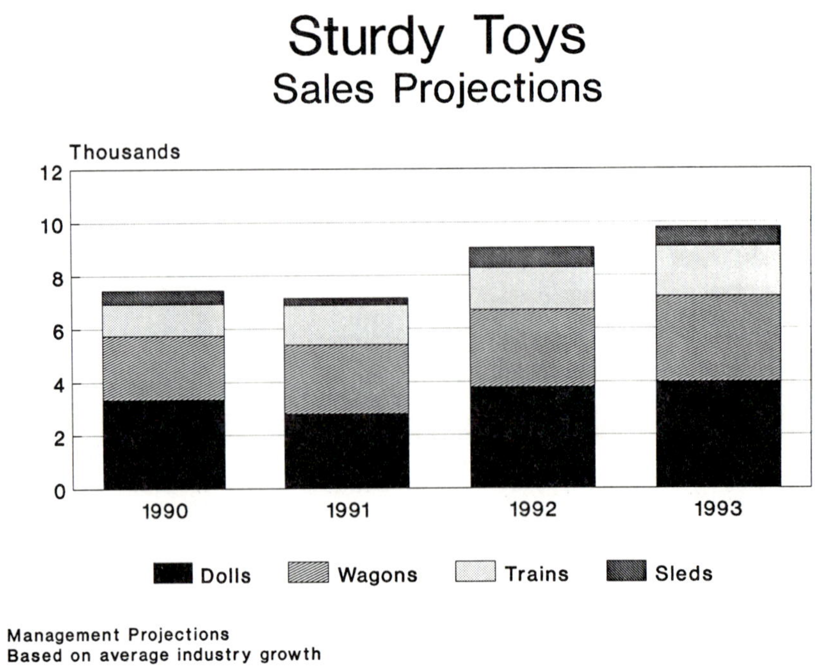

FIGURE 2-17. Stack chart

CREATING A 100% BAR CHART Although the stack graph shows the actual amount that each series contributes to the whole, it takes some calculations to even estimate the percentage contribution for each entry. If you would like to see the percentage contribution of each element, you can use a 100% bar style. The total height of the bar is considered to be 100%, and the amount of each series is measured with the Y scale serving as a percentage indicator.

To look at the Sturdy Toy data with a 100% style bar, follow these steps:

1. Press ESC to return to the Titles & Options form.
2. Press the spacebar to change the Bar style field to 100%.
3. Press F2 (Draw chart). Your chart will look like Figure 2-18.

This chart provides an opportunity for you to see that the doll sales figures account for almost 50% of the total annual sales.

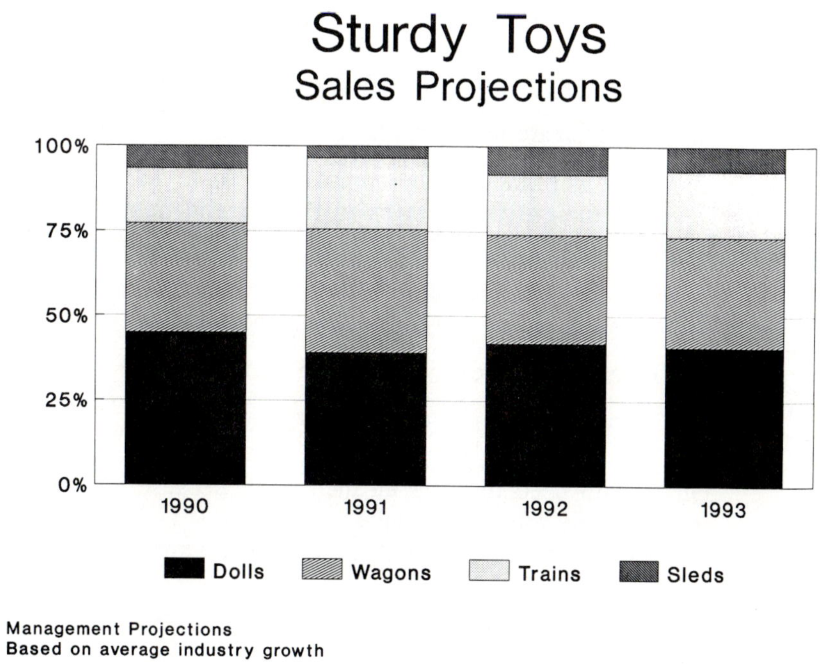

FIGURE 2-18. 100% chart

CREATING A STEP BAR CHART When you choose a step bar style, the bars representing your data values are created with no space between them. This method can be effective to show major changes between the data values. Step style bars can also be used to show a frequency distribution, which measures the values for different observations and groups the data by the number of occurrences of the same value (a frequency count).

If you want to show the variation in occurrences of production line failures in a given month, you can enter a series of values representing the failure rate each day. The one series shown will contain all the values for June, with a data point registered for each date. If you want to create a frequency distribution, you must organize the data differently. Each X data value must represent an observation or interval, like one to three failures. The number of days with one to three failures is measured along the Y-axis, and the height of the bars shows the relative frequency of each interval on the X-axis.

To create a chart to record the production failure that occurs on each date, follow these steps:

1. Press ESC until the Main Menu is on your screen.
2. Select Create new chart from the menu.
3. Select Bar/Line and then press ENTER to acknowledge that you do not want to save the changes to the current graph before creating a new one.
4. Press the spacebar until Month/Day appears in the X Data Type form, and then press ENTER to complete the selection.
5. Type **6/1** and press ENTER.
6. Type **6/30** and press ENTER twice.

There is no need to enter an increment, because the default value of 1 is used any time you do not make an entry.

The Bar/Line Chart Data form is now on your screen.

7. Type **Refrigerator Production** and press ENTER.
8. Type **Mean Production Line Failures** and press ENTER.
9. Type **Head foreman's records** and press ENTER to complete the Footnote field.
10. Press TAB to move to the Series 1 data column.
11. Type a number between 1 and 12 for each date, pressing ENTER after each entry. (If you prefer to use the same numbers used in Figure 2-19, you can look at the bar heights to determine the actual entries.)
12. Press F8 (Options).
13. Press TAB until the Legend Title field entry Series 1 is highlighted.
14. Press CTRL-DELETE to remove the entry.
15. Press PGDN to move to Page 2.
16. With the Bar style field highlighted, press the spacebar until Step is highlighted.
17. Press PGDN to move to Page 3 of the Titles & Options form shown in Figure 2-20 and then press TAB until the cursor is highlighting Linear in the X Axis column.

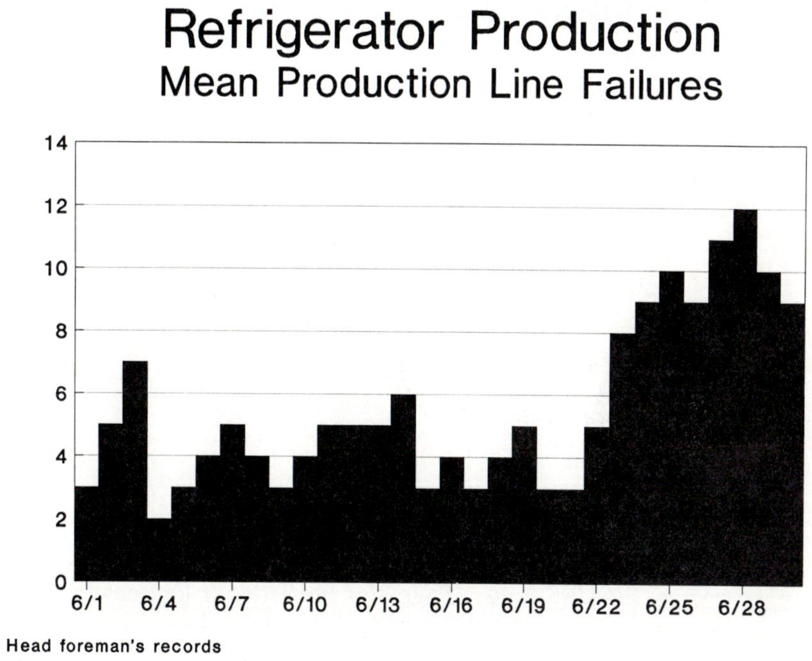

FIGURE 2-19. Step chart

18. Press DOWN ARROW four times, and then type **3**. This changes the interval on the X-axis to prevent crowding of the entries. If you do not make this change, the entries will overlay each other and the result will be a garbled appearance to the X-axis data point entries.
19. Press F2 (Draw chart).

Although your exact entries will determine the appearance of the chart, it will appear similar to the chart shown in Figure 2-19.

20. Press ESC until the Main Menu appears.
21. Press CTRL-S to save the chart.
22. Type **STEP_CHT** and press ENTER.
23. Type **Refrigerator Production Problems** in the Description field and press ENTER.

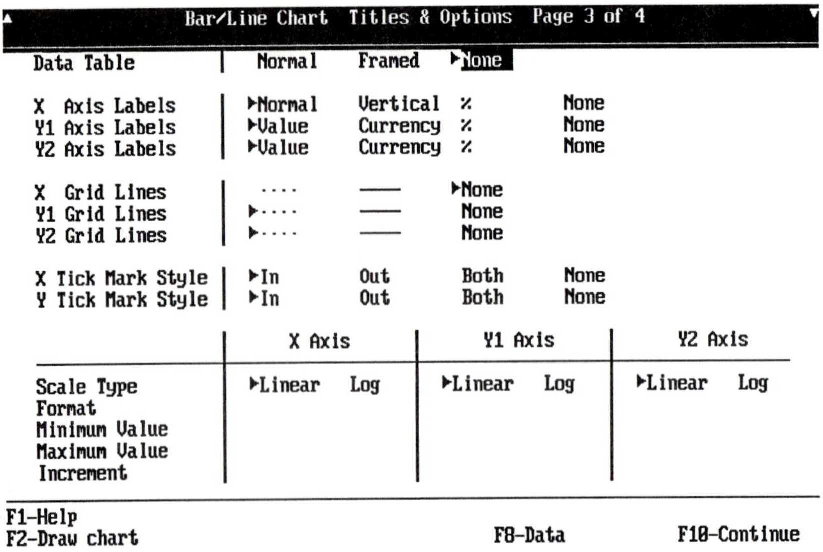

Bar/Line Chart Titles & Options Page 3 of 4

Data Table	Normal	Framed	▸None	
X Axis Labels	▸Normal	Vertical	%	None
Y1 Axis Labels	▸Value	Currency	%	None
Y2 Axis Labels	▸Value	Currency	%	None
X Grid Lines	....	——	▸None	
Y1 Grid Lines	▸....	——	None	
Y2 Grid Lines	▸....	——	None	
X Tick Mark Style	▸In	Out	Both	None
Y Tick Mark Style	▸In	Out	Both	None

	X Axis	Y1 Axis	Y2 Axis
Scale Type	▸Linear Log	▸Linear Log	▸Linear Log
Format			
Minimum Value			
Maximum Value			
Increment			

F1-Help
F2-Draw chart F8-Data F10-Continue

FIGURE 2-20. Page 3 of the Titles & Options form

CREATING A PAIRED BAR CHART A paired bar chart is actually two graphs in one. You can use two different Y-axes, allowing the combination of information that would not otherwise be possible due to different units of measure, such as dollars and unit sales. It is also ideal for series with the same unit of measure but disparate values. For example, the number of sales and headcount can both be measured in units, but the number of units for sales might be measured in thousands and the headcount for each branch office might not exceed ten. If you were to try to show both quantities on the same graph, the Y-axis scaling would prevent the appearance of the headcount entries due to their small magnitude in comparison to sales. If two different Y-axes are shown on the graph, both sets of data are visible.

There is no difference in data entry for a paired style chart and the other charts you have created. You must select the Paired bar style from Page 2 of the Titles & Options window. In addition, you must check which axes each series is assigned to, and you may want to change the color assignments of the series bars.

For a step-by-step look at entering new data ideally suited for a paired style graph, follow these steps:

1. Select Create new chart.

2. Select Bar/Line.
3. Check to be sure that Name appears as the X-axis data type in the form, and press F10 (Continue).
4. Type **Quick Sales** and press ENTER.
5. Type **Headcount/Sales By Office** and press ENTER twice.
6. Type the following X data point names, pressing ENTER after each:

   Akron
   Cleveland
   Gates Mills
   Parma
   Zoar

7. Press HOME followed by TAB to position the cursor for Series 1 entries.
8. Type the following headcount entries for each city, pressing ENTER after each:

   10
   20
   3
   5
   12

9. Press HOME and then press TAB twice.
10. Type the following sales figures for Series 2, pressing ENTER after each:

    550950
    925800
    625000
    300000
    212500

11. Press F2 (Draw chart).

This chart shows the results of graphing data measured in disparate units. Since the headcount numbers are so much smaller than the sales figures, they are indistinguishable from the X-axis.

12. Press ESC to return to the Bar/Line Chart Data form.
13. Press F8 (Options).
14. Press the TAB key seven times to move to the Legend Title for Series 1 and then type **Headcount.**
15. Press ENTER and CTRL-DELETE, then type **Sales.**
16. Press TAB three times to move to the Y-axis field to the right of the legend.
17. Press the spacebar to highlight Y2; that data now is displayed on the second Y-axis.
18. Press PGDN to move to the Bar style field, and press the spacebar five times to change the style to Paired.
19. Press F2 (Draw chart) to view the chart with these changes.
20. Press ESC to return to the Titles & Options form.
21. Press DOWN ARROW twice and type **B**, for Both, to use both patterns and colors to distinguish the series.
22. Press PGDN to move to Page 3 of the Titles & Options form, and then press END to move to the Increment field for the Y2-axis.
23. Type **400000.**

Since the Y-axis on a paired bar style graph displays at the bottom of the graph, this change alters the axis at the bottom. If you do not make this change, the Y2-axis labels will appear too crowded.

24. Press PGDN to move to Page 4, as shown in Figure 2-21. Press TAB eleven times to move to the Marker/Pattern field for Headcount.
25. Type **2** to change the marker pattern and then press DOWN ARROW followed by LEFT ARROW to move to the Marker/Pattern field for Sales.
26. Type **1** and press ENTER.
27. Press F2 (Draw chart) to display the chart with the changes.

Your chart will look like Figure 2-22. The legend and Y-axis title appear too close, but you will learn some techniques later in this chapter for affecting text size and placement that will allow you to correct problems like this.

28. Press ESC until the Main Menu appears.

```
                 Bar/Line Chart  Titles & Options  Page 4 of 4

               Title:        Quick Sales
               Subtitle:     Headcount/Sales By Office

               Footnote:


               X  axis title:
               Y1 axis title:
               Y2 axis title: Thousands
 Legend                          Cum    | Y Label | Color | Marker/ | Line
 Title:                        Yes  No  | Yes  No |       | Pattern | Style

 1 | Headcount                   No     |   No    |   2   |    1    |  1
 2 | Sales                       No     |   No    |   3   |    2    |  1
 3 | Series 3                    No     |   No    |   4   |    3    |  1
 4 | Series 4                    No     |   No    |   5   |    4    |  1
 5 | Series 5                    No     |   No    |   6   |    5    |  1
 6 | Series 6                    No     |   No    |   7   |    6    |  1
 7 | Series 7                    No     |   No    |   8   |    7    |  1
 8 | Series 8                    No     |   No    |   9   |    8    |  1

F1-Help                      F5-Attributes   F7-Size/Place
F2-Draw chart                F6-Colors       F8-Data            F10-Continue
```

FIGURE 2-21. Page 4 of the Titles & Options form

29. Select Get/Save/Remove.
30. Select Save chart.
31. Type **PAIRED** and press ENTER, and then type **Headcount and Sales Chart** and press ENTER.

Adding Enhancements to the Basic Style Types

Now that you have seen all six bar chart styles, you should take a look at some of the enhancements you can add to the bars that make up these graphs. There are three different enhancement options possible. The default setting is to create graphs with no enhancement options added. In the next two sections you will look at the other two enhancement settings that add shadow and three-dimensional (3D) effects to bar charts.

ADDING A SHADOW TO BARS The shadow effect adds depth to a bar by adding a shadow below or to the right of it, depending on whether it is a

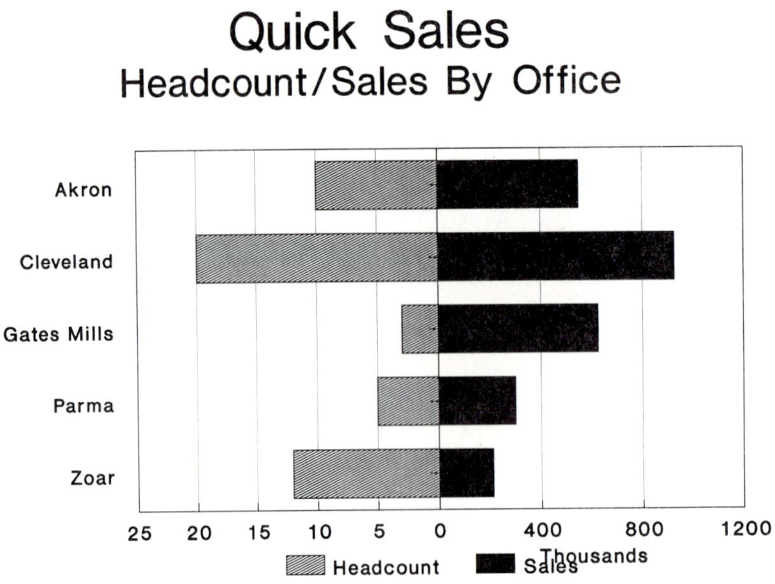

FIGURE 2-22. Paired chart

horizontal or vertical bar. The addition of the shadow does not change the width or height of the bar itself. Since it is still clear where the original bar begins and ends, the shadow effect does not interfere with interpretation of the information presented. The main purpose for adding a shadow is to add visual variety to the presentation of your information.

You can add a shadow to the paired graph you just created. Since a paired graph is displayed with horizontal bars, the shadow effect will appear below the bar. Follow these steps to make the change:

1. Press ESC until the Main Menu returns.
2. Select Enter/Edit chart.
3. Press F8 (Options).
4. Press PGDN to move to Page 2 of the Titles & Options form.
5. Press TAB to move to the Bar enhancements field.
6. Press the spacebar until Shadow is highlighted, and then press ENTER.

7. Press (TAB) to move to the Legend position field.
8. Press the spacebar until Top is highlighted.

In the chart in Figure 2-22, the legend at the bottom of the screen merged with the axis title. The Legend position field sets where the legend will appear in the chart. You will learn other options for legends in the next chapter.

9. Press (F2) (Draw chart).

The graph with the addition of shadows will match Figure 2-23.

USING A 3D EFFECT You can add a three-dimensional (3D) effect to a bar with the 3D option. This adds depth to the bar and can create an exciting visual effect. A plain bar graph like the one in Figure 2-16 looks completely different when you add 3D to achieve results like those shown in

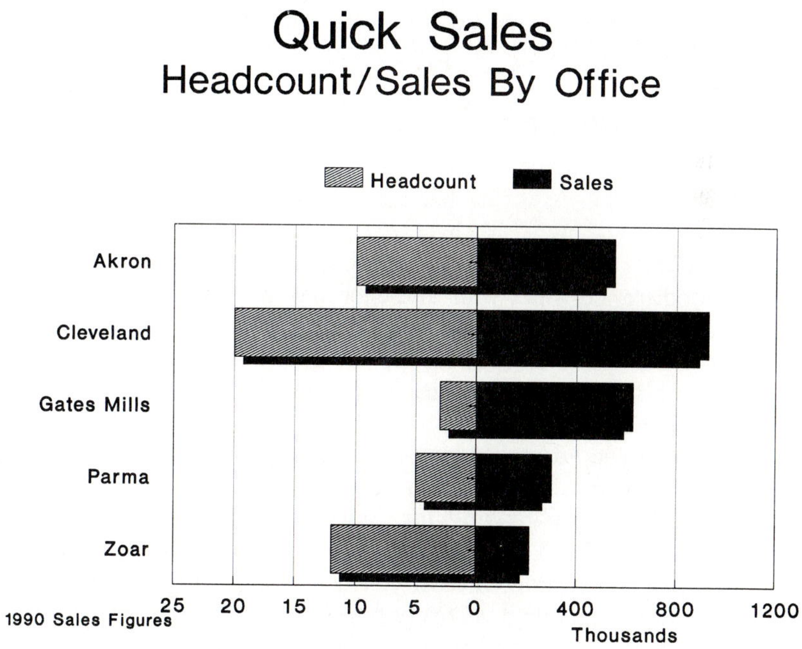

FIGURE 2-23. Paired chart with shadows added

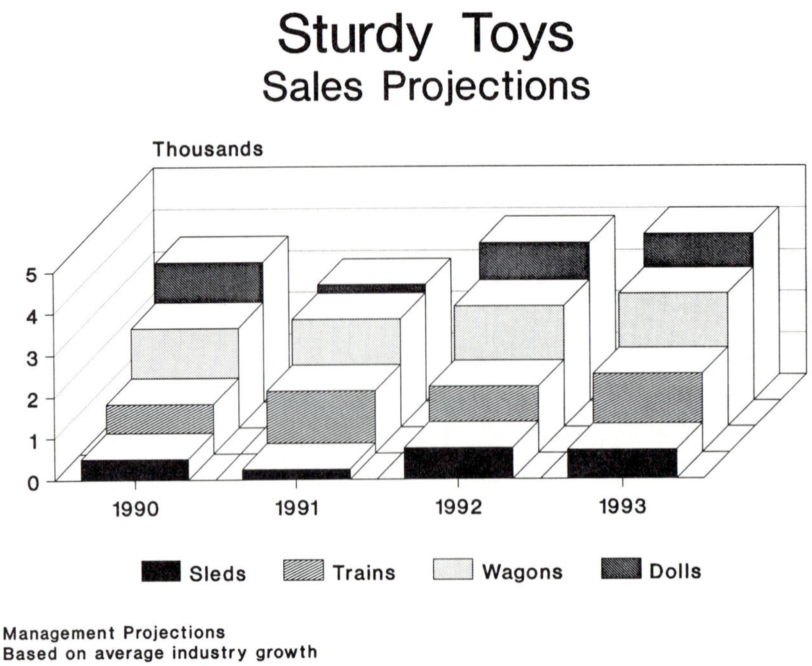

FIGURE 2-24. 3D chart

Figure 2-24. Although this graph achieves a pleasing visual effect, it is not a good choice when your audience has to interpret the value represented by each bar as closely as possible. Although the value is shown by the top line in the bar, many users reviewing the graph will not be certain if it is the top or the bottom of the addition to each bar that is used to determine the magnitude of the data.

You can add a 3D look to a cluster or overlap chart effectively. You can experiment with the other combinations to see which options create the effect you are looking for. With some options, like the combination of overlap and 3D, you may need to change the order of your data to present the smallest values first. If you do not make this change with a 3D overlap chart, the first data values presented may obscure the other series presented.

Create a 3D overlap bar with these steps:

1. Press ESC until the Main Menu appears.
2. Press CTRL-G.

CTRL-G is the speed key for retrieving a chart. It has the same effect as selecting Get/Save/Remove from the Main Menu and selecting Get chart.

3. Move the highlight to PRODUCTS and press ENTER.
4. Press ENTER a second time to confirm that you want to retrieve a chart without saving the changes to the current chart and ESC to remove the PRODUCTS chart from the screen.
5. Press F8 (Options).
6. Press PGDN to move to Page 2.
7. Press the spacebar to change the Bar style field to Overlap, and then press ENTER to move to the Bar enhancement field.
8. Press the spacebar to highlight 3D.
9. Press F2 (Draw chart).

Notice how the first data series obscure the others. Use F6 (Calculate) and the @EXCH function to reorder the data to present the smallest series first.

10. Press ESC to return to the Titles & Options form.
11. Press F8 (Data) to display the Bar/Line Chart Data form.
12. Press TAB to move the cursor to the column for Series 1, Dolls.
13. Press F6 (Calculate).
14. Press TAB and then type **@EXCH(#4)** to cause Series 1 to trade places with Series 4.
15. Press ENTER to make the change.
16. Press TAB to move the cursor to Series 2 data.
17. Press F6 (Calculate) and then press TAB.
18. Type **@EXCH(#3)** and press ENTER.
19. Press F2 (Draw chart).

Your chart should match Figure 2-24. The series progresses from the first (containing the smallest values) to the last (containing the largest values) so you can see all the data in the 3D graph.

MAKING ADJUSTMENTS TO OTHER GRAPH FEATURES

Once you decide on the basic type of bar graph you want to create, you can continue to refine its appearance with other options. You can change the color or pattern assigned to one or more series. You can also alter the placement of the X-axis label or the use of grid lines.

Changing Colors and Patterns

If you have a color monitor, Harvard Graphics automatically displays your graph with bars filled in a color. A new color is automatically used for each series. You can choose whether you want series differentiated by color, patterns, or both by changing the chart's bar fill style. You can also choose to change the particular color or pattern code assigned to a series.

CHANGING THE BAR FILL STYLE A fill style of Color is the default setting for a color monitor. The colors used to fill the bars depend on the type of monitor you are using. Table 2-2 shows the color choices available using the default palette. A palette is a set of sixteen colors that you can use for your graphs. Chapter 8 provides more information on using the twelve palettes Harvard Graphics provides for EGA and VGA monitors. If you print a color graph on a printer that does not support color, Harvard Graphics automatically changes your graph fill style to patterns.

You can choose to display a pattern either in addition to color or in its place as a means of distinguishing one series from another. If you choose patterns, they are assigned codes just like colors. Table 2-3 displays the patterns and the code numbers associated with them.

Color Code	Color
1	White
2	Cyan (dark)
3	Blue
4	Blue (light)
5	Cyan (light)
6	Yellow (light)
7	White
8	Black
9	White
10	Grey (light)
11	Black
12	Red
13	Green
14	Blue
15	Yellow
16	Blue (dark)

TABLE 2-2. Default Color Selections for an EGA or VGA Monitor

If you want to change from Color to Pattern fill style, you will use the Bar fill style field on Page 2 of the Titles & Options form. Make the change to the current graph now, following these steps:

1. Press **ESC** to return to the Bar/Line Chart Data form.
2. Press **F8** (Options).
3. Press **PGDN** to move to Page 2 of the Titles & Options form.
4. Press **TAB** twice to move to the Bar fill style field.

5. Press the spacebar to move the arrow cursor to Pattern.

6. Press (F2) (Draw chart) to view the chart with Pattern as a fill style.

7. Press any key and then repeat steps 5 and 6, selecting Both to view the chart with the bars filled with a color pattern.

CHANGING THE COLOR AND PATTERN ASSIGNMENTS Darker colors can focus attention on a specific series in a graph. The combination of colors can also lend balance to a graph. Using a dark color for the data series with the lowest values and lighter colors for those with larger values can help to achieve this balance. Naturally, you can change the colors for aesthetic reasons or to use the same colors used in your company logo. If you want to change the color or marker pattern for a specific series, you need to use the Color or Marker/Pattern fields on Page 4 of the Titles & Options form. You can change the values separately for each of the eight series possible.

The procedures for changing color and pattern assignments are the same except that you change the Color column entries to change color assignments and change the Marker/Pattern column to change the patterns assigned. If

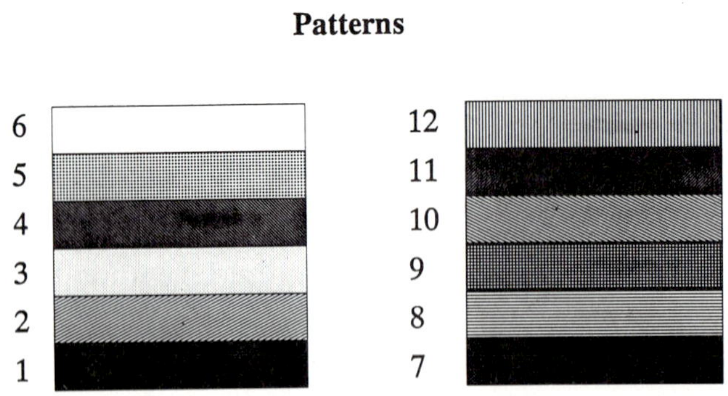

TABLE 2-3. Patterns

you are using patterns to distinguish the different series on your chart, changing the Color settings has no effect on your chart.

The following steps show you how to change the color assignments for a chart:

1. Press ESC to return to Page 2 of the Titles & Options form.
2. Press PGDN twice to move to Page 4 of the same form.
3. Press the TAB key ten times to move to the Color field for Series 1.
4. Press F6 (Colors).

Harvard Graphics displays a list of all the colors that you can use for your chart. In the middle of the table, Harvard Graphics displays the parts of the graph that use the colors. The F6 (Colors) key is only available for colors, not patterns.

5. Highlight Blue and press ENTER.
6. Press ENTER a second time to move to the row for the second series in the Color column.
7. Type **4** and press ENTER.
8. Type **3** and press ENTER.
9. Type **2**.
10. Press F2 (Draw chart) to view the chart with the new colors.

Changing the Frame

The line drawn around the chart area where Harvard Graphics graphs the chart data is the *frame.* The default frame style is a full frame around the bar graph, as shown in Figure 2-24. You can change the frame style with the Frame style options on Page 2 of the Titles & Options form. Harvard Graphics provides four options for frame style: Full, Half, Quarter, and None. The Full option provides a frame line on all sides, and None creates a graph with no frame line. When Half is selected the frame line is shown at the left and bottom of the graph. A selection of Quarter shows the graph with only a line at the bottom.

Complete these steps to change the frame style for the current graph to Half:

1. Press ESC to return to Page 4 of the Titles & Options form.
2. Press PGUP twice to move to Page 2.
3. Press the spacebar five times to change the bar style to Cluster, and then press ENTER.
4. Press the spacebar three times to change the Bar enhancement field to None.
5. Press the TAB key seven times to move to the Frame style field.
6. Press the spacebar to change from the default frame style of Full to Half.
7. Press F2 (Draw chart).

Other options that affect your graph's frame are found in the Frame color and Frame background fields. On a color monitor, you can specify color numbers corresponding to the color selections for bars shown in Table 2-2.

More Bar Customization Options

In the remaining chapters on graphs, you will be introduced to more graph options that can add variety to your presentation. There is one more group of settings that is important to include here since they only affect bar charts.

The Bar width, Bar overlap, and Bar depth fields need not be altered unless you are unhappy with the output. Since these options are located on Page 2 of the Titles & Options form, you can easily make a change to any of them after changing bar style or enhancements.

Unlike earlier custom bar options, these options require you to move to the field and then type your new entry of a number between 1 and 100. The number entry represents the relative width of bars as compared to the space available for the entry. The Bar overlap field uses your entry to indicate what percentage of overlap will be used to make one bar cover another. If you use this setting with a 3D overlap bar chart, the entry controls the overlap between the series in the chart. The Bar depth field allows you to type a number between 1 and 100 in order to control the depth of the bars, with the larger numbers assigning additional depth.

Follow these steps to make a change to an overlap chart:

1. Press ESC to return to the Titles & Options form on your screen.
2. Press HOME so the Bar style field is active.
3. Press the spacebar until the arrow cursor points to Overlap, and then press ENTER.
4. Press TAB until the Bar overlap field is active and type **75**.
5. Press F2 (Draw chart).

Notice the large amount of overlap that is now visible. You can change it back to 50% by repeating steps 4 and 5 in the procedure and typing **50**.

CHANGING THE TEXT FOR GRAPHS

With Harvard Graphics you can create graphs without worrying about the text size or style. Although these characteristics of the text are determined by font selection, you can use the default settings until you want to make a change. By default, Harvard Graphics uses a font called Executive, and selects appropriate sizes for the various titles and other text entries on a graph. If you do not have a problem with the appearance of your graph, you can print it without change. On the other hand there are many options that can improve the appearance of your graphs.

The character style used is determined by two different factors. One is the default font selected. The other determining factor is the size of the text. Figure 2-25 shows a few entries in different sizes. The sizes are already determined by Harvard Graphics for the titles, subtitles, and footnotes shown on the graph. They are represented as numbers that indicate each character's size as a percentage of the smallest side of the paper on which the graph will be printed. When you display the chart, Harvard Graphics shows text in sizes from 3.0 to 4.1 using the EGA or VGA video adapter hardware font. Text sizes less than 3.0 are displayed using a small sans serif font. When you print the chart, Harvard Graphics will output using the selected font. If you press F2 (Draw chart) after selecting Product output from the Main Menu, Harvard Graphics displays the fonts as they appear in the output rather than using the video adapter hardware fonts.

Text elements with a size of at least 6, such as the title with a default size of 8 and the subtitle with a default size of 6, appear in any new font selected with the Setup Defaults Font option. Figure 2-26 provides a sample of the fonts you can select.

FIGURE 2-25. Different sizes of Roman type

Changing the Default Font

With Harvard Graphics you change the font style through the Setup Defaults options. This menu allows you to choose from one of the font styles shown in Figure 2-26. Follow these steps to change a font:

1. Press ESC twice to return to the Main Menu.
2. Press F8 (Options).
3. Press TAB twice until the current font is highlighted.
4. Press the spacebar to move to the font style you want to select.
5. Press ESC to return to the Main Menu.
6. Select Enter/Edit chart.
7. Press F2 (Draw chart) to view the graph with the new font.

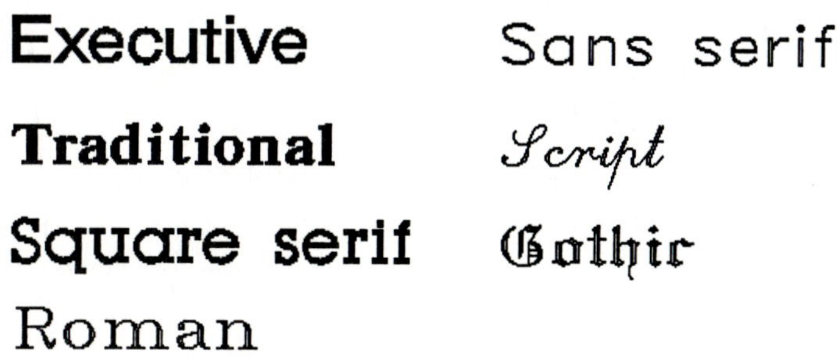

FIGURE 2-26. Fonts

Changing the Size of Entries

You may want to change the point size of titles or footnotes to achieve a more pleasing chart appearance. You may find that your chart looks crowded if you use the standard sizes for exceptionally long title entries. You may also want to reduce the size of X data names if they appear too close to the legend entries. Although you can change the location of legends, there is no option for altering their size.

Changing the size of characters is another aspect of font selection, although this task is completed directly from the Titles & Options form rather than the Setup Defaults menu. Sizes are selected individually for each element of text on the screen. With the default settings, the title entry is shown in the largest size and the footnote entries in the smallest. Pressing F7 (Size/Place) from Page 1 of the Titles & Options form changes the display to match Figure 2-27, which shows the default size for various text options. The size and placement for each line of text in the top of the Titles & Options form appears to the left of the specific lines of text. For example, looking at Figure 2-27, you can see that the subtitle's character size is six and the text is centered. The current point sizes and locations are added to the screen next to fields that can be altered.

To change the size of any text, all you need to do is type a new size next to the appropriate entry. Harvard Graphics accepts entries of between 0 and

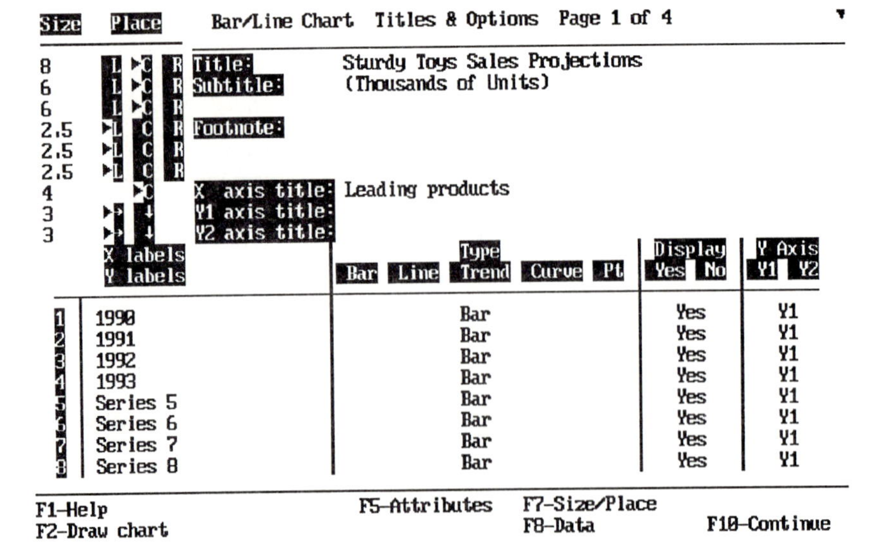

FIGURE 2-27. Size and Place options

100. Selecting 0 is equivalent to hiding the text entry, thus eliminating the need to erase it from the form.

Figure 2-25 provides an example of some of the text size possibilities for the Roman font. You can follow these steps to alter the text sizes for the title and subtitle entries on the current chart:

1. Press (ESC) to remove the chart from the screen.
2. Press (F8) (Options).
3. Press (F7) (Size/Place).
4. Type **10** and press (ENTER) to change the size of the title entry.
5. Type **8** and press (ENTER) to change the size of the subtitle entry.
6. Press (F2) (Draw chart) to display the chart.
7. Press (ESC) and repeat steps 3 through 6, changing the entries back to 8 and 6 as shown originally.

Changing the Location of Entries

Many text entries can be relocated. The current selections for each text entry are marked with an arrow pointer. Most options provide L, R, and C, representing left, right, and center locations for the text. Y-axis title options use an up or a down arrow representation to indicate horizontal or vertical placement of text.

You can move the footnote entries on the current chart to the right by following these steps:

1. Press ESC to return to Page 1 of the Titles & Options form.
2. Press F7 (Size/Place).
3. Press TAB seven times to highlight the L for Left on the first footnote line.
4. Press the spacebar twice to change the field to R.
5. Press TAB twice and then press the spacebar twice to change the entry for footnote line 2.
6. Press F2 (Draw chart) to display the graph with the footnotes to the right.

Creating a Table of Entries with the Chart

Although most of the time you want to replace numeric entries with a graph to convey your message without all the detail, there are situations where you might want to provide the detail for reference along with the chart. Harvard Graphics adds a table of the data values shown on the graph when you select Data Table Normal or Framed. Normal places the data values beneath the chart in rows and columns. Framed places the data values in the same location, except they are framed to set them off from the chart and to provide clear division between entries.

The scaling factor used by Harvard Graphics for the Y-axis affects the appearance of the entries in this table. You might need to change the scaling options if you want your actual values to display as entered. Follow these steps to display the data for your PRODUCTS chart:

1. Press ESC until the Main Menu appears.
2. Select Get/Save/Remove.

3. Select Get chart.
4. Highlight PRODUCTS and press ENTER twice.
5. Press ESC to eliminate the graph display, and then press F8 (Options) to activate the Titles & Options form.
6. Press PGDN twice to move to Page 3.
7. Press the spacebar twice to move the arrow cursor to Framed.
8. Press F2 (Draw chart).

Notice the table contains entries scaled by a factor of 1000 rather than your actual entries.

9. Press ESC to return to Page 3 of the Titles & Options form.
10. Press SHIFT-TAB twice to move to the Increment for the Y1 Axis Linear entries.

This will move the cursor to the second field from the bottom of the form.

11. Type **750.**
12. Press F2 (Draw chart) to see the entries in the table as you originally entered them. Your chart should match the one in Figure 2-28.

The trick to changing the scaling of values in the data table is to choose a value that is less than the scaling factor selected by Harvard Graphics. This means you could have entered any increment less than 1000 to make this change. If you remove the legend, as described in Chapter 3, Harvard Graphics displays the legend information as part of the data table.

CHECKING YOUR SPELLING

All of your hard work in selecting the most attractive graphics options are lost on your audience if the title and legends in your graphs contain spelling errors. These mistakes distract from the message your graph is supposed to convey and focus attention on the defective entries.

The Harvard Graphics Check Spelling option actually provides checks beyond incorrect spelling. It looks for numbers that are punctuated incorrectly, such as 9,45.90. It looks for repeated words, as in "The Year of the the Tiger." Words with incorrect capitalization are also highlighted, as in

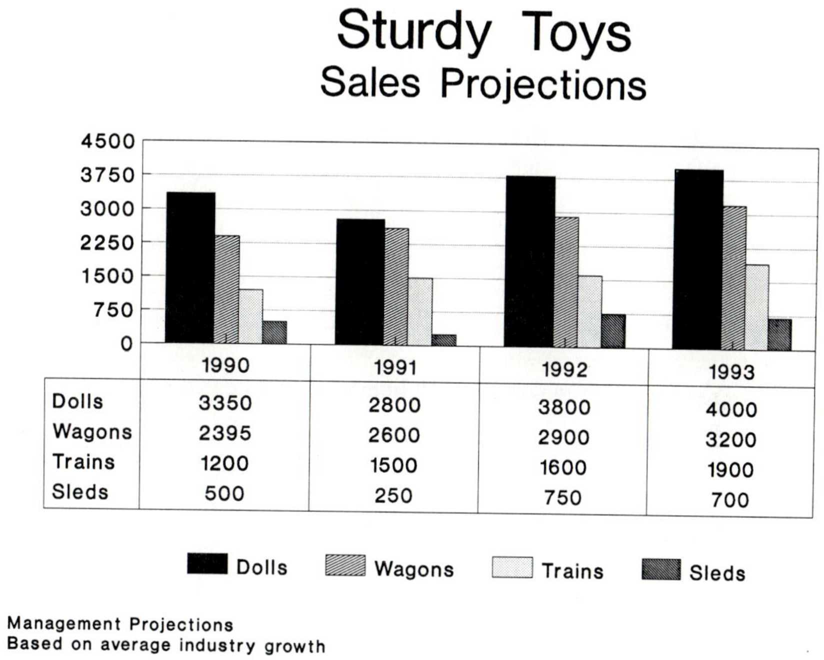

FIGURE 2-28. Chart with data table

"CLeveland." Misplaced punctuation, such as ";profit" is another potential problem. When the Spelling checker option catches these oversights, it saves your making payments for unusable slides or the embarrassment of mistakes in a presentation.

Using the Check Spelling Option

You can check the spelling in the entries on any graph by returning to the Main Menu and pressing F4 (Spell check). Harvard Graphics highlights words that are not in its dictionary and offers you several options.

If the word highlighted as potentially misspelled is correct, press ENTER to select the option Work ok, continue that is marked with the arrow cursor. If the word is correct and you would like to add it to your dictionary, choose the Add to dictionary option.

For words marked as potentially misspelled that are in fact incorrect, you have two other choices. If Harvard Graphics suggests replacements for the word, you can highlight one of the options and press ENTER to make the change. If there are no suggestions or none of the options are correct, you can move the arrow cursor to Type correction and press ENTER. A Type Spelling Correction form will appear for your entry.

Trying the Spelling Checker Option with a Graph

You need to make some deliberate mistakes in entering a new graph to see all the features of the Check Spelling option. Add titles, a footnote, and legends to a new bar chart, but do not enter data since the only purpose of these entries is to try the Check Spelling option. Follow these steps to enter the data and replace incorrectly spelled words:

1. Press ESC twice to return to the Main Menu.
2. Select Create new chart.
3. Select Bar/Line and then press ENTER to acknowledge the warning box concerning data loss.
4. Press F10 (Continue) to accept the default of Name for the X-axis data type.
5. Type **ABC Compny** and press ENTER. Don't correct any of the spelling mistakes at this point, or the exercise will not work correctly for you.
6. Type **Producton Data** and press ENTER.
7. Type **Annual Reprt 1990** and press ENTER.
8. Type the following X-axis entries, pressing ENTER after each:

   Laders
   Brushes
   Hooks

9. Press ESC to return to the Main Menu.
10. Press F4 (Spell check).

The first word highlighted is "ABC," since it is not in the dictionary. If the name of your company was ABC Company, you would probably want to add the word to your dictionary to prevent having to bypass it on many screens. For now, you will bypass it.

11. Press ENTER to select Word ok, continue.

The next word highlighted is "Compny." This word is spelled incorrectly, and one of the replacement words shown in Figure 2-29 is an appropriate correction.

12. Move the arrow cursor to Company and press ENTER.

Notice how the correctly spelled word matches the incorrect one in capitalization. Harvard Graphics moves to the next potentially misspelled word.

13. Move the arrow cursor to Production and press ENTER.
14. Move the arrow cursor to Report and press ENTER.

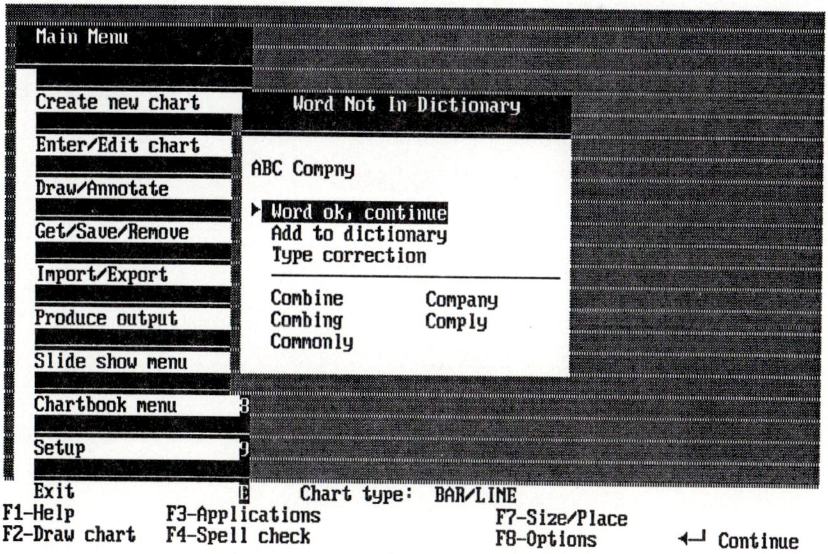

FIGURE 2-29. Suggested spelling corrections

The suggestions for the next incorrectly spelled word, "Laders" are not appropriate, so you must type the correction yourself.

15. Move the arrow cursor to Type correction and press ENTER.
16. Type **Ladders** and press ENTER.
17. Select Enter/Edit chart to view the corrected entries.

chapter 3

CREATING LINE AND AREA CHARTS

Getting Started
New Options for Bar and Line Charts
Area Charts
High/Low/Close Charts
Using Calculations

Now that you have mastered bar graphs, you are ready to explore some of the other chart types that Harvard Graphics supports. This chapter covers additional graph types that can provide important variety to your presentation and maintain the interest of your audience. In this chapter you will learn to use three important new graph types and their variations: line, area, and high/low/close charts. These graph types share many features with bar graphs, and many of the options for bar charts also apply to these chart types. You should, therefore, feel comfortable with creating and modifying these new chart types.

Line graphs graph each series of data with a point and connect each point in a series with a line. You can use line graphs to show trends, and they are a much better choice than bar charts when you have a large volume of data. Using bars with many data values would create a very crowded graph but with a line chart the same data creates an attractive graph that is easy to understand. There are several variations on line graphs: a trend line, a curve line, or a *scatter chart,* which is a line comprised of unconnected points.

Area graphs consist of a line between each point in a series and the area beneath the line filled with a solid color or shaded pattern. Area graphs provide an effective way to show trends and volumes. They can also be combined with a line graph. In a combination graph, revenues might be shown on the area chart and costs shown on a line chart imposed on top of the area chart.

High/low/close graphs are used to chart financial data, like stock or bond prices, as well as error bars or other statistical data. These graphs can show the price range of a financial commodity as well as the opening or closing prices.

Harvard Graphics supports a calculate feature that you can use to rearrange series as you did in Chapter 2 or to compute the values in another series. You can use calculations to make projections and forecasts.

GETTING STARTED

Figure 3-1 shows a line graph that you can create with a few menu selections once you enter the data. Once you create this graph, you can convert it into an area graph. Follow these steps to enter the data and display the chart.

1. From the Main Menu, select Create new chart.
2. Select Bar/Line and press ENTER if Harvard Graphics prompts you about losing the graph in memory.
3. Press F10 (Continue) from the X Data Type menu to accept the default X data type of Name.
4. Type **Mel's Paperbacks** as the title and press ENTER until the cursor is at the entry for the X-axis data point names.
5. Type **East** and press ENTER.
6. Type **North** and press ENTER.
7. Type **West** and press ENTER.
8. Type **South** and press ENTER.
9. Type **Central** and press ENTER.
10. Press the HOME key to move to the first X-axis name.

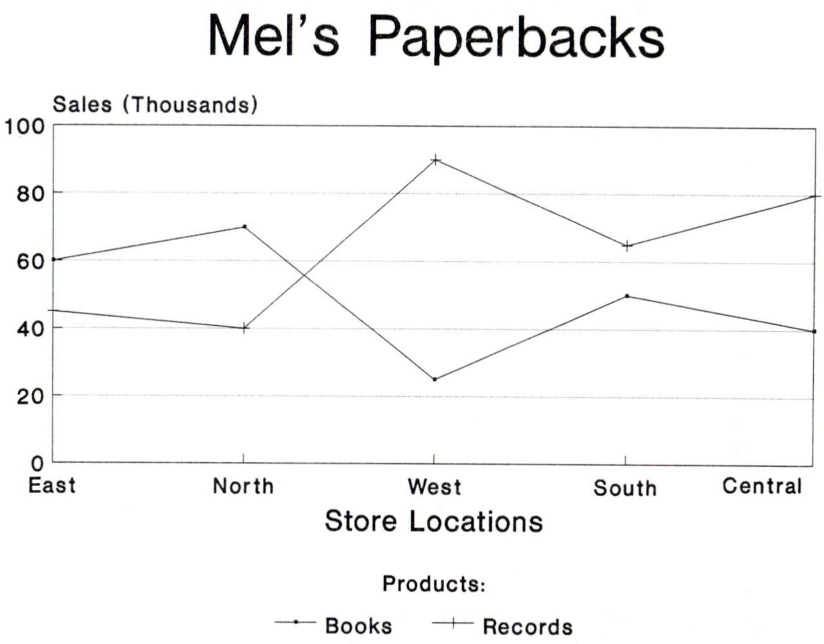

FIGURE 3-1. Line graph to get you started

11. Press (TAB) to move to the first series.
12. Type **60000** and press (ENTER).
13. Type **70000** and press (ENTER).
14. Type **25000** and press (ENTER).
15. Type **50000** and press (ENTER).
16. Type **40000** and press (ENTER).
17. Press the (HOME) key to move to the first X-axis name.
18. Press (TAB) twice to move to the second series.
19. Type **45000** and press (ENTER).
20. Type **40000** and press (ENTER).
21. Type **90000** and press (ENTER).
22. Type **65000** and press (ENTER).
23. Type **80000** and press (ENTER).

24. Press F8 (Options) to display the Titles & Options screen.
25. Move the cursor to the field for the X-axis title.
26. Type **Store Locations** and press ENTER.
27. Type **Sales** and press ENTER to enter a title for the Y1-axis.
28. Move to the Legend Title field.
29. Type **Products:** and press ENTER.
30. Press CTRL-DELETE, type **Books**, and then press ENTER.
31. Press CTRL-DELETE and type **Records**.
32. Press SHIFT-TAB three times to move the Type column for the first series.
33. Select Line and press ENTER to display the first series as a line graph.
34. Select Line and press ENTER to display the second series as a line graph.
35. Press F2 (Draw chart) to create a graph like Figure 3-1.
36. Press ESC twice to return to the Main Menu.
37. Press CTRL-S to select Get/Save/Remove and Save chart.
38. Type **Line1** and press F10 (Continue) to save the graph.
39. Select Produce output.
40. Select Printer.
41. Press F10 (Continue) to print the chart.

NEW OPTIONS FOR BAR AND LINE CHARTS

You may feel that you have seen all the possibilities for altering graphs with the bar chart selections you have used, but there are more. Most of the chart options covered for bar charts in Chapter 2 also apply to line charts. Four pages of options on the Titles & Options form still allow you to customize your line and bar graphs. Several options not discussed in Chapter 2 are covered in this chapter—options that allow you to hide series, draw lines that describe the trend of your data, label the data points, adjust the legend, create grid lines, set how the axes labels appear, change the settings the axes use, and change the line color, marker, and line style Harvard Graphics uses to display the data.

Display Options for Line Charts

While a line chart can be created by simply selecting Line for the series in the first page of Titles & Options, Harvard Graphics has other options that you can use instead of Line. To appreciate the difference between the options, you should enter the data for a new chart that tracks the customer traffic for four different times of the year. A chart like this might be used to schedule employees so additional staff is available on the busiest days, when additional customer assistance is needed.

To create this new line chart, follow these steps:

1. Select Create new chart from the Main Menu.
2. Select Bar/Line.

If you are prompted to keep the current data, select No.

3. From the X Data Type menu, select Month for the X data type and press ENTER.
4. Type **January** and press ENTER to start the X data labels with January.
5. Type **June** to finish the X data labels with June.
6. Press F10 (Continue) to process your entries. Harvard Graphics generates the months as the X data point labels.
7. Type **Mel's Paperbacks** and press ENTER for the chart title.
8. Type **Sales Performance** and press ENTER for the chart subtitle. Press ENTER again, since this graph does not have a footnote.
9. Press TAB to move to the column for the first series.
10. Type **14000** and press ENTER for the first value. Type **17000, 17500, 18000, 13000,** and **22000** in the first series column, pressing ENTER after each one.

11. Press HOME to move to January and then press TAB twice to move to the column for the second series.
12. Type **13000** and press ENTER for the first value. Type **14000, 15000, 14000, 11000,** and **16000** in the second series column, pressing ENTER after each one.
13. Press HOME to move to January and then press TAB three times to move to the column for the third series.
14. Type **16000** and press ENTER for the first value. Type **18000, 18000, 19000, 15000,** and **25000** in the third series column, pressing ENTER after each one.
15. Press HOME to move to January and then press TAB four times to move to the column for the fourth series.
16. Type **2000** and press ENTER for the first value. Type **22000, 23000, 23500, 23500,** and **26000** in the fourth series column, pressing ENTER after each one. The Bar/Line Chart Data form looks like Figure 3-2.
17. Press F8 (Options), and press ENTER until the cursor is at Series 1.
18. Enter the legend text by typing **Anderson, Johnston, Saunders,** and **Williams,** pressing ENTER after each one.

Bar/Line Chart Data

Title: Mel's Paperbacks
Subtitle: Sales Performance
Footnote:

Pt	X Axis Month	Anderson	Johnston	Saunders	Williams
1	January	14000	13000	16000	2000
2	February	17000	14000	18000	22000
3	March	17500	15000	18000	23000
4	April	18000	14000	19000	23500
5	May	13000	11000	15000	23500
6	June	22000	16000	25000	26000
7					
8					
9					
10					
11					
12					

F1-Help F3-Save F5-Set X type F9-More series
F2-Draw chart F4-Draw/Annot F6-Calculate F8-Options F10-Continue

FIGURE 3-2. Data for second line graph

19. Move to Anderson and press TAB to move to the Type column.
20. Make each series a line graph. You can either press RIGHT ARROW, the spacebar, or type **L** and press ENTER for each of the four series.

If you do not make this change the graph will display as a Bar Type chart, because that is the default setting when you choose Bar/Line from the initial chart type menu. When you have finished, the first page of Titles & Options looks like Figure 3-3.

21. Press F2 (Draw chart) to display the line chart which looks like Figure 3-4.

This line chart illustrates many of the default settings that Harvard Graphics uses for line charts. Many of the options that you used for bar charts in Chapter 2 are also available for line charts. For example, if you change the default Type field entry to Line, each data point is marked with a marker. Each data series uses a different marker, and the data points in a series are connected with a line. If your monitor displays colors, you can see that Harvard Graphics distinguishes each series with a different color as well.

Bar/Line Chart Titles & Options Page 1 of 4

Title: Mel's Paperbacks
Subtitle: Sales Performance

Footnote:

X axis title:
Y1 axis title:
Y2 axis title:

Legend Title:		Type (Bar Line Trend Curve Pt)	Display (Yes No)	Y Axis (Y1 Y2)
1	Anderson	Line	Yes	Y1
2	Johnston	Line	Yes	Y1
3	Saunders	Line	Yes	Y1
4	Williams	Line	Yes	Y1
5	Series 5	Bar	Yes	Y1
6	Series 6	Bar	Yes	Y1
7	Series 7	Bar	Yes	Y1
8	Series 8	Bar	Yes	Y1

F1-Help F5-Attributes F7-Size/Place
F2-Draw chart F8-Data F10-Continue

FIGURE 3-3. First page of Titles & Options

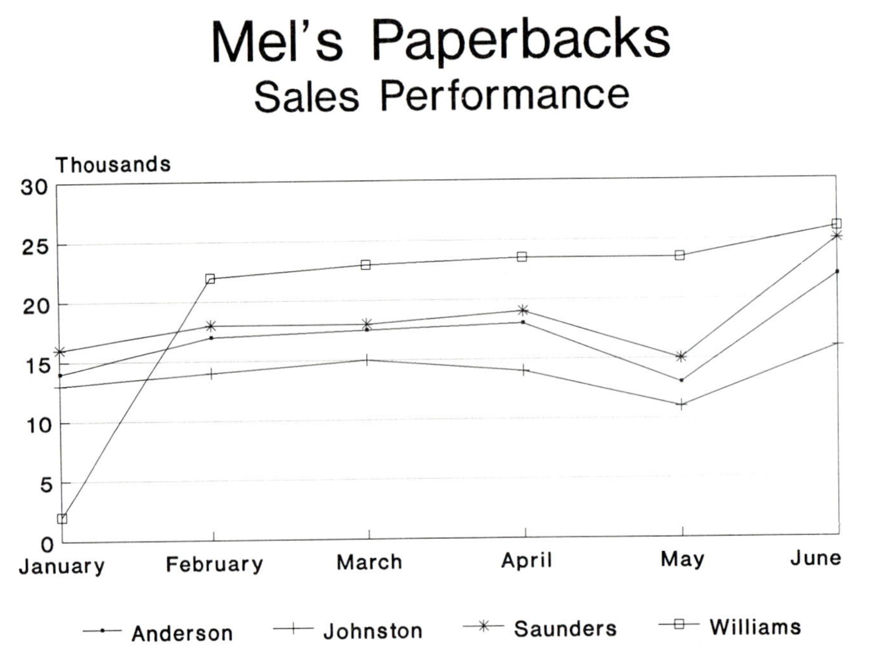

FIGURE 3-4. Line chart created with data from Figure 3-2

You have other Type settings that you can use to control the display of the data. The first page of the Titles & Options form lists Trend, Curve, and Pt in addition to Line and Bar. These three options are variations of a line graph with a different appearance. You can try these graph types with the data you have entered by following these steps:

1. Press any key to return to the Titles & Options screen.
2. Move to the Line selection for the Anderson series.
3. Change the type to Trend for all of the series by pressing (RIGHT ARROW) or the spacebar, or by typing **T** and pressing (ENTER) for each of the series.
4. Press (F2) (Draw chart) to display the line chart, which displays the trends of the data series. This chart looks like Figure 3-5.

A trend chart displays each data point in a series with a marker. Each data series uses a different marker. Instead of drawing a line that connects the points, the line in a trend chart is a straight line that describes the trend

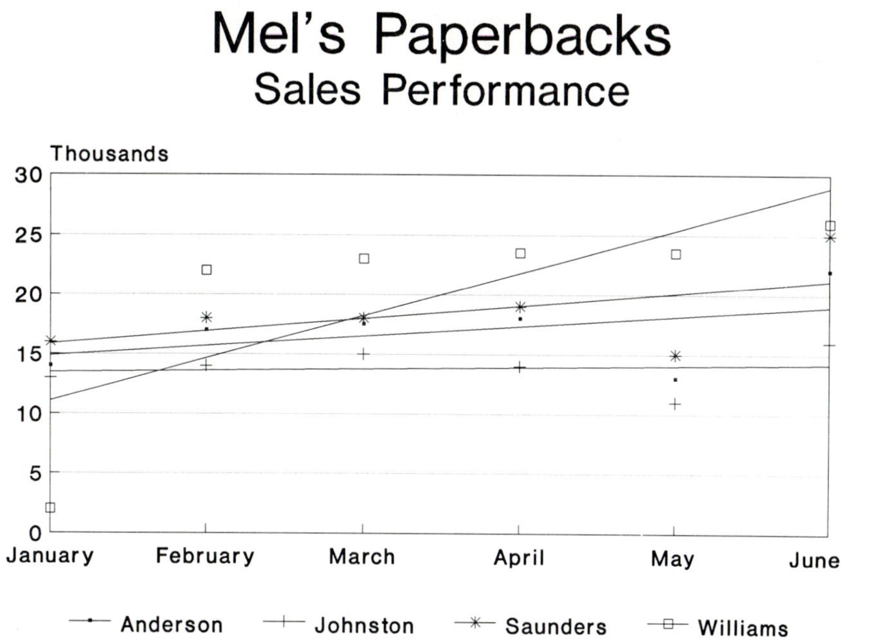

FIGURE 3-5. Chart displayed with Trend type

of the data points (up, down, or steady). Mathematically, Harvard Graphics computes the line that best fits the data points. This computation of a best fit is done with the least-squares method.

5. Press any key to return to the Titles & Options screen.
6. Move to the Trend selection for the Anderson series.
7. Change the type to Curve for all the series by pressing (RIGHT ARROW) or typing **C** and pressing (ENTER) for each of the series.
8. Press (F2) (Draw chart) to display the line chart, which displays the curves of the data series. This chart looks like Figure 3-6.

Like the trend chart, a curve chart displays the data points of each series with a different marker. Unlike the trend chart, the curve chart creates a curved line that represents the trend of the data. The line created with this type of chart will fluctuate more than the line created with the trend type. For example, if you are charting monthly sales for more than one year, a

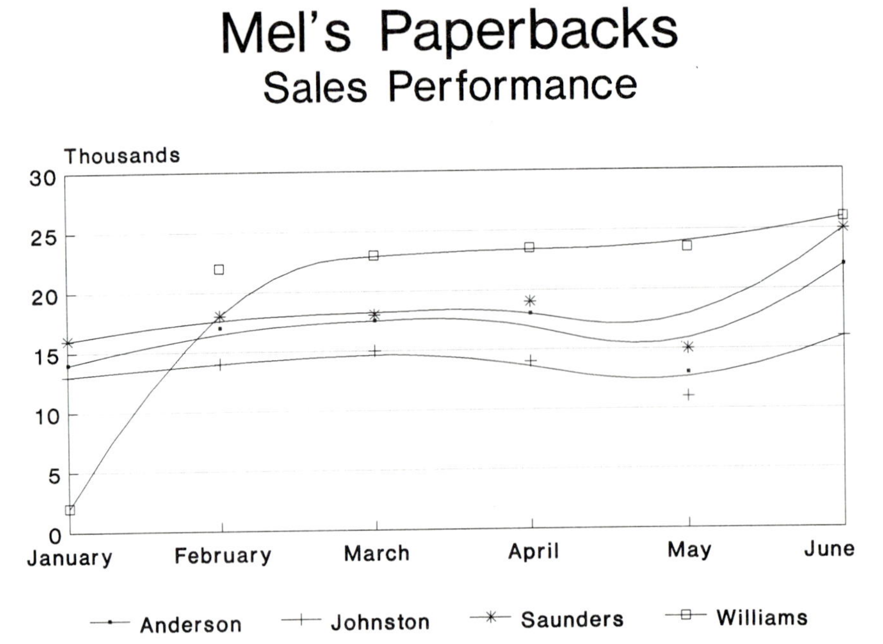

FIGURE 3-6. Chart displayed with Curve type

trend chart might show a sales increase or decrease but would ignore seasonal fluctuations. A curve chart would show a general sales increase or decrease as well as seasonal variations.

9. Press any key to return to the Titles & Options screen.
10. Move to the Curve selection for the Anderson series.
11. Change the type to Pt by pressing RIGHT ARROW or typing **P** and pressing ENTER for each of the series.
12. Press F2 (Draw chart) to display the line chart, which displays the points of the data series. This chart looks like Figure 3-7.

Like line, trend, and curve charts, a points chart displays the data points of each series with a different marker. Unlike the other chart types, the points chart does not connect the values in a data series, nor does it draw any lines. With this type, only the individual data points are displayed. It can be harder to see a trend. Also if there are many data points, it can be difficult to distinguish which data point belongs to each series.

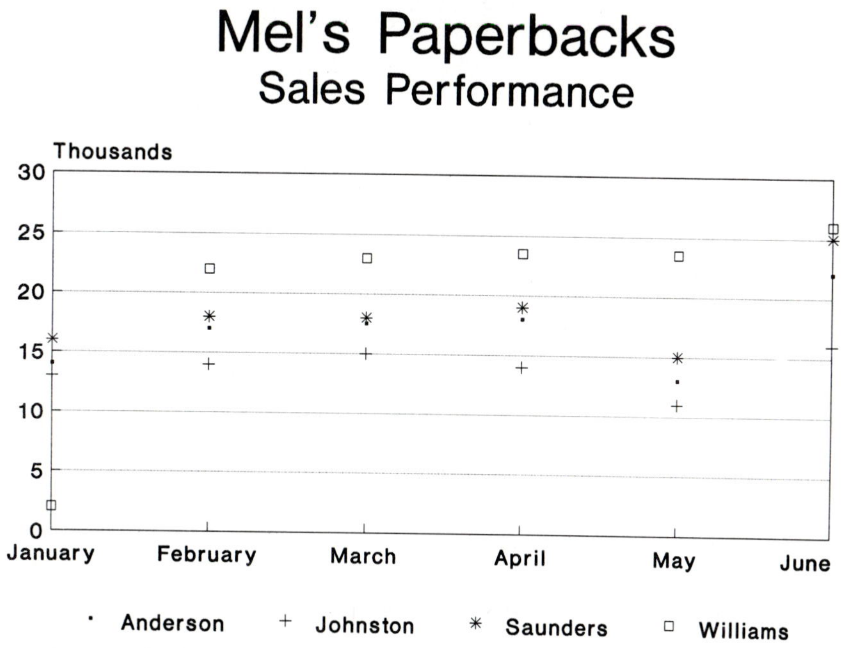

FIGURE 3-7. Chart displayed with Pt type

13. Press any key to remove the graph from the screen.
14. Move to the Type selection for the Anderson series.
15. Change the Type to Line by pressing the spacebar twice or typing **L** and pressing ENTER for each of the series.
16. Press ESC to return to the Main Menu.
17. Press CTRL-S to save the chart.
18. Type **Line2** and press F10 (Continue).

Mixing Display Types

As you have seen in the sample exercises, changing the type for one data series does not change the Type field entry for another data series. This allows you to mix data types. You can combine any of the five types in a chart. To mix display types, select the type you want each series displayed in. You can try mixing graph types with the data entered for the LINE1 graph.

1. Press CTRL-G to get a chart.
2. Select LINE1 from the list and press ENTER.
3. Press any key to remove the graph from the screen.
4. Press F8 (Options) to display Titles & Options.
5. Move to the Type column for the first series (Books).
6. Select Pt and press ENTER.
7. Select Curve for the type for the second series (Records).
8. Press F2 (Draw chart) to view the chart, which looks like Figure 3-8.

While this example presents only one combination, your possible selections are almost endless. You should use only two or three types in a single

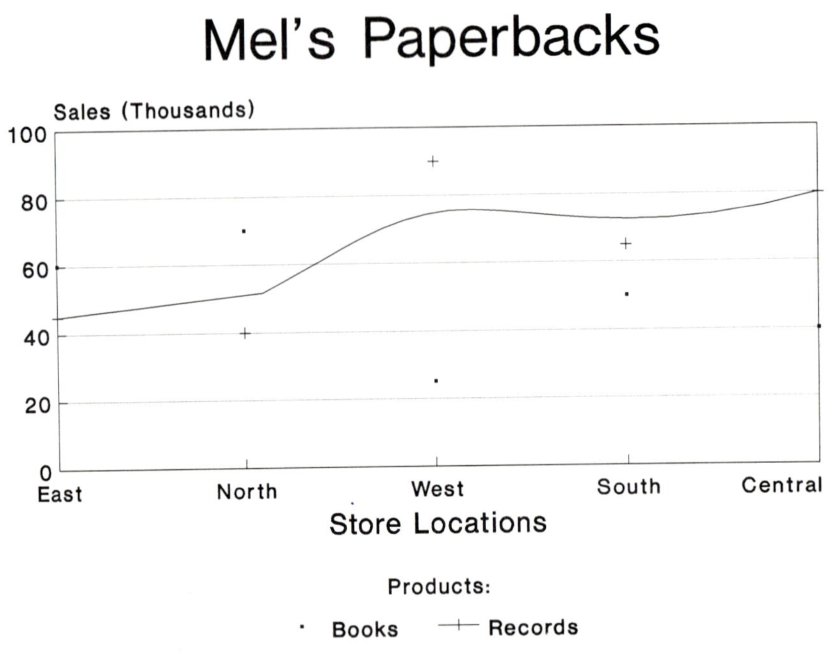

FIGURE 3-8. Chart using two display types

chart. If you try combining all of the types in a single graph, the result will look too busy for the reader to focus on the data.

9. Press any key to leave the graph.

Hiding Data Series

As you use the graphs you create, you may decide to use a graph in a different way. For example, if you are only interested in showing the proportion of books sold at each of Mel's Paperbacks, you need not show the information for records. Harvard Graphics allows you to hide any series and select which data you want to present. To try this feature with the LINE1 chart, follow these steps:

1. Press **ESC** to return to the Main Menu.
2. Select Get/Save/Remove.

You can abandon the changes you have made by retrieving the same chart again.

3. Select Get chart.
4. Select LINE1 from the list and press **ENTER**.
5. Press **ENTER** when Harvard Graphics displays a warning that you have not saved your changes.

You are telling Harvard Graphics to ignore the changes you made since you do not want to save them.

6. Press any key to remove the graph from the screen.
7. Press **F8** (Options) to display Titles & Options.
8. Move to the Display column for the second series (Records).
9. Select No.
10. Press **F2** (Draw chart) to view the graph.

Only the data for books appears because the records data is hidden. You can quickly return the records data to the display.

11. Press any key to leave the graph.
12. Select Yes from the Display column for the second series.
13. Press F2 (Draw chart) to view the graph.

The data for records reappears because you have selected to display the series. By changing the setting in the Display column, you can quickly change which data appears in the chart. Hiding data series becomes especially useful when you start using the calculate feature to create data series from other data series.

14. Press any key to leave the graph.

Options Unavailable for Line Charts

Some of the options that you learned in Chapter 2 for bar charts do not work for line charts. The options for bar style, bar enhancement, bar fill style, bar width, and bar overlap do not affect line graphs. The exception is if you create a line graph that uses the overlap bar style and a 3D bar enhancement. The resulting line graph looks like a ribbon, as shown in Figure 3-9. To create this chart using LINE1, follow these steps:

1. Press PGDN to display Page 2 of the Titles & Options form.
2. Select Overlap and press ENTER.
3. Select 3D and press ENTER.
4. Select Pattern and press ENTER.
5. Press F2 (Draw chart) to view the graph.

In this type of a graph, where each data series appears as a ribbon, you can use the Bar depth option to control the width of the ribbon. You also should label the data points, as described later in this chapter, so you have no difficulty determining the values of the data points that the ribbons connect.

6. Press any key to remove the chart from the screen.
7. Return the lines to their original appearance by selecting Cluster for bar style and None for bar enhancement. You can also return the setting of Bar/Fill style to Color.

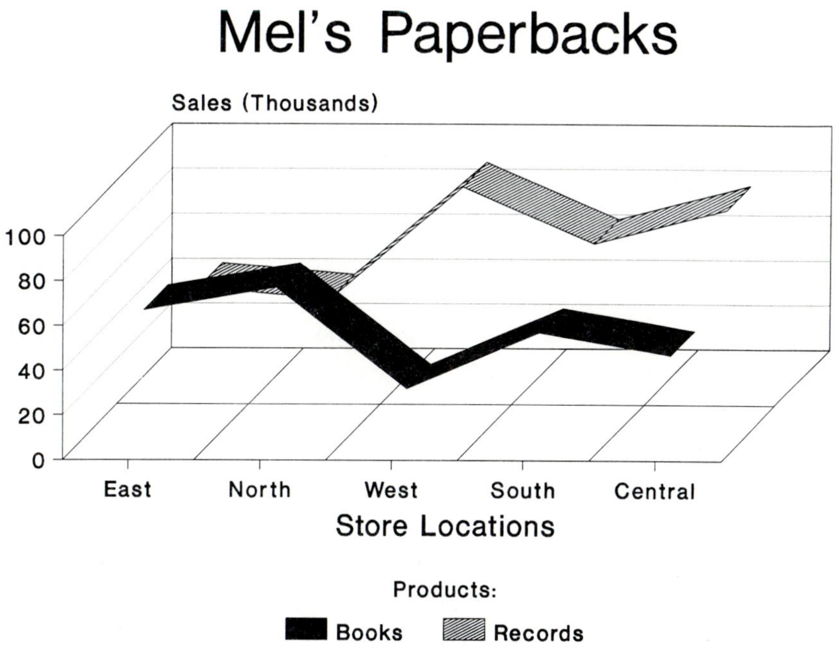

FIGURE 3-9. Line chart with overlap style and 3D enhancement

Setting the Series Appearance

When you look at the charts you created, you can see that Harvard Graphics uses several default settings for how each series appears. For example, each series uses a different color and marker. When the chart has a line for a series, Harvard Graphics uses a solid line. You can change the color, marker, and line style that the chart uses for each series.

CHANGING THE SERIES COLOR In the charts you created, each of the series display is a different color. To change the color of a series, move to Page 4 of the Titles & Options form, shown in Figure 3-10. Move to the Color column for the series you want to change. Each color is represented by a different number. To change the color a series uses, type the new number for the series. The numbers and the colors that represent them (using the default palette on an EGA or VGA monitor) are as follows:

1	White	9	White
2	Cyan (dark)	10	Grey (light)
3	Blue	11	Black
4	Blue (light)	12	Red
5	Cyan (light)	13	Green
6	Yellow (light)	14	Blue
7	White	15	Yellow
8	Black	16	Blue (dark)

An alternative is to press F6 (Colors). A box appears, listing these colors and numbers, from which you can highlight the color you want and then press ENTER.

CHANGING THE SERIES MARKER OR PATTERN In a line, trend, or curve chart, the data points in each series are marked with a unique marker. Both the marker and the line are set in the Marker/Pattern column in the fourth Titles & Options page.

Bar/Line Chart Titles & Options Page 4 of 4

Title: Mel's Paperbacks
Subtitle:

Footnote:

X axis title: Store Locations
Y1 axis title: Sales (Thousands)
Y2 axis title:

Legend Title: Products:		Cum Yes No	Y Label Yes No	Color	Marker/ Pattern	Line Style
1	Books	No	No	2	1	1
2	Records	No	No	3	2	1
3	Series 3	No	No	4	3	1
4	Series 4	No	No	5	4	1
5	Series 5	No	No	6	5	1
6	Series 6	No	No	7	6	1
7	Series 7	No	No	8	7	1
8	Series 8	No	No	9	8	1

F1-Help F5-Attributes F7-Size/Place
F2-Draw chart F6-Colors F8-Data F10-Continue

FIGURE 3-10. Fourth page of Titles & Options

To change the marker or pattern of a series, move to the fourth page of Titles & Options, shown in Figure 3-10. Move to the Marker/Pattern column for the series you want to change. Each marker and pattern is represented by a different number. Type the new number for the series. If you type **0** in the Marker/Pattern column, that series in a line, trend, or curve chart does not use a marker (bar charts are unaffected). The markers and patterns are shown in Figure 3-11.

CHANGING THE SERIES LINE STYLES In line, trend, and curve charts, tne lines are thin and solid with the default setting. You can change the line style to a more appropriate one. For example, if you are creating slides to view from a distance, you may want thicker lines so the people sitting at the rear of the presentation area can see the series lines. Also you may want to make a series containing estimated values appear with a dotted line so the viewers realize that the values are an estimate.

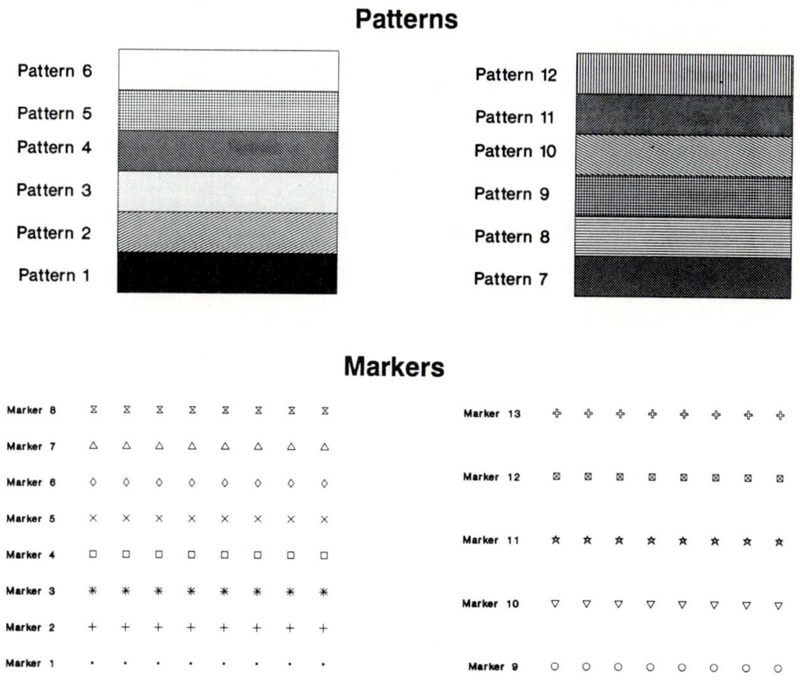

FIGURE 3-11. Patterns and markers available for bar and line charts

To change the line style of a series, move to Page 4 of the Titles & Options form. Move to the Line Style column for the series you want to change. You can enter a new number between 1 and 4. Each number represents a different line style. The numbers and the line styles they represent are as follows.

1 Thin, solid line
2 Thick, solid line
3 Dotted line (....)
4 Dashed line (— —)

Creating a Cumulative Chart

On some charts you might be interested in the total value of all the data point entries. Page 4 of the Titles & Options form provides an option that allows you to chart each series as the cumulative value of all data points in the series. For example, in the LINE2 chart that charts the sales for four salespeople, you may want to graph the data so the chart shows their cumulative sales. To make this change to the LINE2 chart, follow these steps:

1. Press ESC to return to the Main Menu.
2. Press CTRL-S to save the chart.
3. Press F10 (Continue) to save the changes you have made to LINE1.
4. Press CTRL-G to get another chart.
5. Select LINE2 from the list and press ENTER.
6. Press any key to remove the graph from the screen.
7. Press F8 (Options) to display Titles & Options.
8. Press PGUP to move to the fourth page of Titles & Options.
9. Move to the Cum column for the first series (Anderson).
10. Select Yes and press ENTER for each of the four series.
11. Press F2 (Draw chart) to view the graph.

The chart looks like Figure 3-12. Each point in the chart is the salesperson's cumulative total sales up to the month.

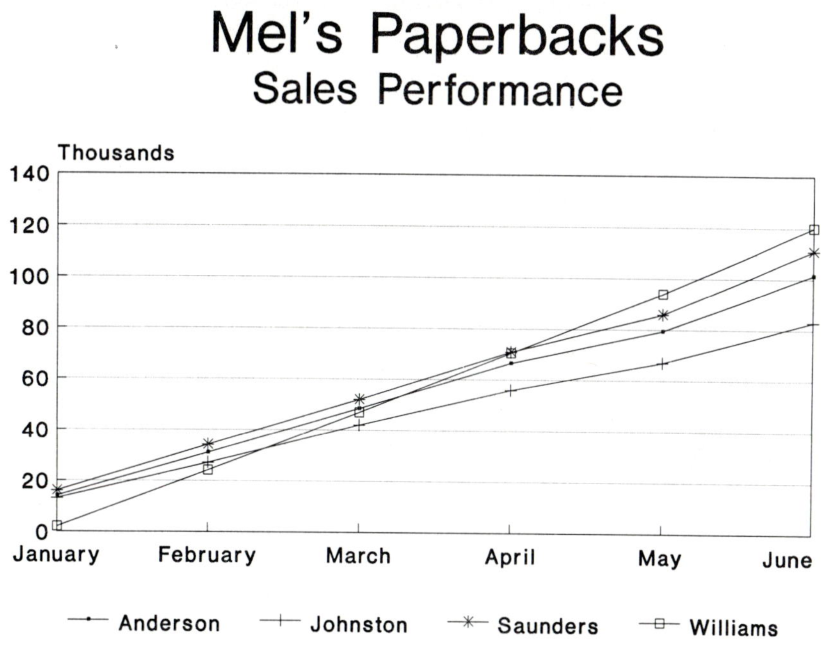

FIGURE 3-12. Line chart showing cumulative values

12. Press any key to remove the graph.

If you want to return the Cum setting to the default, you would change Yes to No for the series in the Cum column. You can also display some series as cumulative and other series as their actual values.

Changing the Legend

In Chapter 2, you learned how to enter the text for a graph's legend. You also learned how to remove legends from a graph. Harvard Graphics offers other options you can use to change the position and appearance of the legend.

CHANGING THE LEGEND'S LOCATION By default, Harvard Graphics positions the legend at the bottom of the chart, below the graphed data. Harvard Graphics lets you select one of 12 positions through a combination of legend location and legend justification.

To reposition the legend, follow these steps:

1. Press ESC to return to the Main Menu.
2. Select Get/Save/Remove.
3. Select Get chart.
4. Select LINE1 from the list and press ENTER.
5. Press ENTER to confirm that you want to lose the changes you made to LINE2.
6. Press any key to remove the graph from the screen.
7. Press F8 (Options) to display Titles & Options. Press PGDN to go to the second page.
8. Move to Legend location.
9. Select the legend position by pressing the spacebar.
10. Press F2 (Draw chart) to view the graph.

Figure 3-13 displays each of the legend positions that are possible using the graph from the LINE1 chart. A chart subtitle is added describing the legend position.

11. Press any key to remove the graph from the screen.

CHANGING THE LEGEND'S JUSTIFICATION In each of the legend locations in Figure 3-13, the legend is centered in its area. You can change the justification of the legend within the legend area by moving to Legend justify and selecting the symbol or word representing the position where you want the legend. If you choose ← or ↑, the legend is placed at the top of the legend area when Legend location is Left or Right. When Legend location is Top or Bottom, the ← or ↑ setting for Legend justify places the legend at the left side of the top or bottom area of the legend area. If you choose Center, the legend is placed in the middle of the legend area. If you choose ↓ or →, the legend is placed at the bottom of the legend area when Legend location is Left or Right. When Legend location is Top or Bottom, the ↓ or → setting for Legend places the legend at the right side of the top or bottom of the legend area.

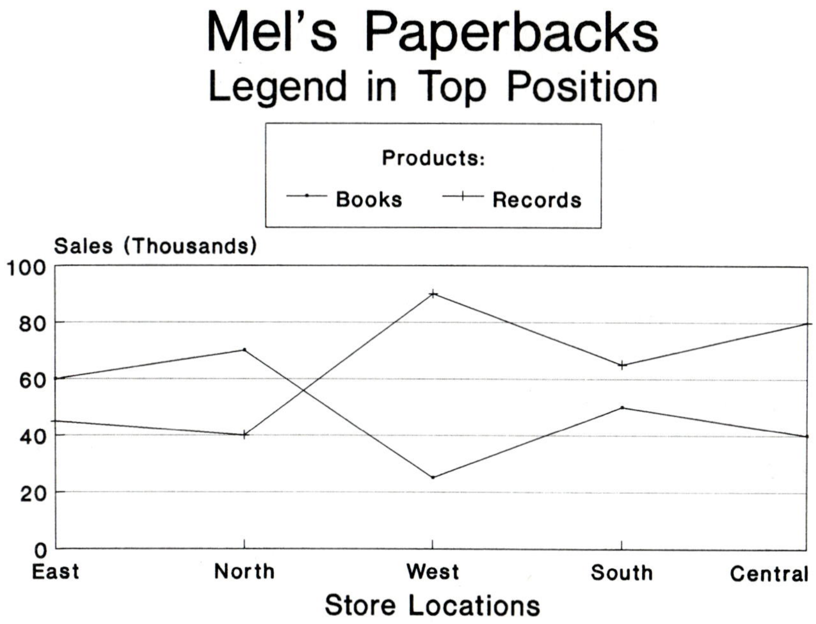

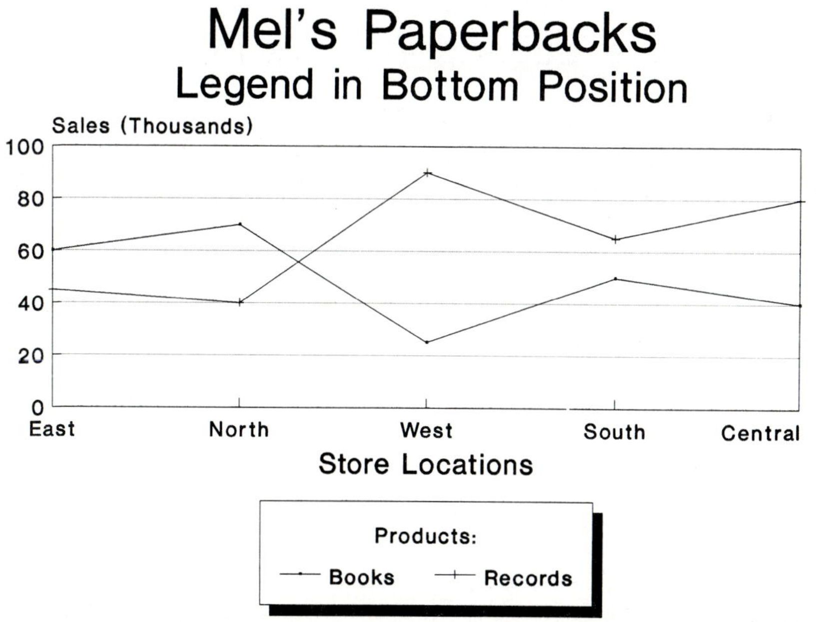

FIGURE 3-13. Charts showing legend position

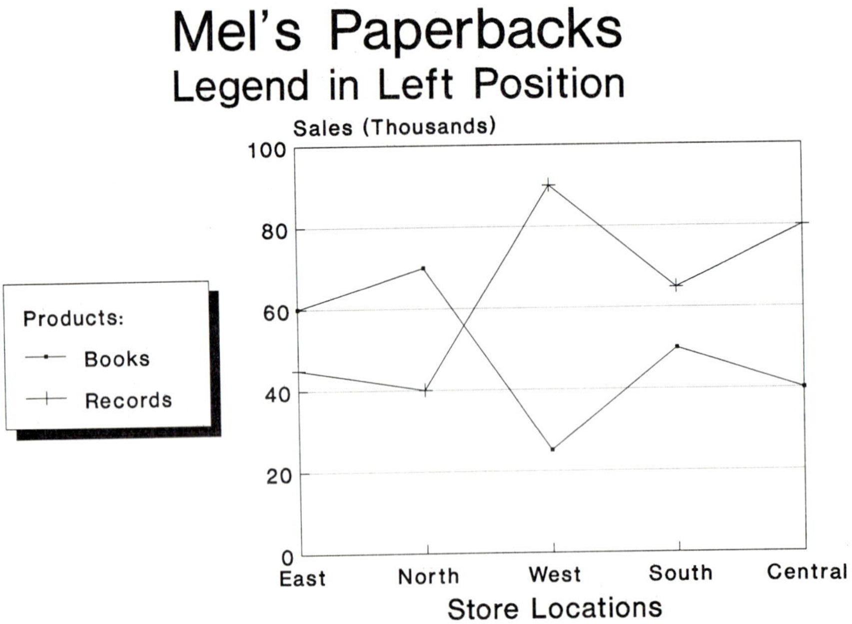

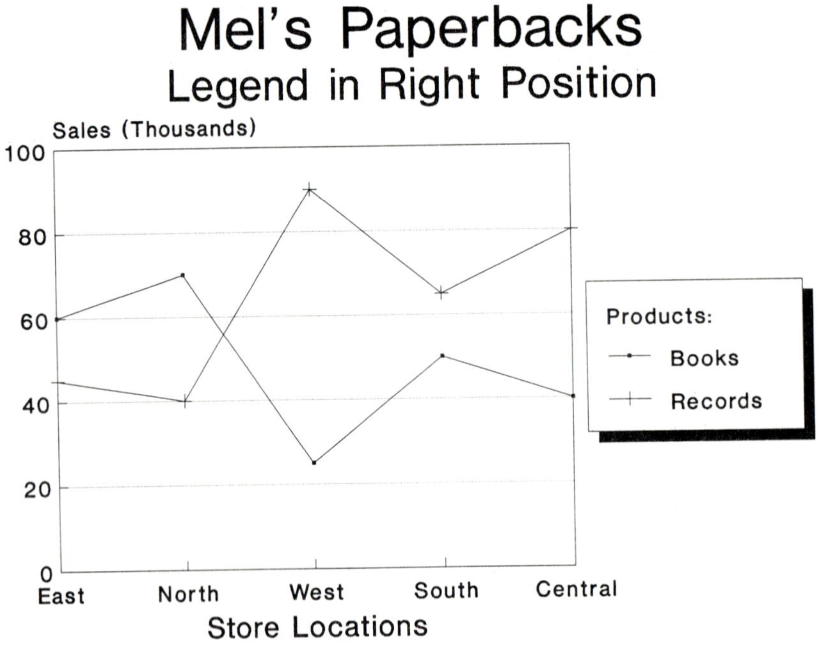

FIGURE 3-13. Charts showing legend position (*continued*)

CHANGING THE LEGEND'S PLACEMENT Another default that Harvard Graphics uses is to put the legend outside of the box containing the chart data. You have the option of putting the legend inside the box containing the chart data. To put the legend in the lower-left corner of the chart data of the LINE1 chart, follow these steps:

1. Move to Legend Location.
2. Select Bottom and press ENTER.
3. Select ← or ↑ for the Legend Justify option and press ENTER.
4. Select In and press ENTER for the Legend Placement option.
5. Press F2 (Draw chart) to view the graph, which looks like Figure 3-14.

When you place the legend inside the graph data area, you want to position the legend where it will not interfere with the data. In the chart in Figure 3-14, you would not want the legend to have a position of Left or Right and Center justification.

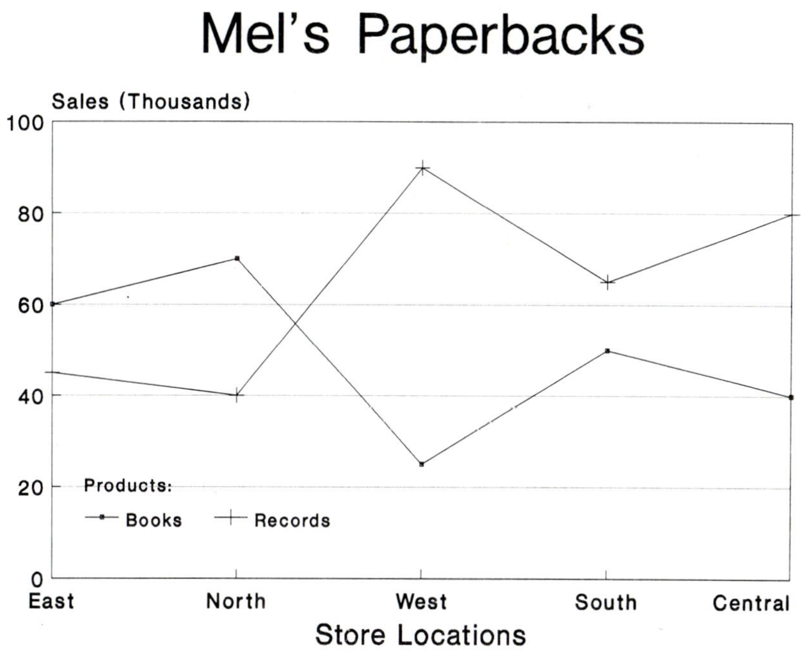

FIGURE 3-14. Chart with legend inside chart data area

6. Press any key to remove the graph from the screen.

ADDING LINES AROUND A LEGEND A legend is an important component of a chart—it is the key that unlocks the meaning of the graph when several sets of data are presented. When you place the legend inside the chart data area, it can be difficult to see. When a legend is outside the chart data area, you may want to distinguish the legend from the graph data. You can emphasize the legend by drawing a box around it.

To draw a box around the legend, using the chart in Figure 3-14, follow these steps:

1. Move to Legend frame.
2. Select Single, Shadow, or None to describe the type of box you want around the legend and press ENTER.
3. Press F2 (Draw chart) to view the graph.

Figure 3-15 shows the graph with a single line and a shadow around the legend. These options have the same appearance when the legend is outside of the chart data area. Selecting None removes the box. When the legend has a frame, the chart information below the legend is hidden. Using the example in Figure 3-15, you cannot see part of a grid line because the legend hides it. When a legend does not have a frame, the information behind the legend appears through the legend.

4. Press any key to remove the graph from the screen.

Changing the Axes

In your initial line chart, you let Harvard Graphics make many of the decisions about the chart's appearance. One of these assumptions is how the axes are scaled. For example, the axes in the line chart use the minimum and maximum values determined by Harvard Graphics. Harvard Graphics also chooses the distance between each value on the axes, the format of the numbers, and the appearance and value of tick marks. You can change these options and set the scale yourself.

CHANGING THE AXES SCALING Most of the charts you create use standard scaling. This means that the interval between every tick mark is the same. For example, in the chart in Figure 3-16, which shows the cumulative

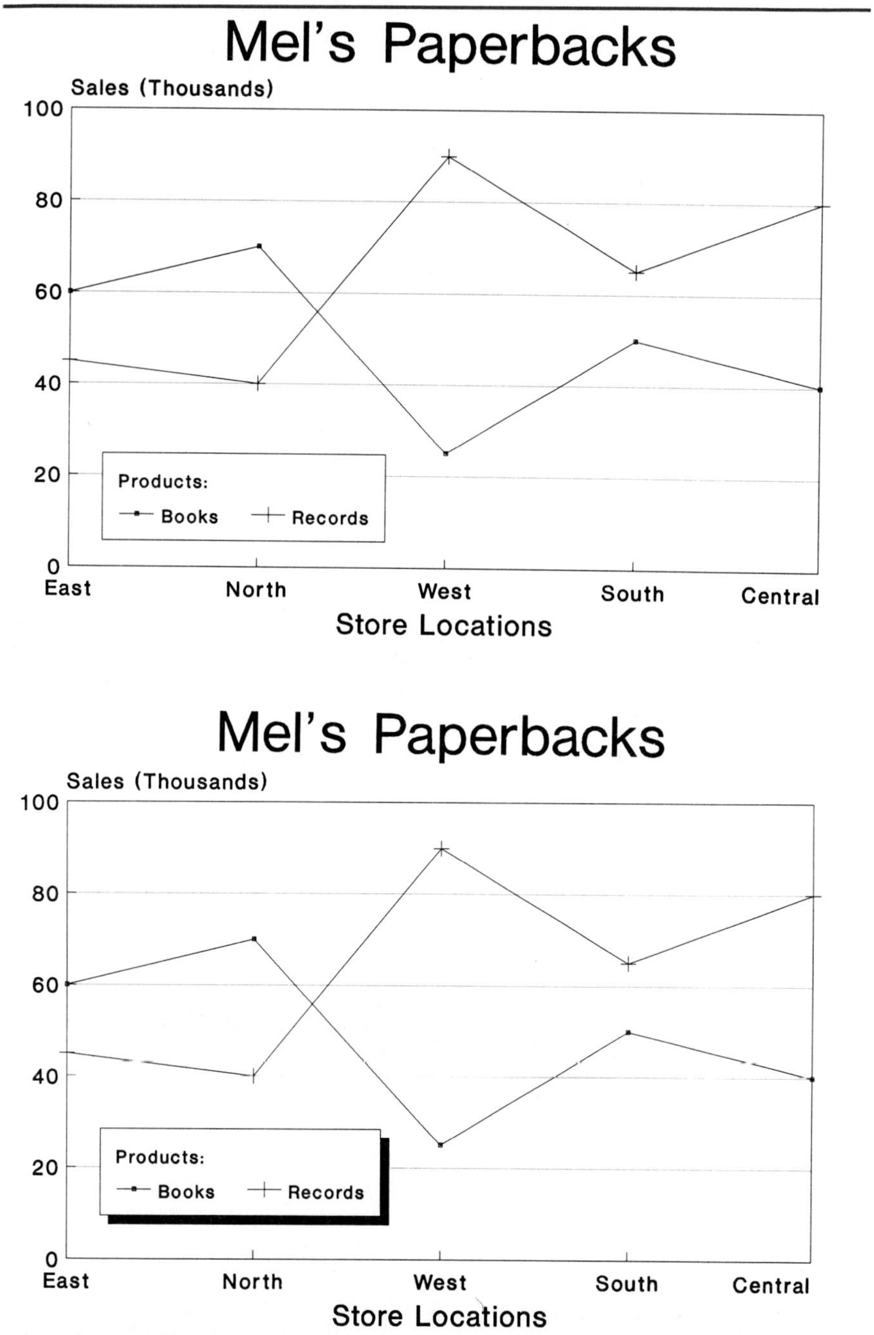

FIGURE 3-15. Charts with boxed legend inside chart data area

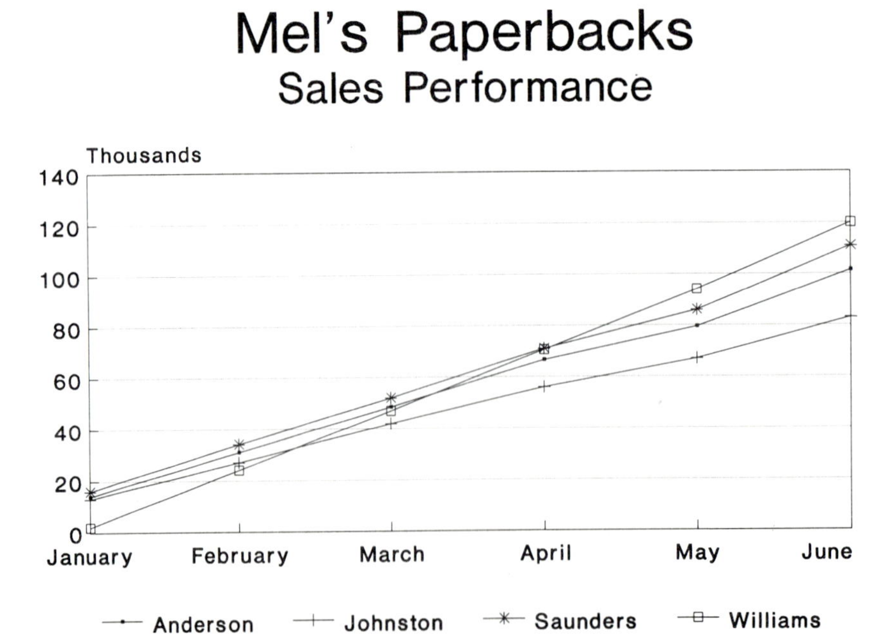

FIGURE 3-16. Chart using standard scaling

amount of sales, the interval between each tick mark on the Y-axis is 20,000. Another option is using a logarithmic scale, in which the increment between each major tick mark on a scale increases by a power of 10. For example, in the chart in Figure 3-17, which charts the same data as Figure 3-16 but uses a logarithmic scale, the interval between the first tick mark and the second tick mark is 90,000. The interval between the second tick mark and the third tick mark is 900,000, or 90,000 multiplied by 10. Logarithmic scaling is often used to graph exponentially growing numbers. When a chart uses logarithmic scaling, it cannot use the 3D option.

To change the axes scaling, move to the third page of Titles & Options. Move the cursor to the Scale Type field in the table at the bottom of the screen, and then move to the X Axis or Y Axis column depending on what you want to change. Harvard Graphics only uses the scale type setting for the X-axis if the values of the X-axis are numbers. Select Linear for standard scaling or Log for logarithmic scaling. If you select Linear, the interval between each tick mark is equal. If you select Log, Harvard Graphics adds minor tick marks (they do not have numbers next to them) to divide the interval into ten. Since the scale is nonlinear, more of the lines are next to the next tick mark.

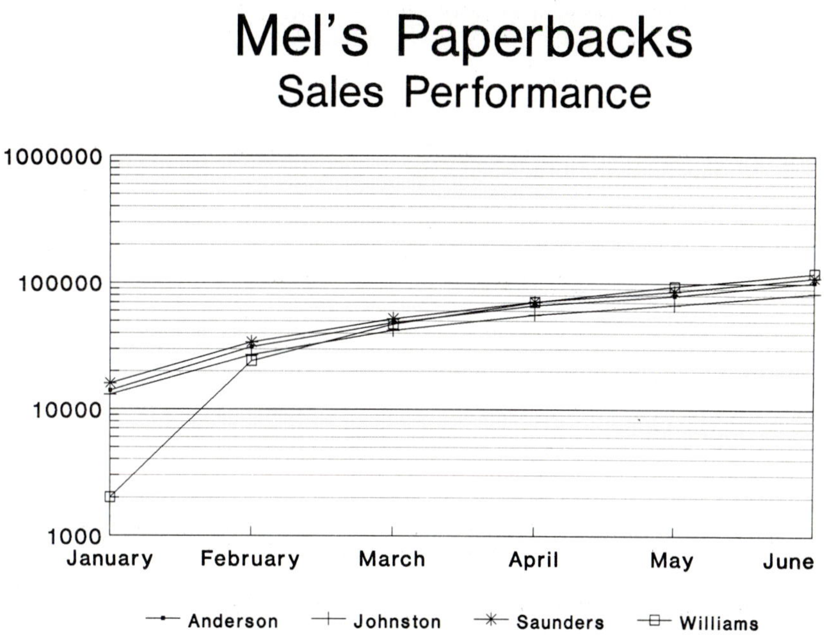

FIGURE 3-17. Chart using logarithmic scaling for the Y-axis

CHANGING THE FORMAT You can change the appearance of the values in a chart by changing the axes labels to currency ($) or percent (%). You can change the format to other styles as well. To change the format of the numbers, move to Page 3 of Titles & Options, shown in Figure 3-18. Then move to the X Axis, Y1 Axis, or Y2 Axis column that represents the axis values you want to change. Harvard Graphics only uses the format setting for the X-axis if the values of the X-axis are numbers. Changing the format of a Y-axis also changes the format of the data series values assigned to the Y-axis. For example, if you set the format of the first Y-axis to display three digits after the decimal point, all of the data series assigned to the first Y-axis will display any labels with three digits after the decimal point. Changing the format of the number does not change the actual values, only the appearance of values.

To set the chart so Harvard Graphics adds a comma before the thousands, type a comma. To have all values with the same number of digits after the decimal point, type the number of digits you want. To place text before the values, type the text followed by a vertical slash (¦). To place text after the values, type a vertical slash (¦) followed by the text. To display the numbers using scientific notation, type an exclamation point. You can com-

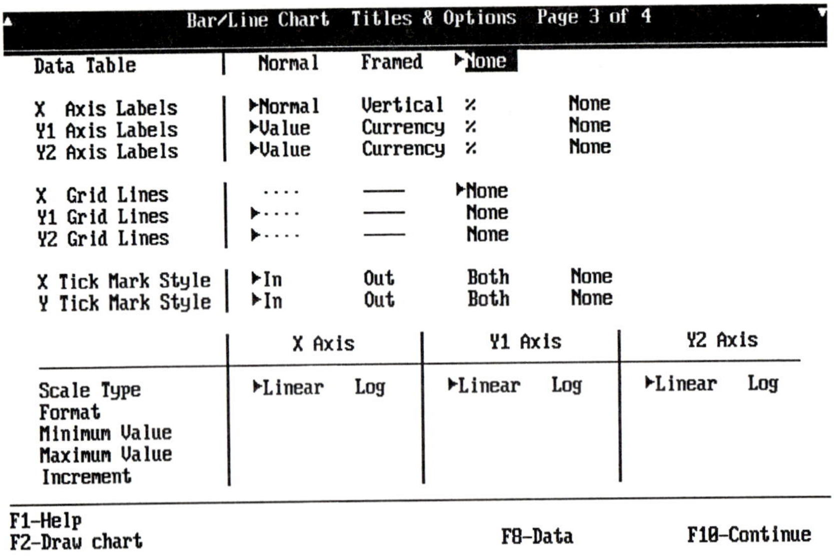

```
Bar/Line Chart  Titles & Options  Page 3 of 4

Data Table        | Normal     Framed     ▸None

X  Axis Labels    | ▸Normal    Vertical   %        None
Y1 Axis Labels    | ▸Value     Currency   %        None
Y2 Axis Labels    | ▸Value     Currency   %        None

X  Grid Lines     |  ....       ——        ▸None
Y1 Grid Lines     | ▸....       ——         None
Y2 Grid Lines     | ▸....       ——         None

X Tick Mark Style | ▸In        Out        Both     None
Y Tick Mark Style | ▸In        Out        Both     None

                  |    X Axis          |    Y1 Axis         |    Y2 Axis
Scale Type        | ▸Linear    Log     | ▸Linear    Log     | ▸Linear    Log
Format            |                    |                    |
Minimum Value     |                    |                    |
Maximum Value     |                    |                    |
Increment         |                    |                    |

F1-Help
F2-Draw chart                            F8-Data           F10-Continue
```

FIGURE 3-18. Third page of Titles & Options

bine them by entering the format codes you want after one another. For example, to use commas and add a pounds sterling sign (£) before the values, type the format code **,£**. If you want to combine text with scientific notation, omit the vertical bar, because Harvard Graphics uses the exclamation point to separate the text and to display the values using scientific notation.

Another possible format code sets the scaling. You can display all the numbers as being divided by another number. For example, you can display numbers divided by 1000 by entering **1000¦**. You can also use this format instruction to use a different base such as hexadecimal (16¦) or decadecimal (12¦).

CHANGING TICK MARK APPEARANCE Tick marks are the markers used for the X- and Y-axes to indicate a data point or a particular value. By default these tick marks point into the chart. This means that the tick marks start from the axes and proceed in the direction of the center of the chart. You can change the tick marks style to point away from the chart, to cross the axis to extend both inside and outside the chart, or you can remove them. To change the tick marks for the LINE2 graph, follow these steps:

1. Move to the Y Tick Mark Style field on Page 3 of the Titles & Options form.

When you change the tick mark style for the Y-axes, you effect both the Y1- and Y2-axes.

2. Press the spacebar to select In, Out, Both, or None, and press (ENTER).

The In option starts the tick marks on the axis and causes them to point toward the inside of the graph. Out starts the tick marks on the axis and causes them to point away from the graph. Both combines the tick marks created with In and Out. None removes all tick marks. All of these options work well with line graphs. With bar graphs, you may want to avoid In for X-axis tick marks, since you will be unable to distinguish them from the bars.

3. Press (F2) (Draw chart).

Figure 3-19 shows the four tick mark styles, with the tick mark style described in the Y-axis title. You can execute the same steps with the X-axis by moving to X Tick Mark Style on Page 3 of the Titles & Options form and selecting the tick mark style.

4. Press any key to remove the chart from the screen.

CHANGING THE TICK MARK VALUES The remaining assumptions Harvard Graphics makes about an axis are the beginning value, the ending value, and the increment between each tick mark. You can change the values Harvard Graphics uses to determine where tick marks are placed. To change the tick mark values of the LINE2 chart, follow these steps:

1. Press (ESC) to return to the Main Menu.
2. Press (CTRL-S) to save the chart.
3. Press (F10) (Continue) to save the changes you have made to LINE1.
4. Press (CTRL-G) to get another chart.
5. Select LINE2 from the list and press (ENTER).
6. Press any key to remove the graph from the screen.
7. Press (F8) (Options) to display the Titles & Options form.
8. Press (PGDN) twice to move to Page 3.
9. Move the cursor to Minimum Value in the table at the bottom of the screen, and then move to the column representing the X- or Y-axis you want to change. In this example, it is the Y1-axis column.

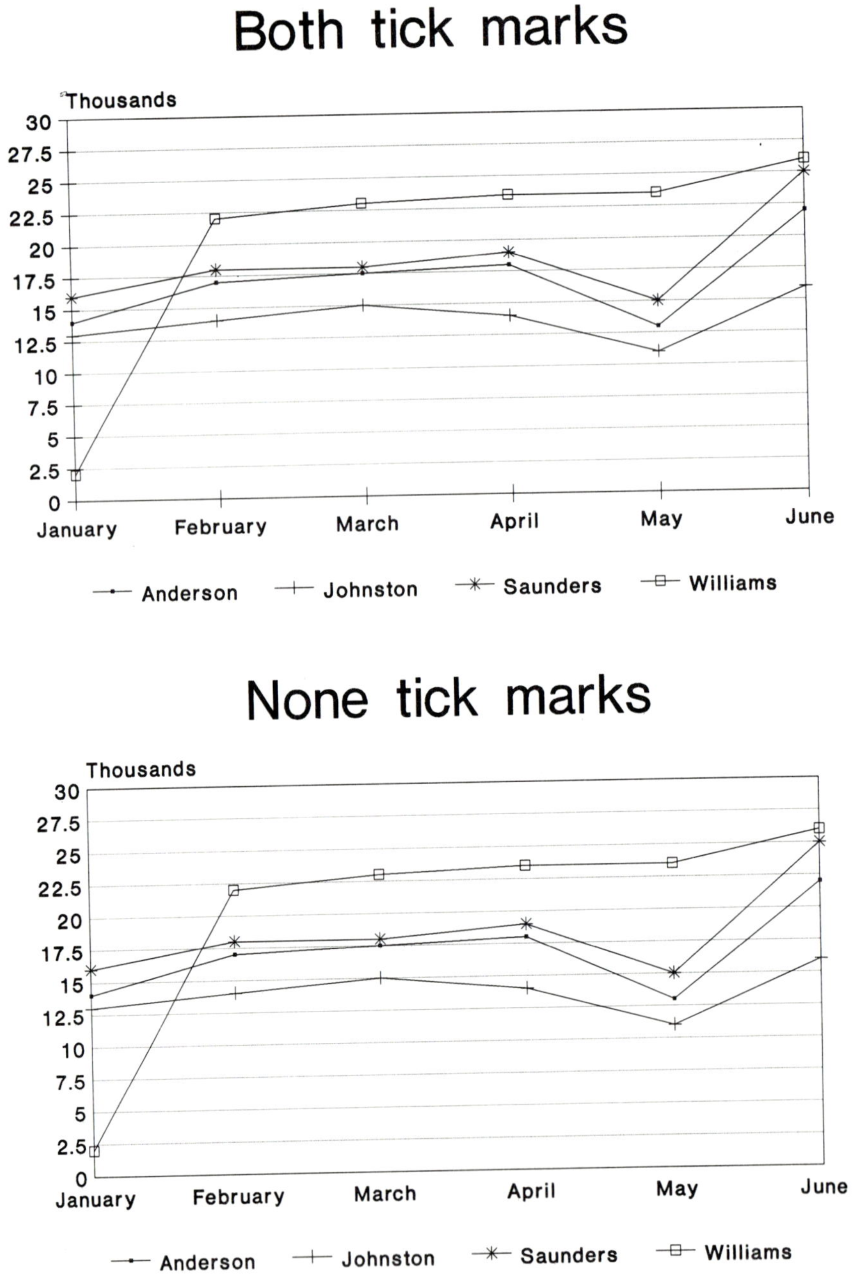

FIGURE 3-19. Charts showing different tick mark styles

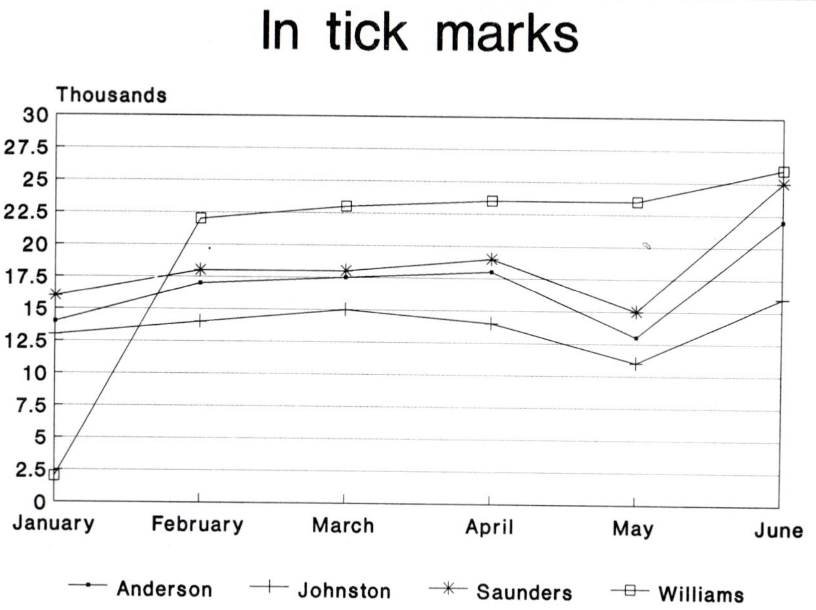

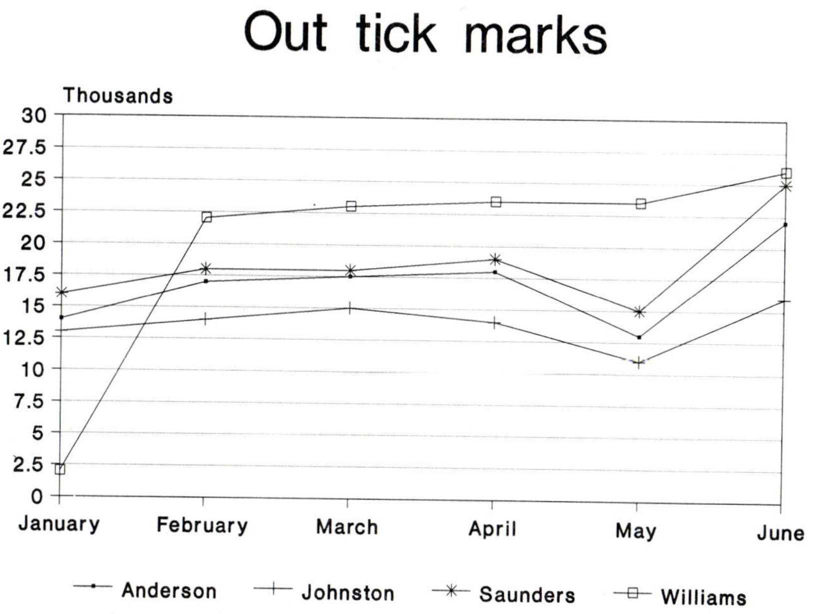

FIGURE 3-19. Charts showing different tick mark styles (*continued*)

10. Type the lowest value the axis will start with and press (ENTER). In this example, it is **10000**.
11. Type the value the axis will end with in the Maximum Value row and press (ENTER). In this example, it is **30000**.
12. Type the value of the increment between each tick mark in the axis in the Increment row. In this example, it is **2500**.
13. Press (F2) (Draw chart) to view the graph in Figure 3-20.

If you do not enter a minimum, maximum, and/or increment value, Harvard Graphics uses the default value it previously used. Harvard Graphics only uses the minimum and maximum settings for the X-axis if the values of the X-axis are numbers.

14. Press any key to remove the graph from the screen.

You can also use the Increment setting to reduce the congestion along an axis that has many values with lengthy labels. You can change the labels

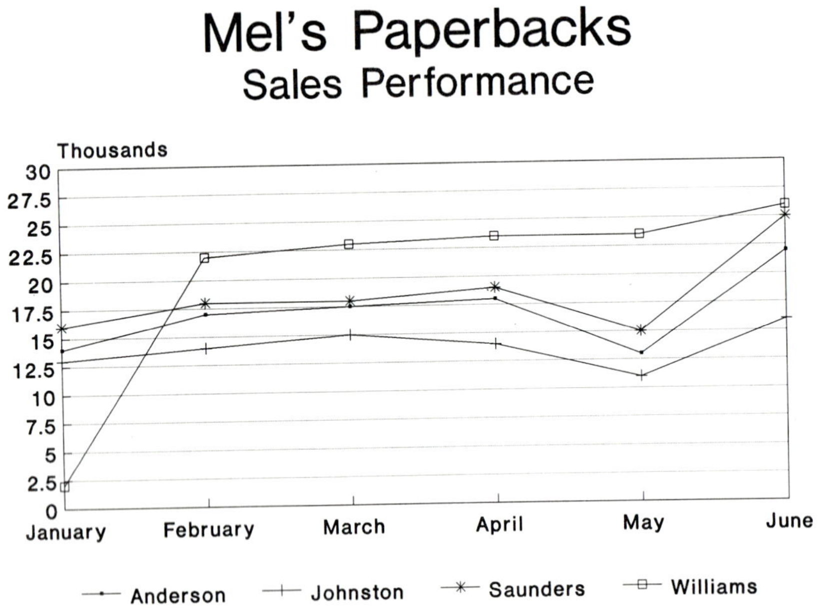

FIGURE 3-20. Chart with Y-axis values set with Titles & Options

in the LINE2 graph so the chart only displays the names of every other month. In a chart with crowded X-axis labels, Harvard Graphics abbreviates months and days when possible. By decreasing the number of X-axis labels, you are increasing the space available for the remaining ones. If months or days are abbreviated, decreasing the number of them provides room for Harvard Graphics to spell the abbreviations out. To change the increment, follow these steps:

1. Move to Increment under X Axis in the third page of Titles & Options.
2. Type **2**.
3. Press F2 (Draw chart) to view the graph shown in Figure 3-21.

Only January, March, and May appear in the X-axis. Later in this chapter you will learn other options, such as displaying the labels vertically and using two rows to display the labels.

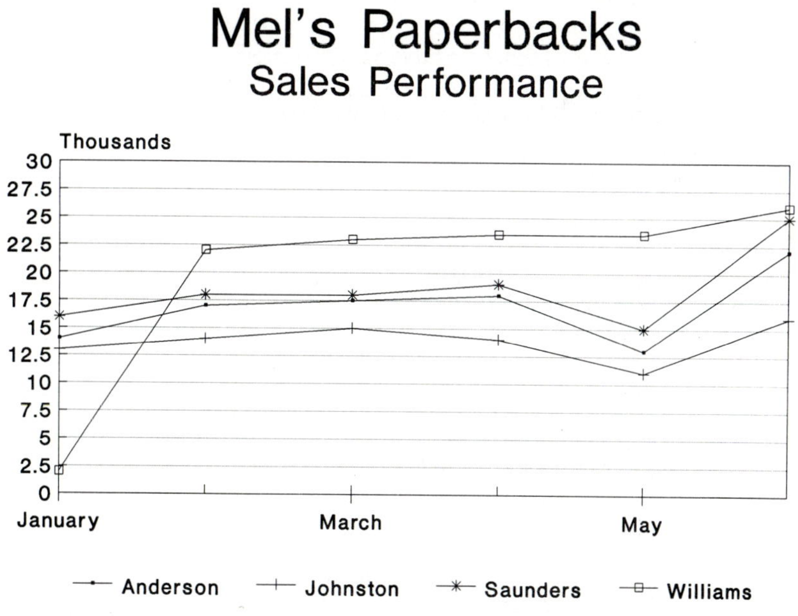

FIGURE 3-21. Chart using an X-axis increment to only show some X-axis values

4. Press any key to remove the chart from the screen.
5. Press CTRL-DELETE to remove the 2.

Deleting an option that you type returns the option to the default.

Adding Grid Lines

Harvard Graphics can add horizontal dashed lines to the line chart you have created to help you determine the values of the data points. These lines make it easy to see where data intersects the Y-axis. The horizontal dashed lines in the line chart are an example of this feature and are called *grid lines*. Grid lines start from the X- or Y-axis and continue horizontally or vertically to the other side. The default for the graph is to display dashed grid lines from the Y-axis. You can change the axis the grid lines start from or remove them altogether.

To change the grid lines, move to Page 3 on the Titles & Options screen shown in Figure 3-18. To create grid lines starting from the X-axis, move to X Grid Lines and select either the periods for dashed grid lines, a solid line for solid grid lines, or None to remove any grid lines. The same step is repeated for the first or second Y-axis. The grid lines start at each tick mark on the selected axis. If you are using two Y-axes, be careful about adding grid lines or your graph will look too busy.

Adding Data Labels

When you create a line graph, you can use grid lines to help a person estimate the value of each data point in the graph. Another option is to display the values next to each data point. To add data labels to the line graph, follow these steps:

1. Press ESC to return to the Main Menu.
2. Press CTRL-S to save the chart.
3. Press F10 (Continue) to save the changes you have made to LINE2.
4. Press CTRL-G to get another chart.
5. Select LINE1 from the list and press ENTER.

6. Press any key to remove the graph from the screen.
7. Press (F8) (Options) to display the Titles & Options screen.
8. Press (PGDN) to go to the second page of Titles & Options.
9. Move to the Value labels option.
10. Select All.
11. Press (F2) (Draw chart) to display the chart. It looks like Figure 3-22.
12. Press any key to return from the chart.

Another option is to selectively display the labels. To only display the labels for the Books series of data, follow these steps:

1. Move to the Value labels option.
2. Choose the Select option.

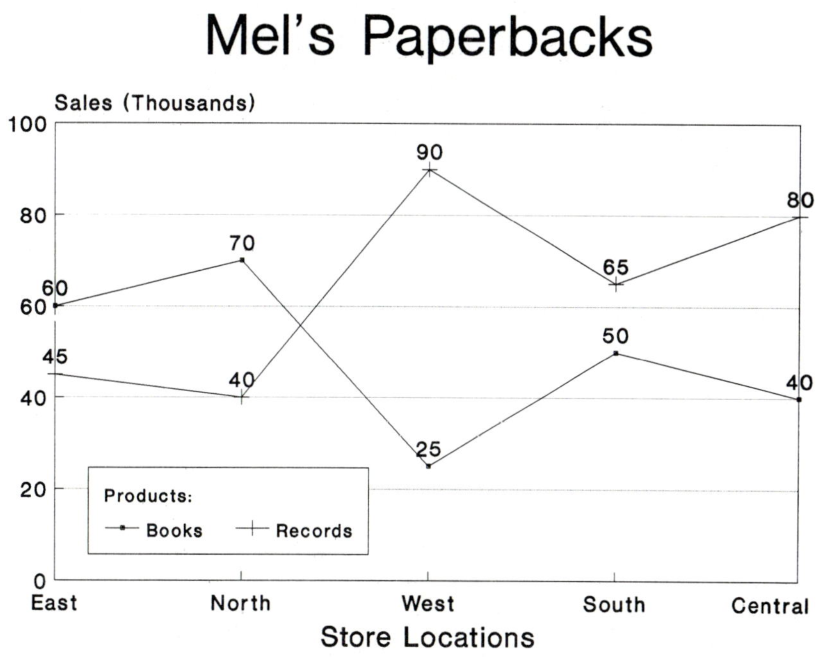

FIGURE 3-22. Chart displaying labels for chart values

Choosing Select means that Harvard Graphics only displays the labels of the data series that you select. To select which series are labeled use the table on the fourth page of Titles & Options.

3. Press PGDN twice to go to the fourth page of Titles & Options.
4. Move to the Books legend line in the table.
5. Press TAB twice to move to the Y Label column.
6. Select Yes.
7. Press F2 (Draw chart) to display the chart. It looks like Figure 3-23.
8. Press any key to return from the chart.
9. Press PGUP twice to go to the second page of Titles & Options.
10. Move to the Value labels option.
11. Select All.

This step returns the chart to display all labels.

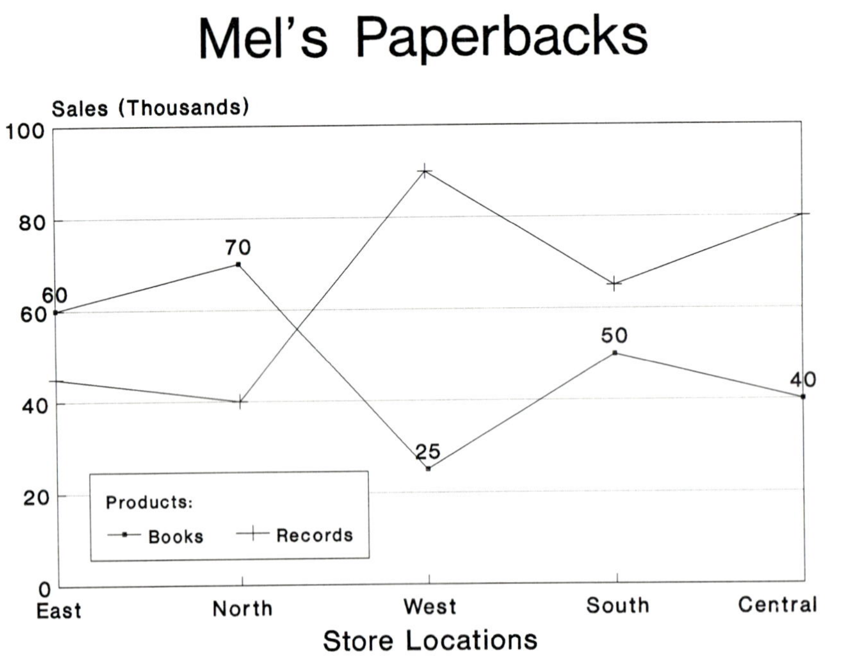

FIGURE 3-23. Chart displaying selected labels for chart values

Axis Label Options

So far, the charts you have created display the X- and Y-axes as you entered them or as they are formatted with the Format option in the bottom of Page 3 of the Titles & Options form. Harvard Graphics has other options that you can use to change the appearance of the axis labels. You can alternate X-axis labels between two rows. You can also display the labels as the values are entered, vertically, as a percentage, or hidden. You can display Y-axis labels as values, as currency ($), as a percentage, or hidden. The default for X-axis labels is to use the labels or values as you enter them in the chart.

When X-axis labels are congested, you can choose to alternate the labels between two lines. To alternate the X-axis labels between two lines for the LINE1 chart, follow these steps:

1. Press **F8** (Data) to display the Bar/Line Chart Data screen.
2. Press **INSERT** to change from the overstrike to the insert mode.
3. Move to North.
4. Type a vertical bar (¦).
5. Press **ENTER** twice to move to South.
6. Type a vertical bar (¦).
7. Press **F2** (Draw chart) to view the graph shown in Figure 3-24.

The X-axis labels that have a vertical bar as the first character are on a second line of labels. In this graph congestion is not a problem, but it may become a problem in other graphs. Splitting the X-axis labels onto two lines can be the remedy.

8. Press any key to return to the Bar/Line Chart Data screen.

Vertical X-axis labels are useful when the labels are running into each other and you do not want to display them using alternate rows. This option does not work well when the X-axis labels are very long, because vertical labels reduce the space left for the chart. To make the X-axis labels of the LINE1 chart vertical, follow these steps:

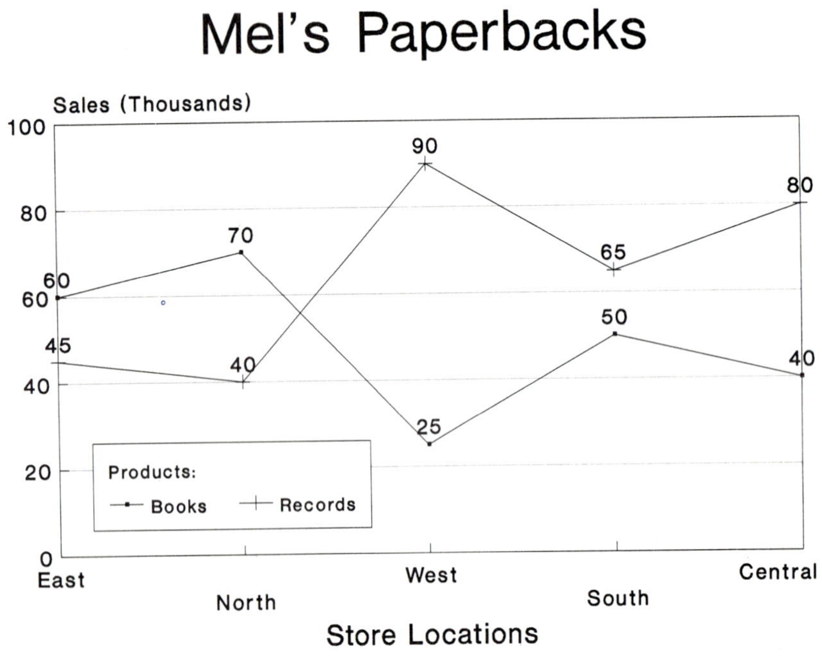

FIGURE 3-24. Chart alternating X-axis labels on two lines

1. Press (DELETE) to remove the vertical bar before South.
2. Press (UP ARROW) twice to move to North.
3. Press (DELETE) to remove the vertical bar before North.
4. Press (F8) (Options) to display Titles & Options.
5. Press (PGDN) to go to the third page.
6. Move to X Axis Labels.
7. Select Vertical.
8. Press (F2) (Draw chart) to view the graph shown in Figure 3-25.

All the store locations are spelled out in the chart. Since the labels take more space, Harvard Graphics uses less space for the actual line chart.

When axis labels are values, you can use the other options to change how the numbers appear. Using currency ($) for the Y-axes labels places a currency symbol before the numbers and adds commas after every third digit

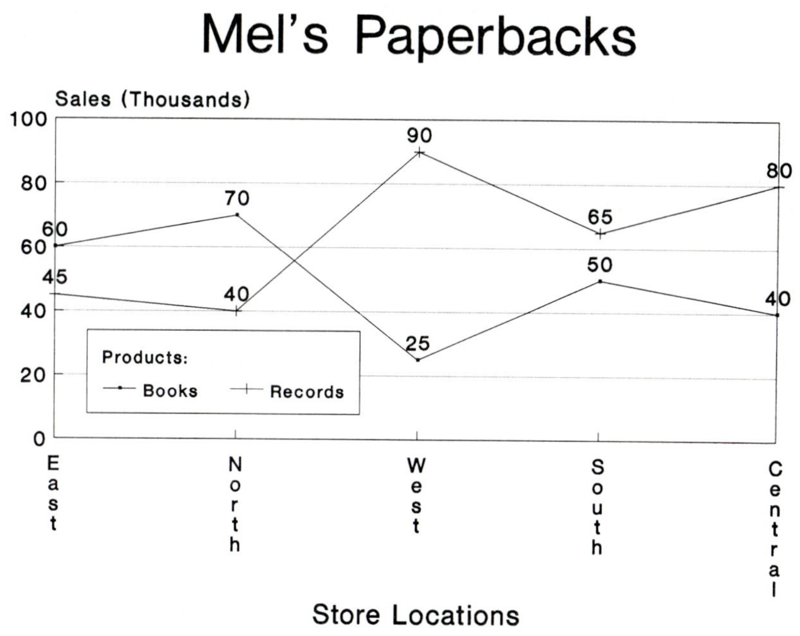

FIGURE 3-25. Chart displaying X-axis labels vertically

to the left of the decimal point. Using percentage for the X- or Y-axes displays the axis labels as multiplied by 100 with a percent sign (%) after the value. You can always hide the values by selecting None or return them to their defaults by selecting Normal for the X-axis and Value for the Y-axis.

To change the format of the Y-axis labels for the LINE1 graph, follow these steps:

1. Press any key to remove the graph from the screen.
2. Move to Y1 Axis Labels.
3. Select Currency.
4. Press F2 (Draw chart) to view the graph shown in Figure 3-26.

Each of the numbers has a $ preceding it.

5. Press any key to leave the graph.

6. Press ESC to return to the Main Menu.
7. Press CTRL-S to save the chart.
8. Press F10 (Continue) to save the changes to LINE1.

AREA CHARTS

In some ways area charts are a combination of bar and line charts. Like line charts, area charts draw lines to each of the data points in a series. Unlike line charts, area charts fill in the area below the line with a color or pattern, which is more like a bar chart. Also like a bar chart, the area chart uses some of the bar chart styles and enhancements, since the area filled with one series would otherwise obscure the other series. Often the series in an area chart are stacked on top of each other.

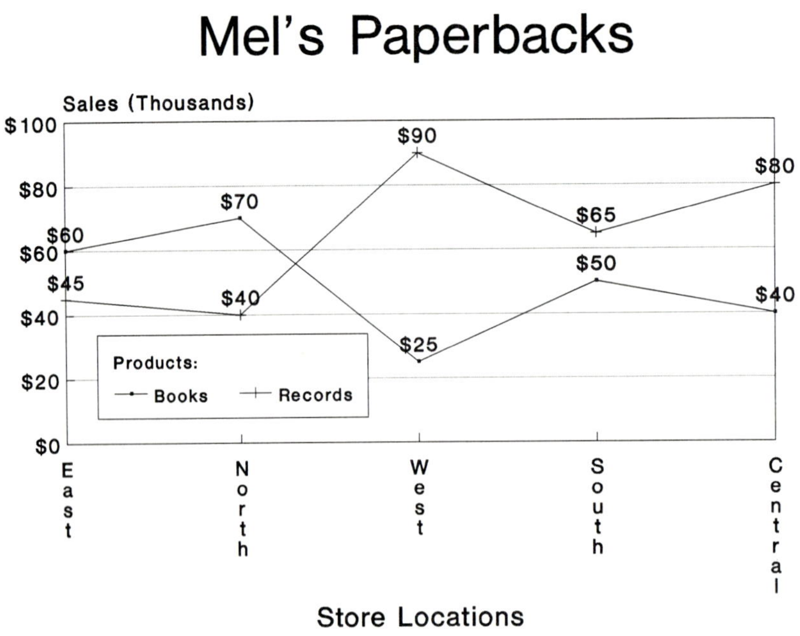

FIGURE 3-26. Chart with Y-axis labels set to $

Creating a Quick Area Chart

Creating an area chart requires the same steps that you performed with line and bar charts. To quickly create an area chart using the data from the LINE1 graph, follow these steps:

1. Select Create new chart from the Main Menu.
2. Select Area and press ENTER.

You will see a message asking you if you want to continue to use the same data. If you select Yes, Harvard Graphics creates a new chart with the settings and data of the LINE1 chart. If you select No, Harvard Graphics erases the data and settings from the last chart so you can start with a new graph.

3. Select Yes and press ENTER.

You will see an Area Chart Data screen that looks identical to the Bar/Line Chart Data screen. Since you chose to keep the data from the LINE1 chart, the values are already entered for you.

4. Press F8 (Options) to see the options the chart uses.

The Titles & Options form looks just like the Titles & Options forms from earlier examples. On Page 1, your Type selections are limited to Area, Line, Trend, and Bar for the types. The Books and Records series are assigned as Line type since these series had this type in the LINE1 graph.

5. Move the cursor to the Type column for the Books series.
6. Make the Books series an area chart by selecting Area. You can press LEFT ARROW or type **A**, and press ENTER.
7. Make the Records series an area chart by selecting Area. You can press LEFT ARROW or type **A**, and press ENTER.

Other options you may want to change are the pattern and color, although first you must move down to Page 4 with the PGDN key.

8. Press PGDN to move to the second page of Titles & Options for the area chart.

In the second page of Titles & Options, the only difference between an area chart and a bar or line chart is that Chart style only includes Stack, Overlap, and 100% in an area chart. Also, Chart enhancement only includes 3D and None in an area chart.

9. Move to Chart fill style and select Both.

10. Press F2 (Draw chart) to view the graph in Figure 3-27.

Each series uses a different pattern and color. Since Chart style is set at Stacked, the first series is on the bottom of the graph. The second series is added on top of the first series. This continues for each of the series.

11. Press any key to leave the graph.

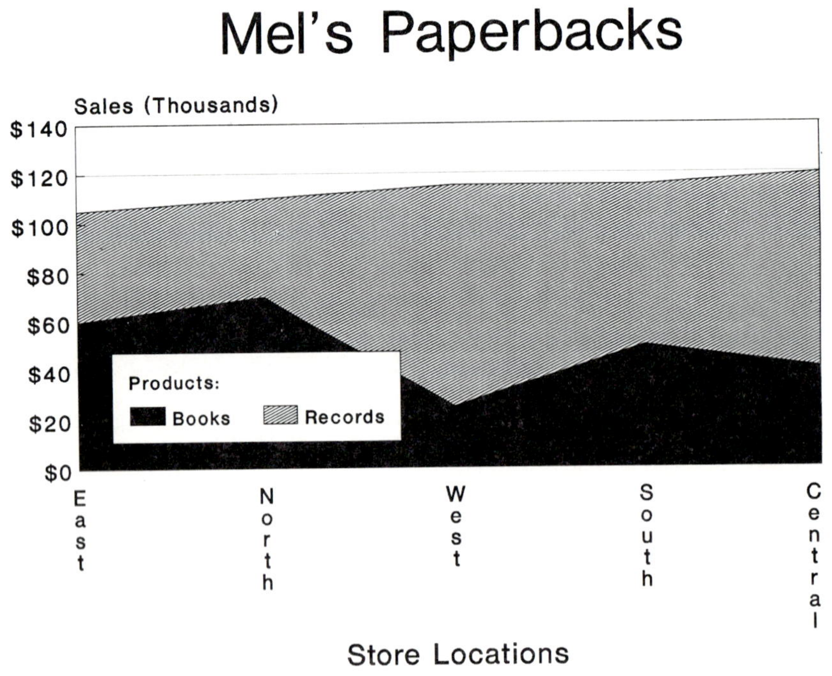

FIGURE 3-27. Area chart

Line and Bar Options Available with Area Charts

Most of the options that you learned to use with line, trend, curve, point, and bar charts also operate with area charts. As discussed in the example of an area chart, Harvard Graphics has only three differences between Titles & Options for an area chart versus the Titles & Options for a bar or line chart. First, the Type options in an area chart are Area, Line, Curve, and Bar versus Bar, Line, Trend, Curve, and Pt in a bar or line chart. Second, the area chart style options are Stack, Overlap, and 100%. Area charts cannot use the Cluster, Step, and Paired options that line and bar charts can. If you select 100%, all of the series are displayed as area charts regardless of the Type choice you made for the series in the first Titles & Options page. Finally area charts do not have the Shadow and Link selections for the Chart enhancement option. All of the other options you learned for line and bar charts also apply to area charts. If you position the legend inside the chart data area, you should add a frame since you will not be able to see the legend text otherwise.

You can show up to 100 X data values with the corresponding series data values in an area chart. If the X data type is calendar based and the X values have a gap in the dates, all of the area type series must either by cumulative or noncumulative. This option is set in the Cum column in the fourth page of Titles & Options. All series must have the same X values. If a series does not have a value for a particular X data value, enter **0**. All of the data points must fit between the minimum and maximum axis values set either by Harvard Graphics or in the third page of Titles & Options.

Another consideration of area graphs is the order of the series; you may want the most stable values as the first series. If your first series varies radically, the area chart will make the other series look more erratic. If all of the series are fairly stable, you should enter the series in the order of their importance. With each of the series graphed as areas, you do not want to assign some area type series to the first Y-axis and other area type series to the second Y-axis.

You can try some of these options by following these steps:

1. Move to Chart style.
2. Select Overlap and press ENTER.

Selecting Overlap places the second series behind the first and so forth for all of the series.

3. Press F2 (Draw chart) to view the graph.

Notice how the data for books is on top of the data for records. The Overlap selection works best when the series are ordered so the first series contains the smallest values and the last series contains the largest values.

4. Press any key to leave the graph.
5. Select 3D and press ENTER.

3D provides an effect similar to what you get with bar charts. The 3D effect is removed if you mix series types, use logarithmic scaling, create a horizontal chart, use two Y-axes, or print the graph to a plotter.

6. Press F2 (Draw chart) to view the graph that appears in Figure 3-28.

This option is similar to creating ribbons for the lines in a line chart, except the area below the ribbon is filled. The data labels, legend, and axes label settings are the same settings you added to the LINE1 chart. Harvard Graphics transfered both the data and the settings to the new chart.

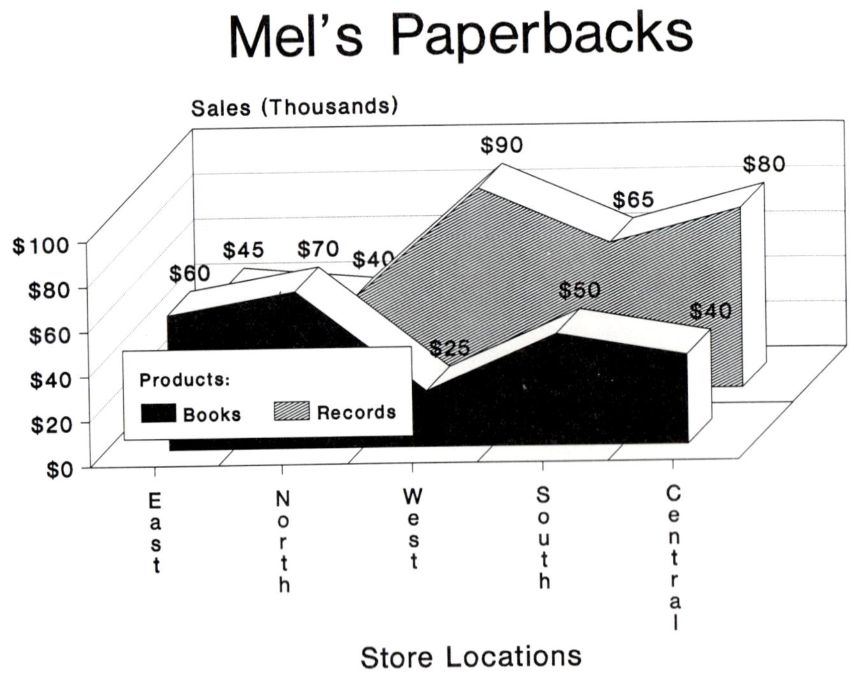

FIGURE 3-28. Area chart with Overlap style and 3D enhancement

7. Press any key to leave the graph.
8. Press ESC to return to the Main Menu.
9. Press CTRL-S to save the chart.
10. Type **AREA1** and press F10 (Continue).

HIGH/LOW/CLOSE CHARTS

When you are tracking the prices of financial commodities, you usually want to know more than the current price. Frequently traded stocks and bonds will vary in price. Often financial reports include the opening, closing, high, and low prices of a stock. Looking at the numbers provides you with the raw data you need to analyze the stock or bond, but it is difficult to see if there is a trend. A high/low/close graph, like the one shown in Figure 3-29, creates a picture of the variations of a financial commodity. Harvard Graphics uses the first four series to chart the high, low, closing, and opening prices. Any additional series may be charted as a bar, line, trend, curve, or points. A line or box is drawn between the high and low values, and tick marks in the line or bar indicate opening or closing prices. Opening prices have a tick mark starting from the line or bar and going to the left. Closing prices have a tick mark starting from the line or bar to the right.

While high/low/close charts were developed for graphing financial commodity prices, you can use this chart to graph other types of data, such as survey responses where the open series represents the average value of the survey's responses and the close series represents the median value of the survey's responses.

Creating a Quick High/Low/Close Chart

High/low/close charts use different data than what you have entered for your line and area charts. To create a high/low/close chart, follow these steps:

1. Select Create new graph from the Main Menu.
2. Select High/Low/Close.

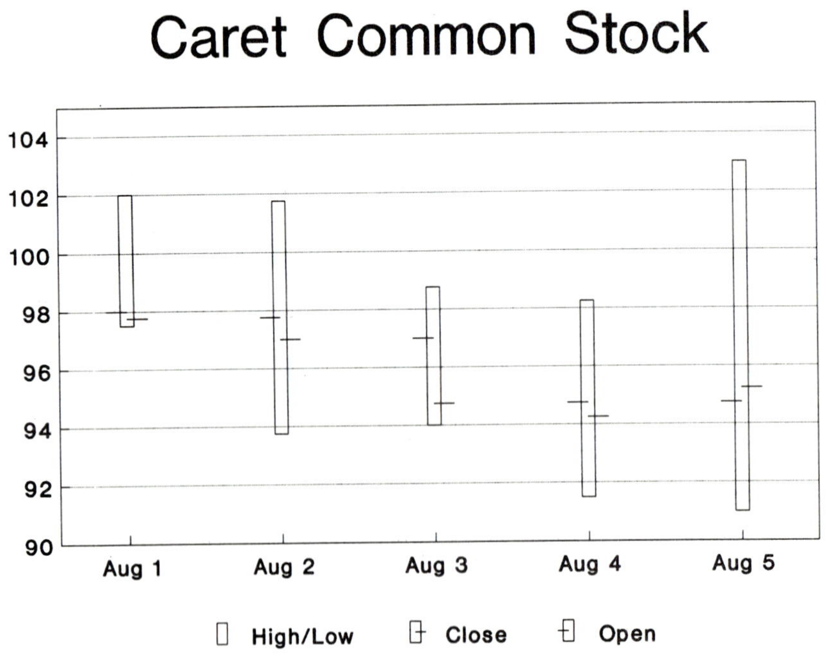

FIGURE 3-29. High/low/close chart

3. Select No and press ENTER when Harvard Graphics prompts if you want to keep the current data.
4. Select Month/Day as the X data type and press ENTER.
5. Type **August 1** and press ENTER to use August 1 as the starting date.
6. Type **August 5** to use August 5 as the ending date.
7. Press F10 (Continue) to accept these values and let Harvard Graphics generate the dates as the X data labels.

The High/Low/Close Chart Data screen already has the first four series labeled High, Low, Close, and Open.

8. Type **Caret Common Stock** and press ENTER for the chart title.
9. Press ENTER twice since this chart does not have a subtitle or footnote.

10. Press TAB to move to the High series column.
11. Type **102** and press ENTER for the first value. Type **101.75**, **98.75**, **98.25**, and **103** in the High series column, pressing ENTER after each one.
12. Press HOME to move to August 1, and press TAB twice to move to the Low series column.
13. Type **97.5** and press ENTER for the first value. Type **93.75**, **94**, **91.5**, and **91** in the Low series column, pressing ENTER after each one.
14. Press HOME to move to August 1 and press TAB three times to move to the Close series column.
15. Type **97.75** and press ENTER for the first value. Type **97**, **94.75**, **94.25**, and **95.25** in the Close series column, pressing ENTER after each one.
16. Press HOME to move to August 1 and press TAB four times to move to the Open series column.
17. Type **98** and press ENTER for the first value. Type **97.75**, **97**, **94.75**, and **94.75** in the Open series column, pressing ENTER after each one. The High/Low/Close Chart Data screen looks like Figure 3-30.

High/Low/Close Chart Data

Title: Caret Common Stock
Subtitle:
Footnote:

Pt	X Axis Month/Day	High	Low	Close	Open
1	August 1	102	97.5	97.75	98
2	August 2	101.75	93.75	97	97.75
3	August 3	98.75	94	94.75	97
4	August 4	98.25	91.5	94.25	94.75
5	August 5	103	91	95.25	94.75
6					
7					
8					
9					
10					
11					
12					

F1-Help F3-Save F5-Set X type F9-More series
F2-Draw chart F4-Draw/Annot F6-Calculate F8-Options F10-Continue

FIGURE 3-30. High/Low/Close Chart Data screen

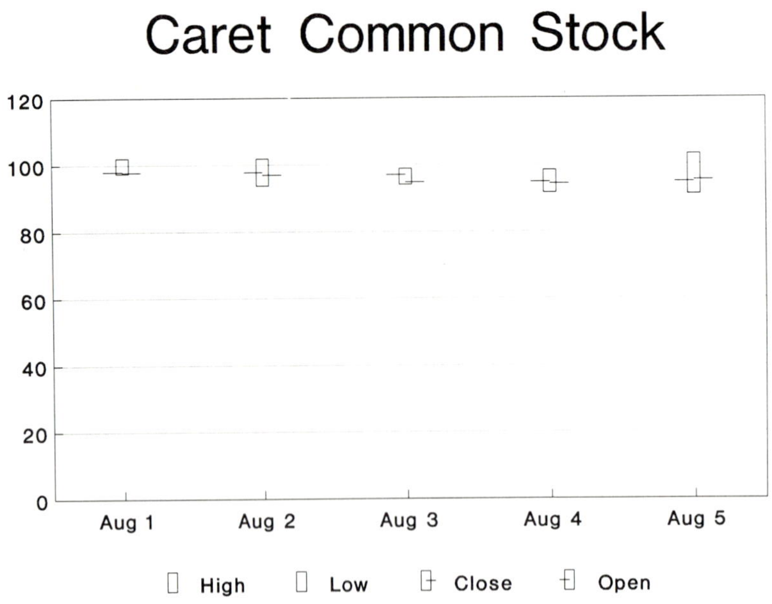

FIGURE 3-31. High/low/close chart created with data from Figure 3-30

18. Press **F2** (Draw chart) to display the chart, which looks like Figure 3-31.

This chart illustrates many of the default settings that Harvard Graphics uses for high/low/close charts. By customizing the options with the Titles & Options screens that appear when you press **F8** (Options), you can change how the data is displayed. You can also include more series in this graph to show how actively the stock was sold.

19. Press any key to return to the High/Low/Close Chart Data screen.

One of the problems with a high/low/close chart is that the Y-axis starts at 0. Since the low values are usually greater than 0, starting the chart from 0 pushes the display of the data to the top part of the chart. The variation of the data is more visible if you set the range to fit within the values ranges. You can see the difference by following these steps, which set the Y-axis from 90 to 105:

1. Press F8 (Options) to display the first page of Titles & Options for the high/low/close chart.

Most of the options in the High/Low/Close Titles & Options form are similar to the Titles & Options for line and bar charts.

2. Press PGDN twice to go to Page 3 of the Titles & Options form.
3. Move to the Minimum value field in the Y1 Axis column.
4. Type **90** and press ENTER to start the axis at 90.
5. Type **105** to end the axis at 105.
6. Press F2 (Draw chart) to display the chart, which looks like Figure 3-32.

Setting the Y-axis range makes the values seem more important because they occupy a larger portion of the chart area.

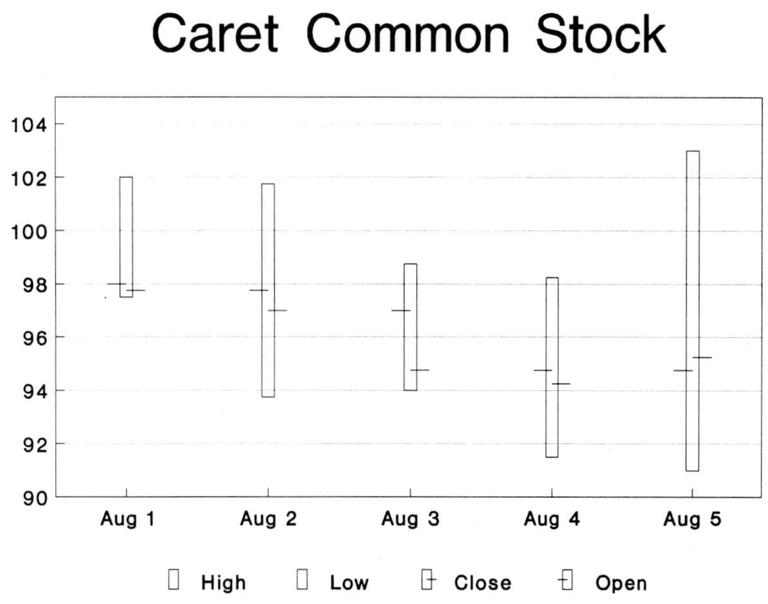

FIGURE 3-32. High/low/close chart with Y-axis range selected

7. Press any key to return to the High/Low/Close Titles & Options form.

High/Low/Close Chart Options

Although most of the options for high/low/close charts are the same as for other types of charts, some options affect only the fifth through eighth series. For a close look at the differences in options, make the following changes to the high/low/close chart you have just created:

1. Press PGUP twice to display the first page of Titles & Options for the high/low/close chart.

In the table that appears in the bottom half of the screen, you can see how Harvard Graphics has already provided legend names and types for the first four series. You can change the legend titles for any series, including the first four, but you cannot change the type of the first four series. If you try to move to the Type column for the first four series, you will notice that the cursor skips from the Legend Title column to the Display column. Since High, Low, Close, and Open do not appear in the Type selections, you cannot select these types for the fifth through eighth series.

2. Move to the High Legend Title.

Since the legend in Figure 3-32 uses the same symbol for High and Low, you may want to combine them.

3. Edit the legend text to read High/Low and press ENTER.
4. Press CTRL-DELETE to remove the Low legend title.

When a legend title is missing, the legend for the series will not appear.

5. Press PGDN to display Page 2 of the Titles & Options form.

On the second page, notice that only the first two options differ from the Titles & Options for bar and line graphs. The Bar style only affects the fifth through eighth series. These produce the same results as the same selections for bar and line charts. The second option, High/Low style, controls how the range between the high value and the low value is connected. The default, Bar, creates a rectangular bar as you saw in Figure 3-32. You can try the other options to see how the graph differs.

6. Select Area and press (ENTER).
7. Select Both for the Bar fill style.
8. Press (F2) (Draw chart) to display the chart, which looks like Figure 3-33.

When the High/Low style is set to Area, the graph contains a polygon connecting the low and high values and fills in the polygon with color and/or a pattern. The pattern the chart uses is selected as the Marker/Pattern number for the High series in the fourth page of Titles & Options.

9. Press any key to return to the Titles & Options screen.
10. Move to the High/Low style option.

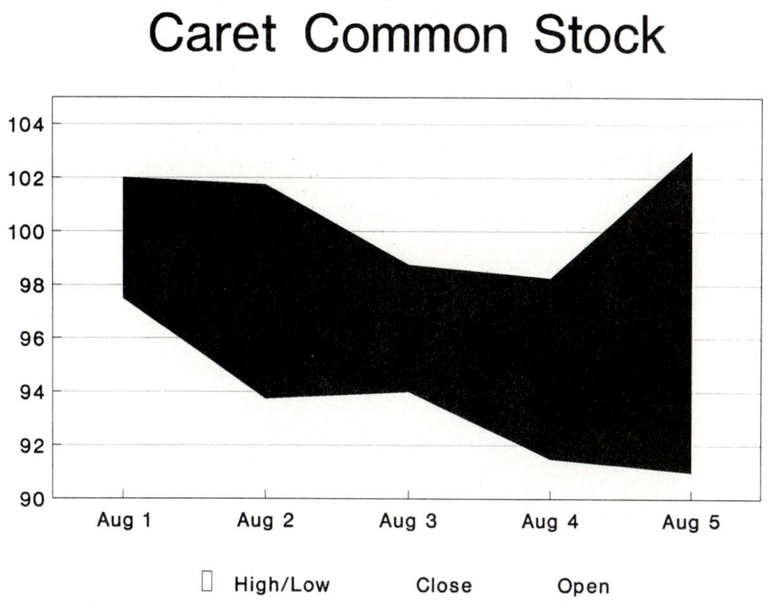

FIGURE 3-33. High/low/close chart with High/Low style set to Area

11. Select Error bar.
12. Press F2 (Draw chart) to display the chart, which looks like Figure 3-34.

When the High/Low style is set to Error bar, the chart draws a line from the high value to the low value and adds horizontal tick marks at both ends of the line for the opening and closing values.

13. Press any key to return to the High/Low/Close Titles & Options screen.

Of the remaining options on the second page of Titles & Options, Bar Width and Bar Overlap affect only the fifth through eighth series. If you display value labels, you can display the High, Low, and fifth through eighth series values. You cannot display labels for the Open and Close series.

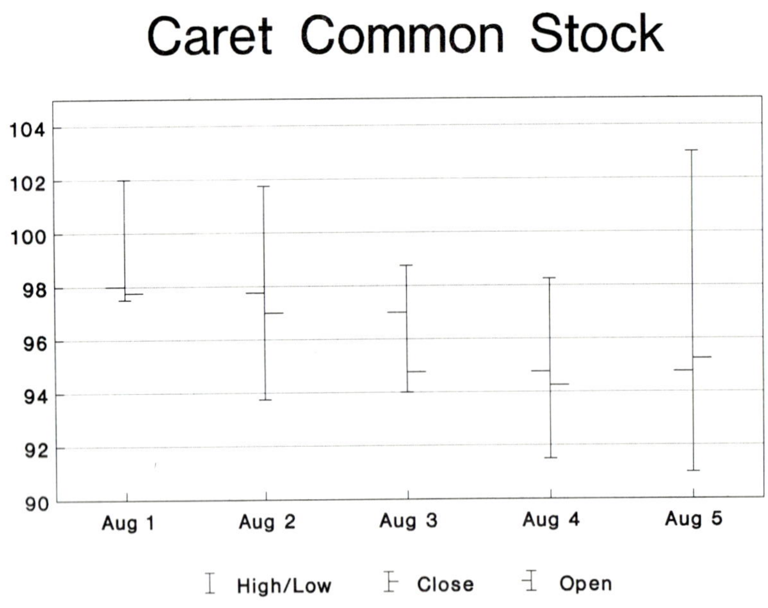

FIGURE 3-34. High/low/close chart with High/Low style set to Error bar

Combining Other Types

The graphs that you create in a high/low/close chart can include other types of information besides the high, low, closing, and opening prices. For example, you may want to include a line chart that graphs how the industry did as an average so you can determine if the particular stock is performing better than average. You may also want to add bar graphs that indicate how much stock was traded. When you add different types of data, you may want to assign the other types of data to the second Y-axis. When you combine different types of data, you may also want to change the Y-axis so the price data does not unintentionally overlay the fifth through eighth series of data. Try the following steps to add a fifth series that contains the column information that displays as bars in the graph:

1. Press F8 (Options) to return to the High/Low/Close Chart Data screen.
2. Press F9 (More series).
3. Press HOME and TAB to move the cursor to the column for the fifth series in the row for August 1.
4. Type **2250** and press ENTER for the first value. Type **2301, 2288, 2303,** and **2321** in the High series column, pressing ENTER after each.
5. Press F8 (Options) to display Page 2 of Titles & Options.
6. Press PGUP to move to the first page of Titles & Options.
7. Move to the Legend title for Series 5.
8. Type **Volume** and press DELETE to remove any extra characters.
9. Press TAB to move to the Type column.
10. Select Bar by typing **B** or pressing LEFT ARROW.
11. Press TAB twice to move to the Y Axis column.
12. Select Y2 by pressing RIGHT ARROW and press ENTER.
13. Press PGDN twice to move to Page 3 of Titles & Options.
14. Move to Y2 Grid Lines.
15. Select None by typing **N** or pressing LEFT ARROW and pressing ENTER.

If you used both Y-axis grid lines, the chart would look busy.

16. Move to 90 for the minimum value in the Y1 Axis column.
17. Type **70**.
18. Press (TAB) to move to the Y2 Axis column.
19. Type **2200** as the initial value of the Y2-axis.
20. Press (F2) (Draw chart) to display the chart, which looks like Figure 3-35.

By adjusting the lower limit of the Y1-axis, the bar chart of the column does not overlay the price data of the first four series.

21. Press any key to return to the High/Low/Close Titles & Options screen.
22. Press (F10) (Continue) to return to the Main Menu.

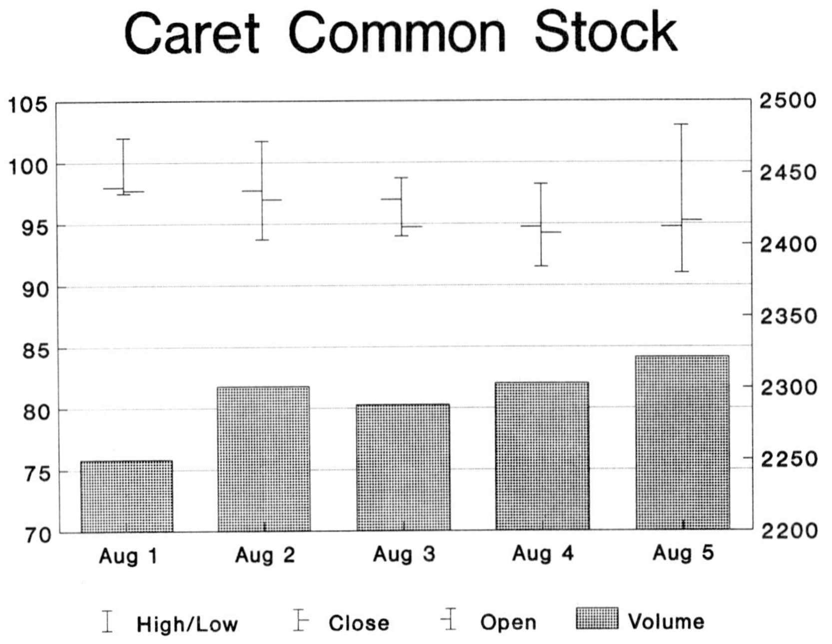

FIGURE 3-35. High/low/close chart using additional series

You can use F10 (Continue) as well as ESC to return to the Main Menu.

23. Press CTRL-S to save the chart.
24. Type **Stock** and press F10 (Continue) to save the chart.

USING CALCULATIONS

Most data you use in a chart you enter through the screens Harvard Graphics creates for each type of chart, or you import it from another source, as covered in Chapter 5. Another option is using the data in the series you have entered to compute values for other series. You can use calculations to create a series that defines a trend, computes an average, or performs series manipulation, like creating a forecast from historic values.

To enter a calculation, display the data entry chart for the bar, line, area, or high/low/close chart you want to use. Move to the column representing the series whose values you want to compute. Next, press F6 (Calculate). Harvard Graphics displays the Calculate overlay, shown in Figure 3-36.

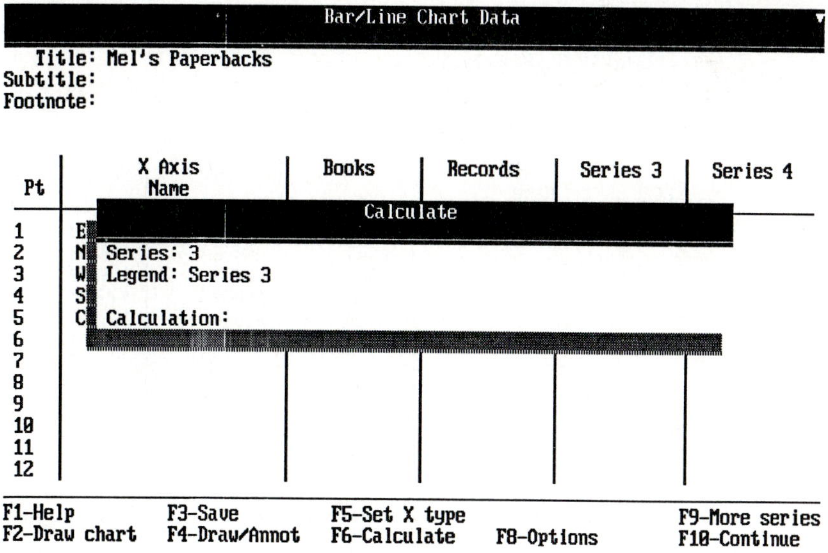

FIGURE 3-36. Calculate overlay

Enter the calculation at the Calculation field and press F10 (Continue). Harvard Graphics computes the values for the series and removes the Calculate overlay. Any entries in a column in which you plan to use a calculation are overwritten as a result of the calculation. If the series already contains calculated values, the calculation that computed the series values last displays as the Calculation field.

Once the values are calculated, you can change the values in the series. When you have finished with the calculation, Harvard Graphics displays a diamond next to the series name if you have entered a true computation. An entry like **@CLR** or **@COPY** does not display a diamond mark because it takes an action that affects the column and the computation does not continue to display. Figure 3-37 provides an example of a calculation that displays the diamond. From the Calculate overlay, you also can change the legend text by typing a new entry.

When you enter the calculations, you frequently refer to values in other series. To use values from other series in a calculation, enter the number sign (#) followed by the number of the series that you want to use. For example, to compute the difference between the first and second series values, you would enter **#1−#2** as the calculation. You cannot reference the series that you are calculating. For example, if you want to reduce the

Bar/Line Chart Data

Title: Mel's Paperbacks
Subtitle:
Footnote:

Pt	X Axis Name	Books	Records	◆ Total	Series 4
1	East	60000	45000	105000	
2	North	70000	40000	110000	
3	West	25000	90000	115000	
4	South	50000	65000	115000	
5	Central	40000	80000	120000	
6					
7					
8					
9					
10					
11					
12					

F1-Help F3-Save F5-Set X type F9-More series
F2-Draw chart F4-Draw/Annot F6-Calculate F8-Options F10-Continue

FIGURE 3-37. Bar/Line Chart Data screen with calculated series first series' values by half, you cannot move to the first series column, press F6 (Calculate) and enter **#1/2** at the Calculation field.

Harvard Graphics has two types of calculations: arithmetic calculations or calculations that use one of Harvard Graphics' predefined functions.

Arithmetic Calculations

Arithmetic calculations use addition, subtraction, multiplication and division to compute a value using another series. Harvard Graphics uses the plus (+) for addition, the minus or hyphen (−) for subtraction, the asterisk (*) for multiplication, and the slash (/) for division. Since Harvard Graphics evaluates the calculation from left to right, be careful of the order that you enter the calculations. For example #1*3+20 is different from 20+#1*3. If one of the values in the first series is 50, the first calculation returns 170; the second calculation returns 210. You cannot use parentheses to change the order of evaluation. If you need to enter a complex formula, you may need to break it into several calculations using different series for each calculation. Remember you do not need to display every series on your chart.

You can try an arithmetic calculation using the data in LINE1. To create a third series that adds the values of the books and records for each store, follow these steps:

1. Select Get/Save/Remove.
2. Select Get chart.
3. Select LINE1 from the list and press ENTER.
4. Press any key to remove the graph from the screen.
5. Press TAB to move the cursor to the third series column.
6. Press F6 (Calculate) to display the Calculate overlay.
7. Press CTRL-DELETE, type **Total**, and press ENTER to enter the legend title for this series.
8. Type **#1+#2** for the calculation.

For each value of the third series, this formula adds the corresponding values of the first and second series.

9. Press F10 (Continue) to continue with the calculation.

The resulting series looks like Figure 3-37. A diamond appears next to Total, indicating that the series contains calculated values.

MAKING CALCULATIONS FOR A SINGLE CELL Sometimes you may want to compute one value in a data series. For example, suppose you are entering the yearly sales for your stores and you only have the quarterly figures for your Central store. You would like Harvard Graphics to compute the yearly sales so you do not have to find a calculator or pencil and paper and compute the yearly sales. To make a calculation for a single cell, omit using any series references. Instead enter the numbers you want to compute. To try this with the LINE1 graph, follow these steps.

1. Press SHIFT-TAB twice to move the cursor to the Books column.
2. Press DOWN ARROW until the cursor is in the row for the Central store.
3. Press F6 (Calculate) to display the Calculate overlay.
4. Press ENTER since you do not want to change the legend.
5. Type **24500+35500** for the calculation.
6. Press F10 (Continue) to finish the calculation. The result of 60000 appears in place of the original 40000. Note that this single cell calculation does not cause a diamond to display and can be overwritten just as you did.
7. Type **40000** to return the Central store's book sales to its original number. Press F6 (Calculate) then press F10 (Continue).

Using Functions in Calculations

Harvard Graphics also provides many functions that you can use in the Calculation field. You have already used the @EXCH function to reorder series in your graphs in Chapter 2. Functions can, among other things, compute statistical data, remove duplicate values, erase a series, sort the data by their X-axis values, and eliminate duplicate entries.

To calculate a series using a function, move to the Calculation field, type @ and the keyword. For some functions, you will need to supply an open parenthesis, any arguments the function uses, and a close parenthesis. You can only use one keyword in a calculation. You cannot combine a function with arithmetic operators.

ROW FUNCTIONS Row functions operate on one row of data at a time. These functions create a series of values that contain the average, the maximum, the minimum, or the total of one or more series of values. The functions @AVG, @MAX, @MIN, and @SUM have the same format. For each function, you must enter the function, an open parenthesis, the series references that you want to use separated by commas, and a close parenthesis. You can use the LINE2 graph to see how these functions work by following these steps:

1. Press ESC to return to the Main Menu.
2. Select Get/Save/Remove.
3. Select Get chart.
4. Select LINE2 from the list and press ENTER.
5. Press ENTER to continue without saving the changes to LINE1.
6. Press any key to remove the graph from the screen.
7. Press F9 (More series) to display the fifth through eighth series.
8. Press TAB to move to the fifth series column.
9. Press F6 (Calculate) to display the Calculate overlay.
10. Press CTRL-DELETE, type **Average**, and press ENTER to enter the legend title for this series.
11. Type **@AVG(#1,#2,#3,#4)** for the calculation.

For each value of the fifth series, this formula averages the corresponding values of the first four series.

12. Press F10 (Continue) to continue with the calculation.
13. Press TAB to move to the sixth series column.
14. Press F6 (Calculate) to display the Calculate overlay.
15. Press CTRL-DELETE, type **Maximum**, and press ENTER to enter the legend title for this series.
16. Type **@MAX(#1,#2,#3,#4)** for the calculation.

For each value of the sixth series, this formula computes the maximum of the corresponding values of the first four series.

17. Press F10 (Continue) to continue with the calculation.

18. Press TAB to move to the seventh series column.
19. Press F6 (Calculate) to display the Calculate overlay.
20. Press CTRL-DELETE, then type **Minimum,** and press ENTER to enter the legend title for this series.
21. Type **@MIN(#1,#2,#3,#4)** for the calculation.

For each value of the seventh series, this formula computes the minimum of the corresponding values of the first four series.

22. Press F10 (Continue) to continue with the calculation.
23. Press TAB to move to the eighth series column.
24. Press F6 (Calculate) to display the Calculate overlay.
25. Press CTRL-DELETE, type **Total,** and press ENTER to enter the legend title for this series.
26. Type **@SUM(#1,#2,#3,#4)** for the calculation.

For each value of the eighth series, this formula totals the corresponding values of the first four series.

27. Press F10 (Continue) to continue with the calculation.

The resulting series looks like Figure 3-38. A diamond appears next to the fifth through eighth series indicating that these series contain calculated values.

SERIES FUNCTIONS Series functions operate on more than one row of data at a time. You can use these functions to perform data reduction (to remove duplicate entries), remove or erase a series, calculate a moving average, copy a series, exchange a series, calculate the proportion to the total for each value in a series, compute the net change between values, compute a cumulative total, and compute regression curves. The functions and a brief description are shown in Table 3-1. The @REDUC function has several unique rules and is covered later.

You can use the LINE2 graph to see how some of these functions work by following these steps:

1. Move to the Minimum series column.
2. Press F6 (Calculate) to display the Calculate overlay.

Bar/Line Chart Data

Title: Mel's Paperbacks
Subtitle: Sales Performance
Footnote:

Pt	X Axis Month	◆ Average	◆ Maximum	◆ Minimum	◆ Total
1	January	11250	16000	2000	45000
2	February	17750	22000	14000	71000
3	March	18375	23000	15000	73500
4	April	18625	23500	14000	74500
5	May	15625	23500	11000	62500
6	June	22250	26000	16000	89000
7					
8					
9					
10					
11					
12					

F1-Help F3-Save F5-Set X type F9-More series
F2-Draw chart F4-Draw/Annot F6-Calculate F8-Options F10-Continue

FIGURE 3-38. Calculated series with row functions

3. Type **Difference in Totals** and press ENTER to enter a new legend title for this series.
4. Press CTRL-DELETE and type **@DIFF(#8)** for the calculation.

For each value of the seventh series, this formula computes the difference between the value of the eighth series on the current row and the previous row.

5. Press F10 (Continue) to continue with the calculation.

Since the first row of the eighth series does not have a previous value to compare against, the first entry for the seventh series is blank. For the remaining values of the series, the @DIFF function computes the difference between the value of the eighth series in the current row and the previous row.

6. Move to the Maximum series column.
7. Press F6 (Calculate) to display the Calculate overlay.
8. Press ENTER to skip entering a legend title.

Function	Format	Results
@CLR	@CLR	Removes the values in the current series.
@COPY	@COPY(#*n*)	Copies the values of the series selected by *n* to the current series.
@CUM	@CUM(#*n*)	Calculates the current series as the cumulative total of the values of the series selected by *n*.
@DIFF	@DIFF(#*n*)	Calculates the net change between values in the series selected by *n*.
@DUP	@DUP(#*n*)	Continuously duplicates the series selected in the current series.
@EXCH	@EXCH(#*n*)	Switches the values and legend text between the current series and the series selected by *n*.
@MAVG	@MAVG(#*n* [*points before*, *points after*])	Calculates a moving average of the values in the series (similar to selecting Curve). The optional *points before* and *points after* arguments range between 1 and 120 and are used to select the number of points before and after the current value. By default, this function uses 1 for each argument. You can actually use any number that exceeds these entries to get an average for the entire series, as in @MAVG(#1,1000,1000).
@MOVE	@MOVE(#*n*)	Moves the values of the series selected by *n* to the current series.
@PCT	@PCT(#*n*)	Calculates the percentage each value in the series selected by *n* is to the total.
@REDUC	@REDUC	Performs data reduction.

TABLE 3-1. Series Functions

Function	Format	Results
@RECALC	@RECALC	Recalculates the values of all calculated series.
@REXP	@REXP(#*n*)	Calculates the exponential regression curve for the series selected by *n*.
@RLIN	@RLIN(#*n*)	Calculates the linear regression curve for the series selected by *n*.
@RLOG	@RLOG(#*n*)	Calculates the logarithmic regression curve for the series selected by *n*.
@RPWR	@RPWR(#*n*)	Calculates the power regression curve for the series selected by *n*.

TABLE 3-1. Series Functions (*continued*)

9. Press CTRL-DELETE, and type **EXCH(#8)** for the calculation.

This function switches the series values and legend title between the current series and the series selected in the parentheses.

10. Press F10 (Continue) to perform the calculation.

When this calculation is performed, Total is the sixth series and Maximum is the eighth series. To copy the Total values to the current column, use the @COPY function. To move the Total series in place of the Maximum series, use the @MOVE function.

11. Move to the Maximum series column.

12. Press F6 (Calculate) to display the Calculate overlay.

The @CLR, @COPY, @EXCH, @REDUC, and @RECALC functions disappear from the function box after you use them.

13. Press (ENTER) to skip the legend title.

14. Type **@CLR** for the calculation.

This function erases the series values and legend title.

15. Press (F10) (Continue) to perform the calculation. The Bar/Line Chart Data screen will look like Figure 3-39.

The values in the Maximum column disappear. Although the legend title still appears, it will not appear in the chart since the series does not have any data.

16. Press (F8) (Options) and (PGDN) to display the second page of Titles & Options.

17. Move to Bar fill style, select Both, and press (ENTER).

18. Press (F2) (Draw chart) to view the graph.

Bar/Line Chart Data

Title: Mel's Paperbacks
Subtitle: Sales Performance
Footnote:

Pt	X Axis Month	◆ Average	Total	◆Difference in Totals	Maximum
1	January	11250	45000		
2	February	17750	71000	6000	
3	March	18375	73500	1000	
4	April	18625	74500	500	
5	May	15625	62500	0	
6	June	22250	89000	2500	
7					
8					
9					
10					
11					
12					

F1-Help F3-Save F5-Set X type F9-More series
F2-Draw chart F4-Draw/Annot F6-Calculate F8-Options F10-Continue

FIGURE 3-39. Series created with series functions

When a chart includes calculated data, the calculated data is treated just as a series in which you enter values. For some charts, you may want to hide one or more series. For example, in the chart you have just created, you might want to hide the first four data series so you can concentrate on the calculated values.

19. Press any key to remove the graph from the screen.
20. Press ESC to return to the Main Menu.
21. Select Get/Save/Remove.
22. Select Save chart.
23. Press CTRL-DELETE to remove the existing filename, and type **CALC** as the new filename.
24. Press F10 (Continue) to save the file.
25. Press ESC to return to the Main Menu.

The @REDUC Function The @REDUC function performs data reduction on a series. Data reduction removes duplicate X-axis labels or values and sorts the chart data so the X-axis labels or values are in order. You may use this when you learn how to import data in Chapter 5. When Harvard Graphics performs the @REDUC function, it does the following steps:

1. Checks if all X-axis and series data is valid. For example, if the X-axis type is Number, Harvard Graphics will display an error message if one of the X-axis values is a label.
2. Checks that any X-axis label or value appears only once. If an X-axis label or value appears more than once and the X type is not Number, Harvard Graphics adds the values for each of the series with the same X-axis label or value. For example, if the LINE2 chart included one row with an X-axis label of West and series values of 10000, 15000, 20000, and 15000, and another row with an X-axis label of West and series values of 25000, 30000, 20000, and 25000, Harvard Graphics would combine it into a single row with an X-axis label of West and series values of 35000, 45000, 40000, and 40000.
3. Sorts the data in ascending order. Any rows that contain series values without X-axis labels or values are at the bottom of the chart data.

To use the @REDUC function, press F6 (Calculate) and enter **@REDUC** at the Calculation field. You can enter this function in any column since this function operates on all of the chart data.

Recalculating Calculated Series

When you have calculated series, you may need to perform the calculations again. You have several methods to recalculate calculated series. To recalculate a series, use one of these procedures:

- Press F2 (Draw chart). Harvard Graphics recalculates calculated series when you display the chart. You will not see the updated numbers until you return to the Bar/Line Chart Data screen.
- Press F10 (Continue).
- Press F6 (Calculate) and F10 (Continue). This procedure updates the values and lets you immediately see the updated numbers.
- Use the @RECALC function in any column. You should enter this in a noncalculated series so you do not overwrite the formula for a calculated column.

When Harvard Graphics updates the values of calculated columns, it calculates the first calculated column and then calculates the next calculated column until all calculated columns are updated.

chapter 4

PIE CHARTS

Pie charts offer a different perspective than the other graph types and are ideal for showing the components of a whole, whether you are examining budget dollars, sales units, or headcount. They are particularly useful in presentations because your audience can identify important issues at a glance. As the chart name implies, a pie chart looks like a pie: the circle represents the whole, and each slice is sized according to the relative size of the data it represents in relation to the whole. Harvard Graphics provides many options for displaying data in a pie chart or in its close relative, a column chart. Features for pie and column charts include linking, 3D, dual pies or columns, and exploded pie slices.

GETTING STARTED

By now you are almost a pro at creating analytical charts, having made bar, line, area, and high/low/close charts. You need to add one final chart type to your list of options—the pie chart. Since pie charts do not use X- and Y-axes, they look very different than the other chart types. Despite the differences, you will find that creating a pie chart is simple; you learned many of the basic features when you created bar and line charts.

To create the pie chart shown in Figure 4-1, follow these steps:

1. Select Create new chart from the Main Menu.
2. Select Pie.

Unlike the bar, line, area, and high/low/close charts, pie charts do not have an X data type. Harvard Graphics assumes that the data in a pie consists of a series of labels and a series of values. The screen for entering the chart, shown in Figure 4-2, contains two pages because you can have two pies in a Harvard Graphics pie chart. Information pertaining to the first pie is entered on the first page with the second page reserved for the second pie. Each pie can contain up to 12 slices.

3. Type **Industry Sales** and press ENTER for the chart title.

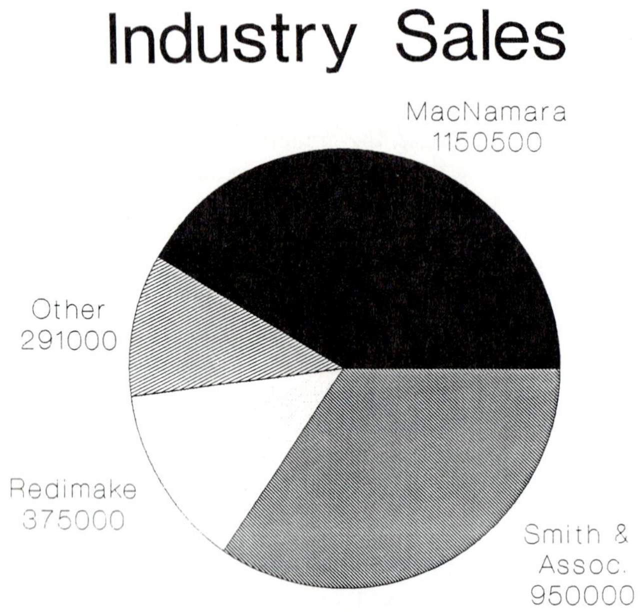

FIGURE 4-1. Sample pie chart

Pie Chart 1 Data Page 1 of 2

Title:
Subtitle:
Footnote:

Slice	Label Name	Value Series 1	Cut Slice Yes No	Color	Pattern
1			No	2	1
2			No	3	2
3			No	4	3
4			No	5	4
5			No	6	5
6			No	7	6
7			No	8	7
8			No	9	8
9			No	10	9
10			No	11	10
11			No	12	11
12			No	13	12

F1-Help F3-Save F9-More series
F2-Draw chart F4-Draw/Annot F6-Colors F8-Options F10-Continue

FIGURE 4-2. Pie Chart 1 Data screen

4. Press ENTER twice to omit entering a subtitle or footnote.

The table in the remaining portion of the screen is where you enter the data that will appear in the pie chart. The first column represents the pie slice and is numbered 1 through 12. The second column is for the label that describes each pie slice. The third column is for the value that the pie slice represents.

5. Type **MacNamara** and press ENTER for the first entry in the Label Name column.
6. Type **Smith & ¦Assoc.** and press ENTER.

The vertical line splits the label into two lines on the chart. You can use this character to break up long labels into shorter lines.

7. Type **Redimake.**
8. Press UP ARROW until the cursor is on MacNamara and TAB to move to the Value column.

9. Type **1150500** and press ENTER.
10. Type **950000** and press ENTER.
11. Type **375000.**

You may want to change the order of the data in the chart. In this example, make the entries in alphabetical order.

12. Press CTRL-UP ARROW.

This moves Redimake before Smith & Assoc. Since the order of the data determines the order of the pie slice in a pie chart, another change you may want to make is to insert data points.

13. Press CTRL-INSERT.

Pressing CTRL-INSERT inserts a new data point at the cursor's location and moves the remaining slices down one position. If you needed to delete a label and its value, you would press CTRL-DELETE.

14. Type **291000** and press SHIFT-TAB to move to the label column.

This enters the data that you want to graph in the pie chart.

15. Type **Other.**

When a pie chart contains slices that are very small, you may not be able to distinguish them easily. It is a good idea to group them into a single category, usually called Other.

16. Press F2 (Draw chart) to display the chart shown in Figure 4-1.

Each of the values in the Value column is represented by a pie slice. The size of the pie slice is determined by the proportion of the slice's value to the total. For example, the first slice represents 1150500 of 2766500 or 41.59%. Next to each pie slice is the descriptive label that you entered in the Label column. Notice how the label for Smith & Associates is split to use two lines.

17. Press any key to remove the graph from the screen.
18. Press F3 (Save) to save the chart.

F3 provides an alternative to CTRL-S and the menu selections for saving a chart. F3 is available from the Data form, eliminating the need to return to the Main Menu to save. When you press F3 (Save), Harvard Graphics displays the same overlay for the directory, file name and description as the other file save options.

19. Type **PIESALE** and press ENTER for the filename.
20. Edit the description so it says **Industry Sales - Pie chart** and press ENTER to save the file.
21. Press ESC to return to the Main Menu.
22. Press CTRL-P to print the chart.

If you want to change any settings, do so at this point. You may want to change whether the chart is printed as a draft or as the final copy.

23. Press F10 (Continue). Your output will look like Figure 4-1 if your printer prints only one color; otherwise each slice will be printed using a different color.
24. Select Enter/Edit chart.

You are now ready to try the features Harvard Graphics provides to enhance the chart's appearance.

SETTING THE SLICE'S APPEARANCE

You can control the appearance of the pie charts by selecting the colors and the fill patterns. You can also explode slices from the pie to pull a piece away from the others so it stands out. You can emphasize slices by selecting bold patterns or bright colors for a particular slice. These options are controlled by the last three columns of the screen in which you entered data.

Harvard Graphics can display the pie slices using different colors, patterns, or both. To control how the pie slices appear, follow these steps:

1. Press F8 (Options) to display the first page of the Pie Chart Titles & Options form, shown in Figure 4-3.

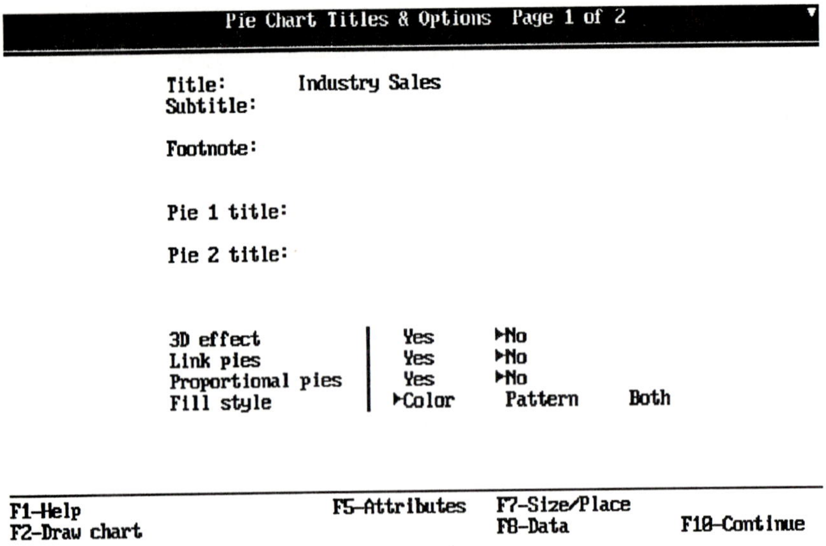

FIGURE 4-3. First page of Pie Chart Titles & Options

While some of the options in this screen are the same as the options you used for bar, line, area, and high/low/close charts, pie charts use other options that are unavailable in other chart types.

2. Move to the Fill style field.
3. Select the fill style you want for the pie chart.

Selecting Color displays each slice filled in a different solid color. Selecting Pattern displays each slice filled with a different pattern. Selecting Both displays each slice in a different color and filled with a different pattern.

The selection you make here determines whether Harvard Graphics uses the color and pattern information supplied in the screen with the data. If you select Pattern, Harvard Graphics ignores the color information. If you select Color, Harvard Graphics ignores the pattern information. All of the figures in this chapter use the Pattern option. You may want to use this selection or Both as you try the examples in this chapter so your charts match the ones in the book.

4. Press F8 (Data) to return to the data entry screen.

Selecting Pie Slice Colors

With the other graph types, you were able to control the way each series of data was displayed. From the Pie Chart 1 Data form, you can determine how each pie slice appears. For example, you can change the color Harvard Graphics uses for each pie slice. This allows you to use colors for emphasis or to achieve a pleasing effect.

To set the color of a pie slice, move the cursor to the Color column and the row that represents the slice for which you want to select a color. Enter the number representing the color you want the slice to use (the numbers for the colors are the same that you used for other chart types). You can also change a color by positioning the cursor on the number representing the color you want to change and pressing F6 (Colors). A list of the color names and their numbers is displayed and you can select one by highlighting the color and pressing ENTER. The color that is listed in this column is used whenever Harvard Graphics displays the pie slices in color.

Selecting Pie Slice Patterns

To set the pattern of a pie slice, move the cursor to the Pattern column and the row of the slice for which you want to select a pattern. Enter a number between 1 and 13, representing the pattern you want the slice to use (the patterns that the numbers represent are the same that you used for other chart types). Harvard Graphics uses the pattern listed in the Pattern column whenever the Fill style field is set to Pattern or Both.

Exploding Pie Slices

One method of emphasizing a pie slice is to pull it away from the center of the pie. This is called exploding a pie slice. In the Pie Chart 1 Data form, move to the row of the slice that you want to explode. Then press TAB until you are in the Cut Slice column. For each pie slice you want to explode, select Yes in this column.

Try exploding the Redimake pie slice in your pie chart by following these steps:

1. Move the cursor to the row for the third pie slice.
2. Press TAB twice to move to the Cut Slice column.
3. Select Yes. You can type Y or press LEFT ARROW and ENTER.
4. Press F2 (Draw chart) to display the chart shown in Figure 4-4. Notice how the slice for Redimake is separated from the other slices.
5. Press any key to remove the chart from the screen.

DISPLAYING TWO PIES

You can add a second pie to a pie chart and use it to break down a pie slice in the first pie. For example, you can add a second pie to the Industry Sales pie chart that breaks down the composition of Other. You can also use a second pie to compare data; a second pie added to the Industry Sales chart could represent next year's sales. When you add a second pie, you can select

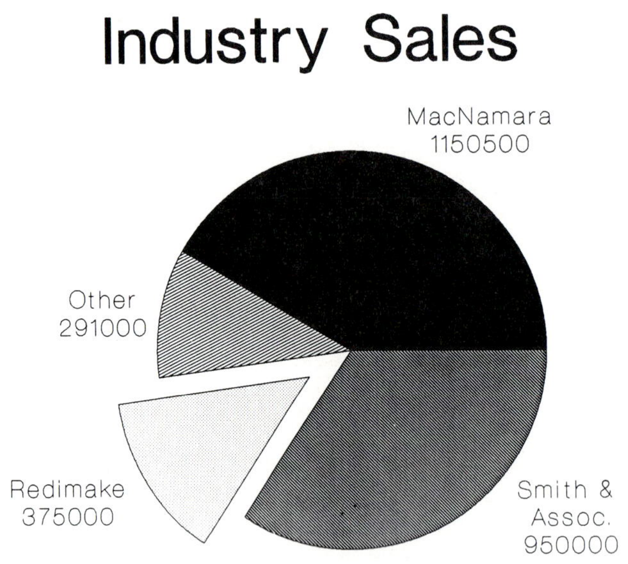

FIGURE 4-4. Pie chart with an exploded slice

options to make the second pie proportional to the first and to link pie slices. The appearance of the second pie is controlled by the same options that controlled the first pie chart.

Adding a Second Pie

To add a second pie, you only have to enter the data that you want to appear in the pie. To add a second pie to the Industry Sales pie chart, follow these steps.

1. Press PGDN.

This displays the Pie Chart 2 Data screen. Harvard Graphics uses this screen to select the data that will appear in the second pie chart. Like the Pie Chart 1 Data screen, you can enter the chart's title, subtitle, and footnote at the top of the screen. The screen's table is identical to the table in the Pie Chart 1 Data screen. The only difference is that the third column is Value Series 2 instead of Series 1. You can enter up to eight series in the Pie Chart 1 Data or Pie Chart 2 Data screen, although you can only use two of the series at a time to display as pie charts.

2. Type **Mardin** and press ENTER.
3. Type **Stattler** and press ENTER.
4. Type **Taylor** and press ENTER.
5. Type **Young & Sons.**
6. Press UP ARROW until the cursor is on Mardin, and TAB to move to the Value Series 2 column.
7. Type **70000** and press ENTER.
8. Type **60000** and press ENTER.
9. Type **90000** and press ENTER.
10. Type **71000.**
11. Press F8 (Options) to display the first page of Pie Chart Titles & Options.

With two pies, you must label what each of them represents. The title will appear below the pies.

12. Move to the Pie 1 title field.
13. Type **1990 Sales** and press ENTER twice for the first pie title.

You can have up to two lines of pie titles.

14. Type **Breakdown of Other** and press ENTER for the second pie title.
15. Press F2 (Draw chart) to display the chart shown in Figure 4-5.

You can customize the second pie in the same way you did the first pie. The second pie uses the color and pattern information you enter in the fifth and sixth columns of the Pie Chart 2 Data screen. If Yes is selected for any series in the Cut Slice column, they are exploded. The Cut Slice, Color, and Pattern columns are separate for each pie. You can change one without affecting the other.

Once you have entered data in the Pie Chart 2 Data screen, Harvard Graphics includes the second pie in the pie chart. If you later want to hide the second pie, you must explicitly do so.

16. Press any key to remove the graph from the screen.

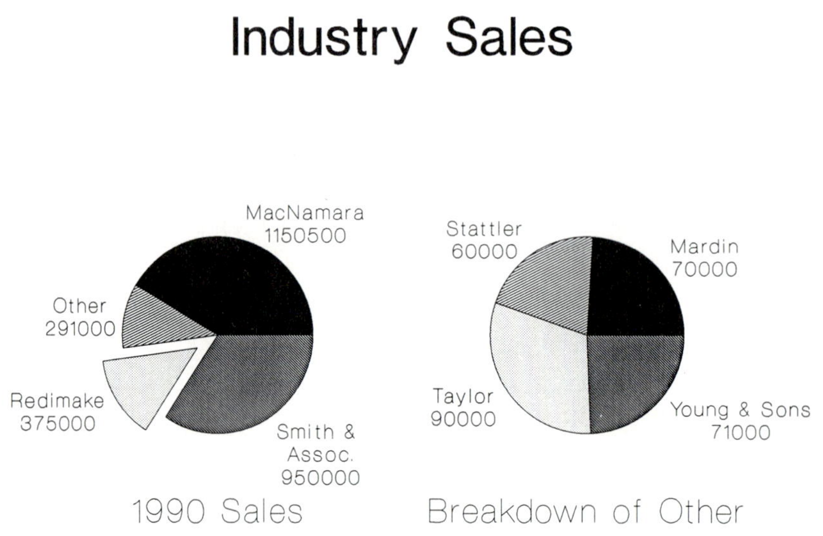

FIGURE 4-5. Two pies in a pie chart

17. Press (PGDN) to display the second page of Pie Chart Titles & Options, which looks like Figure 4-6.

18. Press (TAB) to move to the Pie 2 column for the Chart Style option.

19. Select None.

20. Press (F2) (Draw chart) to display a chart like the one shown in Figure 4-4 with the first pie title added.

Selecting None hides the second pie and the first pie is displayed centered. The None option is only available for the second pie; you cannot hide the first pie.

21. Press any key to remove the graph from the screen.

22. Select Pie for Pie 2 Chart style.

Pie Chart Titles & Options Page 2 of 2

	Pie 1			Pie 2		
Chart style	▸Pie	Column		▸Pie	Column	None
Sort slices	Yes	▸No		Yes	▸No	
Starting angle	0			0		
Pie size	50			50		
Show label	▸Yes	No		▸Yes	No	
Label size	3			3		
Show value	▸Yes	No		▸Yes	No	
Place value	▸Below	Adjacent	Inside	▸Below	Adjacent	Inside
Value format						
Currency	Yes	▸No		Yes	▸No	
Show percent	Yes	▸No		Yes	▸No	
Place percent	▸Below	Adjacent	Inside	▸Below	Adjacent	Inside
Percent format						

F1-Help
F2-Draw chart F8-Data F10-Continue

FIGURE 4-6. Second page of Pie Chart Titles & Options

Adding More Series

In the previous section you learned how you can add a second series and use it to display a second pie. You can add six more series for the chart data. Due to pie chart limitations, you are limited to using any two of the eight available series at one time. The flexibility of changing the series that appear in the pie allows you to enter all your data at once.

You can try out other series, changing which series appear in the pie charts, by following these steps:

1. Press F8 (Data) to return to the Pie Chart 2 Data screen.
2. Press F9 (More series).

The data you entered for the second series disappears, and the third column becomes Value Series 3. Your entries in the second and third columns become the third series data. Any information in the last three columns does not change when you change the series assigned to the pie chart. The information in the Cut Slice, Color, and Pattern columns belongs to the pie, not to the series that is assigned to the pie when the change is made.

3. Type **MacNamara** and press ENTER.
4. Type **Other** and press ENTER.
5. Type **Redimake** and press ENTER.
6. Type **Smith & ¦Assoc.**.
7. Press UP ARROW until the cursor is on MacNamara, and press TAB to move to the Value column.
8. Type **1090000** and press ENTER.
9. Type **291000** and press ENTER.
10. Type **798000** and press ENTER.
11. Type **1200000.**
12. Press F8 (Options) and PGUP to display the first page of Pie Chart Titles & Options.
13. Move to the Pie 2 title field.

The title from the second pie using the second series is still displayed.

14. Press CTRL-DELETE and type **1991 Sales** for the new pie title.

15. Press F2 (Draw chart) to display the chart.

As you can see by the pies, Harvard Graphics draws pies using the series selected in the Pie Chart 1 Data and Pie Chart 2 Data screens. By changing the series that appears in either screen you will change the series that appears in each pie.

16. Press any key to remove the chart from the screen.

17. Press F8 (Data) to display the chart data.

18. Press F9 (More series).

This displays the values for Series 4. You could use this series to enter additional information. If you continue pressing F9 (More series), you will find that you can enter up to eight different series.

19. Press F2 (Draw chart) to display the chart.

The second pie does not appear because the series selected for the second pie does not have any data in the Value column.

20. Press any key to remove the chart from the screen.

21. Press F9 (More series) until Series 3 appears in the Value column.

You can use F9 (More series) to change the series that is used in each pie.

22. Press PGUP to display the Pie Chart 1 Data screen.

23. Press F9 (More series).

Just as you can use F9 (More series) to change the series that appears in the second pie, you can also use this key to change the series that appears in the first pie. You can even use the same series in both pies if you wanted to use pie chart display options to emphasize different points about the same data.

24. Press F9 (More series) until Series 1 appears in the Value column.

OPTIONS FOR TWO PIES

You can use two additional customizing options when you create a chart that contains two pies: You can size the pies based on the total of the values in the two pies, and you can link one pie to the other. Linking the pies creates a visual connection between a slice in the first pie and the second pie.

Making Pies Proportionally Sized

You can size two pies to make them proportional to the values in the pies. This feature allows you to use the overall size of the pies to indicate a proportional increase or decrease. For example, the sales for 1991 are 22% more than the previous year. You can graphically show this on the chart by making the first pie 22% smaller than the second pie. You do not have to concern yourself with computing the percent increase or decrease, because Harvard Graphics will do the computation for you when you select Proportional pies.

To try this feature using the Series 1 and Series 3 data, follow these steps:

1. Press PGDN until you display the Pie Chart 2 Data screen.
2. Press TAB until you move to the Cut Slice column and DOWN ARROW until you move to the row for the Redimake slice.
3. Select Yes.
4. Press F8 (Options) to display the first page of Pie Chart Titles & Options.
5. Move to the Proportional pies field.
6. Select Yes.
7. Press F2 (Draw chart) to display the chart that appears in Figure 4-7.

The first pie is smaller than the second. This provides a quick graphical illustration of the increase of sales in the industry. When you use this option, the totals of the two pies should not be so different that the smaller pie becomes too small to read.

8. Press any key to remove the chart from the screen.
9. Press ESC to return to the Main Menu.

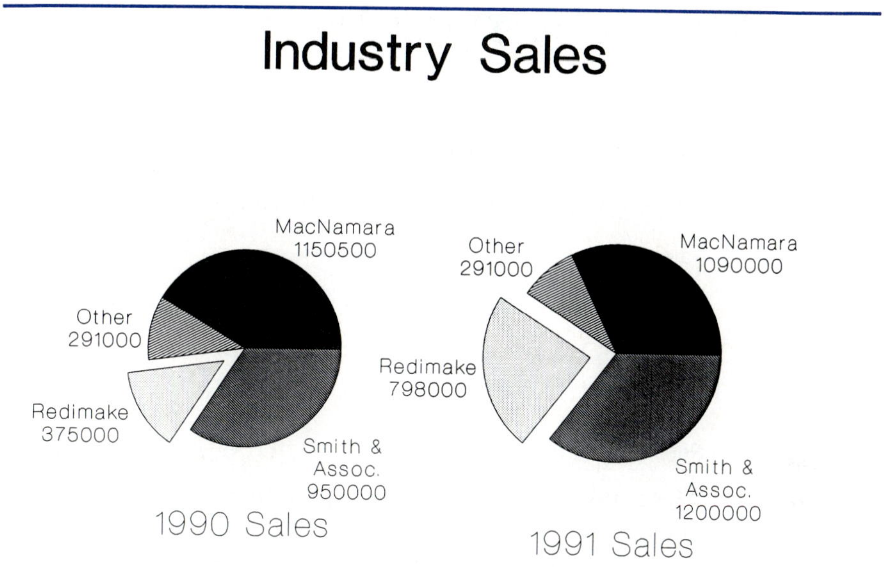

FIGURE 4-7. Pies proportionally sized by their totals

10. Press (CTRL-S) to save the chart.
11. Press (CTRL-DELETE) and type **PIE2** as the filename and press (F10) (Continue).
12. Select Enter/Edit chart.

Linking Pies

In the pie chart that you created earlier, with one pie showing the distribution of sales and a second pie showing the distribution of one slice of the first pie, the title under the second pie is the only explanation of its meaning. To improve this, you can add graphic lines to the pies to connect the Other slice from the first pie to the second pie. First you must explode the pie slice in the first pie chart that defines the other pie chart.

Try linking your pie charts by following these steps:

1. Move to the Cut Slice column in the row for Redimake.

You should only explode the pie slice that you want to link. You exploded this pie slice earlier in the chapter, so you must return it now to its default position.

2. Select No and press ENTER.
3. Move to the Cut Slice column in the row for Other.
4. Select Yes.
5. Press PGDN to display the Pie Chart 2 Data screen.
6. Press F9 (More series) until Series 2 appears below Value.
7. Move to the Cut Slice column in the row for Taylor.
8. Select No and press ENTER.
9. Press F8 (Options) to display the first page of Pie Chart Titles & Options.
10. Move to the Pie 2 title field.
11. Press CTRL-DELETE, and type **Breakdown of Other** for the second pie title.
12. Move to the Link pies option.
13. Select Yes.
14. Press F2 (Draw chart).

As the chart indicates, you do not want to combine linked pies and proportionally sized pies if the second pie will be so small it becomes difficult to read.

15. Press any key to remove the chart from the screen.
16. Move to the Proportional pies option.
17. Select No.
18. Press F2 (Draw chart) to display the chart that appears in Figure 4-8.

The chart now has lines connecting the first pie's Other slice to the second pie. This provides a quick graphical illustration of the title for the second pie chart. Harvard Graphics will rotate the first pie if the exploded slice is not next to the other pie. You can only link a slice of the first pie to the second pie. You cannot link a slice of the second pie to the first pie.

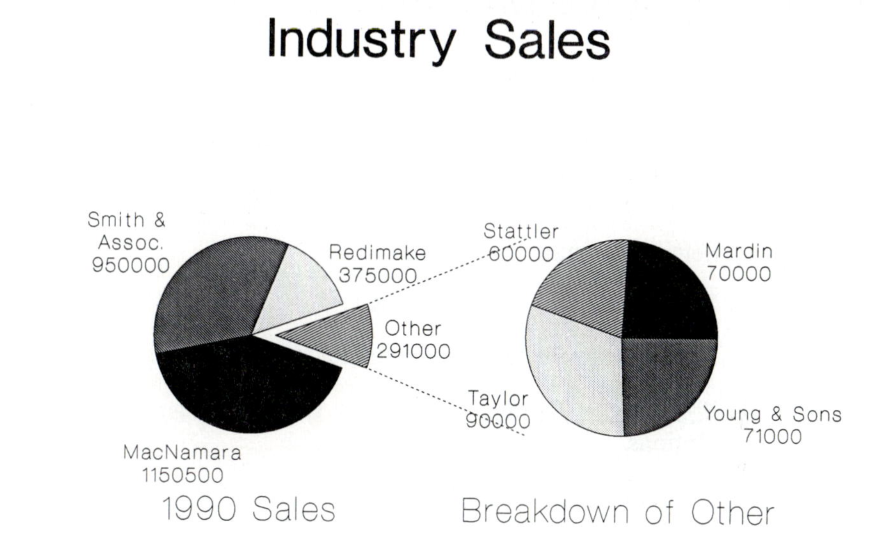

FIGURE 4-8. First pie linked to the second

19. Press any key to remove the chart from the screen.
20. Press ESC to return to the Main Menu.
21. Select Get/Save/Remove.
22. Select Save chart.
23. Type **OTHERPIE** as the filename and press F10 (Continue).

SETTING THE PIE'S APPEARANCE

It is easy to explore the effect of changes on a completed pie chart, so let's look at additional options for enhancing the appearance of a pie chart. Adding 3D, sorting the order of the pie slices, and adjusting the pie size and starting angle are some of the changes you can make to a pie chart.

Displaying Three-Dimensional Pies

The pie charts you have created are flat circles. Although they represent your data accurately, you can make a change that adds depth, improves the chart's appearance, and stimulates reader interest: Add a three-dimensional appearance by following these steps:

1. Select Get chart.
2. Select PIE2 and press ENTER.
3. Press any key to remove the chart from the screen.
4. Press F8 (Options) to display the first page of Pie Chart Titles & Options.
5. Move to the 3D effect field.
6. Select Yes.
7. Press F2 (Draw chart) to display a pie chart like the one shown in Figure 4-9.

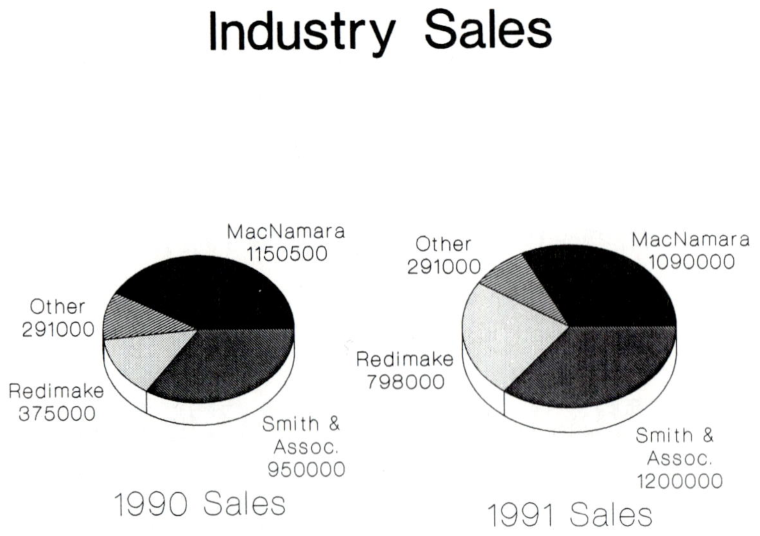

FIGURE 4-9. Displaying pies with a 3D effect

The 3D effect field does not combine with exploded slices. Notice that the Redimake slices are not exploded, even though they are set to be exploded.

8. Press any key to remove the chart from the screen.

Displaying Pies as Columns

Another pie chart option allows you to display certain data in a column, with the column divided into components. Figure 4-10 shows the chart from Figure 4-8 with the second pie displayed as a column instead of a pie. You can make this chart by following these steps:

1. Press ESC to return to the Main Menu.
2. Select Get/Save/Remove.
3. Select Get chart.
4. Select OTHERPIE and press ENTER.

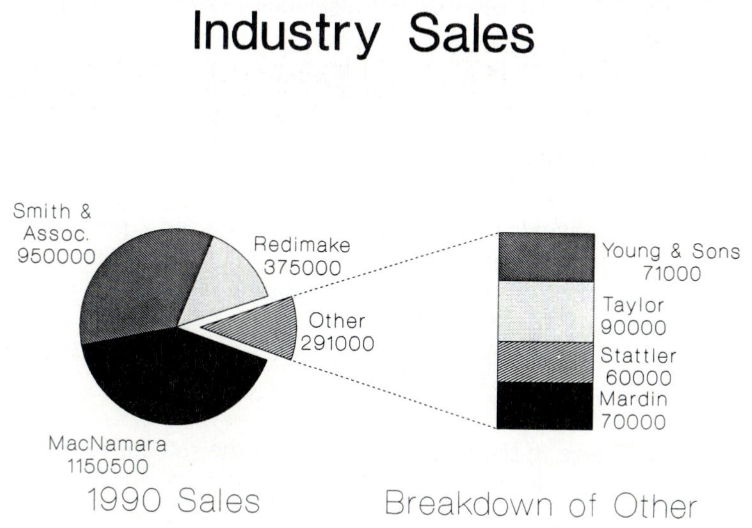

FIGURE 4-10. Displaying a pie as a column

5. Press ENTER to continue when Harvard Graphics displays a warning that the changes have not been saved.
6. Press any key to remove the chart from the screen.
7. Press F8 (Options) to display the first page of Pie Chart Titles & Options.
8. Press PGDN to display the second page of Pie Chart Titles & Options.
9. Move to the Pie 2 column for the Chart style option. You can press RIGHT ARROW until one of the selections is highlighted. Pressing TAB provides a quicker solution for switching between the columns.
10. Select Column.
11. Press F2 (Draw chart) to display the chart that appears in Figure 4-10.

Instead of slices creating a pie, a column has column components that are stacked on each other. The column segments use the colors and patterns selected in the fifth and sixth column of the Pie Chart 1 Data or Pie Chart 2 Data screen. Most of the options that you will use for pie slices also apply to column components, except you cannot explode column components, and the Starting angle field in the Pie Chart Titles & Options screens does not apply to columns.

12. Press any key to remove the chart from the display.

Sorting Pie Slices

You can control the order in which data for a pie chart is entered by using the Sort slices option. For example, you entered the data for the three series in alphabetical order. Another possible option is to order them according to size.

To sort the slices in the pie and column shown in Figure 4-10, follow these steps:

1. Move to the column for Pie 1 in the row for Sort slices.
2. Select Yes.
3. Press TAB to move to the Pie 2 column for the Sort slices option.
4. Select Yes.

5. Press (F2) (Draw chart) to display the pie chart.

Instead of the slices being in the order that you entered them, the slices are arranged from largest to smallest. For pies, the slices are arranged in a counterclockwise fashion. For columns, the column components start from the bottom and work their way up.

6. Press any key to remove the chart from the screen.
7. Press (ESC) to return to the Main Menu.
8. Select Get/Save/Remove.
9. Select Save chart.
10. Press (F10) (Continue) to save the chart with the same settings.

Changing the Pie's Starting Angle

In all of the pie charts you have created, the pies always start at one point and work counterclockwise. This may not present the image you want. For example, you may want a particular slice to appear at the top. You can rotate the pie slices within the pie area by changing its *starting angle,* which is the angle at which the first pie slice starts. The pie continues from this angle around the circle in a counterclockwise direction. Initially, pies use a 0 starting angle, which starts them at the 3 o'clock position in the circle.

Try changing the starting angle to see the effect of this option by following these steps:

1. Select Get chart.
2. Select PIE2 and press (ENTER).
3. Press any key to remove the chart from the screen.
4. Press (F8) (Options) and (PGDN) to display the second page of Pie Chart Titles & Options.
5. Move to the Starting angle option in the Pie 1 column.
6. Type **240.**

The starting angle is a value between 0 and 360. Figure 4-11 shows a circle with several lines and their angles displayed. Notice that as the angle

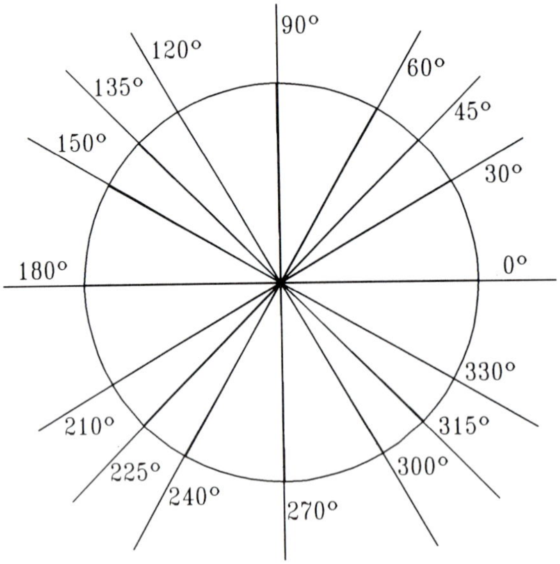

FIGURE 4-11. Circle with angles inscribed

increases, the starting position of the first slice moves counterclockwise. You can use this figure to quickly estimate the angle that you want to use. Once you enter a rough estimate, you can always fine tune the value of the Starting angle option.

7. Press TAB to move to the Pie 2 column.

8. Type **260**.

9. Press F2 (Draw chart) to display the chart shown in Figure 4-12.

You have moved Redimake to the top of the pies. By changing the angle that Harvard Graphics starts drawing the pie slices, you are changing the position of the slices within the circle, but you have not affected the size of any slice of the pie.

10. Press any key to remove the chart from the screen.

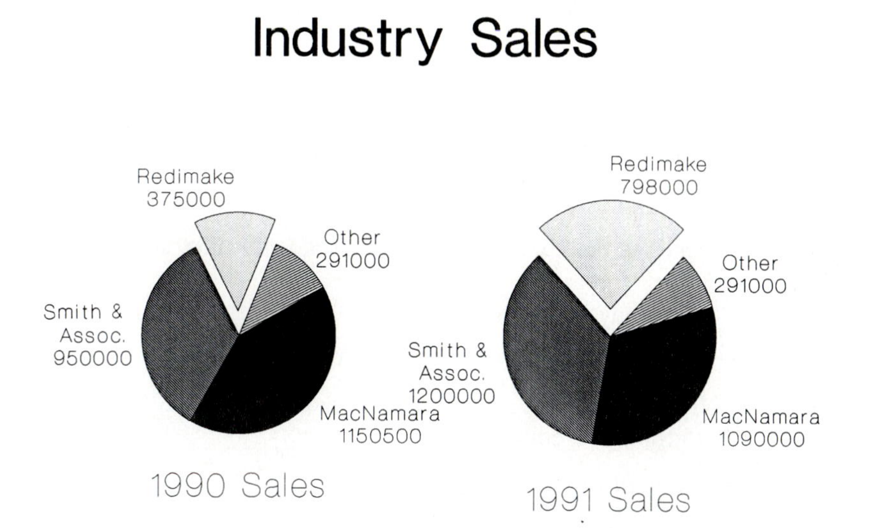

FIGURE 4-12. Entering a starting angle rotates the pies

Changing the Pie Size

With the Proportional pies field you can change the sizes of two pies to make them proportional. Another option is to manually set the size of the pies. This option allows you to control the size of the pies in relation to each other. You may want to manually set the pie sizes if the pie size differential is too great to use the Proportional pies field.

To set the size of the pies, change the value of the Pie size field in the Pie 1 and Pie 2 columns. Although 50 is the default, you can change this number to any value between 0 and 100. As you increase the pie size, the pie may start to run into other objects in the chart, such as titles and footnotes.

Expand your pies in the PIE2 chart to use more of the chart area by following these steps:

1. Press **PGUP** to go to page 1 of the Pie Chart Titles & Options form.
2. Press **TAB** until you move to the Proportional pies field and press the spacebar to change the setting to No.

Although the default setting for this field is No, an earlier exercise set Proportional pies to Yes.

3. Press PGDN to move back to Page 2.
4. Press TAB to move to the Pie size field in the Pie 1 column.
5. Type **20** and press TAB to move to the Pie 2 column.
6. Type **40**.
7. Press F2 (Draw chart).

Both pies in the chart have shrunk, since you have selected smaller values.

8. Press any key to remove the chart from the screen.
9. Press SHIFT-TAB to move to the Pie 1 column.
10. Type **75** and press TAB to replace the entry for the first pie and move to the Pie 2 column.
11. Type **75** for the second pie.
12. Press F2 (Draw chart).

Now both pies are bigger and the same size. Unfortunately, the pies are so big that they hide part of the pie slice labels.

13. Press any key to remove the chart from the screen.
14. Press PGUP to move to Page 1 of the Pie Chart Titles & Options form.
15. Press TAB until the cursor is on the Proportional pies field, and then press the spacebar to change the setting to Yes.
16. Press F2 (Draw chart).

When the pies are proportional, Harvard Graphics only uses the pie size for the first pie and ignores the pie size for the second pie.

17. Press any key to remove the chart from the screen.
18. Press PGDN and then press DOWN ARROW until you move to the Pie size field.
19. Type **50** and press TAB to replace the entry for the first pie and move to the Pie 2 column.
20. Type **50** for the second pie.
21. Press F2 (Draw chart).
22. Press any key to remove the chart from the screen.

Selecting Label Display

Two options in the Pie Chart Titles & Options form are used to determine if the labels appear and to control their size. The Show label field determines if the label appears. If Yes is selected, they appear; if No is selected, they do not. The Label size is the size of the labels relative to the chart size. Like selecting the text size for the title, subtitle, pie titles, and footnotes, the size is the percentage of the chart height the text uses. For example, the default of 3 means the height of the labels is 3% of the chart's height. This number can range between 0 and 20. The label size selected with this option controls all text that is attached to a pie slice, except pie titles. This includes the label in the Label column, the value of the pie slice, and the percentage of the value to the total. To change the label size, type a new value and press (ENTER).

Changing the Value's Appearance

In the pie charts you have created, the values entered in the Value column in the Pie Chart 1 Data or Pie Chart 2 Data screen appeared next to the pie slices because this is the default location. You can decide if the values will appear, where the values will appear, and the format of the values, using the Show value, Place value, Value format, and Currency fields in the middle of the second page of Pie Chart Titles & Options.

The Show value option determines if the values will appear. While Yes, the default, is selected, the values will appear. You can select No if you do not want the values to appear. The Place value field determines the position of the value. Figure 4-13 shows how the different selections change the placement of values. If you select Inside, make sure that the color or pattern can be distinguished from the labels, as in the third pie in the example in Figure 4-13.

The Value format field is just like the format field for the axes in bar, line, area, and high/low/close charts. You can use the same characters and entries to change the format of the appearance. For example, you can enter 2 to display two digits to the right of the decimal point. The Currency field provides a quick method of displaying the values in a currency format. If you select Yes, Harvard Graphics displays the values with a preceding dollar sign. The default of No tells Harvard Graphics to use any formatting you enter for the Value format field.

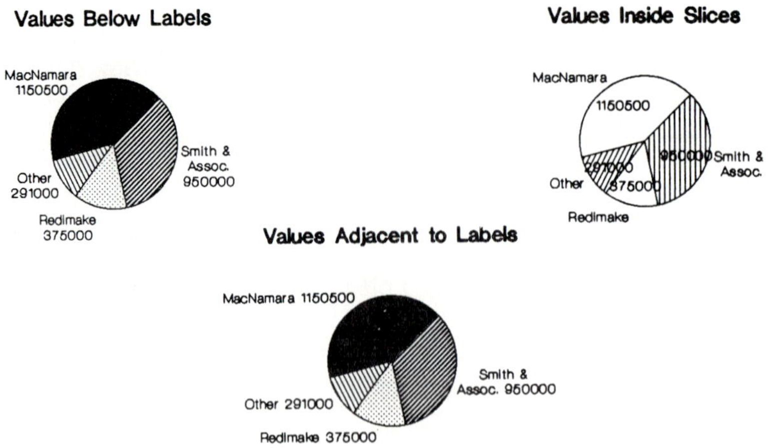

FIGURE 4-13. Place options available for values and percents

Try all these options, using the PIE2 chart, by following these steps:

1. Move to the Value format field in the Pie 1 column.
2. Type **1000|,**.
3. Press TAB to move to the Pie 2 column for the Value format field.
4. Type **1000|,**.
5. Press TAB to move to the Currency field in the Pie 1 column.
6. Select Yes.
7. Press TAB to move to the Pie 2 column for the Currency field.
8. Select Yes.
9. Press PGUP to display the first page of Pie Chart Titles & Options.
10. Move to the second line of the Pie 1 title field.
11. Type **(Thousands)** and press ENTER twice.
12. Type **(Thousands)** for the second line of the Pie 2 title field.

13. Press (F2) (Draw chart) to display the chart that looks like Figure 4-14.
14. Press any key to remove the chart from the screen.

Using Percents

Each of the pie slices or column components is a proportion of the total. You may want to show the proportion each slice is to the total by displaying the percentage. The Show percent, Place percent, and Percent format fields in the bottom of the second page of Pie Chart Titles & Options determine if the percentages will appear, where the percentages will appear, and the format used to display the percentages. They are similar to options for displaying values.

The Show percent field determines if the percentages appear. Select Yes and the percentages appear in the location selected with the Place percent field. The default, No, hides the percentages. The Place percent field determines the position of the value. The selections for this option and the positions where the percentages will appear are the same as the Place value

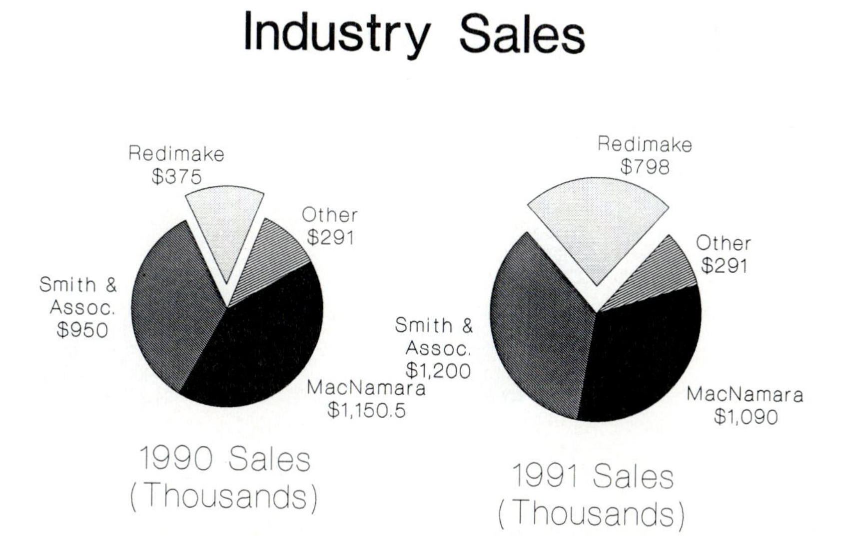

FIGURE 4-14. Pie chart using options to set display of values

field. You cannot place the percent and the value in the same location. The Percent format field is just like the Format option for axes in bar, line, area, and high/low/close charts. You can use the same characters and entries to change the format of the appearance. For example, you can enter **2** to display two digits to the right of the decimal point.

Try these options, using the PIE2 chart, by following these steps:

1. Press PGDN to move to the second page of Titles & Options.
2. Move to the Show percent field in the Pie 1 column.
3. Select Yes.
4. Press TAB to move to the Pie 2 column for the Show percent field.
5. Select Yes.
6. Press TAB to move to the Place percent field in the Pie 1 column.
7. Select Adjacent.
8. Press TAB to move to the Pie 2 column for the Place value field.
9. Select Adjacent.
10. Press F2 (Draw chart) to display the chart that looks like Figure 4-15.

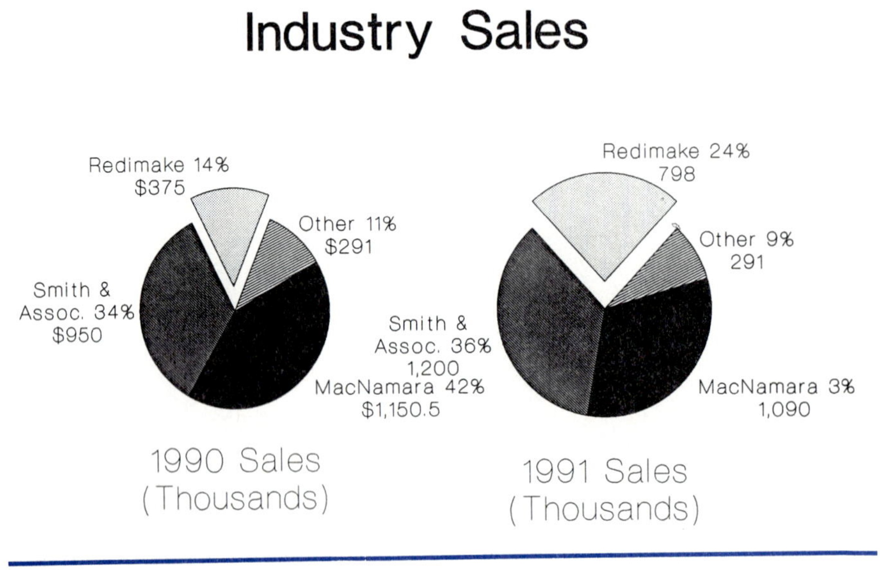

FIGURE 4-15. Pie chart using options to set display of percents

11. Press any key to remove the chart from the screen.
12. Save the chart by pressing ESC to return to the Main Menu, pressing CTRL-S, and pressing F10 (Continue).
13. Press CTRL-P to print the chart.

If you have any settings that you want to change, alter them here. You may want to see how some of the options will affect the final results. For example, you may want to print the chart using Draft and then print it again using Final to see the difference between the quality levels your printer provides.

14. Press F10 (Continue) to print your graph.
15. Press CTRL-S to save the chart again with the altered print settings.
16. Press F10 (Continue) to save the chart with the same name.

chapter 5

IMPORTING AND EXPORTING DATA

In all the charts you have created up to now, you have entered the data using the Harvard Graphics screen for the type of chart you want to create. Often you will have the data stored in another format, such as in a Lotus worksheet that projects sales or in a graph created with PFS:Graph. If the program containing the data or graph is supported by Harvard Graphics, you can bring the data or graph into memory to use with Harvard Graphics without retyping the data. This process is called *importing* the data.

In essence, importing data is bringing data into Harvard Graphics in a format that it can convert to its own data format. Harvard Graphics can import data from Lotus and Excel worksheets or graphs, PFS:Graph files, ASCII files created by word processing programs, database programs that can write their data in reports in ASCII format, and other programs created by Software Publishing Corporation. Harvard Graphics can also convert

CGM Metafiles, the ANSI standard for vector-based graphics files, into Harvard Graphics data format. A utility program is no longer needed to provide these features in Harvard Graphics 2.3.

Another option is *exporting* your Harvard Graphics chart to a file. When you export a chart, you are storing the chart's image in a format that another package can use. Harvard Graphics can export data to Professional Write files; HPGL files, which are a disk image of printed output for Hewlett Packard plotters; Encapsulated Postscript files; and CGM Metafiles. When you export a chart, you are exporting the chart's image, not the chart's data. You can use the exported files to include charts in word processing documents using such packages as Professional Write, OfficeWriter, WordPerfect, or desktop publishing programs such as Ventura Publisher and Aldus PageMaker.

Using import and export features can dramatically reduce data entry time. Entering data more than once to use it with multiple programs is not only frustrating, it is also error prone. You might make a mistake in one of your entries and end up with two sets of data not in agreement when they should be identical. When you are able to import and export data between programs, these problems do not occur.

Use the sections in this chapter selectively. If you do not work with Lotus or Excel spreadsheet packages, you do not need to learn how to transfer data from these packages into Harvard Graphics. The ASCII import features discussed in this chapter may have applicability you are not aware of. Most word processing packages have the ability to create an ASCII file, although the procedure for each word processor is slightly different. The majority of software packages can write reports to disk rather than directly to the printer. When these reports are written to disk they are stored in an ASCII file, making it possible to use the data with Harvard Graphics.

If you do not have an immediate need to transfer data from other sources, skip this chapter for now. In time you will find application for its features as you look for a time-saving approach for using data already stored in another package.

In this chapter you will have an opportunity to import data and graphs from Lotus 1-2-3 and an ASCII file. You will also learn the basic procedure for exporting charts to use them with other programs. All of the import and export options are not covered in detail, although you will find that other file types follow the same basic procedure as the ones shown.

IMPORTING LOTUS AND EXCEL DATA

Harvard Graphics can read data stored in Lotus and Excel worksheet files. This means that you can take budget figures or sales projections from Lotus

1-2-3 or Symphony or Microsoft's Excel and import the data into Harvard Graphics. You can tell Harvard Graphics where this data is located and use all of the charting features offered by Harvard Graphics. You can also import a previously defined graph in the worksheet into Harvard Graphics by specifying the name of the graph. The procedures for importing spreadsheet data and importing a graph are different. The full range of options for importing worksheet data includes 1-2-3 Release 1A, 2.0, 2.01, and 2.2, Symphony, and Excel worksheets. If you have worksheet files with .WKS (1-2-3 Release 1A), .WK1 (1-2-3 Releases 2.0, 2.01, and 2.2), .WRK and .WR1 (Symphony) or .XLS (Excel) filename extensions, you will be able to import their data into Harvard Graphics.

Creating Analytical Graphs with Worksheet Data

When you import spreadsheet data, you must specify range names or cell addresses for each cell or range that you want to use in the graph. When importing a graph you import all the data used to create the graph just by specifying its name. Although the latter approach may seem quicker, importing worksheet data and importing a graph really require about the same amount of time when you consider that you need to specify each individual address or range from within the spreadsheet package to create a graph in the first place. Unless you need to use the graph created in the spreadsheet package for some other purpose, you will do just as well importing the data and not defining graphs from within the spreadsheet package.

Once you import data from a worksheet file, Harvard Graphics will suggest using this file when you make subsequent import requests during the current session. You must use the F3 (Select files) key to request another file.

Since the spreadsheet packages also have graph capabilities, you may wonder why either way of importing data would be of interest. The answer is in Harvard Graphics' ability to create more sophisticated graphs. You can add features like 3D, a shadow effect, and many other options that are not possible if you create graphs directly from these other packages.

Taking a Look at the Worksheet Data

You must understand the layout of the worksheet that contains the data you want to import into Harvard Graphics. Since you must tell Harvard Graphics where to look for legends, titles, and series values, you should note these locations on the worksheet. You can call the worksheet up in memory and jot down these cell addresses, or you can print a copy for reference as you specify your needs to Harvard Graphics. If you plan to bring the data into Harvard Graphics using range names, you may want to use the /Range Name Table command in Lotus 1-2-3 and print a copy of the table containing range names and addresses for reference.

Figure 5-1 shows some data entered on a 1-2-3 worksheet. The entries were created with labels, numbers, and formulas entered into worksheet cells. If you use 1-2-3, this worksheet creation process is very familiar to you. The entries in cells C5..F7 are created with formulas rather than numbers. When the formulas were initially entered in 1-2-3, as many as three decimal digits displayed in these cells. Whole numbers were displayed through 1-2-3's formatting features, which also added the commas in each of the entries. When this data is imported into Harvard Graphics, the full decimal accuracy of each of the numbers is maintained, and some of the numbers will display as many as three decimal digits.

The worksheet file must be saved before you can import the data. The /File Save command in 1-2-3 creates the WKS or .WK1 file that the import feature can read. Symphony and Excel have similar commands for listing named ranges and saving files.

A1: [W12] READY

	A	B	C	D	E	F	G
1			Royston Company				
2			1988 - 1992 Sales				
3							
4		1988	1989	1990	1991	1992	
5	Tires	2,560	2,765	2,986	3,225	3,483	
6	Batteries	3,500	3,815	4,158	4,533	4,941	
7	Chains	4,000	3,500	3,000	2,100	1,000	

FIGURE 5-1. 1-2-3 worksheet data

Harvard Graphics Procedure for Importing Data

To import data you must first define a chart type with the Create new chart command. You must choose an analytical chart type, like pie, bar, or line, rather than a text chart type. If you choose a text chart type, the import procedure will fail.

Once you have defined a chart type, proceed from the chart entry form to the Main Menu by pressing (ESC). Select Import/Export, and a menu matching the one in Figure 5-2 appears. To import Lotus worksheet data, choose Import Lotus data. To import Excel worksheet data, choose Import Excel data. A form like the one in Figure 5-3 appears to allow you to select a worksheet file the first time you use this feature. Highlight the worksheet you want and press (F10) (Continue). Next you are asked to specify the location of the information you want to show on the graph. While this example imports a Lotus 1-2-3 worksheet, the steps for importing an Excel or Symphony worksheet are the same. Cell addresses that supply titles and legends must be preceded by a backslash. This tells Harvard Graphics to use the contents of the cell rather than the letters and numbers in the cell addresses

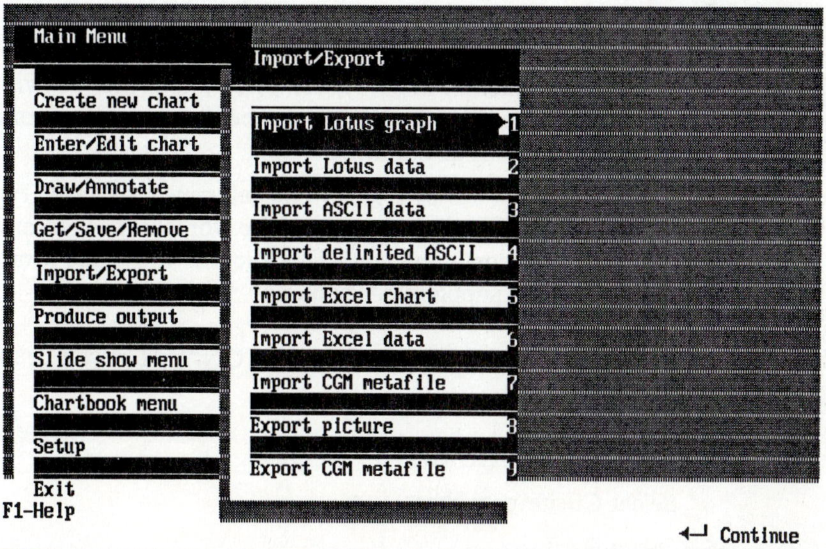

FIGURE 5-2. The Import/Export menu

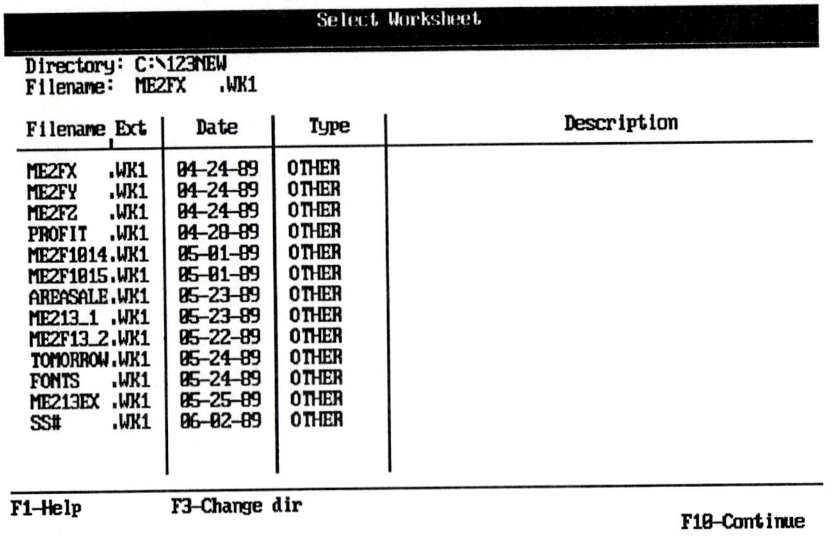

Select Worksheet

Directory: C:\123NEW
Filename: ME2FX .WK1

Filename Ext	Date	Type	Description
ME2FX .WK1	04-24-89	OTHER	
ME2FY .WK1	04-24-89	OTHER	
ME2FZ .WK1	04-24-89	OTHER	
PROFIT .WK1	04-20-89	OTHER	
ME2F1014.WK1	05-01-89	OTHER	
ME2F1015.WK1	05-01-89	OTHER	
AREASALE.WK1	05-23-89	OTHER	
ME213_1 .WK1	05-23-89	OTHER	
ME2F13_2.WK1	05-22-89	OTHER	
TOMORROW.WK1	05-24-89	OTHER	
FONTS .WK1	05-24-89	OTHER	
ME213EX .WK1	05-25-89	OTHER	
SS# .WK1	06-02-89	OTHER	

F1-Help F3-Change dir F10-Continue

FIGURE 5-3. Selecting a worksheet to import

as the text. For example, to use the contents of cell A3 as your title in Harvard Graphics, type **\A3** in the Title field on the Import Lotus Data form.

If you work with 1-2-3 on a regular basis, try this exercise to see how easy it is to transfer data:

1. With 1-2-3 loaded in memory, complete the entries shown in Figure 5-1. Although the entries in C4..F9 can be created with formulas, type the numbers as shown as a quick example.
2. Save the file in 1-2-3 by typing **/** and selecting File Save. Type **ROYSTON** and press ENTER. Print a copy of the worksheet for reference when you attempt to import the data. This creates the same worksheet that is included in the supplementary disk.

1-2-3 saves a file with the name ROYSTON.WK1 if you are using Release 2.0, 2.01, or 2.2.

3. Exit 1-2-3 and start Harvard Graphics.
4. Select Create new chart.
5. Select Bar/Line.

6. Select Name as the X data type and then press F10 (Continue).

It is important for the X data type to match the type of data in the worksheet that you plan to use for the X-axis labels.

7. Press ESC to return to the Main Menu.
8. Select Import/Export.
9. Select Import Lotus data from the Import/Export menu.

Harvard Graphics displays the names of the worksheet files in the current directory. If there are none, Harvard Graphics displays a message at the bottom of the screen: "No files were found." You can change the directory by pressing UP ARROW, typing a new drive and directory designation, and pressing ENTER. Figure 5-4 shows the directory now changed to C:\123OTHER, where the 1-2-3 file for the example is stored.

Another way to change the directory is to press F3 (Change dir). Harvard Graphics displays both parent and subordinate directories. The parent directory is indicated by two periods (..). You can highlight the directory you want and press ENTER. Press F3 (Select files) once you are

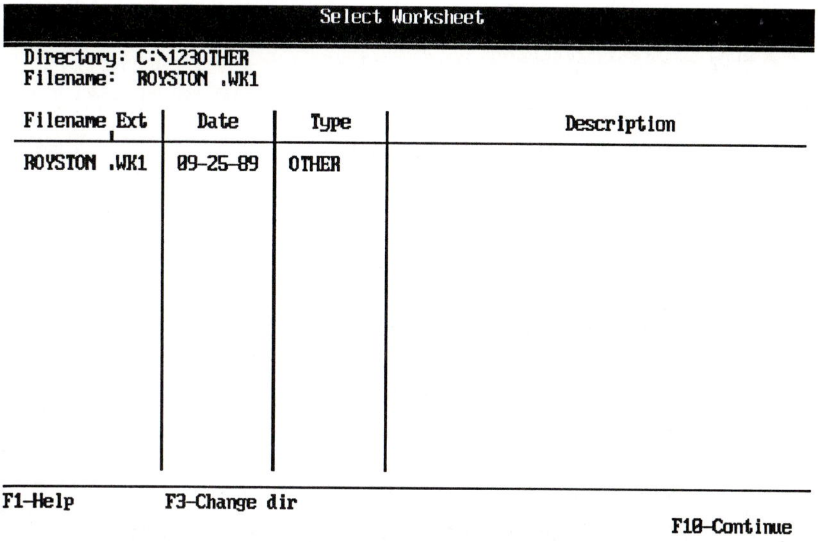

FIGURE 5-4. Changing the directory to locate 1-2-3 files

in the desired directory, since this function key allows you to toggle between choosing directories and choosing files. In the example shown, a new directory name was typed since the desired directory is neither a parent nor a subordinate of the original directory shown.

If you import spreadsheet data from the same directory regularly, you can use Setup Defaults from the Main Menu and specify an import directory that Harvard Graphics will automatically use.

10. Select the worksheet to use by highlighting the name of the desired file and pressing F10 (Continue).

The Import Lotus Data screen appears for you to specify the range names or addresses that you want to use.

11. Type **\c1** for the Title field and press ENTER.

The backslash (\) tells Harvard Graphics to use the contents of the cell for the title. This is the same convention that 1-2-3 uses.

12. Type **\c2** for the Subtitle field and press ENTER.
13. Type **Unit sales** for the Footnote field and press ENTER.
14. Type **A5.A7** for the X axis data field and press ENTER.
15. Type **B5.B7** for the Series 1 Data Range and press ENTER.
16. Type **C5.C7** for the Series 2 Data Range and press ENTER.
17. Type **D5.D7** for the Series 3 Data Range and press ENTER.
18. Type **E5.E7** for the Series 4 Data Range and press ENTER.
19. Type **F5.F7** for the Series 5 Data Range and press ENTER.

Your entries should match Figure 5-5. Notice the function-key assignments shown at the bottom of the screen. F4 (Clear ranges) can be used to clear ranges when you want to make major changes to the appearance of the current graph.

F6 (Range names) is another important function key. When you press this key, Harvard Graphics lists the range names created in the worksheet. Using range names is easier than cell addresses since they are easier to

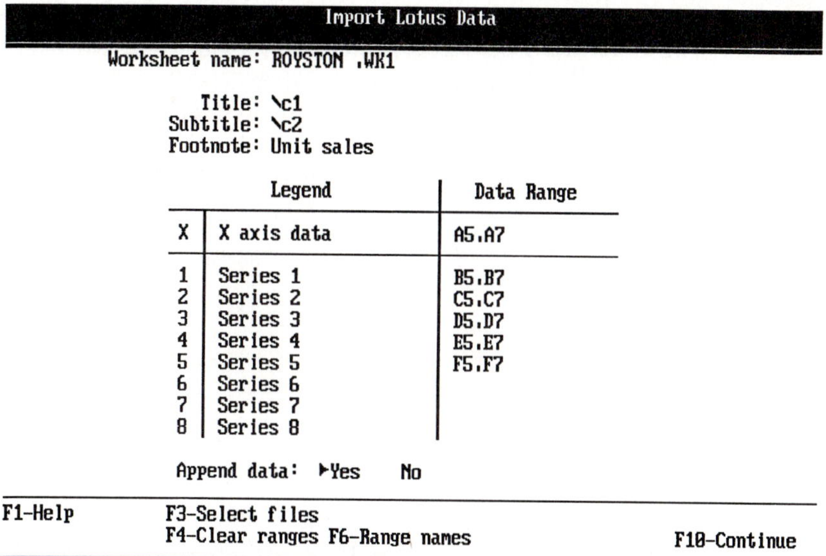

Import Lotus Data

Worksheet name: ROYSTON .WK1

Title: \c1
Subtitle: \c2
Footnote: Unit sales

	Legend	Data Range
X	X axis data	A5.A7
1	Series 1	B5.B7
2	Series 2	C5.C7
3	Series 3	D5.D7
4	Series 4	E5.E7
5	Series 5	F5.F7
6	Series 6	
7	Series 7	
8	Series 8	

Append data: ▸Yes No

F1-Help F3-Select files
F4-Clear ranges F6-Range names F10-Continue

FIGURE 5-5. Import Lotus Data form

remember. When you select a range name from the list, Harvard Graphics adds the range name at the cursor's position. You can also enter range names directly without using the F6 (Range names) key.

20. Press END to highlight the Append data field.
21. Press the spacebar to change the entry to No to ensure that the data will replace any data in memory rather than add to it.
22. Press F10 (Continue).

The Bar/Line Chart Data screen shown in Figure 5-6 now appears.

23. Press F8 (Options) to display the Titles & Options screen.
24. Press TAB until the cursor is in the Legend Title field for Series 1.
25. Press CTRL-DELETE to remove the existing entry, type **1988**, and press ENTER.
26. Repeat the process for the next four legend entries, assigning **1989**, **1990**, **1991**, and **1992** consecutively to the series, as shown in Figure 5-7.

Bar/Line Chart Data

Title: Royston Company
Subtitle: 1988 - 1992 Sales
Footnote: Unit sales

Pt	X Axis Name	Series 1	Series 2	Series 3	Series 4
1	Tires	2560	2764.8	2985.984	3224.863
2	Batteries	3500	3815	4158.35	4532.601
3	Chains	4000	3500	3000	2100

FIGURE 5-6. Data from the Lotus worksheet imported into Harvard Graphics

27. Press F2 (Draw chart).

28. Press ESC twice to return to the Main Menu. Now you can save and print the chart.

When printed, the chart that is currently displayed will look like Figure 5-8.

Importing 1-2-3 and Excel Graphs

When Harvard Graphics imports a 1-2-3 graph, it imports the data from the graph definition stored on a spreadsheet in a .WK1 file. It does not import the picture of the graph that you may have saved in a .PIC file with the 1-2-3 /Graph Save command. When you import an Excel chart, Harvard Graphics imports both the data and the graph settings that are stored in the Excel chart files (the files with an .XLC extension). Although it may not seem to

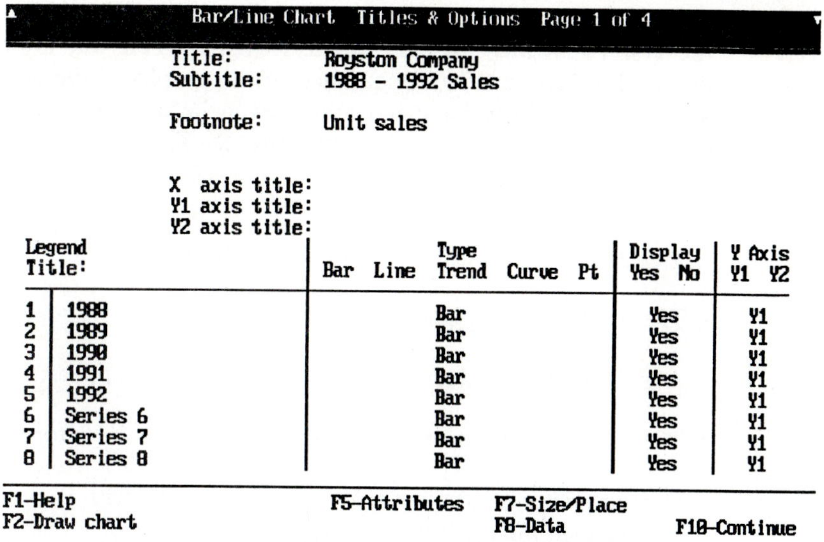

Bar/Line Chart Titles & Options Page 1 of 4

Title: Royston Company
Subtitle: 1988 - 1992 Sales

Footnote: Unit sales

X axis title:
Y1 axis title:
Y2 axis title:

Legend Title:		Type: Bar	Line	Trend	Curve	Pt	Display: Yes	No	Y Axis: Y1	Y2
1	1988			Bar			Yes		Y1	
2	1989			Bar			Yes		Y1	
3	1990			Bar			Yes		Y1	
4	1991			Bar			Yes		Y1	
5	1992			Bar			Yes		Y1	
6	Series 6			Bar			Yes		Y1	
7	Series 7			Bar			Yes		Y1	
8	Series 8			Bar			Yes		Y1	

F1-Help F5-Attributes F7-Size/Place
F2-Draw chart F8-Data F10-Continue

FIGURE 5-7. Adding a title and legends

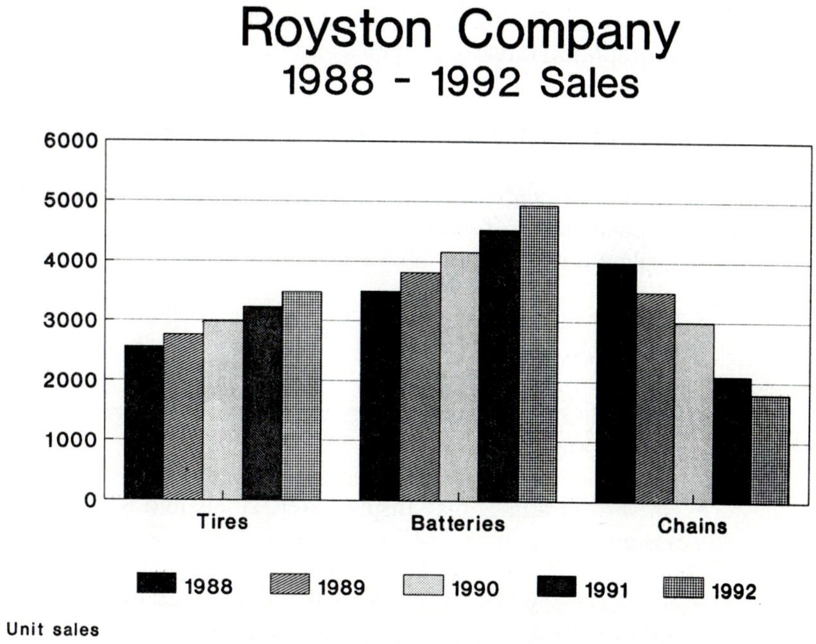

FIGURE 5-8. Completed chart created from 1-2-3 data

matter, the distinction is important because when you import a graph into Harvard Graphics, you will have access to all the data values used to create the graph that are not part of the .PIC file. You will notice some subtle differences between the appearance of the graphs in the spreadsheet package and that of the imported graph, even before you make enhancements with Harvard Graphics' expanded features. The imported graph differs in the following ways:

- Tick marks are placed inside the graph frame.
- The Y-axis title is placed horizontally rather than vertically.
- Any data labels added in the 1-2-3 graph do not appear.
- The display of dates and times may not match 1-2-3's format.
- High/low/close charts use a Y scale that begins with 0, unless you specifically change the scale in Harvard Graphics.
- Y-axis scaling on other bar/line charts may differ from Lotus' scale.

When you import an Excel chart, you may notice these differences between your graph in Harvard Graphics and in Excel:

- Harvard Graphics imports only the first 40 characters of a title.
- Harvard Graphics only imports up to eight data series and 240 data points for each series. If your Excel chart contains more data, Harvard Graphics displays a warning.
- Harvard Graphics does not import text attributes of the text in an Excel chart. You must add these features separately in Harvard Graphics.
- Harvard Graphics may display the data in a different order than Excel for pie and area charts.
- Harvard Graphics may display axes, labels and bars in a slightly different position.
- Harvard Graphics only imports the data stored in the chart which does not include the data in linked spreadsheets.

- Harvard Graphics may display complex combination charts differently than Excel.

When importing a Lotus or Excel graph, you have a choice between importing just the data or the data and the basic chart type. Importing the data alone allows you to bring a Lotus or Excel graph into a template or predefined chart format.

IMPORTING THE GRAPH DATA You must have a named graph in your Lotus worksheet to import the graph from 1-2-3. You do not name the chart in Excel. Figure 5-9 shows a basic graph named PIE that is defined in the 1-2-3 worksheet saved as ROYSTON. A graph stored in a Lotus .PIC file is not acceptable because Harvard Graphics must be able to access the actual data in the worksheet that is defined by the named graph on the 1-2-3 worksheet.

When you imported spreadsheet data you had a choice of adding the new data to the current chart data or replacing it. When you import a graph, the data defined by the graph always replaces any data in the current chart.

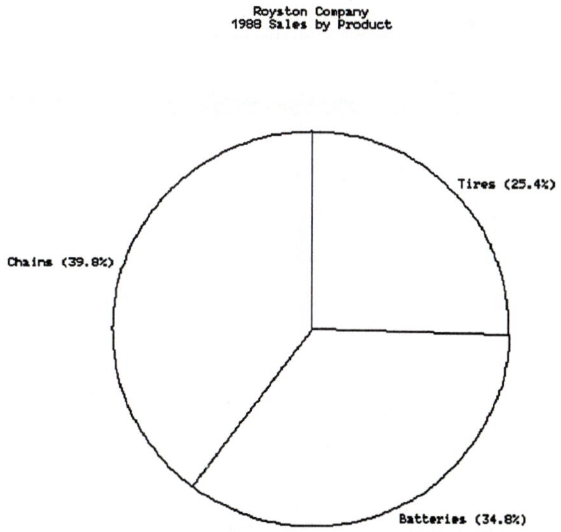

FIGURE 5-9. Pie chart displayed on the 1-2-3 screen

If you have a graph defined and named on a Lotus worksheet follow these steps to import it:

1. Select Create new chart and then select Pie.
2. Press ESC to return to the Main Menu.
3. Select Import/Export.
4. Select Import Lotus graph.

For an Excel chart, you would select Import Excel chart.

5. If this is the first worksheet you have imported in the current session, a list of all worksheet files in the current directory appears. You can highlight a file and press F10 (Continue) or change the directory to select from another drive or directory. If you have already imported from a worksheet file, the Import Lotus Graph screen shown in Figure 5-10 appears instead. Press F3 (Select files) if you need to activate the Select Worksheet form to use another worksheet. The same is true for importing Excel charts.

Figure 5-10 highlights a few interesting things that can be potential problems. In the first entry, the graph called BAR shows \c1 as a title and \c2 as a subtitle. This is because the backslash option was used to supply the data for

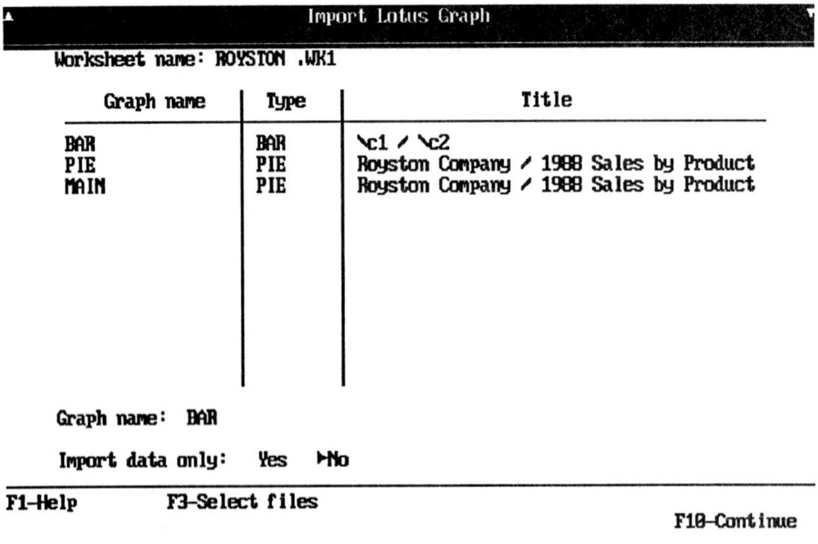

FIGURE 5-10. Selecting the graph to import

these two fields in 1-2-3. Instead of converting the cell references to the contents of these cells, the addresses display. Another problem is not using unique title and subtitle entries, as evidenced by the entries for the graphs PIE and MAIN.

6. Highlight a named graph and press TAB to move to the Import data only field. In this example PIE was selected.
7. Press the spacebar until this field is set to Yes and then press F10 (Continue).

The Lotus graph displays as the current graph, as shown in Figure 5-11. Since the Import data only field was set to Yes, the chart uses the settings of the current graph. If you had set this field to No, the graph would be the same type that was defined in the 1-2-3 file. When this field is set to No, the graph settings of the imported chart replace all the settings of the current chart.

IMPORTING THE GRAPH In addition to importing the graph data you can also import the graph type. The only difference between importing the graph and the graph data is that in the former case, the graph type in the Lotus file will determine the graph appearance. To import the entire graph, make sure that the field Import data only field is set to No.

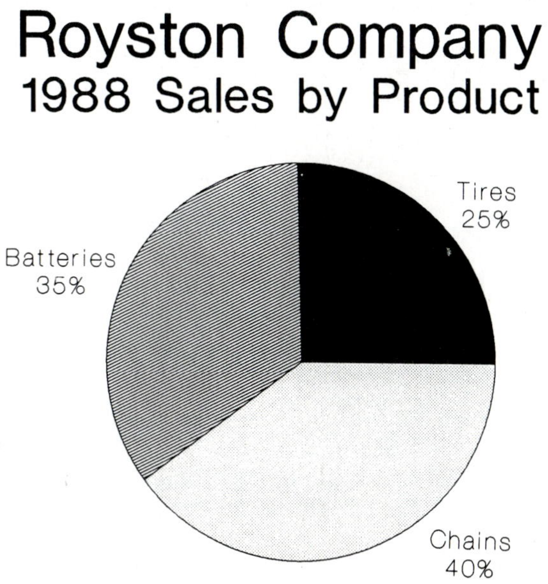

FIGURE 5-11. Graph imported from 1-2-3

IMPORTING ASCII DATA

ASCII data has even broader applicability than 1-2-3 data, since almost any word processing package can write out data in ASCII format. In addition, many other programs provide an option for printing reports and listings to disk rather than a printer. The copy of the report on disk is typically stored in ASCII format.

Just what is ASCII format and how special is it? ASCII files are nothing more than text files. The text in them is devoid of any special codes that may instruct your printer how to print certain text. In essence ASCII codes are the plain text, with everything else stripped away. The procedure for creating ASCII files varies from program to program; check the index of the manual for your software package under either "ASCII" or "text files."

When you bring ASCII data into Harvard Graphics you can choose to place the data in either analytical or text style charts. Regardless of the type of text chart chosen, Harvard Graphics always uses the free-form text chart style and overwrites any data that may have been in the current chart. The first line in the text file is used for the title, and the other lines are placed in the text area. No entries are recorded in the Subtitle and Footnote areas. You can even choose what parts of the file you want to import while you view data from the chart. The keys shown in Table 5-1 show you how the function and special keys affect your view of the data in the text file.

Since Harvard Graphics can import lines as long as 256 characters, it is possible that an entire line of text will not fit within a line of the text chart. In this case the line is wrapped to additional lines on the chart.

Choosing the Correct Settings for Importing Text

There are a number of selections that you need to make once you start the import process. First, you need to tell Harvard Graphics whether to import the text data by line or by column. This setting determines how Harvard Graphics divides the data it reads into series. You want to import the text by line when the first value in each line of the file is your X data value. This assumes that each line in the file contains the X data value, followed by the values for each of the series. If the first value at the top of each column contains your X data labels, you should import the data by column. This assumes that each line in the file contains the values for different series. For

Key Sequence	Purpose
CTRL-RIGHT ARROW	Scrolls 10 characters to the right
CTRL-LEFT ARROW	Scrolls 10 characters to the left
CTRL-UP ARROW	Scrolls up 1 line
CTRL-DOWN ARROW	Scrolls down 1 line
CTRL-HOME	Moves to the upper-left corner of the file
CTRL-END	Moves to the lower-right corner of the file
CTRL-PGUP	Moves to the first line in the current column
CTRL-PGDN	Moves to the last line in the current column
PGUP	Scrolls the screen 13 lines up
PGDN	Scrolls the screen 13 lines down
HOME	Moves to the beginning of the current line
END	Moves to the end of the current line

TABLE 5-1. Keys for Reviewing the Contents of Data To Be Imported

example, the first line contains the X data values, the second line contains the first series data values, and so on up to the eighth series. You can treat pie chart slice labels exactly like X data labels for making the determination of line versus column.

The fields Read from line and to line at the bottom of the screen allow you to enter the line numbers in the ASCII file where you want to begin importing. For example, if you are importing text created as a report from another program, you may want to skip the first six lines if they contain the report title and other introductory information.

If the data in your ASCII file is arranged in tabular columns, as in Figure 5-12, leave the setting for the Tabular data format field set to Yes. Otherwise, you can change this field to No.

The fields Read from column and to column allow you to specify where to begin and end within lines. If you want to start at character or column 5, you can type **5** for Read from column. For example, if your data file contains line numbers in the first four columns, you would start importing the text starting in column 5 to omit these line numbers.

```
                    Taylor University
               School of Business Enrollments

Degree            1987     1988     1989     1990
B.A.              1200     1150     1100     990
M.B.A.            500      600      650      700
Ph.D.             140      120      150      175
```

FIGURE 5-12. ASCII data

Once you finalize your entries on the Import ASCII Data screen, an Import Titles and Legends overlay prompts you to specify whether a title and legends should be imported if you have selected a graph type before importing the file. Selecting Yes in the Import title and subtitle field uses the first nonblank line as the title and the next two lines as the subtitle in the imported chart. In the second line in the overlay, setting the Import first line (or column) as series legends field to Yes uses the first line selected with the Read from line field as the legend text. Use this for the legend text when the selected line contains descriptive text of the records below it, such as Name, Amount, and Description. Select No when the first record contains data you want graphed in the chart rather than used as legend text.

Trying the Import Process for ASCII Data

All of this may seem a little complicated, but it will fall into place as you use it to import the data shown in Figure 5-12, which is in the file TAYLOR on the supplementary disk. These instructions assume that you have created this file before entering Harvard Graphics. Follow these steps to complete the import process for the ASCII file:

1. Select Create new chart from the Main Menu.
2. Select Bar/Line.
3. Press (F10) (Continue) to accept Name as the X-axis data type.
4. Press (ESC) to return to the Main Menu.
5. Select Import/Export from the Main Menu.
6. Select Import ASCII data.
7. Highlight the file you want to use or type the name of the file.

If you want to use a file in another directory you can use (UP ARROW) to move to the Directory field and type a new drive and/or directory.

8. After highlighting or typing the filename, press (ENTER).

An Import ASCII Data form will display with data from your file visible on the screen. Note the line numbers at the left and the column numbers at the bottom. The initial assumption is that you want to use the tabular data that starts in row 4 and all five columns.

9. Press the spacebar to read the data by column, as shown in Figure 5-13.

This method creates three series: B.A., M.B.A., and Ph.D.

10. Press (F10) (Continue).

The following Import Titles and Legends form is displayed:

```
Import Titles and Legends

Import title and subtitle:               ▸Yes  No
Import first column as series legends:   ▸Yes  No
```

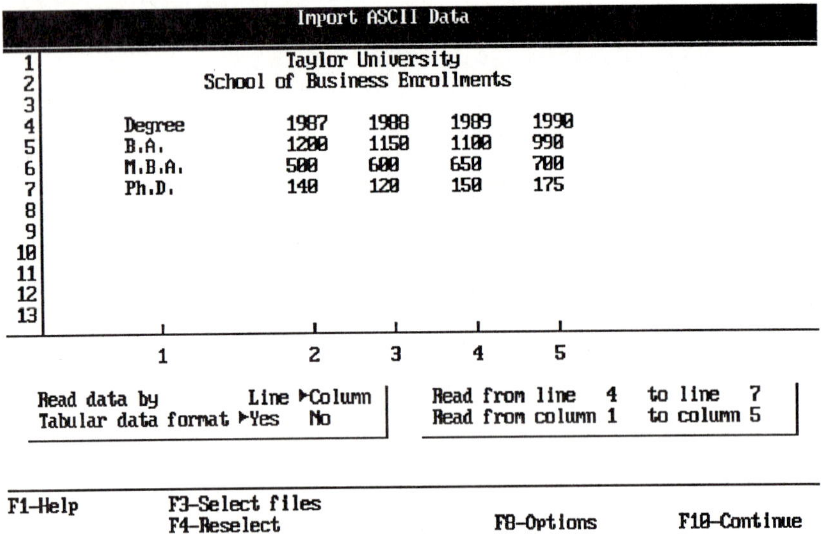

FIGURE 5-13. Import ASCII Data form

11. Check to ensure that both the Import title and subtitle field and the Import first column as series legends field are set to Yes.

If you need to make a change, you can tab between fields and use the spacebar to change the setting.

12. Press (F10) (Continue).

The Bar/Line Chart Data form shown in Figure 5-14 is displayed.

13. Press (F2) (Draw chart) to create a display like the one shown in Figure 5-15.
14. Press (ESC) twice to return to the Main Menu.
15. Press (CTRL-S) to save the file, type in **TAYLOR** and then press (F10) (Continue).

IMPORTING DELIMITED ASCII DATA

Database programs, accounting packages, and some spreadsheet products can create ASCII data in a *delimited ASCII format.* This means that the text

Bar/Line Chart Data

Title: Taylor University
Subtitle: School of Business Enrollments
Footnote:

Pt	X Axis Name	B.A.	M.B.A.	Ph.D.	Series 4
1	1987	1200	500	140	
2	1988	1150	600	120	
3	1989	1100	650	150	
4	1990	990	700	175	
5					
6					
7					
8					
9					
10					
11					
12					

F1-Help F3-Save F5-Set X type F9-More series
F2-Draw chart F4-Draw/Annot F6-Calculate F8-Options F10-Continue

FIGURE 5-14. Data imported from the ASCII file

used to separate text and numeric fields. Double quotes (" ") are normally used around label entries, and a comma is normally used as a field separator, although Harvard Graphics will allow you to specify other characters in place of the double quotes and the comma.

Figure 5-16 shows some delimited data that was written to a file by a database program. This file is called SELLERS.PRN, which is included on the supplementary disk. The file contains the name of each salesperson, the number of cars sold in 1989, and a field for each component of their address, including the ZIP code.

When you import this data into Harvard Graphics, the first field supplies X-axis data labels, the second supplies the values for Series 1, and the sixth field, the only other numeric field, places ZIP code entries in Series 5. You can use the @CLR function to eliminate these ZIP code entries.

Follow these steps from the Main Menu to import the delimited data:

1. Select Create new chart.
2. Select Bar/Line.
3. Press **F10** (Continue) to accept Name as the X-axis data type.
4. Press **F8** (Options) and then press **PGDN**.

in individual fields is encased in a special character, another character is used to separate text and numeric fields. Double quotes (" ") are normally used around label entries, and a comma is normally used as a field separator, although Harvard Graphics will allow you to specify other characters in place of the double quotes and the comma.

Figure 5-16 shows some delimited data that was written to a file by a database program. This file is called SELLERS.PRN, which is included on the supplementary disk. The file contains the name of each salesperson, the number of cars sold in 1989, and a field for each component of their address, including the ZIP code.

When you import this data into Harvard Graphics, the first field supplies X-axis data labels, the second supplies the values for Series 1, and the sixth field, the only other numeric field, places ZIP code entries in Series 5. You can use the @CLR function to eliminate these ZIP code entries.

Follow these steps from the Main Menu to import the delimited data:

1. Select Create new chart.
2. Select Bar/Line.
3. Press F10 (Continue) to accept Name as the X-axis data type.
4. Press F8 (Options) and then press PGDN.
5. Press TAB six times and then press the spacebar to change the graph to Horizontal.
6. Press ESC to return to the Main Menu.
7. Select Import/Export.
8. Select Import delimited ASCII.
9. Highlight the file containing the delimited ASCII data and press ENTER. If you need to change the directory, you can do that before highlighting the file using either the Directory field or the F3 (Change dir) key.
10. Harvard Graphics displays an ASCII Delimiters overlay form like the one shown here:

```
ASCII Delimiters

Quote character        : "
End of field delimiter : ,
End of record delimiter: #13#10
```

These are the standard characters used. You can change the quote character, the end of field delimiter, and the end of record delimiter. If you are not certain what your file contains, you can either take a look at it with a text editor or give these defaults a try by pressing F10 (Continue).

11. Press F10 (Continue) to use the delimiters.

Harvard Graphics displays an overlay that contains an Import first record as series legend field. Since the first record does not contain text that you want to use for the legend text, press the spacebar and then ENTER to select No. If the first record contained text like "Name","Cars Sold",

```
"Eliza Smith",500,"842 Euclid Avenue","Elyria","OH",44136
"John Von Steiner",300,"2507 E. 115 Street","Pompano","OH",44192
"Greg Bond",250,"4602 Lorain Avenue","Elyria","OH",44130
"Joan Ostrosky",670,"9114 Chester Avenue","Painesville","OH",44157
"Mary Hull",900,"2766 Ivanhoe","Gates Mills","OH",44196
"Karen Larson",716,"6002 W. 107th Street","Elyria","OH",44196
"Dave Doe",650,"9629 East Blvd","Cleveland","OH",44116
"Sue Winchester",400,"2918 Snow Road","Gates Mills","OH",44108
"Keith Campbell",817,"9727 Riverside Street","Shaker Heights","OH",44189
"Frank Grant",320,"3442 Cornell Road","Shaker Heights","OH",44198
"Heather Petrowski",652,"4772 Jefferson Avenue","Gates Mills","OH",44163
```

FIGURE 5-16. Delimited ASCII data

"Address","City","State","Zip Code" you would press ENTER to select Yes since this text describes the data in the subsequent records. You will see the X data names displayed and the values for Series 1. The three fields after the number of cars sold contained character data so Harvard Graphics did not import the addresses, cities, and states.

12. Press F2 (Draw chart) for a display like the one in Figure 5-17.

At first glance, you may be surprised to see Series 5 displayed. Series 5 is generated by the ZIP code entries.

13. Press any key to return to the Bar/Line Chart Data form.
14. Type **Tricia's Classic Automobiles** in the Title field and press ENTER.
15. Type **1989 Sales** in the Subtitle field and press ENTER.
16. Press F9 (More series) to display additional series.
17. Press TAB until the cursor is on the first entry for Series 5.
18. Press F6 (Calculate), and then press TAB to move to the Calculation field.

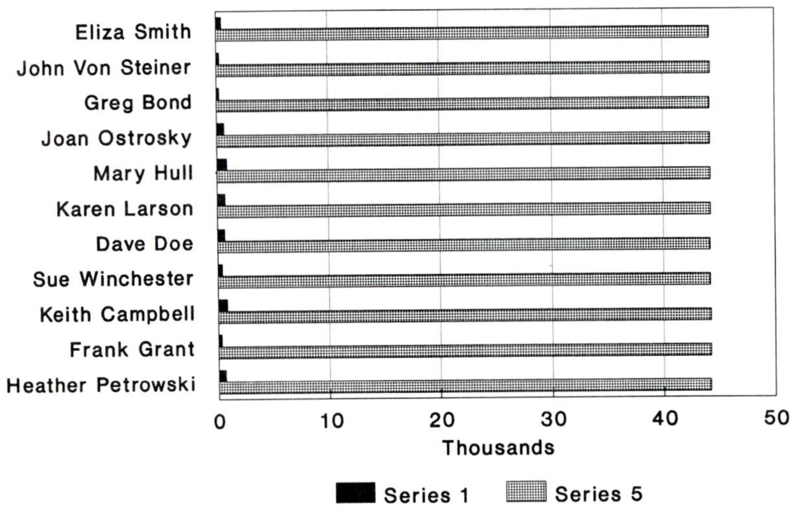

FIGURE 5-17. Chart showing sales and ZIP codes

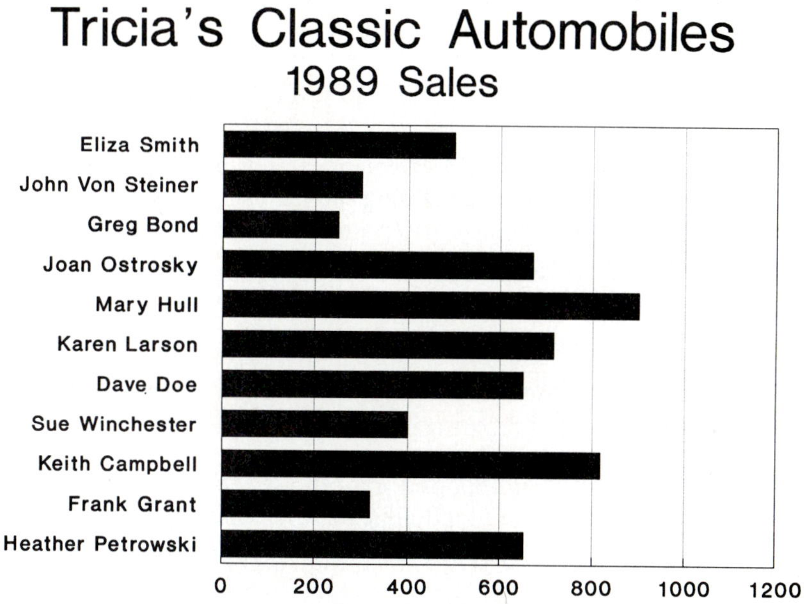

FIGURE 5-18. Chart with corrections showing sales data

19. Type **@CLR** to clear the data values for this series and press ENTER.
20. Press F8 (Options) and then press TAB until you move to the Series 1 entry in the Legend Titles field.
21. Press CTRL-DELETE to remove the legend.
22. Press F2 (Draw chart) to draw a chart that looks like Figure 5-18.
23. Press ESC twice to return to the Main Menu.
24. Press CTRL-S, type **TRICIA**, and press F10 (Continue) to save the chart.

IMPORTING FILES FROM A METAFILE FORMAT

CGM Metafile is a file format that is sometimes used to store graphic images. These graphs can be created with other graphics programs. Once you create these graphs in the other programs, you can import the graphs into Harvard Graphics.

To import a graph stored in a CGM Metafile, follow these steps:

1. Select Import/Export from the Main Menu.
2. Select Import CGM metafile.
3. Highlight the file containing the CGM Metafile and press ENTER.

The file has a .CGM extension. If you need to change the directory, you can do that before highlighting the file using either the Directory field or the F3 (Change dir) key. After a few minutes of processing, Harvard Graphics displays the imported chart.

4. Press any key to remove the chart and return to the Main Menu.
5. Press CTRL-S to save the file, type a file name and press F10 (Continue).

Once the file is imported you can use the other Harvard Graphics features to change how the graph appears. The chart may look different than in the package it was created in. The most common differences are

- The text uses a different font.
- Some text is truncated since Harvard Graphics only uses the first 60 characters of each text element (title, footnote, label on the X axis, and so on).
- The colors do not match the original since Harvard Graphics uses a different palette. You will learn in Chapter 8 how you can change the color palette Harvard Graphics uses to display your charts.
- Single color chart elements now have an outline of a different color. You can use the Draw/Annotate or Draw Partner features to change the colors Harvard Graphics uses to print the chart elements.
- Patterns may be different.
- Line styles and widths may be different.
- Polylines and polygons that have more than 200 sides or lines may not be complete.

Sometimes Harvard Graphics may not be able to import a metafile if the file is too large. If this occurs, Harvard Graphics displays a message. To import the image into Harvard Graphics, you must modify the image in the package that you created the chart in and simplify it, for example, by removing footnotes.

EXPORTING DATA

You can export a chart picture from Harvard Graphics to several other file formats. These other formats allow the chart to be printed with information from the program you are transferring the data to. Before exporting, you should display the graph on your screen to ensure that the image you are exporting is correct.

Follow these steps to create an export file in one of the available formats:

1. After defining and reviewing a chart, press ESC to return to the Main Menu and then select Import/Export.
2. Select Export picture.

The Export Picture form shown in Figure 5-19 is displayed.

3. If you need to change the directory where the file will be written, press UP ARROW, type a new drive and directory name, and then press ENTER.

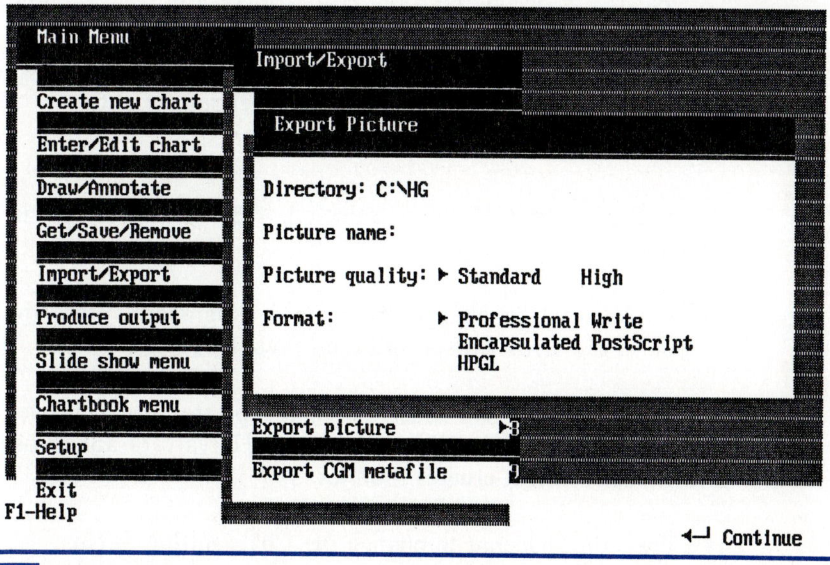

FIGURE 5-19. Specifying export options

4. Type a filename for storing the exported data. Remember you do not want to exceed eight characters in the filename and you should avoid spaces. For this example, PFSBAR was used as the filename. Press ENTER after typing whatever name you choose.
5. Press the spacebar to change the Picture quality field to High.

Standard quality charts save the text the chart uses. This allows you to edit the text in the program you will use later with the exported chart. On the other hand, the font the text will use in the other package is entirely determined by the other program. You will not be able to use the Harvard Graphics' fonts. Choosing the High quality setting of Picture quality to export your graph exports the text in the graph as polygons, which are filled in with lines. Instead of the file containing the text in the graph, it contains the shapes of the text in the chart. The resulting chart maintains the same font as the original text in Harvard Graphics, but you cannot change the text in the other program you will use with the exported graph. Since the high-quality charts must store the polygons for the text as well as the lines that fill them, these files are larger and take longer to print. You can reduce the size and printing time by using any font other than Executive and Square Serif. You will want to use the Standard picture quality if you want to use the fonts of the other graphics package or you will want to edit the text in the other graphics package.

6. To change the file format to Encapsulated Postscript or HPGL, which is an image of the chart for plotters that can be transferred to Ventura Publishing or other desktop publishing packages, press the spacebar until the arrow cursor points to the desired format.
7. Press F10 (Continue).

When Professional Write is selected, the overlay shown in Figure 5-20 appears.

8. If you want to change the printer assignment, press the spacebar to move the arrow cursor and then press ENTER.

The printer assignment must match the printer you will eventually use to print your Professional Write document. Harvard Graphics uses the printer information when it creates the files.

9. Press the spacebar to change the Color setting to No.
10. Press F10 (Continue) to write the file to disk.

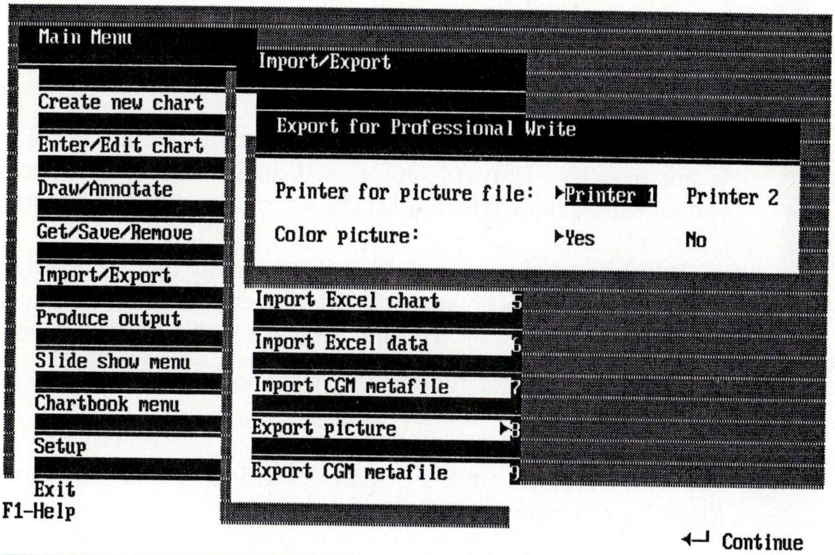

FIGURE 5-20. Configuring for exporting to Professional Write

To incorporate the chart into a Professional Write document, you must include within the file the name of the file you saved it under, encased in asterisks.

EXPORTING FILES TO A METAFILE FORMAT

The other choice you have for exporting charts is to export using the CGM metafile format. The metafile format creates better-looking charts in other programs than HPGL or EPS. HPGL cannot display Harvard Graphics' 3D effect and does not display overlapping objects correctly. Metafiles can be used by other programs, such as Freelance Plus, Manuscript, Ventura Publishing, and other desktop publishing programs.

To export a chart in a Metafile format, you must first install the Virtual Device Interface (VDI) as described in Appendix A. To export a chart to a CGM Metafile, follow these steps:

1. Make the chart you want to export the current chart.
2. Select Import/Export from the Main Menu.
3. Select Export Metafile.

Harvard Graphics displays the Export Metafile overlay on the screen. If VDI is not installed, Harvard Graphics displays a message indicating that you cannot export the chart to a Metafile format until VDI is installed.

4. If you do not want to save it to the directory that the overlay box displays, press SHIFT-TAB and edit the Directory field so it contains the directory where you want to store the chart in the Metafile format.
5. Type the name of the file you want to use to save the chart and press ENTER.

Harvard Graphics adds a .CGM extension. Other programs that accept Metafiles will expect a .CGM extension.

6. Select either Yes or No at the next option to determine whether the chart in the Metafile will use Harvard Graphics fonts.

If you select Yes, the chart uses the Harvard Graphics' fonts. Since the file will need to store the font information, the file will be larger than if you select No. If you select No, the chart will use fonts from the program you later use with the Metafile format.

7. Press F10 (Continue) to save the file.

Once the file is created, you can import the file into other programs. The chart may look different in the other program since each program may interpret data such as color and pattern information differently.

chapter 6

CREATING TEXT CHARTS

Although text charts lack some of the pizzazz of analytical charts, they are often the backbone of a presentation. They provide the key introductory points, serve to summarize some of the data presented in analytical charts, and display recommendations and conclusions at the end of a presentation.

Text charts can serve a useful purpose for both the speaker and the audience. For the audience they provide a reinforcement of the speaker's main points. Since learning can be increased by stimulating both the senses of hearing and sight, a greater retention of information is often noticed when verbal presentations are accompanied by visuals.

An experienced speaker will often find that notes are not necessary when key points are summarized in text graphs. There is no need for fumbling with notes or losing one's place in the pages since the speaker's words are guided by the contents of the text charts. The final product can be produced as a 35-millimeter slide or a transparency, so professional-quality output is possible.

Harvard Graphics supports a variety of text charts, so you should be able to select a chart type that meets your needs. You can also add needed variety to the presentation when you use different style text charts.

Text charts are easy to create, and in one sense, anything you want to enter on the chart is fine. There are some techniques that you will find helpful in preparing all types of text charts. Figure 6-1 shows a chart that is extremely busy and violates many of the points of good design. The chart in Figure 6-2 was made for the same presentation but was streamlined to show phrases rather than sentences. This chart also incorporates more white space and uses a combination of upper- and lowercase letters rather than all uppercase. As you look through the examples in this chapter, you will learn other techniques to help you create the best text charts possible.

GETTING STARTED

Now that you have mastered analytical charts, you will find that text charts are easy. There are no Titles & Options forms to be completed. You simply

FIGURE 6-1. Text chart with poor design

Meeting Agenda
February 1990

Compensation Package
Pay raises
New benefit package

Hiring needs
Assembly workers/clerical positions
$500 bonus opportunity for referrals

Employee discount program
Geauga Lake/Cedar Point
Restaurants

FIGURE 6-2. Improving the appearance of the text chart

enter your information on the chart and change basics, like size and placement of the information.

Follow these steps to create the first screen in a presentation:

1. Select Create new chart from the Main Menu.
2. Select Text.
3. Select Title chart.

Your screen will look like Figure 6-3 as Harvard Graphics presents an empty Title Chart form for your entries. This screen is actually divided into three different areas—top, middle, and bottom sections that each consist of three lines. You can make entries on any or all of the lines in each section.

4. Type **High Performance, Inc.** and then press ENTER three times.
5. Type **Achievement Awards** and then press ENTER three times.
6. Type **February 15, 1990.**

7. Press F2 (Draw chart) to view the entries shown in Figure 6-4.
8. Press any key to return to the Title Chart form.
9. Press F3 (Save) to save this chart.
10. Type **INTRODCT** and press ENTER.
11. Type **Introduction to Awards Banquet** and press ENTER.
12. Press ESC to return to the Main Menu.
13. Press CTRL-P to print the chart.
14. Check the settings to see if you need to make any changes, and then press F10 (Continue) to print.

If you have never printed a chart, the various print options are described in more detail in Chapter 2.

In 14 steps you have entered all the data for a three-line title chart, saved a copy of the chart to disk, and printed it. As you learn a few new options you will find that another step or two allows you to make dramatic changes

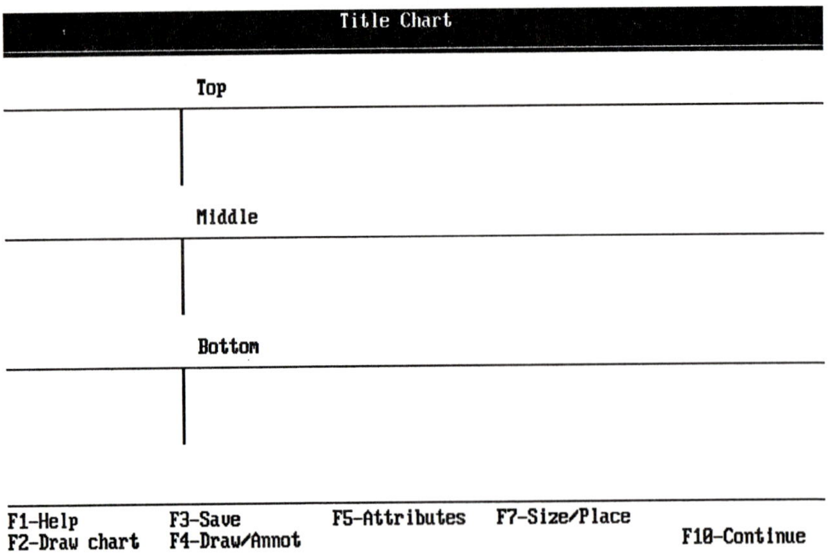

FIGURE 6-3. Title Chart form

FIGURE 6-4. Title chart

to the appearance of the chart. You will have an opportunity to explore title charts more fully and will also be introduced to the other text chart options offered by Harvard Graphics as you continue in this chapter.

CREATING MORE TITLE CHARTS

Title charts can be used for more than the beginning of a presentation. They can be used as dividers to segment your presentation when you have several major areas to cover. Each new area may start with another title chart. An entry placed in the top section of the Title Chart form will automatically be larger than the text placed in either of the other two sections of the chart, allowing you to use the top area to present the theme for the new section.

You can enter as many as 60 characters across a title chart if the size of the text is small enough. Table 6-1 shows you how many characters can fit across a chart in a variety of text sizes. You might not want to approach the upper limit, since your audience can absorb your ideas more quickly if you use short entries composed of short words. Often you will find phrases more

Character Size	Number of Characters Across
20	12
15	17
12	21
10	25
8	32
6	42
4	58
2	60

TABLE 6-1. Characters That Appear on an 8½-by-11-inch Page Printed in Landscape Mode

effective than sentences in a presentation. Although you have been taught to always use sentences to convey written and spoken ideas, if you attempt to use them on a chart you will be adding many unnecessary words. You also need not use all the lines on a chart. Blank lines improve readability and often make it easier for the reader to focus. Another chart can always be added to the presentation for the additional information.

Regardless of which section of the Title Chart form you use, the default is to center each line. If you want to deviate from this standard text alignment, you must look at the text size and placement options covered later in this chapter.

Changing the Size and Placement of Text Entries

Although the content of your message is important, its appearance is a vital factor in how you convey your message. The correct placement and sizes of text can highlight information for the reader and present a professional image. Also, the size of the characters affects both the number of characters and the number of lines that will fit on a chart. If you ever display a chart with either lines or characters truncated, you will want to alter the character size so you can see all of the text. With Harvard Graphics it is easy to change the size of the text and alter its placement on your output.

CHANGING TEXT SIZES Each type of text chart has its own defaults for the character size in different lines of the chart. Typically, titles and subtitles are larger than the detail lines, and footnote lines are the smallest of all the defaults. The default text size settings for a title chart are 8 for the top section of three lines, 6 for the three middle lines, and 4 for the bottom three lines. Reducing the size of any entries much below 4 makes it difficult for your audience to read these entries from a distance. You can increase the size of the first two sections or even choose to make the middle and bottom sections the same size. Use the F7 (Size/Place) option that worked with bar graphs to make the change. You will find that you can change each of the nine lines individually, and you are not required to make the same selection for each line in a section. Figure 6-5 shows the size and placement options that appear when you press F7 (Size/Place) for a title chart. You can move from option to option with TAB and change the current setting by typing a new size number.

CHANGING THE PLACEMENT OF LINES ON THE SCREEN Placement of text in the title chart is also important. You can control some of the

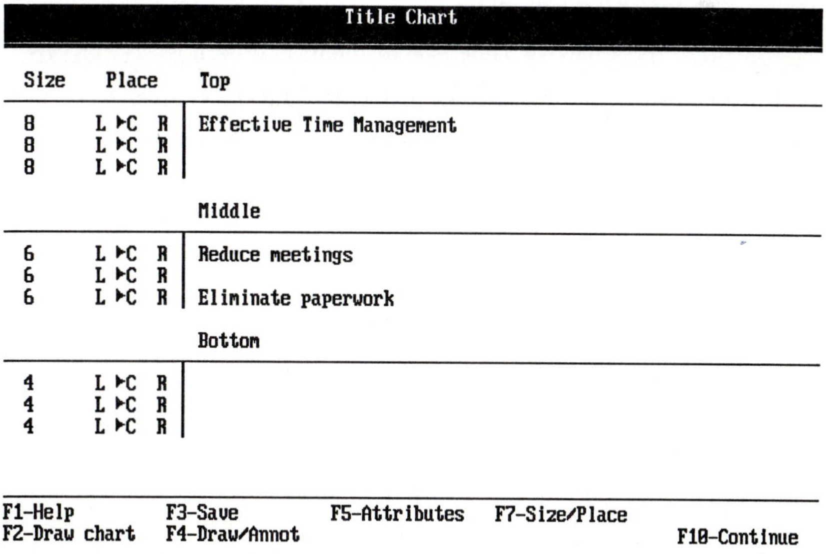

FIGURE 6-5. Size and Place options

spacing with blank lines. These lines are added by pressing ENTER without making an entry on the line. If you need two lines in the top section and two lines in the middle section you might consider placing your entries in lines 1, 2, 5, and 6. Another approach would be to use 1, 3, 5, and 6. Either of these alternatives is better than using lines 1, 2, 3, and 4, because they add important space between elements on a slide or transparency.

CHANGING TEXT PLACEMENT WITHIN A LINE Another option for changing the position of the text alters its placement within a line. The default for title charts is to center each entry, but you can use left or right alignment for any or all of the lines on a title chart. The change is effected on a line-by-line basis with F7 (Size/Place).

TRYING OUT SIZE AND PLACEMENT CHANGES Although you could alter the title chart you created in the first exercise, a few practice entries will help you master your new chart-building skill. You will create a title chart that will be used to introduce a new section of a management presentation.

Follow these steps to enter the data and make the changes to size and location:

1. Select Create new chart.
2. Select Text.
3. Select Title chart.
4. Type **Effective Time Management** and then press ENTER three times.
5. Type **Reduce meetings** and press ENTER twice.
6. Type **Eliminate paperwork** and press F2 (Draw chart).

Concise entries were used to create the new section opener for the presentation. The two entries in the middle section are used to show the two major areas that will be discussed. You will see in a later section that a simple list could have been used to convey this information as well.

7. Press ESC to return to the Title Chart form.
8. Press F7 (Size/Place).

Your screen will look like Figure 6-5.

9. Type **10** to change the size of the entry in the top line.

10. Press TAB until the cursor is in the Place field for the first line in the middle section.
11. Press the spacebar until the arrow cursor points to L for Left.
12. Press TAB four times to move to the Place field for the last line in the middle section.
13. Press the spacebar until the arrow cursor moves to L for Left.
14. Press F2 (Draw chart) to see the difference.
15. Press ESC and then press F7 (Size/Place).
16. Type 8 and press DELETE to return the size of the top line to the default setting.
17. Press TAB until the cursor is in the Place field for the first line in the middle section.
18. Press the spacebar until the arrow cursor points to C for Center to return Place to its default setting.
19. Press TAB four times to move to the Place field for the last line in the middle section.
20. Press the spacebar until the arrow cursor moves to C for Center, resetting Place to its default setting.
21. Press F2 (Draw chart).

Changing the Font in a Text Chart

Just as a change in your voice inflection conveys a different message to your audience, changing the font in your chart can present a different slant to the information your message contains. The default Executive font is clear and striking. At the other extreme is the Gothic font, which is much more elaborate. The Executive style might be an appropriate choice for presenting a marketing plan. On the other hand, Gothic might be a good choice if you are making a presentation on architecture or the Middle Ages. All the other fonts presented in Chapter 2 can also be used to change the style of your text as you wish.

Use the same process that worked for you in Chapter 2, when you wanted to change the font for bar chart titles and legends. Follow these steps to change the font for the current text chart using F8 (Options):

1. Press ESC twice to return to the Main Menu.
2. Press F8 (Options).

Although the display is not exactly the same as when you select Setup and Defaults from the menu, you can use the same technique to change the font.

3. Press TAB until the Font field is highlighted.
4. Press the spacebar until the arrow cursor moves to the Gothic font.
5. Press ESC to return to the Main Menu.
6. Press F2 (Draw chart) to display a chart that looks like Figure 6-6.
7. Press ESC to return to the Main Menu.
8. Press F8 (Options).
9. Press TAB twice to move to the Font field, and then press the spacebar until the arrow cursor points to Roman.
10. Press ESC to return to the Main Menu.

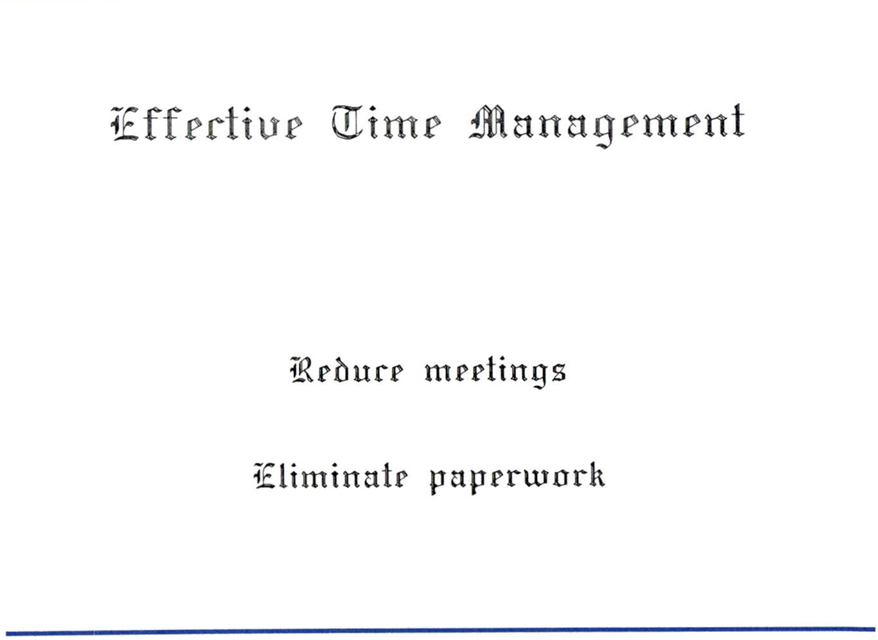

FIGURE 6-6. Using a Gothic font

11. Press F2 (Draw chart) to view the change. The chart will look like Figure 6-7.
12. Press ESC to return to the Main Menu.
13. Press F8 (Options).
14. Press TAB twice to move to the Font field, and then press the spacebar until the arrow cursor points to Executive.
15. Press ESC to return to the Main Menu.

Checking the Spelling of Your Entries

In Chapter 2 you learned to check bar charts for spelling errors in titles and legends. Since text charts have even more potential for spelling mistakes than analytical charts, you must be sure to check each one from the Main Menu before creating an output copy. Such checking can prevent costly mistakes in output.

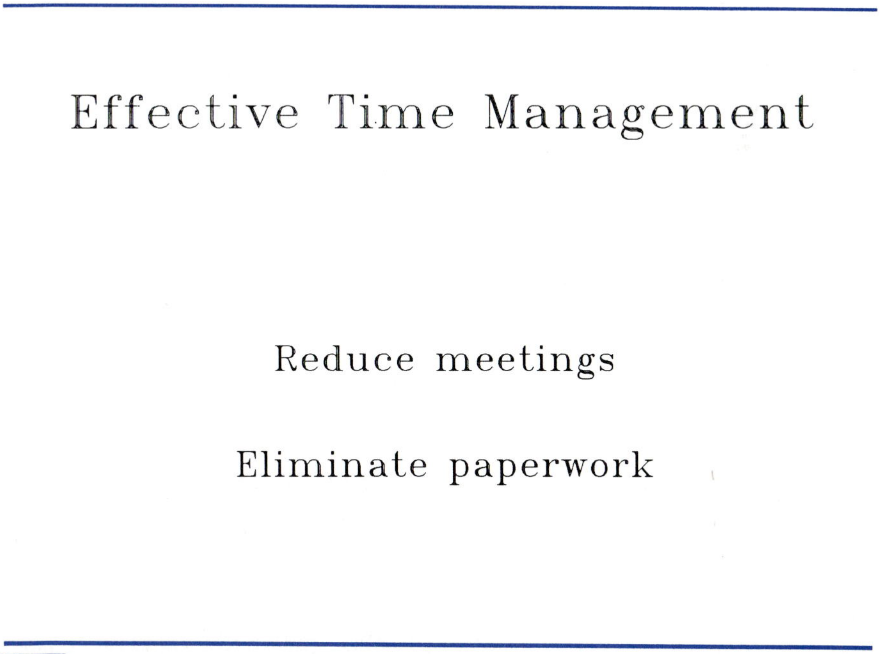

FIGURE 6-7. Using a Roman font

Follow these steps to introduce some errors in the current title chart and then make the necessary corrections:

1. Select Enter/Edit chart.
2. Move to the first "f" in "Effective" and press DELETE.
3. Move to the first "e" in "Management" and press DELETE.
4. Press ESC to return to the Main Menu.
5. Press F4 (Spell check).

Harvard Graphics highlights the first word in the chart that contains a potential misspelling.

6. Press DOWN ARROW until "Effective" is highlighted, and then press ENTER.
7. Press DOWN ARROW to move the arrow cursor to "Management" and press ENTER.

Since there are no more misspelled words, Harvard Graphics displays a message indicating that the Spelling checker procedure is complete.

8. Press ENTER to return to the Title Chart form.

Changing Other Text Attributes

You can change the attributes of the text in any graph, but such changes are even more significant in text charts, since all you have is the words on the chart to convey your message. You can use features like underlining and italics to draw emphasis to a particular entry. You can also vary the use of fill for characters to determine if you have the outline of characters or solid letters. Boldface is used to control the emphasis on words and phrases. If you are designing charts for a color output device, you can customize the color of any text on the screen.

The basic features for changing text attributes work the same whether you are working on an analytical chart or a text chart. Just as you did with bar and line charts, you can press F5 (Attributes) and then press TAB to move to the particular attribute you wish to change. Pressing the spacebar either adds or removes an arrow cursor from the current attribute. Attributes marked with an arrow cursor are on and those without the mark are off. Once the attribute settings are selected, use the arrow keys to select the text to be affected and press ENTER. Alternatively, you can invoke attributes with SHIFT-F5 rather than F5 by itself to mark an entire line of any chart for change without using the arrow keys to expand your selection.

ELIMINATING FILL AND BOLD All text is automatically marked with the attributes Fill and Bold. You can turn either attribute off if you want to eliminate it. Try this now with the current chart:

1. Press SHIFT-F5 (Attributes).

This tells Harvard Graphics that you want to use the selected attributes on the entire line of the chart. If you want to include multiple lines, press DOWN ARROW.

2. Press the spacebar to eliminate the Fill attribute.
3. Press TAB to move to the Bold attribute.
4. Press the spacebar to eliminate Bold.
5. Press ESC twice to return to the Main Menu.
6. Press CTRL-P to print your chart.
7. Check your current settings, make any required changes, and then press F10 (Continue). The top line in your printed chart will appear lighter than the other two lines since Bold is turned off.
8. Select Enter/Edit chart.
9. Press SHIFT-F5 (Attributes) and then press the spacebar to turn Bold back on.
10. Press SHIFT-TAB to move to the Fill attribute.
11. Press the spacebar to turn Fill back on.
12. Press ENTER.

USING ITALICS You can use Italics for emphasis in addition to Bold, or as a substitute for Bold. The same keys used for Fill and Bold are used to invoke the Italics attribute, depending on whether you want to use it for the entire line.

You can use italics for the two meeting topics if you follow these steps:

1. Move the cursor to the first line in the middle section of the Title Chart form.

Check to ensure that the cursor is on the first character in this line.

2. Press SHIFT-F5 (Attributes) then press DOWN ARROW twice.
3. Press TAB twice to move the highlight to Italics.
4. Press the spacebar to place an arrow cursor next to this entry.
5. Press F2 (Draw chart) to preview the chart.

The last two lines of the chart will appear in italics, as shown in Figure 6-8.

CREATING LIST CHARTS

List charts are an effective presentation method when you have a number of items. These items might represent features of a new product, parts of a meeting agenda, or an action plan for the rollout of a new product. You can

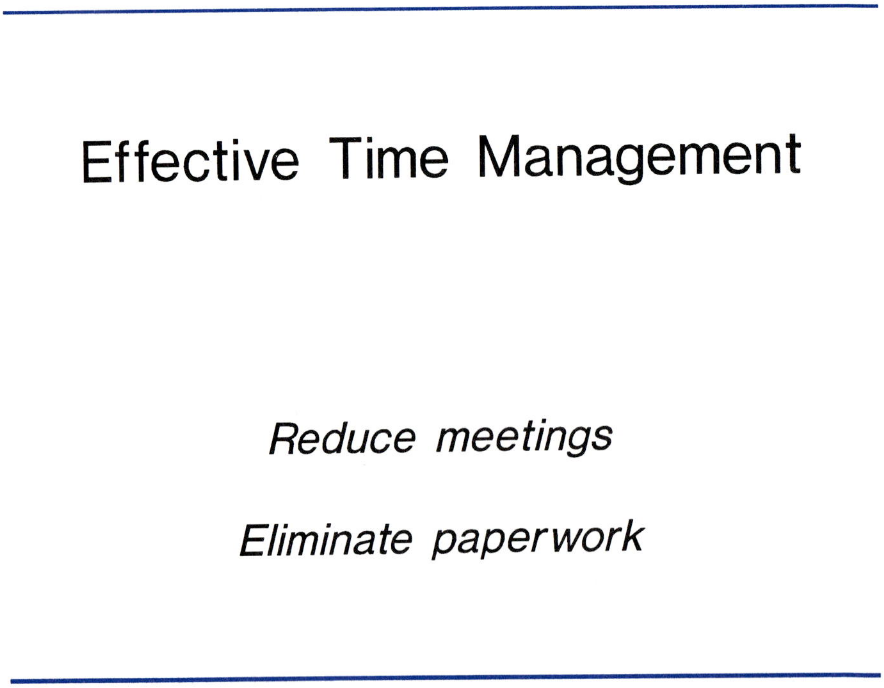

FIGURE 6-8. Detail entries in italics

use a list to present items in order from most to least important, or you can list all your entries in a random sequence.

List charts provide a way to convey many different ideas on one chart. A *simple list chart* consists of a maximum of 48 lines, with one item per line. A *bullet list chart* has a special symbol in front of each entry and a blank line between entries if Harvard Graphics adds the bullet markers. You can show only 24 bulleted lines on a bullet list chart.

As you enter either type of list, your aim should be to use a parallel structure for each of the list items. When you use parallel structure, the same parts of speech are used to start each phrase. If one phrase begins with a verb, every phrase should start with a verb. For example, you might need to list an item indicating a need to run an ad for new personnel in a local paper and another to schedule interviews with applicants. If you use the words "Place ad" for the first item, "Interviews with applicants" would be a poor choice for the second entry since the structures of the phrases are not parallel. It would be better to use "Interview applicants" for the second entry. Although the change may seem minor, a parallel structure helps to create a more professional image in your charts with little additional work.

Simple List Charts

A simple list chart allows you to display a title, a subtitle, and individual list elements. The elements in the list are shown one per line but are not numbered or marked in any special way.

You can create a list of the items you want to cover at your next staff meeting in just a few minutes. Try these entries as an example:

1. Press (ESC) twice to return to the Main Menu.

2. Select Create new chart.

3. Select Text and then select Simple list.

4. Press the spacebar and press (ENTER) twice to indicate that you do not want to save the data.

5. Type **Staff Meeting** in the Title field and press (ENTER).

6. Type **March 12, 1990** in the Subtitle field and press (ENTER) twice.

7. Type each of the following lines, pressing ENTER after each line:

   Discuss hiring needs
   Assign temporary construction parking
   Review current projects
   Request volunteers for charity breakfast
   Discuss company picnic

Notice the parallel construction used for each phrase, with a verb beginning each entry. Although Harvard Graphics does not require this consistency, it improves your presentation.

8. Press F2 (Draw chart).

Your chart looks like Figure 6-9.

9. Press ESC to return to the Simple List form.
10. Press F3 (Save) to save your chart.
11. Type **SIMPLELT** and press F10 (Continue).

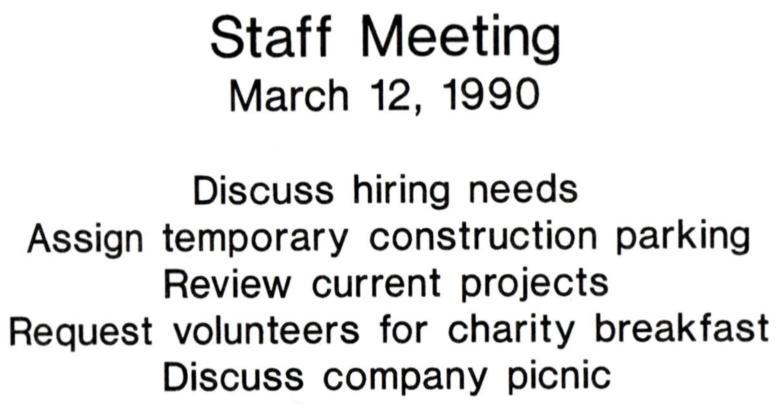

FIGURE 6-9. Simple list chart

CHANGING THE BORDER OPTION FOR A LIST CHART Harvard Graphics default settings produce charts that print exactly as they show on the screen, with no borders around the text. Two options, selected with either F8 (Options) or through Setup Defaults, allow you to add either a single- or a double-line border around the edges of your chart. If you choose either Single or Double for the Borders field, border lines appear when the graph is printed, but they do not display when you preview the chart.

Try this now with the staff meeting entries in the current chart:

1. Press ESC to return to the Main Menu.
2. Press F8 (Options).
3. Press TAB to move to the Border field and press the spacebar twice to change the setting to Double.
4. Press ESC to return to the Main Menu and press CTRL-P to print the chart.
5. Check your settings, and then press F10 (Continue) to produce a chart that looks like Figure 6-10.
6. Repeat steps 2 and 3 except change the Border field back to None.

Harvard Graphics 2.3 has a new option, No margin. This option removes any border on the chart. This option is used when you want to print the chart with the chart using the full area of the page without leaving space for margins.

USING SPECIAL SYMBOLS IN YOUR LIST CHARTS *Special symbols* are character representations beyond what you see on your keyboard. They may be foreign characters, monetary units other than dollars, Greek letters, or arrow heads.

The use of special symbols is not restricted to a list chart. You can use them anywhere you enter text, including bar chart axes titles and legends.

To add a special symbol to the chart you are creating, look up the ASCII code for the special character you want. Table 6-2 shows examples of the special symbols in the Executive font. You can test the availability of characters in other fonts by entering the ASCII codes when each font is active. You can then press the ALT key and, while holding it down, type on the numeric keypad the three-digit code representing the character you want. When you release the ALT key, the special character appears.

Follow these steps to create a chart listing international representatives for a company:

1. Press ESC to return to the Main Menu.

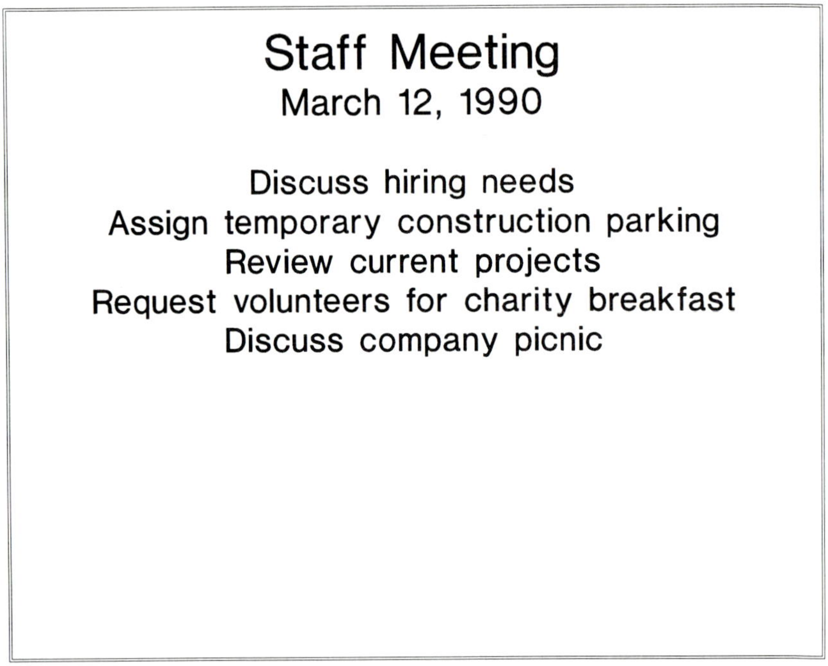

FIGURE 6-10. Double border added to a simple list chart

2. Select Create new chart and then select Text.
3. Select Bullet list and press the spacebar and ENTER to change Keep current data to No. Press ENTER to indicate that you do not want to save the data.
4. Type **International Representatives** and then press ENTER three times.
5. Type **Fran** but do *not* press ENTER. The next letter you need requires a special symbol ç (cedilla).
6. Press ALT and hold it down while you type **135** (ALT-**135**) from the numeric keypad.

It is necessary to use the numeric keypad; the numbers along the top row of your keyboard will not have the same effect.

7. Type **ois Monet - France** and press ENTER twice.

Symbol	Entry Code	Symbol	Entry Code	Symbol	Entry Code
§	Alt 21	Å	Alt 143	í	Alt 161
Ç	Alt 128	É	Alt 144	ó	Alt 162
ü	Alt 129	æ	Alt 145	ú	Alt 163
é	Alt 130	Æ	Alt 146	ñ	Alt 164
â	Alt 131	ô	Alt 147	Ñ	Alt 165
ä	Alt 132	ö	Alt 148	ª	Alt 166
à	Alt 133	ò	Alt 149	º	Alt 167
å	Alt 134	û	Alt 150	¿	Alt 168
ç	Alt 135	ù	Alt 151	¡	Alt 173
ê	Alt 136	ÿ	Alt 152	«	Alt 174
ë	Alt 137	Ö	Alt 153	»	Alt 175
è	Alt 138	Ü	Alt 154	ß	Alt 225
ï	Alt 139	ø	Alt 155	µ	Alt 230
î	Alt 140	£	Alt 156	§	Alt 245
ì	Alt 141	Ø	Alt 157	✓	Alt 251
Ä	Alt 142	á	Alt 160	■	Alt 254

TABLE 6-2. Special Symbols Printed in Executive Font and Their Entry Codes

8. Type **Margaret Müller - Germany**, using ALT-**129** to create the ü (u umlaut). Press ENTER twice.

9. Type **Klaus Weiß - Austria**, using ALT-**225** to create ß (the German sharp s). Press ENTER twice.

10. Type **Wilhelm Bö - Switzerland**, using ALT-**148** to create the ö (o umlaut). Press ENTER twice.

11. Type **José Núñez - Spain**, using ALT-**130** for the first é (which is an e acute), ALT-**163** for the ú (u acute), and ALT-**164** for the ñ (n with tilde).

12. Press F2 (Draw chart) to preview the chart, which now looks like Figure 6-11.

13. Press ESC twice to return to the Main Menu.

14. Select Get/Save/Remove and Save chart.

15. Type **INTERNAT** and press F10 (Continue) to save the chart.

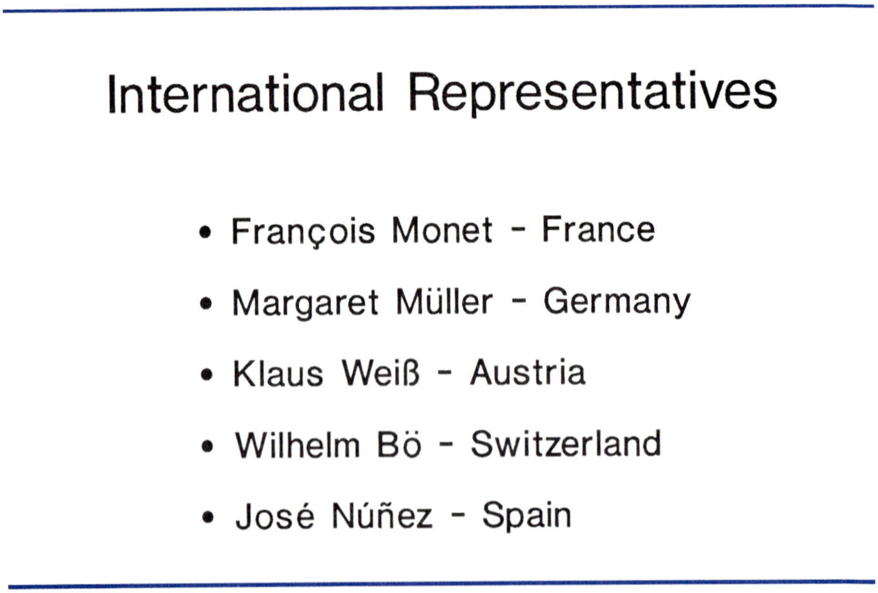

FIGURE 6-11. Chart with special characters

Bullet List Charts

A *bullet list* is similar to a simple list. In fact, the only real difference is that bullet markers are added at the front of each item in the list and the default justification places each entry at the left rather than the center of a line. The standard bullet marker is a large dot centered on the line, although you can change it to other symbols. To have Harvard Graphics add the bullet markers for you automatically you need to skip a line between each entry in the list by pressing ENTER twice.

You can create a bullet list with additional detail items under each bullet item. You can even choose to use bullet markers in front of these items, but usually you use CTRL-B to add them because they do not follow the standard default entry method for Harvard Graphics bullets.

CREATING A BULLET LIST CHART In the sample chart you will create in this section, the data is transferred from the existing simple list chart. Later you will learn more about the risks and advantages of transferring data between charts. For now, all you need to do is follow these steps to transfer the data to a new bullet list chart:

1. Select Get chart.
2. Type **SIMPLELT** and press ENTER to display the chart containing staff meeting notes displayed as a simple list.
3. Press ESC to display the Simple List form and then press ESC a second time to display the Main Menu.
4. Select Create new chart and then select Text.
5. Select Bullet list.
6. Press ENTER to accept Yes when prompted about keeping the current data.

The Bullet List form will appear with a bullet next to the first line. To display each line with a bullet at the front you would need to add a blank line between each of the entries.

7. Move your cursor to the "A" in "Assign" and press CTRL-INSERT.
8. Move your cursor to the "R" in "Review" and press CTRL-INSERT.
9. Move your cursor to the "R" in "Request" and press CTRL-INSERT.
10. Move your cursor to the "D" in "Discuss" and press CTRL-INSERT.

Each line in the old chart appears in the new bullet chart with a bullet at the front of each entry. If you preview the chart it will look like Figure 6-12.

CHANGING THE SHAPE OF BULLETS Although the centered dot, which is the default symbol for bullet entries, is the standard symbol used for bullets, you can change it for variety. This change can be helpful if you are using a two-level outline structure on a bullet chart. The second level might use a different symbol than the first level. Entries that represent a check list are also effectively presented when you change the bullet symbol to a checkmark.

You can change the symbol used for each bullet as you enter it if you use the CTRL-B option for entry. All you need to do in this situation is highlight a different symbol with the spacebar or RIGHT ARROW before pressing ENTER. Although it is easy to make the change, you should limit the symbols you use on any one chart to one or two, or the symbols will distract from the message presented in your text.

Use the CTRL-B option to add a second level of entries beneath each of the main points using this approach:

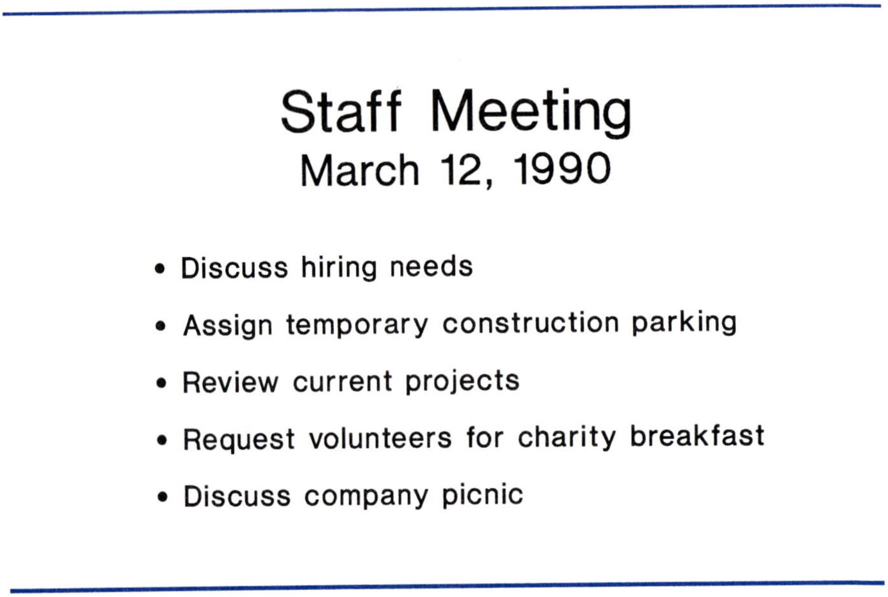

FIGURE 6-12. Bullet list

1. Move to the blank line under the first occurrence of "Discuss" at the top of the screen.
2. Press CTRL-INSERT, press the spacebar five times, and then press CTRL-B.
3. Press RIGHT ARROW to highlight the hyphen and then press ENTER.
4. Press the spacebar to add a blank space, then type **Programmers**, and press ENTER.
5. Press CTRL-INSERT and CTRL-B.
6. Press ENTER to accept the hyphen character, which is still highlighted from the last time you used it.
7. Press the spacebar, type **Clerical staff**, and then press ENTER.
8. Press ENTER twice to move to the blank line below "Assign."
9. Press CTRL-INSERT and then press the spacebar five times to indent.
10. Press CTRL-B and then press ENTER.

11. Repeat steps 4 through 6, entering all three items shown under "Assign temporary construction parking," as shown in Figure 6-13.

12. Press F7 (Size/Place) and then TAB six times to move to the size of the chart's text.

13. Type **4.0** and press F10 (Continue) so all of the text will fit in the chart.

14. Press F2 (Draw chart) to display the chart shown in Figure 6-13.

If you want to change the symbol used for the bullets that are added by Harvard Graphics every time you press ENTER twice, you must use a different approach. This change is made by pressing F7 (Size/Place). After the size and place features are added to the screen you will see the Bullet Shape field at the bottom of the new information. You need to press TAB to move to this field and use the spacebar to choose the desired setting.

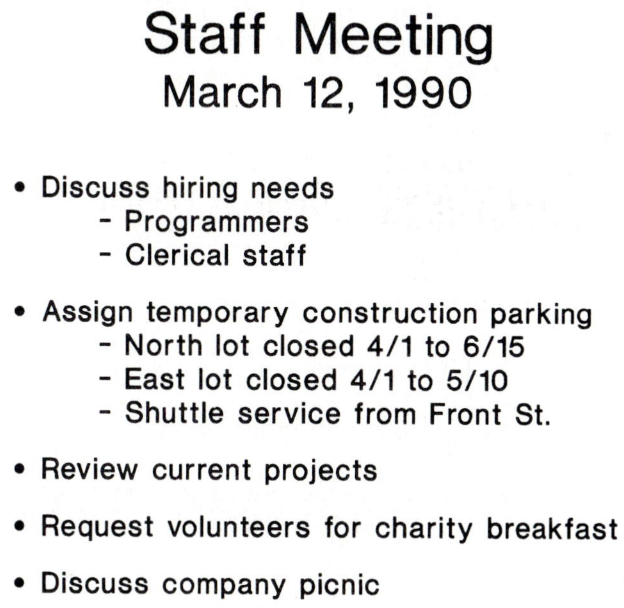

FIGURE 6-13. Bullet list with two bullet styles

CREATING A NUMBERED LIST Sometimes you want to emphasize the order of steps in the information presented. A numbered list can help reinforce the sequence of activities by putting a number to the left of each item in the list. Harvard Graphics adds these numbers for you and automatically assigns the next highest number to each new entry if you choose the # symbol in the Bullet Shape field.

Follow these steps to change the bullet style and enter a new chart:

1. Press ESC twice to return to the Main Menu.

2. Select Create new chart and then select Text.

3. Select Bullet list. Press ENTER to remove the warning that the chart has not been saved.

4. Type **Product Testing Phases** and press ENTER three times.

5. Press F7 (Size/Place).

6. Press SHIFT-TAB twice to move to the Bullet Shape field.

7. Press the spacebar or RIGHT ARROW to move the arrow cursor to the pound sign symbol (#) and then press ENTER twice.

8. Type **Laboratory trials** and press ENTER twice.

Don't panic when you still see #; numbers are not substituted until you preview or print the chart.

9. Type **Limited customer sites** and press ENTER twice.

10. Type **Full beta program** and press ENTER twice.

11. Type **Final testing with gamma release.**

Your screen will display the pound signs as shown in the example in Figure 6-14.

12. Press F2 (Draw chart) to change the display to match the entries in Figure 6-15.

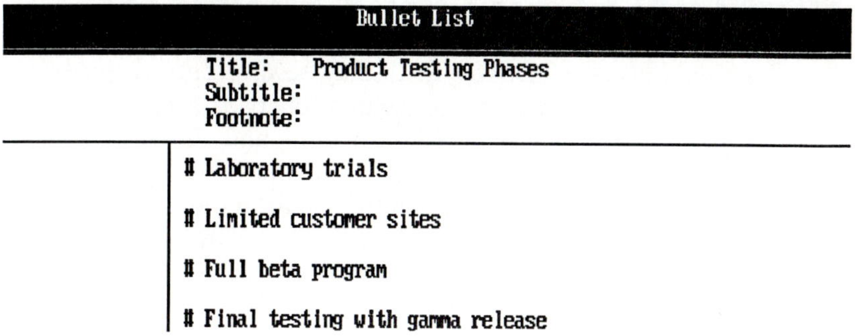

FIGURE 6-14. Screen display of numbered entries

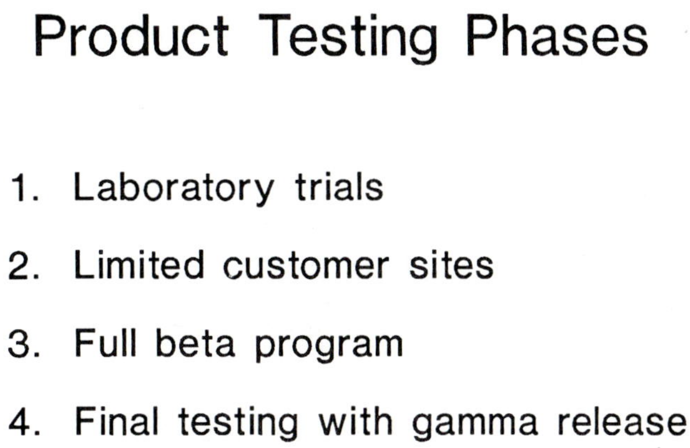

FIGURE 6-15. Preview of a numbered list

CREATING COLUMN CHARTS

Column charts allow you to display several entries under each main chart entry. You can think of the column chart as a table in which each column contains a different type of information, and all the data about an individual or a project appears across a row of the table. You can create tables that have either two or three columns of information. If you choose to do all the work yourself, you can use the free-form chart covered later to have more than three columns.

Creating a Two-Column Chart

A two-column chart can be an effective way to present the exact sales figures for the top five sales personnel. Likewise, it can showcase the result of your top three divisions. You can enter as many as 23 lines in a two-column chart, although you will want to limit your entries to fewer lines unless you plan to use a very small character size.

Follow these steps to create a chart showing new products in 1990 and their date of introduction:

1. Press ESC twice to return to the Main Menu.
2. Select Create new chart, Text, and Two columns.
3. Select No if you are prompted about transferring data and press ENTER to acknowledge that you do not want to save changes.
4. Type **Innovative Marketing** and press ENTER.
5. Type **New Products in 1990** and press ENTER twice.
6. Type **Product** and press ENTER.
7. Continue to enter these product names in the first column, pressing ENTER after each:

   Quick-Rol
   Sof-Tex
   Heat-Away
   Seal R More
   Sports Score
   Time Save

8. Press UP ARROW until the cursor is on Product and then press TAB.
9. Complete these entries, pressing ENTER after each:

   Introduced
   February 15
   March 10
   June 22
   August 1
   November 3
   December 22

10. Press SHIFT-TAB, and then press UP ARROW a sufficient number of times to move to Quick-Rol.
11. Press SHIFT-F5 (Attributes).

Notice that Harvard Graphics considers the line to extend only within the current column and highlights the entire entry in the first line of column 1.

12. Press DOWN ARROW until Time Save is highlighted.
13. Press TAB to move to Bold, and then press the spacebar to remove the arrow cursor. Press ENTER.
14. Press TAB to move to February 15.
15. Repeat steps 11 through 13 to remove Bold from the detail entries in column 2.
16. Press F2 (Draw chart).

Your preview screen will look like Figure 6-16. You can use F7 (Size/Place) to change the space between columns. The default value is M, but you may also select S, L, or X, where S is small, L is large, and X is extra large.

Creating a Three-Column Chart

A three-column chart provides the same type of format as a two-column chart except there is an additional column. Also, you are limited to 14 lines in a three-column chart. Rather than enter all new data, you can take the

Innovative Marketing
New Products in 1990

Product	Introduced
Quick-Rol	February 15
Sof-Tex	March 10
Heat-Away	June 22
Seal R More	August 1
Sports Score	November 3
Time Save	December 22

FIGURE 6-16. Two-column chart

entries in your two-column chart and convert them into a three column chart. Your final product will only require entries in column three. Follow these steps:

1. Press ESC twice to return to the Main Menu.
2. Select Create new chart and then select Text.
3. Select Three columns.
4. Select Yes to use the data from the current chart.
5. Press TAB five times to move to the top of column three.
6. Type **Developer** and press ENTER.

7. Complete the entries in column three as follows:

   High Tech
   Textiles Unlimited
   Kool King
   Work Savers
   Broadcasters
   Efficiency Experts

8. Press F2 (Draw chart)

Notice that boldface has reappeared for the detail entries. If you want to remove the boldface you would need to repeat steps 11 through 13 for each column to remove boldface from the entries after completing these steps. Your chart would look like Figure 6-17 if you printed it.

Innovative Marketing
New Products in 1990

Product	Introduced	Developer
Quick-Rol	February 15	High Tech
Sof-Tex	March 10	Textiles Unlimited
Heat-Away	June 22	Kool King
Seal R More	August 1	Work Savers
Sports Score	November 3	Broadcasters
Time Save	December 22	Efficiency Experts

FIGURE 6-17. Three-column chart

CREATING FREE-FORM CHARTS

Free-Form charts allow you to create a chart with no restrictions other than a limit of 48 lines. This means you can create several columns with widths that vary to suit your needs. This allows you to group entries differently than the predefined options do. You enter text just as you want to see it.

The instructions that follow are somewhat tedious because you want to line up the columns to align the decimals in the numbers. The text that you enter at the beginning of each line is automatically left aligned. Follow these steps to create a simple four-column free-form chart:

1. Press ESC twice to return to the Main Menu.
2. Select Create new chart and then select Text.
3. Select Free form.
4. Press the spacebar to highlight No when you are prompted about using the data from the previous chart. Press ENTER twice.
5. Type **Major Customers** and press ENTER two times.
6. Type **Based on 1990 Sales** and press ENTER.
7. Type **Company.**
8. Press the spacebar 12 times and then type **Unit Volume.**
9. Press the spacebar 5 times, type **#Emp.**, and press the spacebar 7 more times.
10. Type **First year** and press ENTER twice.
11. Type **Green & Sons** and then press the spacebar 7 times.
12. Type **25,000,** press the spacebar 10 times, and then type **10.**
13. Press the spacebar 11 times and then type **1986.**
14. Press ENTER and then type **Jacobs Brothers.**
15. Press the spacebar 4 times and then type **22,000.**
16. Press the spacebar 10 times and then type **15.**
17. Press the spacebar 11 times and then type **1989.**
18. Press ENTER and then type **Smith Kline.**
19. Press the spacebar 8 times and then type **15,999.**
20. Press the spacebar 10 times and then type **15.**

21. Press the spacebar 11 times and then type **1988.**
22. Press F2 (Draw chart) to preview the chart, as shown in Figure 6-18.

While these instructions create a well-structured chart, you can also use this chart type to position text anywhere on the screen.

CHANGING THE STYLE OF AN EXISTING CHART

You have already changed a simple list chart into a bullet list chart. You have also transformed a two-column chart into a three-column chart. These

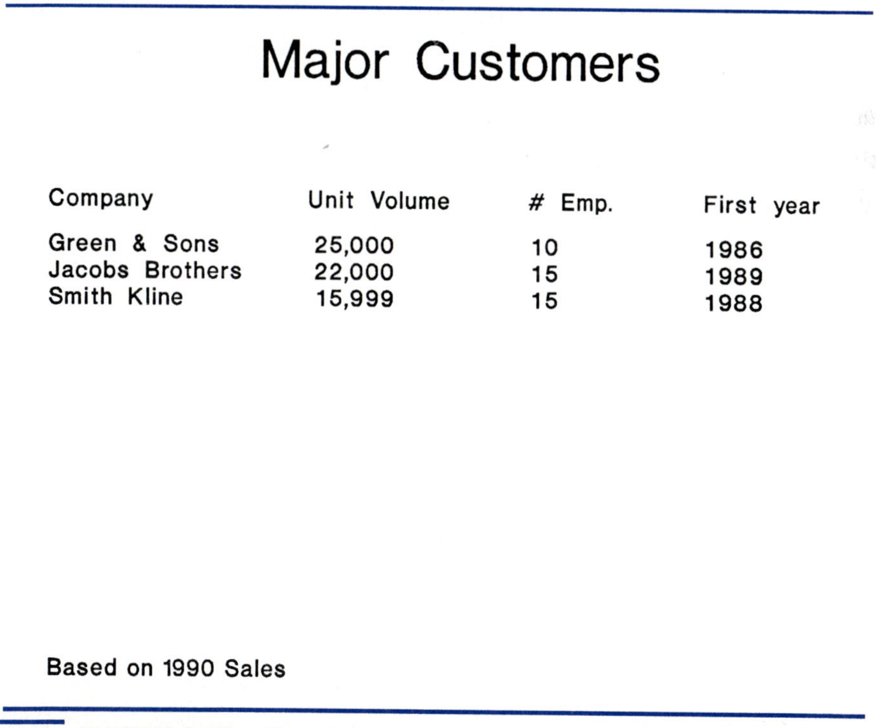

FIGURE 6-18. Free-form chart

capabilities are useful if you enter data and decide you do not like the chart style. You can make a style change without reentering all the data. Although the ability to change chart styles can save reentry when changing between some chart types, it cannot always solve your problem. If you enter data in a three-column chart that was intended for two columns, you can transfer the data in the first two columns to the two-column chart, but the data in the third column will be lost. Also, when changing from either a two- or a three-column chart to a title or list chart, the orientation of the entries is changed. Entries placed across each of the columns in a three-column chart will be placed down a column in the title or list chart.

One practical application for changing the chart type was the creation of your two-column chart and its transformation as you needed another column of information. The transition to a three-column chart proceeded smoothly since there was space for each of the new entries. Changing from a simple list to a bullet chart is another easy change to make if you decide that you want bullets in front of your entries. Remember, if you make a change like transforming a three-column chart into a two-column chart, you will lose the data in the third column.

To change the chart type you need to select Create new chart from the Main Menu. After selecting Text and then the type of chart that you want, you can select Yes when prompted about saving the data. Harvard Graphics will transfer the data to the new chart.

chapter 7

CREATING ORGANIZATION CHARTS

Organization charts are used to show the hierarchical structure representing a company, division, region, or department. Typically, organization charts are composed of a series of boxes in a pyramid shape, with the names and positions of managers in the organizational unit written in each box. Typing an organization chart has always been a nightmare for a typist trying to size the boxes properly in order to fit all of the names inside the boxes and still place them symmetrically on the page. Harvard Graphics eliminates this problem because it automatically sizes all the boxes on a chart for you, making sure that all the boxes at the same level are the same size. Boxes at a lower level are also never made larger than boxes at a higher level. Not only are these boxes quick to create initially, but they also are a breeze to revise; making modifications, deletions, and additions requires only a few seconds.

Harvard Graphics allows you to enter names, titles, comments, and abbreviations as you create your charts. You can use as many as eight levels of entries, and you can control the appearance of the charts in a number of ways.

If you are creative you may find that the organization chart format can be used for other things. Figure 7-1 shows an organization chart for an accounting system that is composed of a series of program modules. The module name, description, and programmer's name are all entered in fields normally used to prepare an organization chart. After working only a few minutes, you have a graphical representation of the relationships between the programming modules and can tell at a glance who to contact if you experience a failure in any program module.

GETTING STARTED

Creating an organization chart (or *org chart,* as they are frequently called) is easy with Harvard Graphics. You can focus on your organization structure

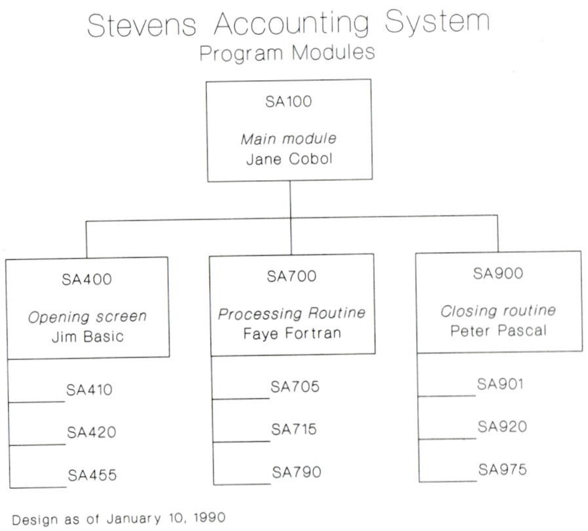

FIGURE 7-1. Using an organization chart for program modules

without any concern for where the entries should be placed. The chart that you will create in this exercise has only two levels of entries, but later in the chapter you will learn how to revise it to increase the complexity of the organizational structure. Follow these steps to create the chart:

1. Select Create new chart from the Main Menu.
2. Select Organization.

The Organization Chart form shown in Figure 7-2 appears on your screen. The form includes fields for special entries, like names and titles of managers to be included in the organization chart, but also allows for the entry of standard Title, Subtitle, and Footnote fields.

3. Type **Mesopotamia Metals** in the Title field and press ENTER.
4. Type **Organization Chart** in the Subtitle field and press ENTER.
5. Type **June 15, 1990** in the Footnote field and press ENTER.

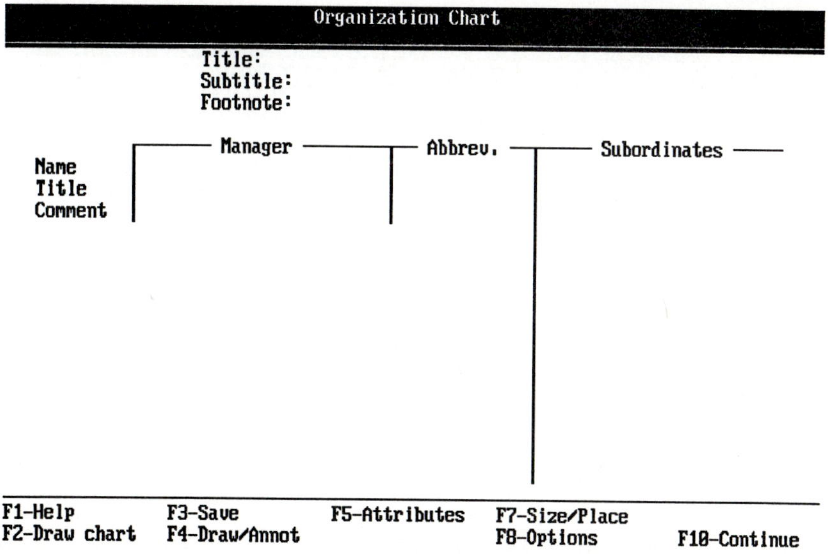

FIGURE 7-2. Blank Organization Chart form

The cursor moves to the Name field in the Manager column. This entry will be the highest level in the chart.

6. Type **Jane Steel** in the Name field and press ENTER.
7. Type **President** in the Title field and press TAB to move to the Abbrev. column, where abbreviations can be entered for Name, Title, and Comments fields. These entries cannot exceed 11 characters.
8. Press UP ARROW to move to the field for the Name abbreviation.
9. Type **Steel** to supply the last name as the name abbreviation and press ENTER.
10. Type **Pres.** to supply an abbreviation for the Title, and then press TAB to move to the first field in the Subordinates column.
11. Type the following names, pressing ENTER after each:

    Tom Iron
    Hilda Copper
    Jim Brass

Your Organization Chart form should match Figure 7-3. Each of these entries represents the subordinates of Jane Steel. For now these two levels

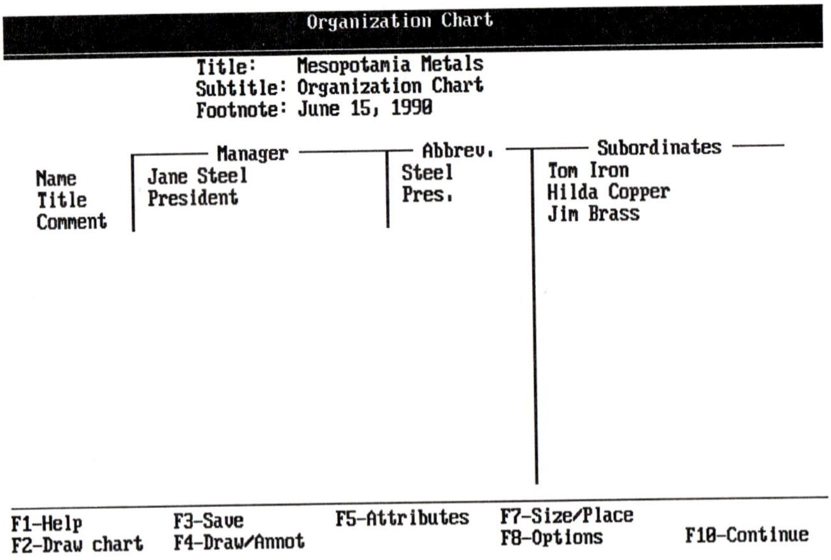

FIGURE 7-3. Completing entries for the first two levels

are sufficient. Later you will learn how to add descriptive information for these entries and how to add additional levels of subordinates.

12. Press (F2) (Draw chart).

Notice that a box is drawn for the top level that includes the name on two lines with the title on the third line. Since the second level is also the last level, the names are not shown horizontally. By default, the last level of an organization chart is displayed vertically.

13. Press (ESC) twice to return to the Main Menu.
14. Press (F8) (Options).

The first option in this overlay determines the orientation that Harvard Graphics uses for print output. The default of Landscape prints the graph as shown in previous examples. The alternative, Portrait, rotates the output 90 degrees.

15. Press the spacebar and (ESC) to select Portrait orientation and return to the Main Menu.
16. Press (CTRL-P) to print your chart.
17. Check the settings and change any that are incorrect by pressing (TAB) to highlight the field you want to change and using the spacebar to select a new option for the field.
18. Press (F10) (Continue) to print a chart that looks like Figure 7-4. Notice how the output is rotated.
19. Press (F8) (Options).
20. Press the spacebar and (ESC) to return the orientation to Landscape and return to the Main Menu.
21. Press (CTRL-S) to save the chart.
22. Type **ORG1** as the chart name.
23. Press (F10) (Continue) to write the file to disk.

The Landscape orientation works better with Organization charts since the charts frequently need the horizontal space to list everyone at a particular level.

24. Select Enter/Edit chart.

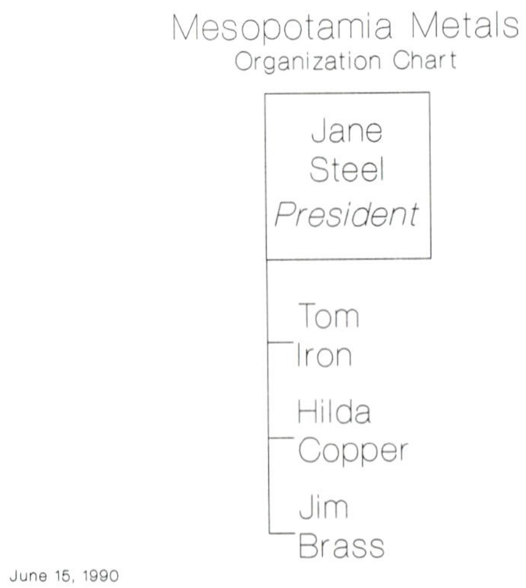

FIGURE 7-4. Displaying the first two levels with default settings

In just a few minutes you have mastered the basics of organization charts. Now you can continue to build on your skills with organization charts by adding more levels and changing the appearance of your entries.

MAKING ADDITIONS TO THE BASIC ORGANIZATION CHART

Although you have mastered the basic procedure, you will need to make a few additions to the basic chart. In most companies there are more than two levels in the organization hierarchy, and you need to learn how to add these extra levels. Also, since Harvard Graphics allows you to add one staff position to a chart, you can try this feature by adding a staff position reporting directly to the president.

Adding More Levels

Since you can have as many as eight levels in a Harvard Graphics organization chart, you are nowhere near the limit. You can add subordinates beneath any of the individuals that report to Jane Steel. You will complete an Organization Chart form for each individual with subordinates. To bring this form to your screen you need to highlight the name of the subordinate for whom you want to add a new level of subordinate and press CTRL-PGDN.

Follow these steps to add subordinates to the individuals who report to Jane Steel:

1. Move the cursor to Tom Iron with the TAB key.
2. Press CTRL-PGDN and a new Organization Chart form appears with Tom's name in the Manager field.

Your cursor will be in the top line of the Subordinates column.

3. Press SHIFT-TAB to move to the Abbrev. field and type **Iron.**
4. Press SHIFT-TAB to move to the Name field, and press DOWN ARROW to move to the Title field.
5. Type **Foundry Manager** and press TAB to move to the Abbrev. column.
6. Type **Foundry** and press TAB to move to the Subordinates column.
7. Type the following names, pressing ENTER after each name:

   Paula Tin
   George Silver
   Mary Gold

8. Press CTRL-PGUP to return to the first level that shows Jane Steel in the Manager field.
9. Move the cursor to Hilda Copper and then press CTRL-PGDN to add subordinates.
10. Press SHIFT-TAB and type **Copper.**
11. Press SHIFT-TAB followed by DOWN ARROW.
12. Type **Office Manager** and press TAB.
13. Type **Off. Mgr.** and press TAB.
14. Type the following subordinate names, pressing ENTER after each:

Steve Chrome
Larry Lead

15. Press CTRL-PGUP to move to the first level with Jane Steel in the Manager field.

16. Move your cursor to Jim Brass and press CTRL-PGDN.

A shortcut approach that eliminates a step is pressing PGDN to move directly from the Copper entry to the one for Brass.

17. Press SHIFT-TAB to move to the Abbrev. field and type **Brass.**

18. Press SHIFT-TAB followed by DOWN ARROW, then type **Purchasing Manager.**

19. Press TAB and type **Purchasing.**

20. Press TAB and type the following names in the Subordinates column, pressing ENTER after each.

    Martha Molybdenum
    Nancy Nickel
    Zelda Zinc

21. Press F2 (Draw chart).

Notice that the chart no longer shows Tom Iron, Hilda Copper, and Jim Brass vertically. Vertical display is reserved for the lowest level.

22. Press ESC until the Main Menu appears.

23. Press CTRL-P to print your chart.

24. Make any changes to settings that you want and press F10 (Continue) to produce output like Figure 7-5.

25. Press CTRL-S to save your chart.

26. Type **ORG2**, and press F10 (Continue).

If you want you can enter a different description before pressing F10 (Continue).

If you decide to create additional levels, you would use the same procedure, adding a form any place you need a new level. CTRL-PGDN will always open a subordinate level beneath the current chart when one does

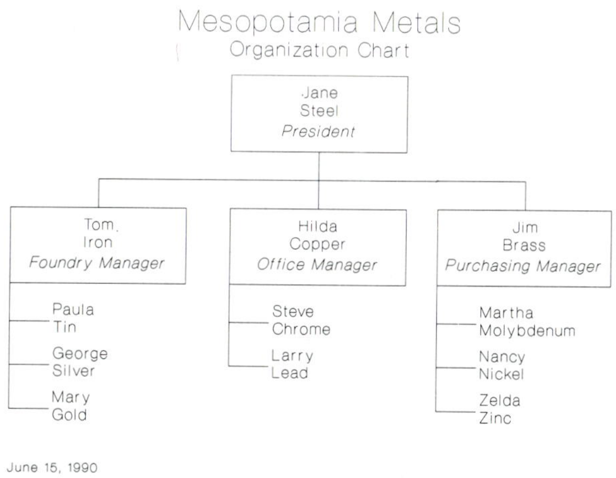

FIGURE 7-5. Adding a third level

not exist. With CTRL-PGDN you can also access the Organization Chart forms for the last level of entries, even if there are no subordinates. You can use the forms for the last level to add a title, comments, and abbreviated entries.

Adding a Staff Position

You can add a staff position to the organization chart by entering **Staff** in the Title field. Harvard Graphics also offers display options that allow you to use a unique pattern of entries to make it easy to detect differences between staff and line positions with subordinates reporting. These options are discussed later in this chapter.

Another special feature of Harvard Graphics allows you to add one staff position to any chart, using a special half-box format for this staff entry. The process is easy: just type an asterisk before typing the name. Add a staff position reporting directly to the president with these entries:

1. Select Enter/Edit Chart.
2. Press CTRL-PGUP and move to below Jim Brass in the Subordinates column for Jane Steel.
3. Type ***Lucy Lithium** and press ENTER.

The Organization Chart form looks like this:

```
                          Organization Chart

              Title:    Mesopotamia Metals
              Subtitle: Organization Chart
              Footnote: June 15, 1990

         ┌──── Manager ──────┬─ Abbrev. ─┬──── Subordinates ───
Name     │ Jane Steel        │ Steel     │ Tom Iron
Title    │ President         │ Pres.     │ Hilda Copper
Comment  │                   │           │ Jim Brass
                                         │ *Lucy Lithium
```

4. Press F2 (Draw chart). Your chart looks like Figure 7-6.

Notice that Lucy Lithium's name is placed in an open-topped box.

5. Press any key to return to the Organization Chart form and then press F3 (Save) to save your changes.
6. Press F10 (Continue) to save the chart using the same file information.

ALTERING THE APPEARANCE OF THE ORGANIZATION CHART

There are numerous options for changing the chart appearance. You can change the style of the text used for entries, the presentation of information in the last level, the placement of names and other information in boxes, and the layout of text on the page.

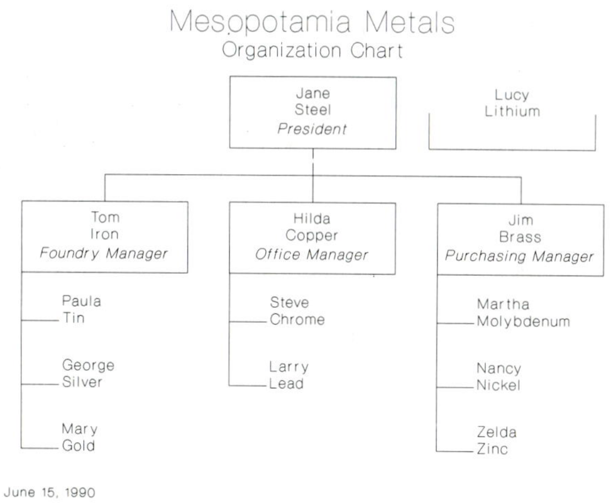

FIGURE 7-6. Printed copy of the chart showing the staff position

Adding Shadow Effect to the Boxes

You can add depth to the organization chart display if you choose to add a shadow effect to the boxes on the chart. Like many other changes, you can effect this change by pressing F8 (Options) with any of the Organization Chart forms on the screen. The Org Chart Options form shown in Figure 7-7 appears.

Follow these steps to add the shadow effect to the current chart:

1. Move to Lucy Lithium in the Subordinates column for Jane Steel and press CTRL-PGDN.

2. Press SHIFT-TAB twice and the DOWN ARROW once. Type **Administrative Assist.** for Lucy's title.

3. Press F8 (Options) to display Figure 7-7.

4. Press TAB five times to move to the Shadow field.

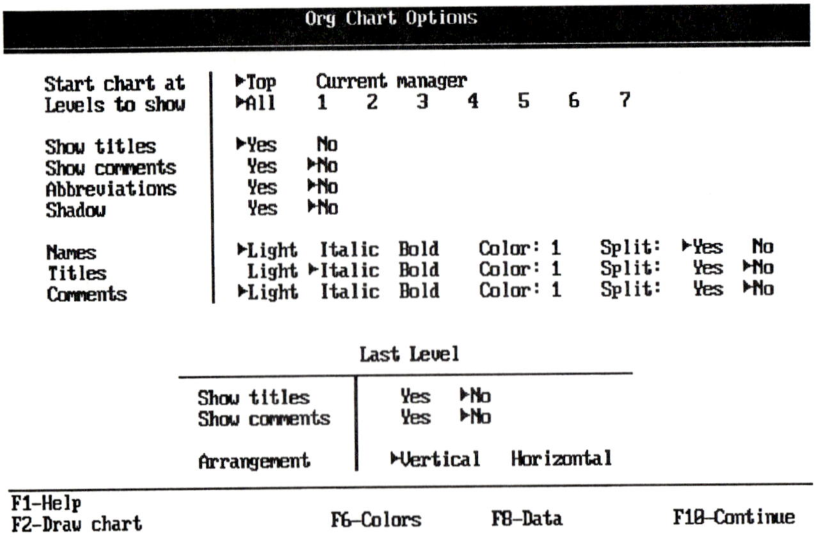
Org Chart Options

Start chart at	▸Top	Current manager									
Levels to show	▸All	1	2	3	4	5	6	7			
Show titles	▸Yes	No									
Show comments	Yes	▸No									
Abbreviations	Yes	▸No									
Shadow	Yes	▸No									
Names	▸Light	Italic	Bold	Color: 1	Split:	▸Yes	No				
Titles	Light	▸Italic	Bold	Color: 1	Split:	Yes	▸No				
Comments	▸Light	Italic	Bold	Color: 1	Split:	Yes	▸No				

Last Level

Show titles	Yes	▸No
Show comments	Yes	▸No
Arrangement	▸Vertical	Horizontal

F1-Help
F2-Draw chart F6-Colors F8-Data F10-Continue

FIGURE 7-7. Default settings for the Org Chart Options form

Notice the current default setting of No.

5. Press the spacebar to change the entry to Yes.
6. Press F2 (Draw chart).

Your chart looks like the one in Figure 7-8, with the shadow effect on the four complete boxes. Notice that no shadow was added to the staff box.

Displaying the Last Level

The last level in the hierarchy has displayed vertically on each organization chart you have created, because the default Arrangement setting for the last level is Vertical. You can change this setting to Horizontal so Harvard Graphics displays the last level of entries as boxes. This may be appropriate for the current chart since there are not too many entries in the last level. If each of the last-level entries contained five or six names, vertical placement would be the only option.

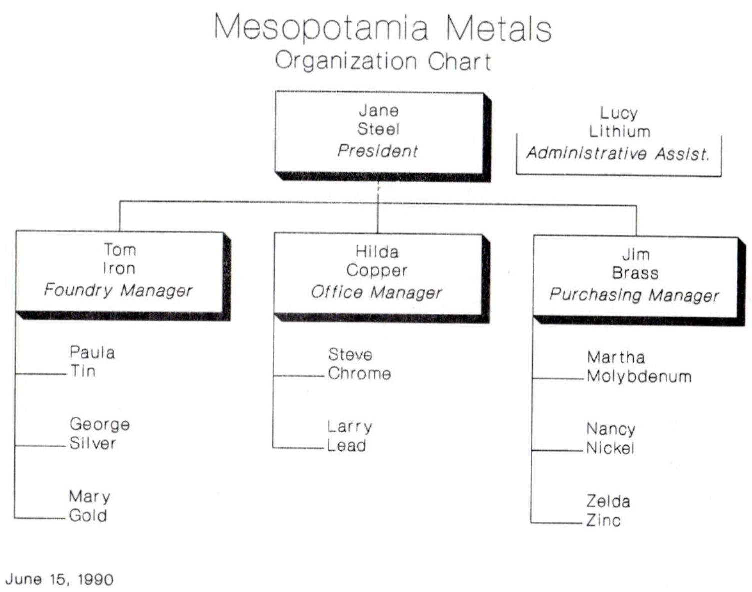

FIGURE 7-8. Adding shadows to the boxes

You can also use options in the Last Level section of the Org Chart Options form to show titles or comments, although the default is not to display either. If you choose either of these options, you must remember to use CTRL-PGDN to make your last-level entries. To display the last level of the current chart horizontally, follow these steps:

1. Press any key to return to the Org Chart Options form.
2. Press TAB until you move to the Arrangement field in the Last Level section of the Org Chart Options form.

Another option is to press END to move to the end of the form.

3. Press the spacebar to change the setting to Horizontal.
4. Press F2 (Draw chart) to display on your screen a chart like the one shown in Figure 7-9.

Since the Shadow setting is still set to Yes, even the new boxes have shadows. The new boxes do not display titles for two reasons. First, title

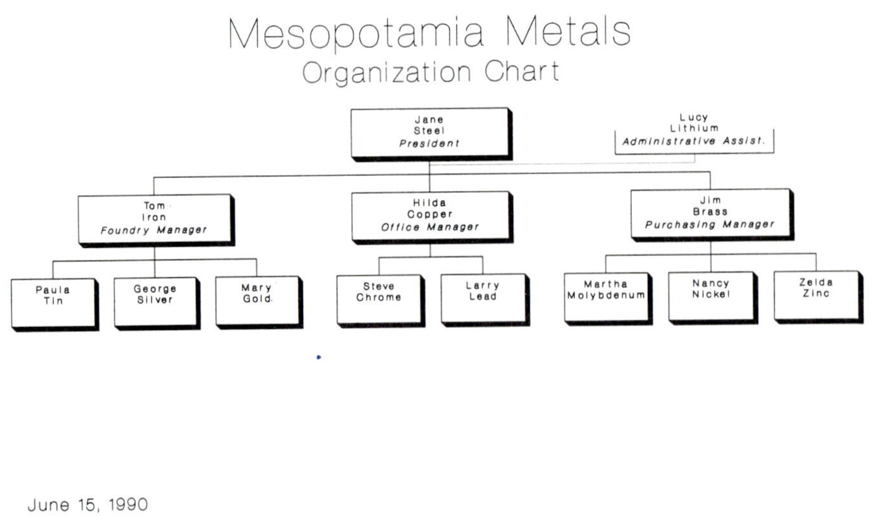

FIGURE 7-9. Showing the last level horizontally

entries were never added to the last level. You need to use CTRL-PGDN with each entry at this level to add a title. Second, even if you added titles they would not display because the Show Titles field in the Last Level section is set to No.

5. Press any key to return to the Org Chart Options form.
6. Press SHIFT-TAB until the Shadow field is highlighted and press the spacebar to change it to No.

Changing the Text Style

Harvard Graphics has a number of options that affect the style of the text used in the organization chart. Some of these options can only be used with the title and subtitle, while others apply to information in the boxes on the chart. You can make changes to the text through the Org Chart Options form, the F5 (Attributes) key, and the F8 (Options) key on the Main Menu.

USING THE ORG CHART OPTIONS FORM The Org Chart Options form allows you to change some of the options for text in three different areas. Names, titles, and comments can be affected separately. You can select either Light, Italic, or Bold for the text in these areas. In addition you can change the assigned color number or decide to split the entry between two lines. The default settings for Names are Light, Color: 1, and Split: Yes, which splits the name between two lines. Titles are shown in Italic as the default. They also use Color: 1 but are not split between lines. The default settings for Comments are Light, Color: 1, and Split: No. You can change any of these settings by pressing TAB to move to the appropriate field and using the spacebar to pick another option.

USING THE F5 (ATTRIBUTES) KEY You have used F5 (Attributes) in other chapters to change text like titles and Y-axis labels. With organization charts, the only text fields that you can affect with F5 are Title, Subtitle, and Footnote. You can still determine whether characters are filled, bold, italic, or underlined. You can also set the color of the text. SHIFT-F5 (Attributes) works for an entire line of text at once. If you move to the text for an organization chart box and press F5 (Attributes), the menu of options will not appear at the bottom of the screen, because they are only valid for specific fields.

CHANGING THE FONT FOR THE CHART In earlier chapters you looked at changing the font for a chart with the F8 (Options) key at the Main Menu. Once you press this key you can TAB to the Font field and select any of the options with the spacebar. All the text will display in the font you select.

Change the display for the current chart with these steps:

1. Press ESC to return to the Main Menu from the Org Chart Options form.
2. Press F8 (Options).
3. Press TAB until the Font field is highlighted.
4. Press the spacebar until the arrow cursor moves to Gothic.
5. Press ESC to return to the Main Menu.
6. Press F2 (Draw chart).

Notice that Gothic is used for all of the text. In Chapter 9 you will learn how you can change the font of individual fields.

7. Press (ESC) and press (CTRL-P) to print the chart.
8. Make any changes you want before pressing (F10) (Continue) to create a chart like the one in Figure 7-10.

Changing the Levels Displayed

The default setting is to display all the levels in the chart. You can change what is displayed in two ways. The Org Chart Options form provides the Start chart at and Levels to show fields that alter what is displayed. The default setting for Start chart at is Top, but you can change it to Current Manager. If you make this change, Harvard Graphics looks at which page of the Organization Chart form is on your screen before creating the chart. The manager that is on the current page will be placed at the top level of the chart that is created.

The Levels to show field allows you to display up to eight levels with the All option. Choosing any of the number selections will cause Harvard

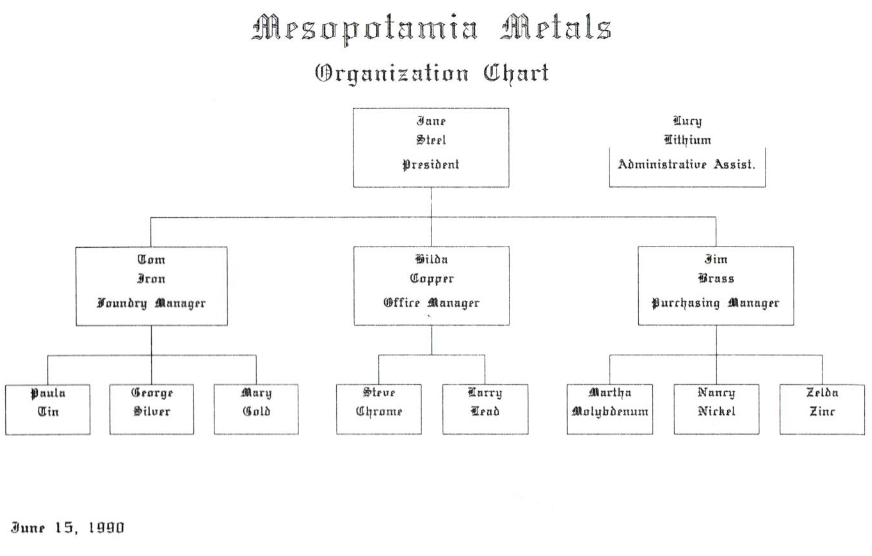

FIGURE 7-10. Using the Gothic font

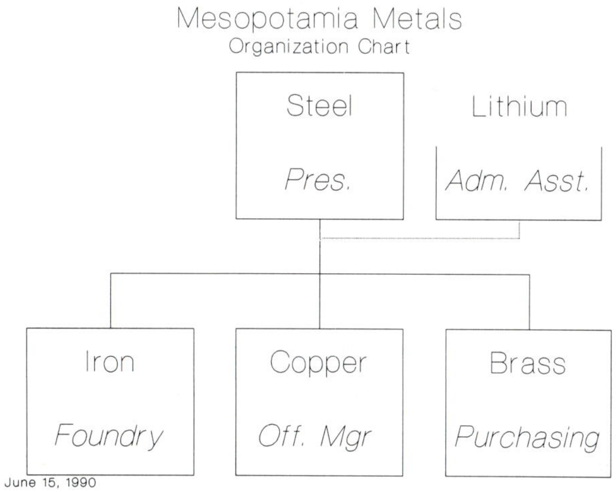

FIGURE 7-12. Showing abbreviations

SIZE AND PLACE CHART ENTRIES You have already used F7 (Size/Place) to alter text on other charts. With organization charts you can change the placement of titles, subtitles, or footnotes to left, right, or center. You can also change the size that is expressed as a percentage of the smallest edge of the paper the chart will be displayed on.

To change text size and alignment, select Enter/Edit chart. Next press F7 (Size/Place) to display the following options.

Size	Place	Organization Chart
6	L ▸C R	Title: Mesopotamia Metals
4	L ▸C R	Subtitle: Organization Chart
2.5	▸L C R	Footnote: June 15, 1990

To change Size, TAB to the appropriate setting and type a new number. To change the placement of text, TAB to the Place field for the text you want to change and press the spacebar to make the change.

SIZE AND PLACE FROM THE MAIN MENU Although you have not yet used it on any of the charts, the F7 (Size/Place) option works differently when you use it from the Main Menu. You can use this feature to alter the size and placement of the entire chart in relationship to the page. Although the following exercise demonstrates this feature with an organization chart, you can use it with any of the other text or analytical charts.

When you press F7 (Size/Place), an image of your chart is displayed on the screen, and you can define the beginning and ending corners of a box that will define the chart size. You then use the arrow keys as well as the special key combinations shown in Table 7-1 to move the cursor and thus define the corners of the box.

Follow these steps to retrieve a previous copy of the chart and resize it:

1. Press CTRL-G to get a chart.
2. Type **ORG2** and press ENTER.
3. Press ESC twice to return to the Main Menu.
4. Press F7 (Size/Place).

A copy of the current chart is displayed on your screen, as shown in Figure 7-13. Notice the message near the bottom on the left that indicates you should select the first corner of the box that will define the size and placement of the chart on the paper, which is represented by the white area on your screen.

Key	**Function**
Arrow Keys	Move in the direction indicated
CTRL-ARROW	Moves to the edge of the paper in the direction indicated
BACKSPACE	Allows you to reposition the first corner of the box
CTRL-HOME	Moves to the upper-left corner
CTRL-END	Moves to the lower-left corner
CTRL-PGDN	Moves to the lower-right corner
CTRL-PGUP	Moves to the upper-right corner

TABLE 7-1. Keys to Use in Size/Place from the Main Menu

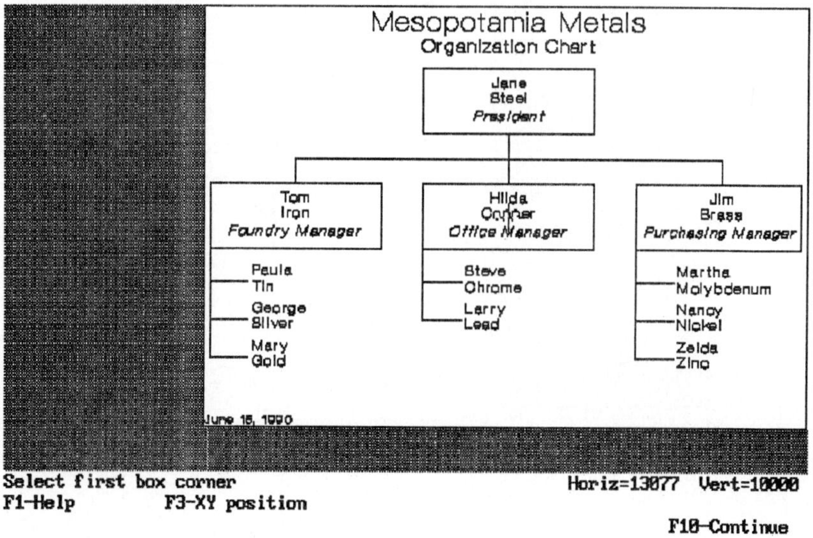

FIGURE 7-13. Initial display after requesting Size/Place from the Main Menu

5. Press CTRL-HOME to move to the upper-left corner and press RIGHT ARROW to move in from the edge of the paper a little.
6. Use the DOWN ARROW key to move down from the top of the page. Exact placement is not important, but the location of the plus symbol marking your position should be similar to the one shown in Figure 7-14.
7. Press ENTER after positioning the plus sign.
8. Move with RIGHT ARROW and DOWN ARROW until the box defining the size and placement of the chart looks something like Figure 7-15.
9. Press ENTER to accept the current location.

Harvard Graphics displays the chart within the new boundaries established by the box you just defined, as shown in Figure 7-16. This box defines the position of the chart as well as the size Harvard Graphics can use in order to fit all the information within the box.

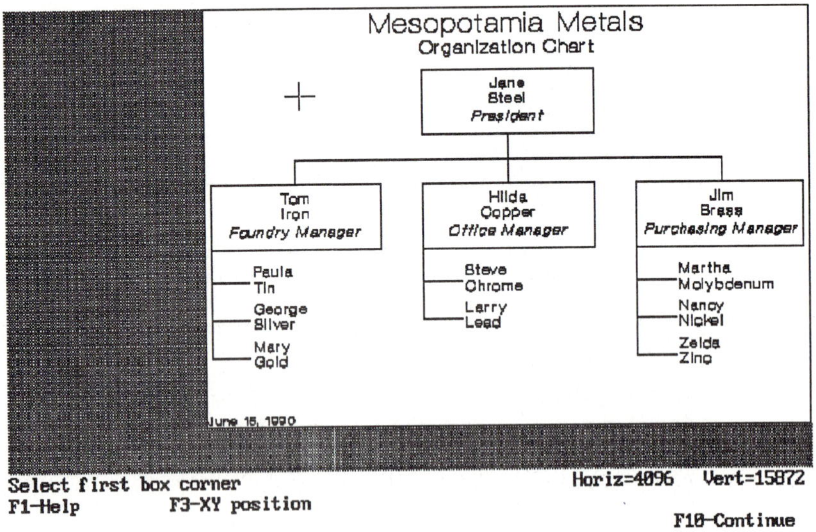

FIGURE 7-14. Defining the first box corner

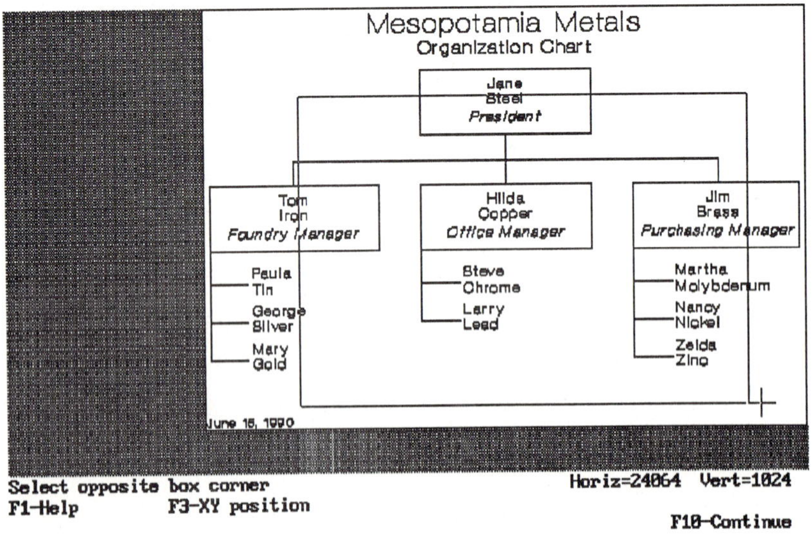

FIGURE 7-15. Defining the opposite box corner

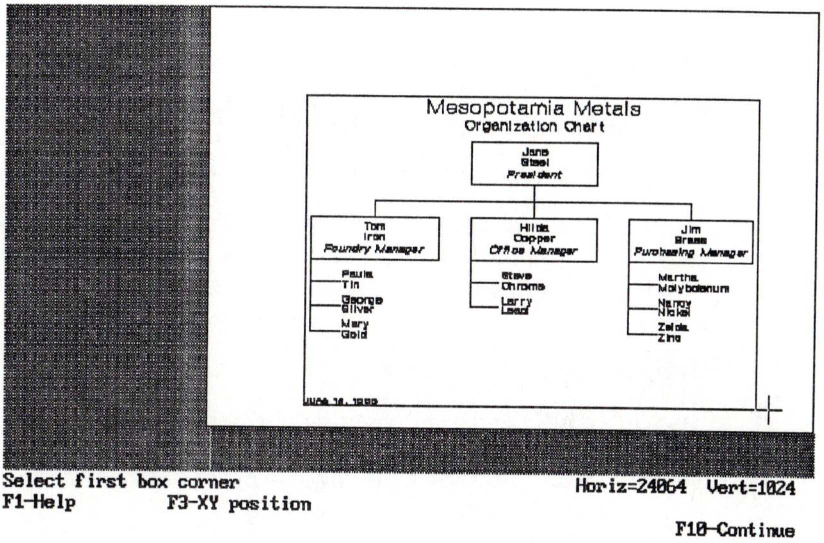

FIGURE 7-16. Organization chart with new size and placement

RESPONDING TO A REORGANIZATION

Normally the details of a reorganization are kept confidential until the last minute. If you are the person making the reorganization decisions, you will find this package easy enough to use that you can create a new organization chart for your announcement meeting without any outside help. If you are lower down the organization chain and have responsibility for creating an organization chart quickly, this package will make your chore a breeze. It is possible to add subordinates or change the names of people or responsibilities with little time invested. The keys listed in Table 7-2 provide features you need to move between screens and make fast editing changes.

Changing Entries

You can change the Name, Title, or Abbrev. fields by typing new entries. Alter a few of the name entries with these steps:

1. Press ESC until the Main Menu appears.

2. Press CTRL-G to get another chart.
3. Select ORG4 from the list and press ENTER twice to select the file and confirm that you do not want to save the modified ORG2 chart.
4. Press ESC to remove the chart from the screen.
5. Move to the page showing Jane Steel's subordinates with CTRL-PGUP.
6. With your cursor positioned on the "T" in the name Tom Iron, check to make sure you are in overstrike mode—the cursor is a line rather than a flashing box character. If the cursor is a box you must press INSERT to change it to a small line before proceeding.
7. Type **Ian** to replace Tom.
8. Press ENTER and then type **Carla** to replace Hilda.
9. Press ENTER and then type **Ben** to replace Jim.

Changes can be made to titles, comments, and abbreviations in the same way.

Key	**Function**
CTRL-PGUP	Moves to the level above the current level, if one exists
CTRL-PGDN	Moves to the level below the current level, if one exists
PGDN	Moves to the form for the next subordinate on the current level
PGUP	Moves to the form for the previous subordinate on the same level
INSERT	Toggles between insert and overstrike modes
CTRL-UP ARROW	Moves the current subordinate entry up one in the subordinate list
CTRL-DOWN ARROW	Moves the current subordinate down one in the subordinate list

TABLE 7-2. Keys for Editing Organization Chart Entries

Adding a Subordinate Entry

You can add a subordinate entry to any of the lists. After positioning your cursor, all you do is press CTRL-INSERT to add a blank line above the current location and place a new entry in the blank spot. Add a new entry above Carla Copper with these steps:

1. Position your cursor on Carla Copper and then press CTRL-INSERT.
2. Type **Molly Magnesium.**

If you want to add a title or subordinates you will need to use CTRL-PGDN to access the page for Molly.

Changing the Position of Subordinate Entries

You can alter the order for any of the entries in a subordinate list by moving the cursor to the subordinate entry you want to move and pressing either CTRL-UP ARROW or CTRL-DOWN ARROW, depending on whether you want to move the current entry up or down.

Deleting a Subordinate Entry

You can delete any subordinate entry that is not also a manager by positioning the cursor on the entry in the Subordinates column and pressing CTRL-DELETE. If the subordinate is also a manager, Harvard Graphics will not allow you to delete the entry. It will display the message "Cannot delete manager with subordinates."

Delete the subordinate entry for George Silver who reports to Ian Iron with these steps:

1. Move the cursor to Ian Iron.
2. Press CTRL-PGDN to move to the sheet containing Ian's subordinate entries.
3. Move the cursor to George Silver and then press CTRL-DELETE.

The entry immediately disappears, and the entry beneath it moves up to the second line in the Subordinate area.

4. Press PGDN to move to the page for Molly Magnesium.

Notice that PGDN takes you to the form for the next subordinate on the same level rather than the next level.

5. Press PGDN to move to the page for Carla Copper.
6. Press PGUP to move back to Molly Magnesium's page.

PGUP takes you to the next form on the same level rather than the previous level.

7. Move to the Title field by pressing SHIFT-TAB twice and then pressing DOWN ARROW.
8. Type **Marketing Director** and press ENTER.
9. Press F8 (Options) and TAB to move to the Levels to show field. Press the spacebar until the arrow cursor points to All.
10. Press TAB three times to move to the Abbreviation field. Press the spacebar to change the Yes to No.
11. Press TAB until you move to the Show titles field under Last Level. Press the spacebar to change the Yes to No.
12. Press F2 (Draw chart) to create a chart like the one in Figure 7-17.

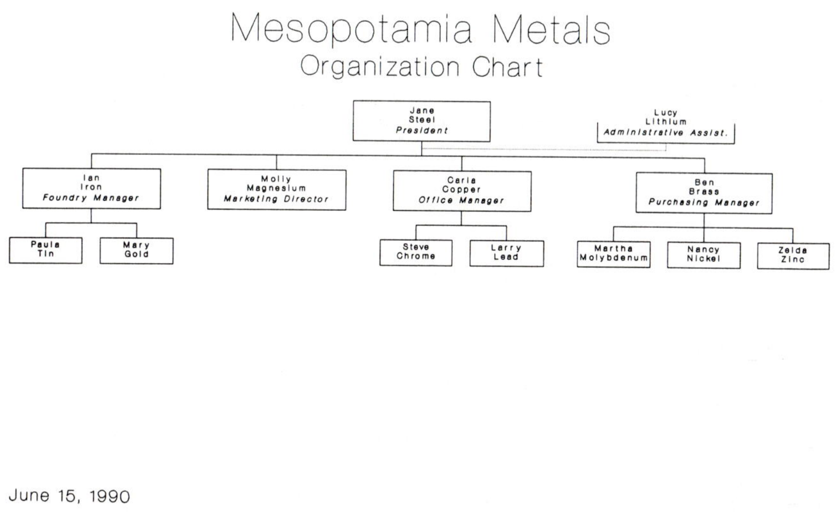

FIGURE 7-17. Organization chart showing addition, deletion, and changes

13. Press (ESC) twice to return to the Main Menu and press (CTRL-S) to save the chart.
14. Select Save chart, type **ORG5**, and then press (F10) (Continue) to save this chart.

chapter 8

USING CHART GALLERIES

A *gallery* is a predefined graph option. Galleries contain sample data, so you can evaluate the visual impact of each chart style before making your selection. You can select a visual image from a gallery rather than a specific graph type. Using this visual image, you can select the graph type that most closely matches your needs without a lot of trial and error and without having to define your exact requirements. Once you select the appearance you want to achieve, you can edit the sample data values or clear the data form and make all new entries. Although galleries were available as accessories in earlier releases of Harvard Graphics, the complete set of chart gallery options is part of the Release 2.3 package.

Galleries allow you to build sophisticated charts without taking the time to understand all of the selections necessary to create the chart. The use of gallery selections also ensures compatible color selections and allows you to create an entire presentation with a consistent appearance. If you have an EGA or VGA monitor, you can select from among the chart galleries' 11 color-coordinated palette options for a graph.

CREATING A CHART FROM THE GALLERY

You can create a variety of charts without selecting a myriad of options. When you create a chart, all you need to do is specify that you want to create a chart from the gallery options. You can choose to display the chart with the sample data that is part of the gallery, or you can clear the data and enter your own. Using the palette options, you can change the colors assigned to the chart before you enter you own data. After entering your data you must assign colors to various components separately or use the Setup menu options to change the palette assigned to the chart.

Viewing Gallery Options

There are nine chart galleries from which you can select. Each gallery offers a family of related chart options. To display the gallery choices, follow these steps:

1. Select Create new chart from the Main Menu.
2. Select From gallery.

Harvard Graphics displays the gallery choices shown in Figure 8-1. The nine sections of the screen each represent a gallery option containing between four and nine specific chart definitions. The numbered box in the upper-left corner of each section of the screen allows you to choose the gallery you want to explore. The numbers for the gallery options and the type of gallery they represent are as follows:

1	Text
2	Pie
3	Bar
4	Line
5	Area
6	High/low/close
7	Organization
8	Bar/line mix
9	Combination

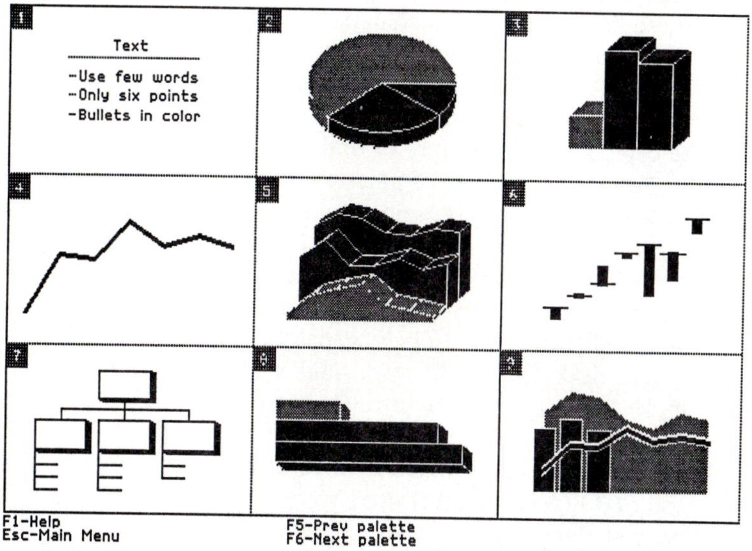

FIGURE 8-1. Gallery options

You worked with all these graph types in previous chapters, and more descriptions of the various types of graphs are given in those chapters. If you decide that you want to change the chart settings for a chart you see in the gallery, you can press F8 (Options) after proceeding to the data form for the chart that you select from the gallery. When you save the chart, your changes to the data and chart definition are saved under the name you supply, although the gallery definition is not altered. Before exploring the various galleries, you will want to see how you can change the impact of the various options through a change in the default color palette.

Changing Assigned Palette Colors

A palette is a file with a coordinated set of color selections you can use for chart background, data, text, and symbols. Palette files have 16 different color assignments for the various elements of the graph. Harvard Graphics provides 11 default palette files for use with EGA or VGA monitors. All of these files have a .PAL filename extension.

The default palette file is automatically used when you display the gallery options. You can change quickly to any of the remaining ten palettes. You can make the color change from the main gallery display or once you have selected a specific gallery of options.

To see the next set of palette colors, press F6 (Next palette). To return to the previous palette selection, press F5 (Prev palette).

When you display the data in Figure 8-1 on a monochrome monitor, you cannot see any differences in the display. If you use a color EGA or VGA monitor, the default colors are dark cyan, blue, light blue, light cyan, and white. If you press F6 (Next palette), the colors change to dark blue, dark green, dark cyan, light cyan, and white. Pressing F6 (Next palette) five more times cycles you through more of the 11 palette options to show a display where red, red gray, brown, and orange are the selected colors. You can use F5 (Prev palette) to return to previous selections, or continue to use F6 (Next palette) until you cycle through all the options and you are back at the first color palette again.

Although you can always change the color palette with the function keys, color assignments vary depending on your monitor. You must have an EGA or VGA monitor to utilize all 11 palette options provided by Harvard Graphics.

Selecting a Specific Gallery

Once you display the gallery options shown in Figure 8-1, you can select one of the numbered options. Each option corresponds to a type of chart and presents related options for the type of chart selected. You can again use F5 (Prev palette) or F6 (Next palette) to move between the palette options, or you can type one of the numbers to select a particular type of bar chart.

If you type **3**, the nine bar charts shown in Figure 8-2 are presented in a more detailed gallery. You also can use the mouse to make gallery selections, clicking the mouse on the desired selection. The numbered options in the bar graph gallery represent the following:

1 Cluster
2 Overlapped
3 Stacked
4 3D cluster
5 3D stacked
6 3D overlapped
7 Dual Y-axis
8 Highlighted bars
9 Step

To select one of the options for a new chart, type the number. If you type **4**, a 3D cluster graph patterned after the sample shown in box 4 of Figure 8-2 is displayed on your screen. The data that determines the height of the

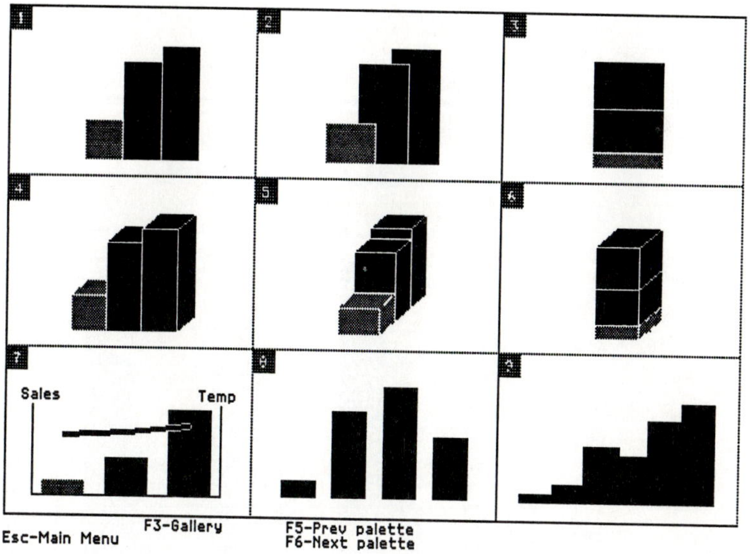

FIGURE 8-2. Bar chart gallery

bars is sample data. The text entries for the labels on the graph are also sample data entries that show the size and placement of chart labels. Figure 8-3 shows 3D Cluster used as the sample title for a graph. You can save the settings and erase the data or edit the entries one by one.

You have one last chance to change the color of this chart using F5 (Prev palette) and F6 (Next palette). Once you leave the gallery by proceeding to the data form, F5 (Prev palette) and F6 (Next palette) no longer cycle through the color palettes. Although you can change the colors for the graph later, if you do not change it now you must alter individual elements separately or return to the Setup menu selections to choose a different palette.

Entering Your Data in the Gallery Selection

You can enter your own data in the selected chart in two ways. You can leave the sample data in the chart and type your entries over the existing

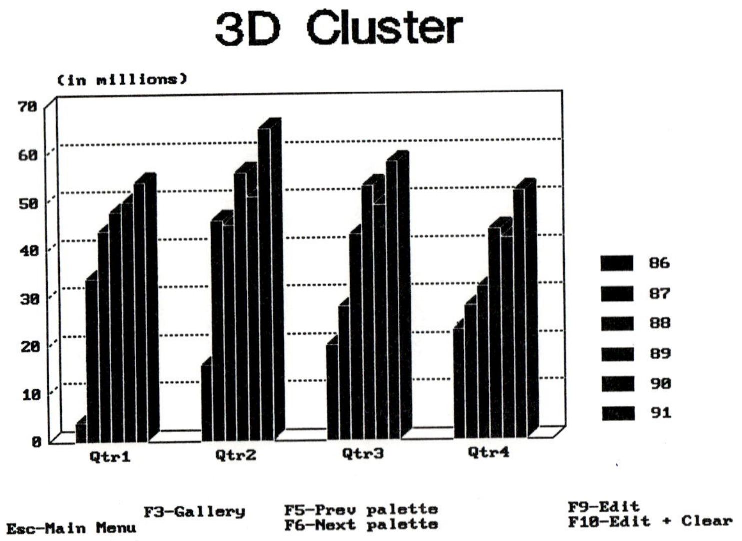

FIGURE 8-3. 3D Cluster chart

Bar/Line Chart Data

Title: 3D Cluster
Subtitle:
Footnote:

Pt	X Axis Name	86	87	88	89
1	Qtr1	4	34	44	48
2	Qtr2	16	46	45	56
3	Qtr3	20	28	43	53
4	Qtr4	23	28	32	44
5					
6					
7					
8					
9					
10					
11					
12					

F1-Help F3-Save F5-Set X type F9-More series
F2-Draw chart F4-Draw/Annot F6-Calculate F8-Options F10-Continue

FIGURE 8-4. Bar chart data form

entries, or you can clear the entire data form and start over with a blank form. The best approach depends on whether you want to use the existing data as a guide to where you need to make entries.

EDITING THE SAMPLE DATA You can proceed from a display of the graph to the data form, shown in Figure 8-4, by pressing F9 (Edit). By leaving the existing entries on the chart, you know exactly where you need to supply information. You can move from entry to entry with the TAB key and type the new entries. If your replacement entry is shorter than the current entry, you can use DELETE to remove the extra characters after you type the new entry, or use CTRL-DELETE before typing to delete an entire line from the data form.

Follow these steps from the Main Menu to create a 3D cluster graph of Allied Lighting's headcount projections for 1990 to 1995:

1. Select Create new chart from the Main Menu.
2. Select From gallery.
3. Type **3** to select the bar chart gallery.

4. Type **4** to select a 3D cluster chart.
5. Press F9 (Edit) to move to the data form.
6. Press HOME to move to the top of the data form.
7. Type **Allied Lighting** for the title and press ENTER.
8. Type **Headcount projections** and press ENTER.
9. Press F8 (Options).
10. Press TAB until the cursor marking your place on the Titles & Options form is on the 8 in legend 86.
11. Type **90** and press ENTER.
12. Continue typing new year numbers and pressing ENTER until you have replaced the original legend 91 with 95.
13. Press F8 (Data) to return to the data form. Notice that the F8 key takes on a different meaning depending on whether you are in the data form or the options form.
14. Press TAB until the cursor that marks your place on the form moves to the Qtr1 row in the column labeled 90.
15. Type **50**, press TAB, type **76**, press TAB, type **90**, press TAB, and type **120.**
16. Press HOME to move to Qtr1, and then use the DOWN ARROW key to move toward the appropriate line for each entry.
17. Continue marking the entries for the years 90 to 93, using the following entries and pressing TAB after each entry except the last:

60	**72**	**100**	**125**
40	**45**	**52**	**50**
30	**32**	**50**	**42**

18. Press F9 (More Series) to display the last two series for 94 and 95.
19. Press HOME followed by TAB.
20. Complete these entries using the arrow keys or TAB to position the cursor for each entry:

130	**156**
130	**165**
45	**47**
52	**45**

21. Press F2 (Draw chart) to display the chart.
22. Press ESC twice.
23. Press CTRL-S, type **ALLIED**, and press F10 (Continue) to save the chart.

There was no need to change option settings to get the 3D and cluster effects. Even the size of the font used for the title was preselected when you chose the gallery option that came closest to your needs. You can always return to the data form and use F8 (Options) to make additional changes, but the gallery gives you a professional appearance and harmonizing colors without all the work.

You can still change the color of a chart once you have entered data, but a different approach is needed. The last section in this chapter provides specific how-to tips, but for now you will want to explore the galleries for other chart types.

USING THE GALLERY CHOICE WITH A BLANK DATA FORM If you want to use the gallery selection but start the data form with a clear slate, just press F10 (Edit + Clear) when the chart shown in Figure 8-3 is presented. The data form for the type of chart you selected will be blank. You proceed in the same way you did when editing the form in the previous section. The only difference is that the previous entries do not mark your place on the data entry form to remind you where to supply entries. As you become more familiar with Harvard Graphics, this is less of a problem than with your first few charts.

A LOOK AT THE OTHER GALLERIES

With nine different galleries to select from, you can create all types of charts from the gallery options. In this section you can create a quick chart from each of the other galleries to see the wide range of possible selections.

Creating a Text Chart from the Gallery

Harvard Graphics gallery options offer the following nine text charts, as shown in Figure 8-5:

1 Bullet
2 Bullet with subtitle
3 Bullet* with different color selections
4 Simple List
5 Title Chart
6 Numbered List
7 2 Column
8 3 Column
9 Free Form

* Appears as Build on screen

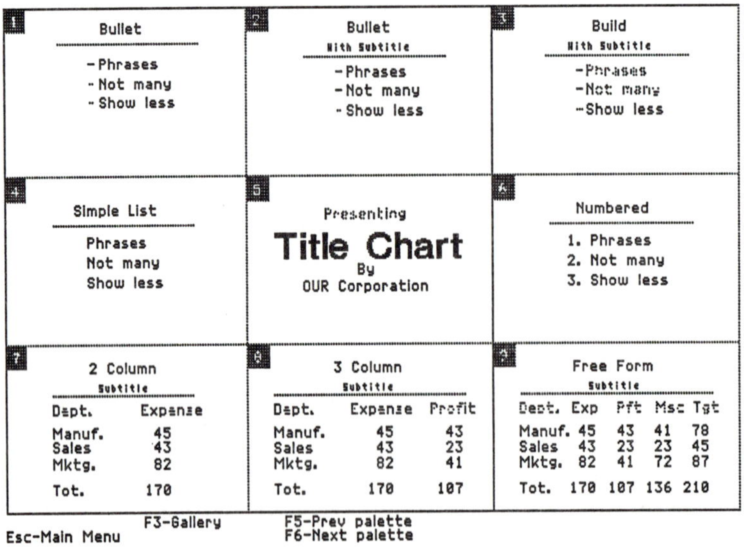

FIGURE 8-5. Gallery of text charts

Follow these steps to create a title chart for a sales presentation:

1. Select Create new chart from the Main Menu.
2. Select From gallery.
3. Type **1** to select the text chart gallery shown in Figure 8-5.
4. Type **5** to select Title Chart.
5. Press F10 (Edit + Clear) to clear the data from the data form.
6. Press TAB twice to move the cursor to the third line in the top section.
7. Type **Presenting** and press ENTER.
8. Type **Sales Awards** and press ENTER.
9. Type **By** and press ENTER.
10. Type **ABC Corporation.**
11. Press F2 (Draw chart).

Your chart will look like the one in Figure 8-6, with the font sizes automatically set by the gallery selection you chose.

12. Press ESC twice to return to the Main Menu.
13. Press CTRL-S, type **ABC**, and press F10 (Continue).

FIGURE 8-6. Text chart created from the gallery

Creating a Pie Chart from the Gallery

The gallery offers nine pie chart options, as shown in Figure 8-7. These include charts with two pie charts and pie/column chart combinations, as shown in the following list of selections:

1 Pie with title
2 Pie with title and subtitle
3 Pie with slice exploded and column
4 3D pie with title
5 3D pie with title and subtitle
6 3D pie with column
7 2 pies
8 2 3D pies
9 2 proportional pies

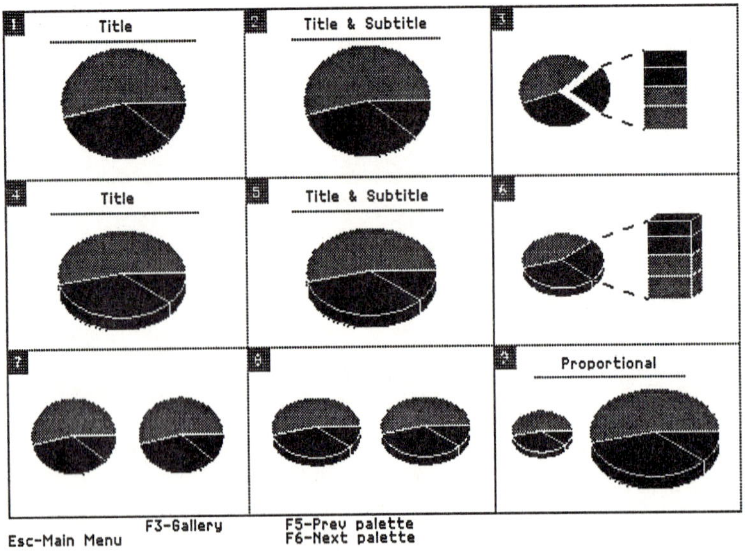

FIGURE 8-7. Pie chart gallery

Pie charts are useful when you want to show the percentage each element is of the whole. If you want a pie chart option that is a little more sophisticated, as part of a budget presentation for example, you can choose a pie/column chart to show the relative size of each budget component to expand information about one particular piece of the pie with the column chart. Because the chart is a combination of two different types of charts, you must enter two data series. Follow these steps to select the chart options and complete the chart:

1. Select Create new chart from the Main Menu.
2. Select From gallery.
3. Type **2** to select the pie gallery.
4. Type **3** to select the pie/column chart combination, in which the column chart displays additional detail for the exploded piece.

The chart will then show a pie chart with six slices. The associated column chart for the exploded pie slice will contain eight different sections. When you enter your data, you are not required to use all of them. If you want to use fewer pie slices and column sections, clear the data form with F10 (Edit + Clear) rather than F9 (Edit).

5. Press F9 (Edit) to display the data form.
6. Type **Salaries**, press TAB, type **2500**, and then press TAB four times to move to the next line.
7. Type **Benefits**, press TAB, type **800**, and then press TAB four times.
8. Type **Rent**, and then press DELETE three times to delete the last three characters in the sample entry. Press TAB, type **1000**, and press TAB four times.
9. Complete the following budget account entries using the same procedures followed in steps 6 through 8:

Postage	**900**
Phone	**650**
Material	**1500**

10. Press HOME and type **1991 Expenses** as the title.
11. Press PGDN to display the Pie Chart 2 Data form.

The entries for this series are used to supply the data for the column chart.

12. Press TAB three times, type **Wood,** press TAB, and then type **200.** Press TAB four times to move to the next line.

13. Complete the remaining entries for the breakdown of the material budget using one line for each entry and using the same procedure followed in steps 6 through 8 and 12:

Wood	**200**
Paint	**100**
Glue	**200**
String	**250**
Nails	**250**
Glass	**500**

14. Press CTRL-DELETE to remove the entries for pie slice seven, and press CTRL-DELETE again to remove the entries for pie slice eight.

15. Press F8 (Options) and then press TAB four times to move to the Pie 2 title.

17. Type **Material Breakdown.**

18. Press F2 (Draw chart) to display the graph as shown in Figure 8-8.

Figure 8-8 displays patterns rather than the color or monochrome shades that will display on your screen.

19. Press ESC twice to return to the Main Menu.

20. Press CTRL-S, type **MATERIAL,** and press F10 (Continue) to save the chart.

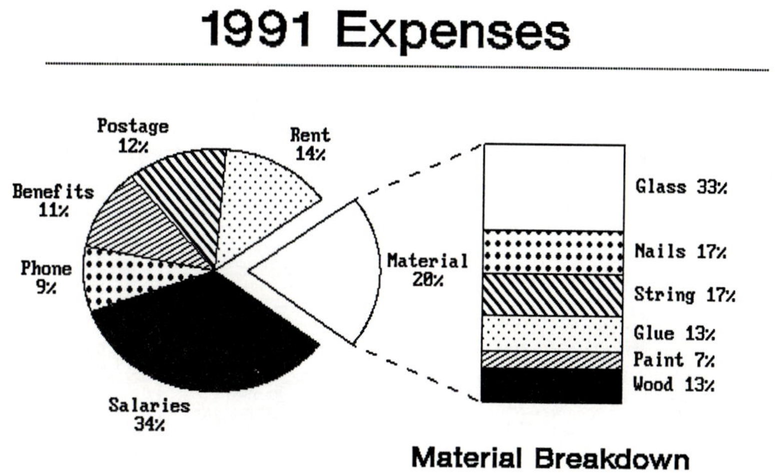

FIGURE 8-8. Pie/column chart

Creating a Line Chart from the Gallery

Harvard Graphics provides nine options in its gallery of line charts. These charts are accessed from the gallery by typing **4**. The following line chart options are available, as shown in Figure 8-9:

1 Overlap
2 Curve
3 Trend
4 Point
5 Logarithmic
6 Bar & line
7 Overlap
8 3D overlap
9 Data table

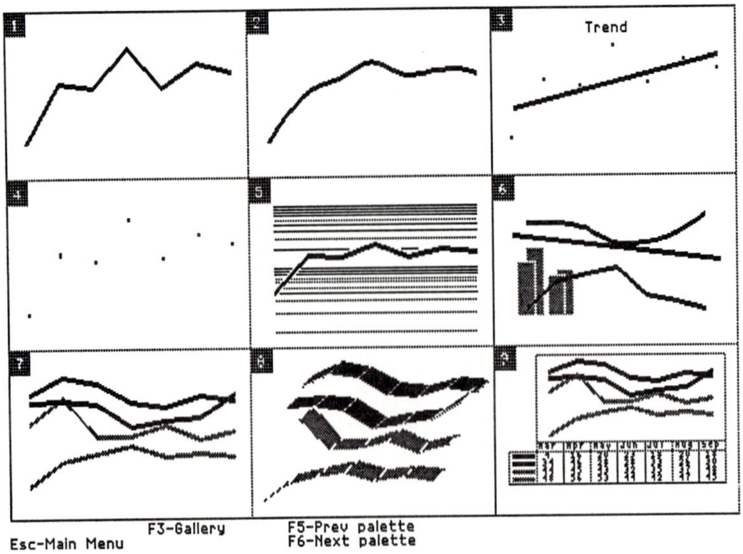

FIGURE 8-9. Line chart gallery

You can look at one of the line chart options and make a few customizing changes without entering a full set of data values. To make a few changes to a data table line chart, follow these steps:

1. Select Create new chart from the Main Menu.
2. Select From gallery.
3. Type **4** to view the line chart gallery.
4. Type **9** to select the data table chart.
5. Press F9 (Edit) to activate the data form for the chart.
6. Type **Jan** to replace the first month name and press ENTER.
7. Continue typing the following month names, pressing ENTER after each:

Feb
Mar
Apr
May
Jun
Jul

8. Press HOME twice to move to the Title entry.
9. Type **Element Table** and press ENTER.
10. Type **Monthly measurements** and press ENTER.
11. Press F2 (Draw chart).
12. Press any key to return to the Bar/Line Chart Data form.
13. Press F3 (Save) to save the chart.
14. Type **ELEMENT** and press F10 (Continue).
15. Press ESC to return to the Main Menu.

Creating an Area Chart from the Gallery

Harvard Graphics provides a gallery of six different area chart designs. There are three basic selections of overlap, stacked, and 100%, but all three choices can also be obtained in 3D. Figure 8-10 shows the gallery of options:

1	3D Overlap
2	3D Stacked
3	3D 100%
4	Overlap
5	Stacked
6	100%

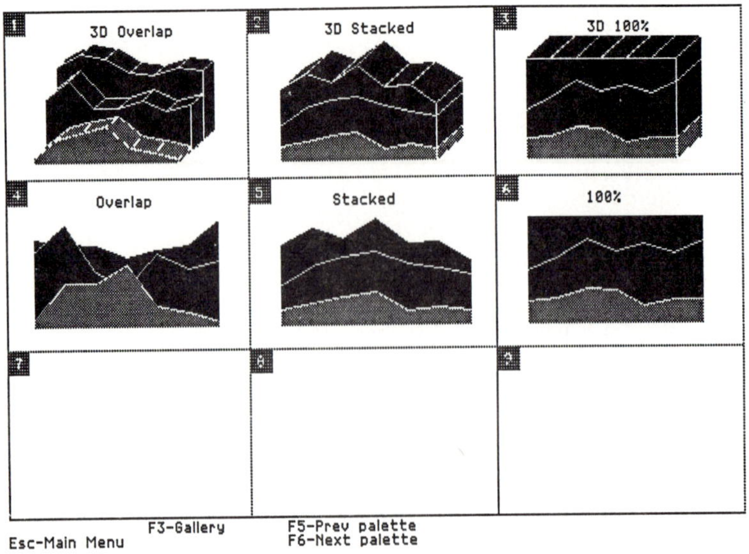

FIGURE 8-10. Area chart gallery

To create a 3D stacked area chart, follow these steps:

1. Select Create new chart.
2. Select From gallery.
3. Type **5** to select the area chart gallery.
4. Type **2** to select 3D Stacked.
5. Press F9 (Edit) to move to the data form.
6. Press F8 (Options).
7. Type **Kitty Kat, Inc.** for the title and press ENTER.
8. Type **Peak season sales** for the subtitle.
9. Press TAB six times.

10. Type **87** and press (ENTER).

11. Continue typing year numbers and pressing (ENTER) after each until you have typed **92**.

12. Press (F2) (Draw chart).

Your chart should look like Figure 8-11, except your screen displays different colors or monochrome shades rather than patterns.

13. Press (ESC) twice to return to the Main Menu.

14. Press (CTRL-S), type **KITTY**, and press (F10) (Continue).

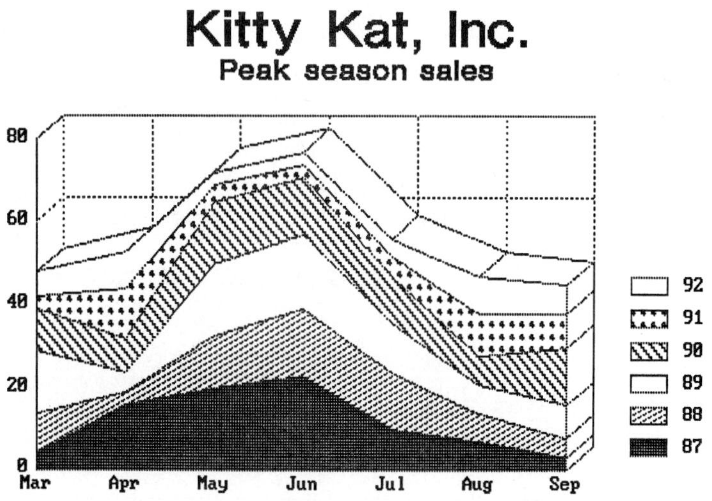

FIGURE 8-11. Area chart created from a gallery option

Creating a High/Low/Close Chart from the Gallery

Harvard Graphics provides six different high/low/close charts for monitoring stock, bond, and commodity prices, as shown in Figure 8-12. The six gallery options are as follows:

1 Stocks by Day
2 Stocks by Hour
3 Area
4 Moving Average (includes line graph)
5 Moving Average
6 Error

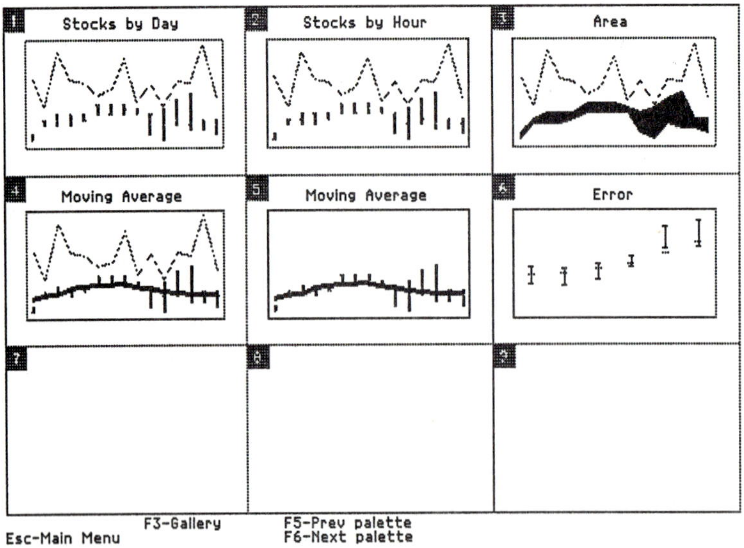

FIGURE 8-12. High/low/close chart gallery

To create a Stocks By Hour chart using the sample data, follow these steps:

1. Select Create new chart from the Main Menu.
2. Select From gallery.
3. Type **6** to select a high/low/close chart, and then type **2** to select Stocks by Hour.
4. Press F9 (Edit) to move to the data form.
5. Press HOME, type **Geauga Homebuilders, Inc.**, and press ENTER.
6. Type **June 15, 1990 Prices.**
7. Press F2 (Draw chart).
8. Press ESC twice.
9. Press CTRL-S, type **HOMEBLD**, and press F10 (Continue).

Creating an Organization Chart from the Gallery

The gallery of organization charts provides four options, as shown in Figure 8-13. You can choose to show the last level either vertically or horizontally and you can choose whether or not to use a shadow effect on the boxes in the chart. Unlike other gallery options, the organization charts are not numbered consecutively. The numbers and associated selections are:

1	Vertical last level
2	Vertical last level with shadow effect
4	Horizontal last level
5	Horizontal last level with shadow effect

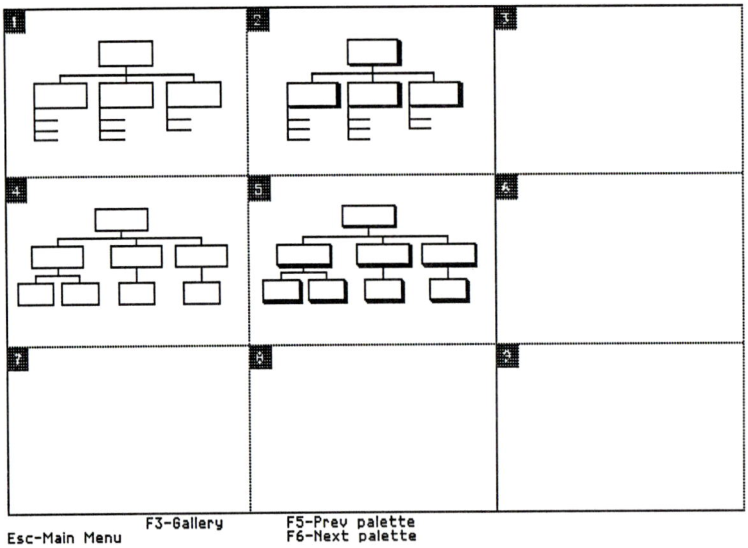

FIGURE 8-13. Organization chart gallery

To create an organization chart with a horizontal last level and shadow effect from the sample gallery data, follow these steps:

1. Select Create new chart.
2. Select From gallery.
3. Type **7** to select the organization chart gallery.
4. Type **5** to select the gallery option with a horizontal last level and shadow effect.
5. Press F9 (Edit) to move to the data form.
6. Press TAB until the cursor is on Ron Brandson.
7. Press CTRL-PGDN twice to move down two levels. You can change a name at any level.
8. Press CTRL-PGUP twice to return to the first level.
9. Press F2 (Draw chart).

10. Press ESC twice.
11. Press CTRL-S, type **ORG_H**, and press ENTER.

Creating a Bar/Line Mix Chart from the Gallery

The bar/line mix gallery offers the following nine selections, as shown in Figure 8-14:

1 3D cluster
2 3D stacked
3 Stacked
4 Bar overlap
5 Combination overlap
6 Area overlap
7 Paired bar
8 Line overlap
9 Logarithmic

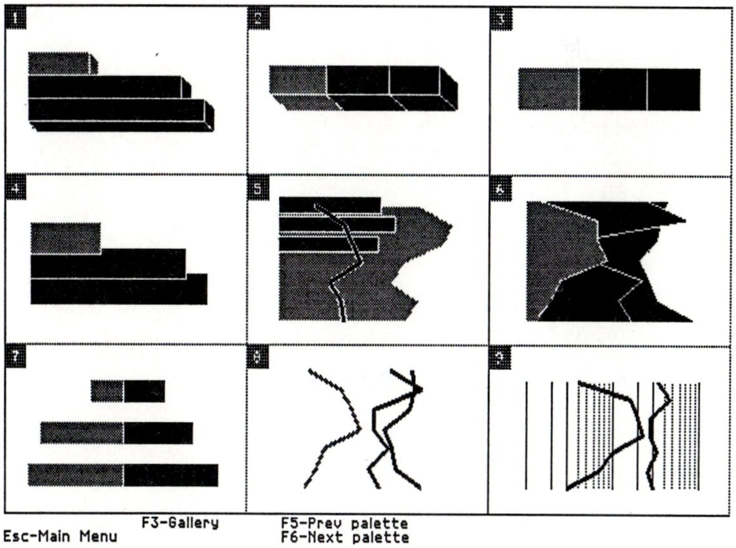

FIGURE 8-14. Bar/line mix gallery

To create a paired bar chart from the gallery, follow these steps:

1. Select Create new chart.
2. Select From gallery.
3. Type **8** to select the Bar/Line Mix gallery.
4. Type **7** to select the paired bar option.
5. Press F9 (Edit) to display the data form.

Create a chart that shows headcount for a publisher and the number of books published by year.

6. Type **1990** and press ENTER to change the X-axis name for point 1.
7. Continue entering new X-axis names using 1991 through 1995 for your entries.
8. Press HOME to move to 1990, and then press TAB to enter the value for the first series.
9. Type **5** and press ENTER.
10. Continue entering the following series 1 values, pressing ENTER after each:

    35
    40
    40
    50
    60

11. Press HOME to place the cursor on 1990, and press TAB twice to move to the second series.
12. Type **10** and press ENTER.
13. Continue typing the following numbers, pressing ENTER after each:

    100
    120
    120
    125
    130

14. Press F8 (Options).
15. Type **ABC Books** and press ENTER to provide a title.
16. Type **Headcount/Title Projections**, and then press TAB six times to move to the legend title for series 1.
17. Type **Emp**, press DELETE three times, and press ENTER.
18. Type **Books** and press ENTER.
19. Press F2 (Draw chart) to create a chart like Figure 8-15.
20. Press ESC twice.
21. Press CTRL-S, type **PUBLISH** and press F10 (Continue).

Creating a Combination Chart from the Gallery

Although you have seen combination charts in the bar/line mix gallery, the charts in the combination gallery provide sophisticated options with as many

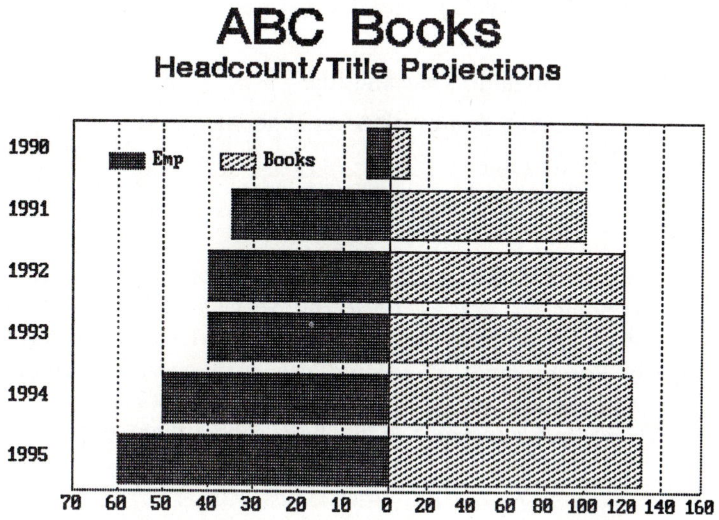

FIGURE 8-15. Paired bar chart

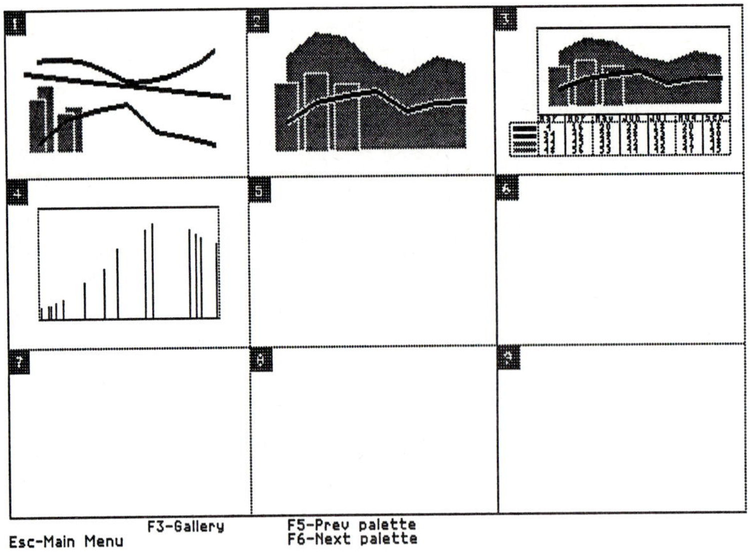

FIGURE 8-16. Combination gallery

as three chart types used on one chart. The options in the combination gallery, as shown in Figure 8-16, are as follows:

1 Combination bar and line

2 Combination overlap bar, line, and area

3 Data table

4 Numeric X data

A *numeric X data chart* allows you to provide a series of values for the X-axis point and graphs the second series as Y values. This type of chart is useful when you have two different measurements you want to show on the graph. For example, you could use it to chart the quantity of pollutants found in random soil samples taken at different depths.

To create a numeric X data chart, follow these steps:

1. Select Create new chart.
2. Select From gallery.
3. Type **9** to select the combination gallery.

4. Type **4** to select the numeric X data option.
5. Press F9 (Edit).

You can type new data values just as you did for the other gallery charts.

6. Press F2 (Draw chart).
7. Press ESC twice to return to the Main Menu.
8. Press CTRL-S, type **POLLUTE**, and press F10 (Continue).

CHANGING CHART COLORS

When you switch to the data form, the sample data for the gallery selection you made is placed on the data form along with other settings to create the style chart you selected. You cannot switch to another gallery selection without returning to the Main Menu and selecting Create new chart again. Selecting Create new chart clears the current data form.

Rather than use F5 (Prev palette) or F6 (Next palette) to change the palette, you can use F8 (Options) to change the color for a particular setting. This requires you to handle the color coordination yourself. In Chapter 9 you will learn another way Harvard Graphics lets you change the color of chart elements.

Changing the Color of a Particular Chart Element

You can change the color of a pie slice, a series of bars, or the text on a chart. The method you use to change the color of an individual element depends on the element you want to change and the type of chart that you are working with.

With a text chart, you use F5 (Attributes) after moving your cursor to the text on the data form for the chart. You can choose a color as well as other text attributes.

To change the color of a pie slice in a pie chart, you can use the Pie Chart Data form. The codes in the color column control the color of each piece. To change one, move to the color column for the appropriate pie slice and press F6 (Colors). Although you could type a new color code in the column, using F6 displays the color numbers and names for your selection. To change the color of text on a pie chart, you move the cursor to the text you want to change in the options form for the chart type and use F5 (Attributes).

To change the color of bars for a series on a bar chart, you use F8 (Options). The colors for bars are on page 4 of the options form for the chart type. Once you activate this page by pressing PGDN three times, you can move to the color column and use F6 (Colors) to make a selection for each series of bars. The text for bar charts is changed with the same procedure as the text in a pie chart.

Changing the Color Palette for the Current Graph

If you want to switch to a different palette after proceeding to the data form, you must return to the Main Menu to change the palette and use F8 (Options). If you have an EGA or VGA monitor, try using a different palette on the current graph following these steps:

1. Press F2 (Draw chart) to display the current chart. Notice the colors the chart currently uses.
2. Press any key to remove the chart from the screen.
3. Press F8 (Options) to display the Options menu overlay.
4. Press END to move the cursor to the last field. This is the chart's current palette setting. Remember this entry so you can return it to the setting in step 10.
5. Type **10** and press ENTER. Harvard Graphics includes palette files that are numbered 1 through 11.
6. Press F2 (Draw chart) to display the current chart using the new palette. Notice the colors the chart now uses.
7. Press any key to remove the chart from the screen.
8. Press F8 (Options) to display the Options menu overlay.
9. Press END to move the cursor to the last field.
10. Type the entry you replaced in step 4 and press ENTER.

Changing the palette this way changes the setting that only the current graph uses. The palette setting is stored in the chart files that also contain the data for the chart.

Changing the Default Color Palette from Setup

If you want to switch to a different palette to use for the charts you subsequently create, you have to return to the Main Menu. The Setup option in the Main Menu allows you to select another palette. Follow these steps to make the change from a data form screen:

1. Press ESC to return to the Main Menu.
2. Select Setup.
3. Select Color palette.
4. Select the third selection, Select palette.
5. Highlight one of the .PAL files in the list presented. You can also change the directory that Harvard Graphics uses to list palette files.
6. Press F10 (Continue) and ESC to return to the Main Menu.
7. Press F2 (Draw chart) to view the chart with the new color selection.
8. Press any key to return to the Main Menu.

chapter 9

DRAWING

Besides creating charts from text and numeric entries, you can also use draw features to create or enhance a chart. The additions made through the Draw options include geometric shapes, arrows, and lines. Pictures, known as *symbols,* and text can also be added. The geometric shapes and text that you add with Draw are called *objects.*

When you draw a chart or annotate an existing one, a mouse can make your task easier. A mouse lets you quickly point to the object in a chart you want to use or specify where you want to position an object. Remember that you can press the left mouse button when the directions instruct you to press ENTER and press the right button when the directions instruct you to press ESC.

Since charts drawn in the Draw/Annotate screen have more flexibility in positioning objects, you may find that the objects in your charts vary slightly from the ones shown in the figures in this chapter. Also, as you create charts you will find that objects appear in color, even though the figures illustrating these examples are in black and white with patterns where different colors appear.

When you first start using the draw features, they seem to offer unlimited capabilities, especially when you consider how many symbols are available to you as part of the package. As your skill level increases you may want to change symbols or extend the features in other ways. Harvard Graphics includes a supplemental Draw Partner package that enhances the basic draw features. Draw Partner is linked to Harvard Graphics 2.3 to allow you to use it with any chart with just a keystroke. This means you do not need to leave Harvard Graphics or save your chart to access Draw Partner's features. You will see a few of the ways that Draw Partner can benefit you later in this chapter.

GETTING STARTED

You have already learned how you can create charts to show data and text. Although the chart you create in this exercise contains some text, it is not added as a title or footnote. The text in this chart is added through the Draw/Annotate screen and can be placed anywhere on the chart. Follow these steps to add a symbol and text through the Draw options:

1. Select Create new chart, Text, and Free form, and then press (ESC) to return to the Main Menu if you have been editing another chart.

These steps remove an existing chart from Harvard Graphics memory. If you have just loaded Harvard Graphics, the current chart is already blank.

2. Select Draw/Annotate from the Main Menu and then select Symbol.
3. Select Get and highlight HUMANS4.SYM in the list. Press (ENTER).
4. Press (PGDN) repeatedly to move to the group silhouette symbol in the bottom line and press (ENTER) twice.

The first (ENTER) selects the symbol and the second fixes the box that represents it on the screen.

5. Press (ESC). Your screen currently looks like Figure 9-1.
6. Select Add and then select Text.
7. Type **ALLBEN, INC.** and press (ENTER).
8. Move the text above the silhouette and press (ENTER).

In this example Horiz is equal to 13056 and Vert is set to 13824.

9. Type **Benefits for all employees** and press ENTER.
10. Move below the silhouette and press ENTER to create an image that looks something like Figure 9-2.
11. Press ESC three times to return to the Main Menu.
12. Press CTRL-P to print the chart.
13. Check the settings and change any that are incorrect by pressing TAB to highlight the field you want to change and using the spacebar to select a new option for the field.
14. Press F10 (Continue) to print and create a chart that looks like Figure 9-3.
15. Press CTRL-S to save the chart.
16. Select Save chart and type **PEOPLE** as the chart name.
17. Press F10 (Continue) to write the file to disk.

FIGURE 9-1. Draw/Annotate screen with symbol added

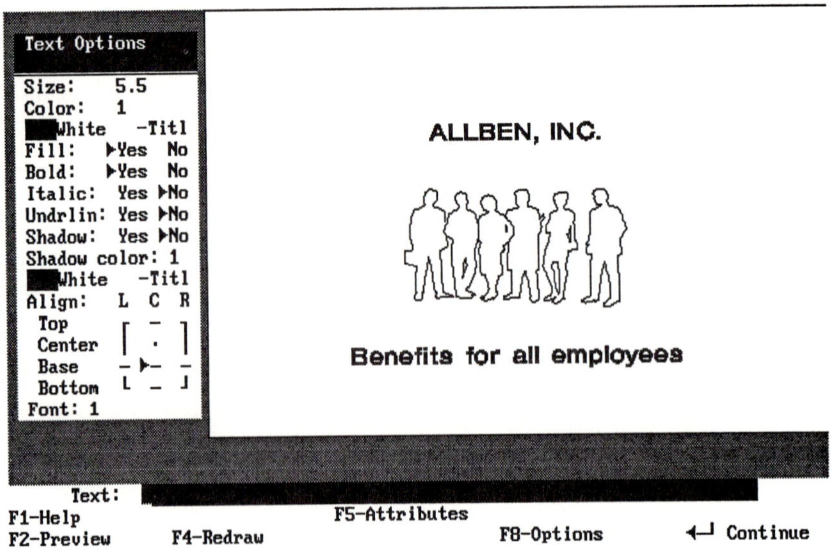

FIGURE 9-2. Draw/Annotate screen with text added

FIGURE 9-3. Printed chart created with Draw/Annotate screen

A chart like this can be the perfect lead-in to a presentation. With the available symbol files you can create this chart in only a few minutes.

USING THE DRAW FEATURES IN HARVARD GRAPHICS

There is a wide variety of tasks you can perform with the draw features of Harvard Graphics. Objects like symbols, text, and geometric shapes can dramatically alter the appearance of existing charts or create brand new transition charts that do not classify as either text or analytical charts.

Using an Existing Chart Versus Creating a New One

In Harvard Graphics you can use the draw features using charts you create, define, and display with Create new chart from the Main Menu, or you can start with a blank screen and draw all objects that appear on the chart. When you select Draw/Annotate from the Main Menu or press its speed key equivalent CTRL-R, you can use the current chart as you add objects. In the example in "Getting Started," your initial chart was blank.

When you edit an existing chart in the Draw/Annotate screen, you cannot change the chart defined with one of the forms you learned to use in previous chapters. For example, you cannot change the color a series uses for a bar chart since this information is set in the Bar/Line Titles & Options form. While you are working in the Draw/Annotate screen, the chart created with a chart data form and the enhancements created with the Titles & Options form seem invisible; you cannot even select the basic chart to change titles or other chart features. You may want to think of the basic chart as the background image on which your Draw/Annotate screen objects are written.

When you add objects to a blank screen, as in the example in "Getting Started," you draw everything that appears in the chart. You could use this method to create a company logo for a slide show or you might use this in place of a text chart. To create a chart that contains only the objects that you add from the Draw/Annotate screen, select Create new chart, Text, and Free form. When Harvard Graphics displays the screen to enter text for a free-form chart, press F4 (Draw/Annot) or press ESC to return to the Main Menu and then select Draw/Annotate. This procedure removes any chart data that Harvard Graphics remembers from the last chart you used. Another option is to exit Harvard Graphics, load Harvard Graphics, and then select Draw/Annotate.

ADDING OBJECTS

Once you are in the Draw/Annotate screen, the first change you will want to make is to add an object. An object can be a line, shape, text, or symbol. To add any of these objects, select Add from the Draw menu. Then select the object you want to add: Text, Box, Polyline, Line, Circle, or Polygon. Once you select the object, Harvard Graphics displays the options box for the object and prompts you for information such as the text you want to add or the starting position of the object you want. Your position on the screen is marked with *cross-hairs,* which resemble a large plus sign. You can use the arrow keys to position the cross-hairs. The HOME key moves the cross-hairs up and to the left. The PGUP key moves the cross-hairs up and to the right. The PGDN key moves the cross-hairs down and to the right. The END key moves the cross-hairs down and to the left. Combining these keys with the CTRL key moves the cross-hairs to the extreme edge of the chart in the direction selected. You can increase the amount the arrow keys move the cross-hairs by pressing the grey + key. You can decrease the amount the arrow keys move the cross-hairs by pressing the grey − key. Press the asterisk (*) and the arrow keys move the cross-hairs the original distance or increment. These keys are shown in Figure 9-4 with other key combinations you can use to move in the chart box.

If you want to change the settings for the object, press F8 (Options). When the cursor is at the first field in the options box, move the cursor to the field you want to change and make the change. For options such as outline or fill color, you can press F6 (Choices) to display a list of the available colors. When you have finished setting the options, press F8 (Draw) to return to entering the information about the object.

The information you must enter in the options box depends on the object you are adding. For each of the following objects, you will need to supply the following information:

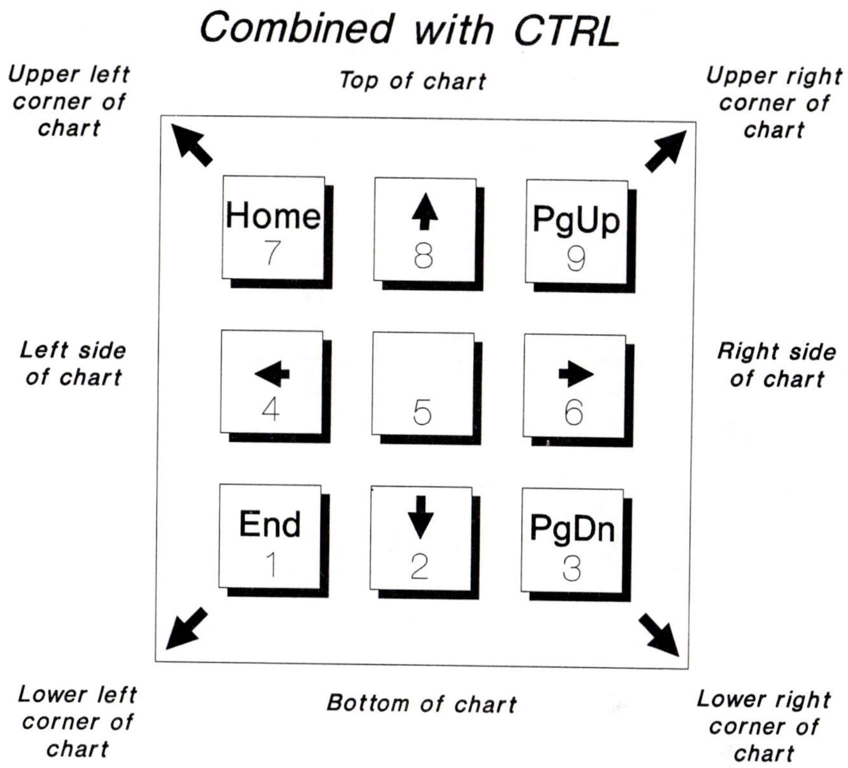

FIGURE 9-4. Keys to use in the Draw/Annotate screen

- *Text* First supply the text you want to add. Press ENTER, and then position the text where you want it placed. Harvard Graphics displays a box that represents the size of the object. When you position the box where you want and press ENTER, the box changes into the text you entered earlier.

- *Box* First supply one corner of the box by moving the cross-hairs to the beginning point and pressing ENTER. Next you must position the cross-hairs to the opposite corner and press ENTER. Harvard Graphics uses the horizontal and vertical positions of the two points you have selected to determine the lines of the box.

- *Polyline* First supply the starting position of the first line of the polyline by moving the cross-hairs to the beginning point and pressing ENTER. Then you must move the cross-hairs to the ending point of that line and press ENTER. You will continue pointing and pressing ENTER until you have drawn all of the connected lines you want. After selecting the last point on the polyline, press ESC to complete the object.
- *Line* First move the cross-hairs to the beginning point of the line and press ENTER. Then move the cross-hairs to where you want the line to end and press ENTER.
- *Circle* First supply the center of the circle, and then move the cross-hairs diagonally away from the center to create a box that the circle or ellipse will fill. Harvard Graphics draws the largest circle or ellipse that can fit inside the box created with the horizontal and vertical positions of the two points you selected.
- *Polygon* First supply the first corner of the polygon by moving the cross-hairs to the beginning point and pressing ENTER. Then you must move the cross-hairs to where you want a corner of the polygon and press ENTER. You will continue pointing and pressing ENTER until you select all of the corners of the polygon. After selecting the last point of the polygon, press ESC to complete the shape. You do not have to return to the starting position of the polygon since Harvard Graphics draws the last side of the polygon for you.
- *Button* First supply a button number 1 through 10 and press ENTER. You can also enter the numbers 211 through 217 which are assigned specific functions. Next, position the cross-hairs to the first corner of the button and press ENTER. Move the cross-hairs to the opposite corner and press ENTER. Harvard Graphics draws a dotted outline of the box. More information on using buttons is supplied in Chapter 10, "Creating Multiple Chart Screens and Slide Shows" since buttons are a feature that you use with slide shows.

After you create one of these objects, you see a prompt that allows you to make a new object of the same shape. If you want to add the same type of object, select the next object's position. If you want to return to the Add menu to select another object type or to discontinue adding objects, press ESC. You can press ESC from the Add menu to return to the Draw menu.

When you are drawing lines, polygons, and polylines, you may want to combine the SHIFT key with the mouse or the arrow keys. When you press SHIFT and move the mouse or press the arrow keys, the cross-hairs move in a straight horizontal or vertical motion, not a combination of both.

For example, if you are drawing a polyline, you may want to press SHIFT as you move the mouse or press the arrow keys so the lines do not slant. You must also hold down the SHIFT key as you press ENTER to select one of the object's points.

Creating a Chart and Adding Embellishments with Draw

You have read about many Draw options for building a chart. Although the draw features can be used alone, as in the "Getting Started" example, they can also be used to add enhancements to existing charts. You can create a bar chart and add annotations by following these steps:

1. Select Create new chart from the Main Menu.
2. Select Bar/Line.
3. Press F10 (Continue) to accept the default of Name for the X data type.
4. Type **Acme Industries** and press ENTER for the chart title.
5. Press ENTER twice to omit entering a subtitle and footnote.
6. Type **Books** and press ENTER for the first entry in the Label column.
7. Type **Magazines** and press ENTER.
8. Type **Periodicals** and press ENTER.
9. Type **Kitchen Paper Prod.**
10. Press HOME and TAB to move to the column for the first series data.
11. Type **50500** and press ENTER.
12. Type **95000** and press ENTER.
13. Type **75000** and press ENTER.
14. Type **35000** and press ENTER.
15. Press F8 (Options) and PGDN to move to the second page of the Titles & Options form.
16. Move to the Bar fill style field and select Pattern.
17. Move to the Horizontal chart field and select Yes.

18. Move to the Legend location field and select None.
19. Press (PGDN) twice to move to the fourth page of the Titles & Options form.
20. Press (TAB) to move to the Markers/Patterns column in the table for the first series.
21. Type **6** for a hollow pattern.
22. Press (F2) (Draw chart) to display the chart.

At this point the chart could use some enhancements. Besides the enhancements available in the Bar/Line Titles & Options form, you can also add enhancements by *annotating* the chart, which means adding objects to a chart you have already created with the other Harvard Graphics choices. You can use the annotation features to add arrows to the bars of the chart.

23. Press (ESC) twice to return to the Main Menu.
24. Select Draw/Annotate. This displays the screen shown in Figure 9-5.

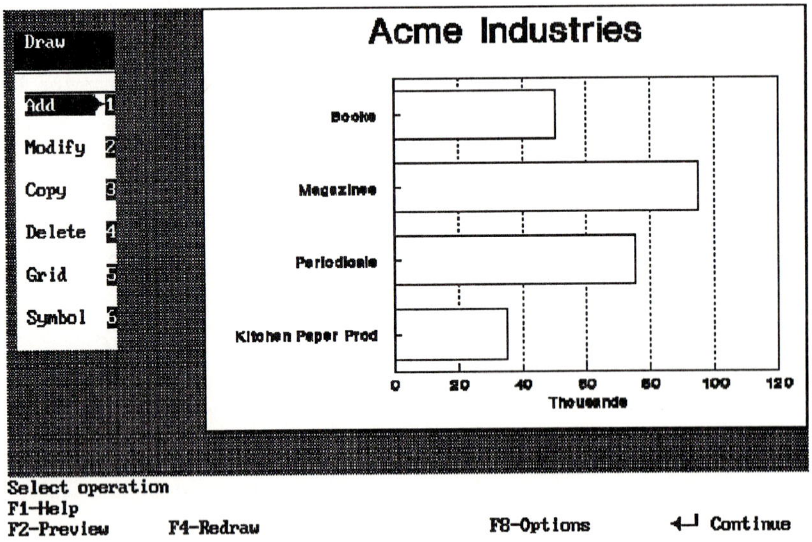

FIGURE 9-5. Initial Draw/Annotate screen

This screen displays the current chart in the chart box. On the left is the Draw menu, which you can use to add graphics to your charts.

25. Select Add.

The Add menu displays the objects you can add by drawing them.

26. Select Line.

Harvard Graphics displays the Line Options box on the left side of the screen. In the bottom of the screen, Harvard Graphics prompts you for a point of the line.

27. Press F8 (Options) so you are at the Arrows field.
28. Press DOWN ARROW twice and press ENTER to select a line with an arrow at the right end of the line.
29. Press F8 (Draw) so you can draw the lines.

Harvard Graphics prompts for the beginning position of the line.

30. Point to the tick mark for the Books bar on the X-axis and press ENTER.

Harvard Graphics prompts for the next point on the line. This will be the ending position of the line. As you move the cross-hairs, Harvard Graphics displays a temporary line representing where the line will be drawn.

31. Press RIGHT ARROW or move the mouse until the line goes to the middle of the right side of the bar and press ENTER. Harvard Graphics prompts for the next line you want to add.
32. Point to the tick mark for the Magazines bar on the X-axis and press ENTER.
33. Press RIGHT ARROW or move the mouse until the line goes to the middle of the right side of the bar and press ENTER.
34. Point to the tick mark for the Periodicals bar on the X-axis and press ENTER.
35. Press RIGHT ARROW or move the mouse until the line goes to the middle of the right side of the bar and press ENTER.

36. Point to the tick mark for the Kitchen Paper Prod bar on the X-axis and press ENTER.
37. Press RIGHT ARROW or move the mouse until the line goes to the middle of the right side of the bar and press ENTER.
38. Press ESC three times to return to the Main Menu.
39. Press CTRL-S to save the chart.
40. Type **ACMESALE** and press ENTER for the filename.
41. Edit the description so it says **Acme Industries - Annotated**, and press ENTER to save the file.
42. Press CTRL-P to print the chart.

If you want to change any settings, do so at this point. You may want to change whether the chart is printed as a draft or as the final copy.

43. Press F10 (Continue). Your output looks like Figure 9-6.
44. Press CTRL-R to return to the Draw/Annotate screen.

Adding More Objects

You are not limited to one draw feature. A single chart can use many of the features to add symbols, text, and other enhancements. Try adding some objects to your chart by following these directions:

1. Select Add.
2. Select Text.

Harvard Graphics prompts for the text you want to enter. Since you do not want to use the default settings shown in the Text Options box on the left side of the chart box, change the settings before you add the text.

3. Press F8 (Options).
4. Press CTRL-DELETE to remove the current text size.
5. Type **3** for the new text size.

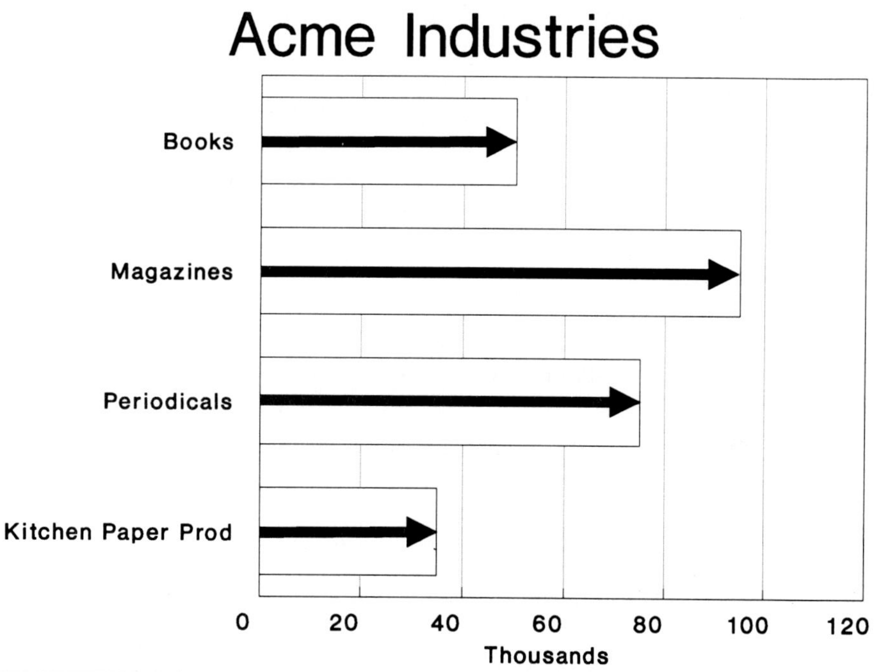

FIGURE 9-6. Chart with arrows added with Draw/Annotate screen

6. Press F8 (Draw) to return to the prompt to enter text.
7. Type **Sun Days** and press ENTER.

Harvard Graphics now prompts for the location for the text and displays a box that represents the size of the text you are positioning.

8. Move the cross-hairs below the "M" in the Magazines X-axis label and press ENTER.

Harvard Graphics prompts you for the next text you want to add. Since the next text uses the same settings as Sun Days, you do not have to press F8 (Options) to change the settings in the Text Options box.

9. Type **News Express** and press ENTER.

Harvard Graphics again displays a box showing the size of the object and prompts you for where you want it positioned. Unlike before, Harvard Graphics suggests a position below Sun Days. When you add multiple text objects, Harvard Graphics suggests a location for you. While you do not have to use the suggestion, you can use it to quickly position additional objects of the same type.

10. Press (ENTER) to accept Harvard Graphics' suggestion for the text position.
11. Type **Gracious Living** and press (ENTER) for the next text you want to add.
12. Press (ENTER) to accept Harvard Graphics' suggestion for the text position.
13. Press (ESC) to return to the Add menu since you do not want to add another Text object.
14. Select Box.

Harvard Graphics prompts for the beginning position of the box.

15. Press (F8) (Options) since you want to change how the box appears.

Each type of object has a unique Options box that is customized for the type of information the object uses.

16. Move to the Style field.

Rather than just drawing a simple box, you can choose from 21 different options for how the box will look. These options are shown in Figure 9-7.

17. Press (F6) (Choices) to select the box type you want, then select Rounded, pressing (ENTER) to finalize.
18. Move your cursor to Center Fill and select No.
19. Press (F8) (Draw) to return to drawing the box.
20. Move the cross-hairs to below and to the left of the "G" in Gracious so the box you draw contains the three magazine names.
21. Press (ENTER).

Harvard Graphics prompts for the opposite box corner.

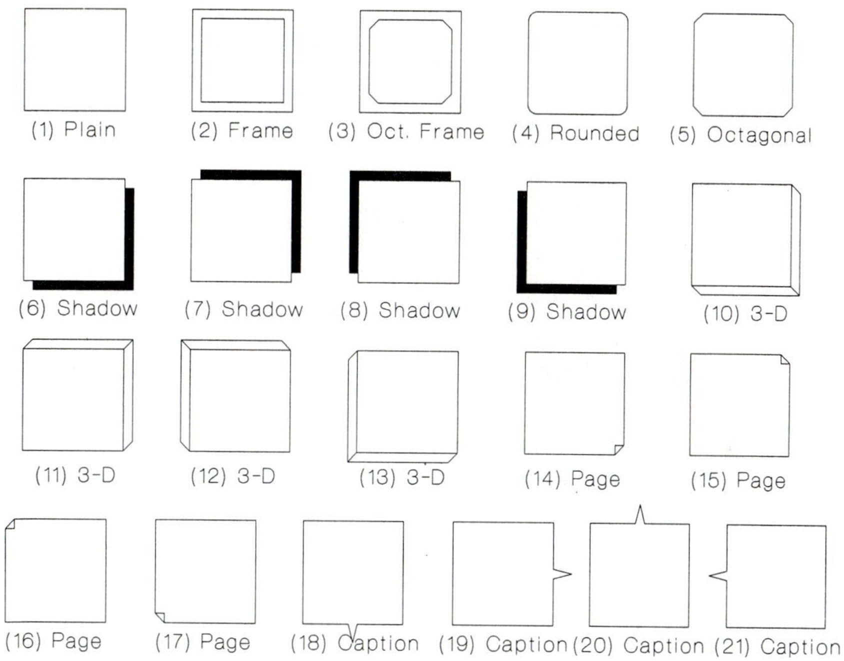

FIGURE 9-7. Available box styles

22. Move the cross-hairs next to the X-axis and above Sun Days.

As you move the cross-hairs to the opposite corner, Harvard Graphics lightly draws the box using the position you selected and the current cross-hairs position. You can use this box to judge if the box you are creating is positioned and sized correctly.

23. Press ENTER.

Harvard Graphics draws the box using the two corners you selected.

24. Press ESC since you do not want to draw another box.
25. Press ESC again to return to the Draw menu. The chart looks like the one in Figure 9-8.

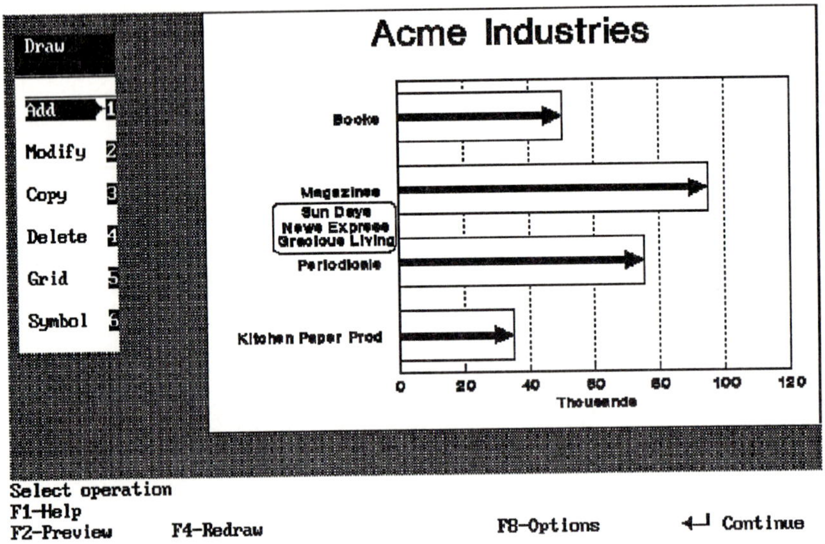

FIGURE 9-8. Chart with text and box objects added

As you become more proficient at drawing, you will find that you want to change the defaults of the object types. While this topic is beyond the scope of this chapter, you should be aware that you can change the defaults of object types by pressing F8 (Options) from the Add menu. If you are not satisfied with the objects, you can modify the objects using the Draw/Annotate screen.

MODIFYING AN OBJECT

As you create a chart, you may want to change certain aspects of the chart appearance, such as the position of objects, the size, or the color. Harvard Graphics has several changes you can make to an object. From the Modify menu, select Move, Size, Options, Front, or Back. Once you select one of these options, you must select the object or objects you want to change.

As you modify the chart, you may want to redraw it without viewing the chart on the full screen. For example, when you move an object, Harvard Graphics erases the object in the old position and draws it in the new position. Since Harvard Graphics does not redraw the chart behind the erased copy of the moved object, this area appears blank. To redraw the chart in the Draw screen, press F4 (Redraw). Of course you can continue to view the chart using the whole screen by pressing F2 (Preview).

Selecting Objects

Selecting objects is the process of telling Harvard Graphics the objects you want to work with. You can select one or more objects. Once objects are selected, you can continue to modify, copy, and delete them.

To select one object, point to that object with the cross-hairs when Harvard Graphics prompts for the object you want. To make sure that you are pointing to the object you want, you should point to the center of the object. Press ENTER to select the object you are pointing to, and Harvard Graphics marks the object with four dots around it. To the left of the chart box, Harvard Graphics displays the Options box for the object you selected. If Harvard Graphics selects the correct object, press ENTER to select Choose this from the bottom of the screen. If it did not select the object you want, tab to Select next below the chart box and press ENTER. When the object you want is selected, highlight Choose this and press ENTER. Harvard Graphics draws a rectangle the size of the object. You will use this box when you move, size, or copy an object to indicate its size and position. At this point, the next step you take depends on how you are modifying the object.

You can select multiple objects at the Harvard Graphics prompt by pointing to a position that will be a corner of a box that will contain all the objects you want. After you press ENTER to select the current position, Harvard Graphics prompts for the opposite corner. Move the cross-hairs so the box it draws will contain all of the objects you want; an object must be entirely in the box for Harvard Graphics to select the object. Press ENTER. Harvard Graphics marks each of the objects with four dots. The options box to the left of the chart box contains the options for a group rather than for a specific type of object. If the marked objects are the ones you want, press ENTER to select Choose this from the bottom of the screen. If Harvard Graphics did not select the correct objects, point to Select next below the chart and press ENTER. You may instead want to select Retry and try again. When the objects you want are selected, highlight Choose this and press ENTER. The box used to select the objects continues to appear since you will use this box to indicate the size and position of any object you move, size, or copy. At this point, the next step you take will depend on how you are modifying the object. You will get practice selecting objects both ways later in the chapter.

Moving Objects

When you create a chart that uses the Draw/Annotate screen, you probably will not design it perfectly when you add the elements. You may want to reposition the objects to improve its appearance. For example, if your chart has many objects, you may want to position them so the chart does not appear crowded. You may also need to reposition objects that point to chart data that changes. For example, if your chart has an arrow pointing out your division's sales, you will want to reposition the arrow as the data for your division changes.

Try moving the box and the text inside it that you added to the chart by following these directions:

1. Select Modify from the Draw menu.
2. Select Move from the Modify menu.

Harvard Graphics prompts for the object you want to move.

3. Point to a position above and to the left of the box around the magazine titles.

Since there is no object here, you are forcing Harvard Graphics to prompt for a box containing objects to move.

4. Press ENTER to select the current position.

Harvard Graphics prompts for the opposite corner.

5. Move the cross-hairs to below the lower-right corner of the box.
6. Press ENTER.

Harvard Graphics marks the three text objects and the box. Since Magazines and Periodicals are part of the underlying chart, you cannot accidentally select them.

7. Press ENTER to select Choose this from below the chart box.

Harvard Graphics displays a box representing the size of the objects you are moving and prompts you for where you want to move the objects.

8. Move the cross-hairs to the left so the right side of the box is below the "z" in the Magazines label.
9. Press ENTER to select the chosen location.

Harvard Graphics erases the box and text in the old position and draws them in the new position.

Another method of selecting a position is to enter the horizontal and vertical positions in the Horiz and Vert fields. You can use this method any time you are pointing to a location on the screen. This method is useful when you are aligning objects that you want to start with the same vertical or horizontal position.

As you have moved the cross-hairs to place and reposition objects, you may have noticed changes in the numbers next to the Horiz and Vert fields below the chart box. Harvard Graphics assigns each point on the chart a unique horizontal and vertical position. The horizontal positions start at the left side with 0 and continue to the right side with 26017. The vertical positions start at the bottom with 0 and continue to the top with 20000. To position objects using these fields, press F3 (XY position), type the horizontal position you want, press ENTER, type the vertical position you want, and press ENTER again. After you finalize the vertical position by pressing ENTER, Harvard Graphics moves the cross-hairs to the position you selected. For example, for step 8 of the previous example, you could have pressed F3 (XY position), typed **3500**, pressed ENTER, typed **8500** and pressed ENTER.

Sizing an Object

Another change you will want to make to an object is to resize it. For example, you may want to reduce the box and text that you added to the bar chart. Later, when you learn to add symbols, you may want to resize them if you are not satisfied with the size you first selected. When you size an object, you can change its height-to-width ratio. For example, if you size a polygon, you can make the resulting object appear elongated or contracted by making the ratio between the height and width different. You can also change an object's size and force the height-to-width ratio to remain the same.

You can try changing the size of the box and text inside it that you added to the chart by following these directions.

1. Select Size from the Modify menu.

Harvard Graphics prompts for the object you want to size.

2. Point to a position above and to the left of the box around the magazine titles.
3. Press ENTER to select the current position.

Harvard Graphics prompts for the opposite corner.

4. Move the cross-hairs to below the lower-right corner of the box.

This selects the box and the three text objects. Magazines and Periodicals cannot be selected.

5. Press ENTER to select the other corner of the box that will select objects.
6. Press ENTER to select Choose this from below the chart box.

Harvard Graphics displays a box representing the size of the objects and prompts you to position one of the corners. When you select a corner of the box, Harvard Graphics draws the selected objects so they have the same proportion to each other as they did originally. The selected objects are expanded or contracted depending on the increase or decrease in the size of the box.

7. Press SHIFT-LEFT ARROW.

When you hold down SHIFT as you press an arrow key or point with the mouse, Harvard Graphics preserves the height-to-width proportion. That is why, as you moved the corner to the left, the corner also moved up so the height of the box would be diminished by the same proportion as you diminished the width by pressing the LEFT ARROW. If you do not hold down SHIFT, you can change the height without changing the width or change the width without changing the height.

8. Press SHIFT-ENTER to select the chosen size.

Harvard Graphics erases the selected objects and draws them in their new size.

When you resize text, you do not change the height-to-width proportion. If you increase the size of the box that selects text objects, you also increase the text size. The proportion between height and width is determined by the text size. Changing the size of a text object cannot elongate the height or width independently.

Changing Object Options

Another change you may want to make is in the options an object used. When you added objects, you set how each object would appear by pressing F8 (Options) and setting the fields. Frequently when you are drawing, you may add an object and realize that you forgot to change the color or text size before you added the object. Rather than removing the object and drawing it again, you can change the settings for it. After you select Options from the Modify menu to change the options for an object, you must select the object or objects you wish to change. Once the objects are selected, Harvard Graphics displays the Options box for the object type selected. If multiple object types are in the group of objects selected, Harvard Graphics displays a Group options box which lets you select the fill color, outline color, and shadow color. The options box is set to the object's current selections. Any change you make in this box affects the current object.

You can try changing options by changing some of the attributes of the objects you have added to your chart. To change these object options, follow these steps:

1. Select Options from the Modify menu.

Harvard Graphics prompts for the object you want to change.

2. Point to a corner of the box and press ENTER.

By pointing to a box corner, you are away from the text so Harvard Graphics will correctly select the box as the object you want to change.

3. Press ENTER to select Choose this.

Harvard Graphics displays the Options box for boxes.

4. Press TAB to move to the Style field.

5. Type **6** to select a three-dimensional effect with the shadow going to the upper right.
6. Press F10 (Continue) since you are finished with selecting the options for this object.

Unlike Move and Size from the Modify menu, Harvard Graphics does not prompt you to select the next object to modify.

7. Select Options from the Modify menu.
8. Move the cross-hairs to the left of the "G" in "Gracious."

Move it further to the left than the box. Also, move it above the bottom line of the box. By specifically omitting part of the box, it will not be included in the box of objects you will select.

9. Press ENTER.
10. Move the cross-hairs to include all three text objects inside the box and press ENTER.

Since you omitted the bottom of the box, you can include the top of the box without selecting the box as an object to modify. You do not have to worry about selecting the chart data you added with a Chart Data form, because Harvard Graphics will not let you select this object.

11. Press ENTER to select Choose this.

Harvard Graphics displays the Options box for text. Notice that the text size is smaller than the 3 you entered initially; you reduced the text size when you reduced the size of the text objects.

12. Press TAB three times to move to the Bold field.
13. Select No so the text objects will not be boldface. The Text Options box has additional options. For example, you can select the color, italicize the text, or change the alignment. In the Font field you can select the font of the text.
14. Press F10 (Continue) since this is the only option setting you want to change.
15. Press ESC to return to the Draw menu.

Deleting Objects

While you are busy adding objects to the chart, you may also want to remove objects. The steps you learned to remove characters and field settings from chart data and forms do not affect drawn objects. You must select Delete from the Draw menu to remove an object. You then select Choose to remove a single object, Undo to restore an object you have removed, or All to remove all drawn objects in the current chart and start over. When you select All you cannot restore the chart's drawn objects later.

You can try deleting an object and restoring it by following these directions to delete and restore the box you drew:

1. Select Delete from the Draw menu.
2. Select Choose from the Delete menu.

Harvard Graphics prompts for the object you want to remove.

3. Point to the box corner to select this as the object you want to delete and press ENTER.

By pointing to a box corner, you are away from the other objects so Harvard Graphics will correctly select the object you want to change.

4. Press ENTER to select Choose this.

The box disappears and Harvard Graphics returns to the Delete menu.

5. Select Undo.

Harvard Graphics restores the last deleted object, which is the box you just deleted in this example. The undeleted object has the original position and attributes the object had when you deleted it.

6. Press ESC twice to return to the Main Menu.
7. Press CTRL-S to save the chart.
8. Press F10 (Continue) to save the chart using the same information.

Copying Objects

For some charts, you will be creating multiple copies of the same object. For example, in the chart in Figure 9-9, each of the keys is a box. Rather than creating a box for each key, it is simpler to add a box for the first key and copy it to the new locations. In charts like this where the same object is used more than once, making the object once and copying it is quicker than adding the object each time.

To copy one or more objects, select Copy from the Draw menu. Then select the objects you want to copy using the steps you performed previously to move, size, and set the options of objects. Harvard Graphics draws a temporary box indicating the size of the objects you will copy. Press the arrow keys or move the mouse in the direction you want to move the entire

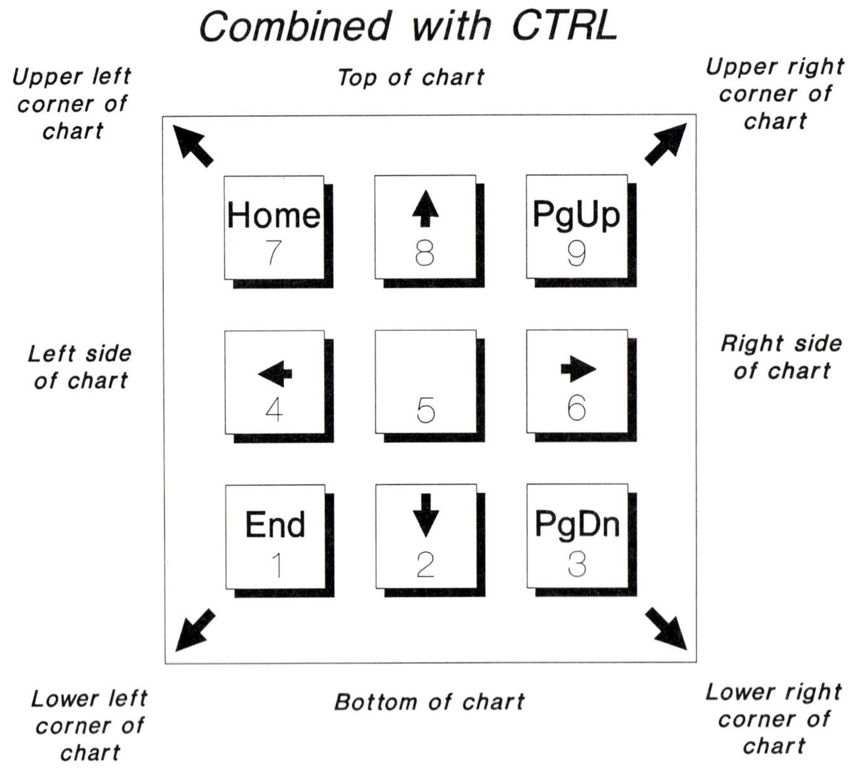

FIGURE 9-9. Chart created by copying box objects

box. When the box is positioned where you want the copy, press ENTER. Harvard Graphics assumes that you want to create additional copies until you press ESC. Therefore, after you make the first copy, another box is displayed. Harvard Graphics uses the direction and distance between the original and the first copy to determine where you want the next copy placed (provided the suggested placement fits on the chart). You can use this suggestion to make repeated copies at similar intervals.

Earlier in this chapter, Figure 9-7 displayed the possible styles for boxes. These boxes were created by repeatedly copying boxes to the next position. Once the boxes were copied, the style field was changed for each box using Options from the Modify menu.

You can try copying objects by following these steps:

1. Select Create new chart, Text, and Free form to remove the current chart from memory.
2. Press F4 (Draw/Annot) to change from the Free Form Text form to the Draw/Annotate screen.
3. Select Add.
4. Select Text.

Harvard Graphics prompts for the text you want to add.

5. Press F8 (Options) to change how the text will appear.
6. Press SHIFT-TAB twice to move to the Align field.
7. Press LEFT ARROW once and ENTER twice to left align the text.

As you add more text objects, Harvard Graphics will left align the text instead of centering, which is the default.

8. Type **Advantages** and press ENTER.

Harvard Graphics prompts for the text's location.

9. Press F3 (XY position).
10. Press CTRL-DELETE, type **2000** for the Horiz field, and press ENTER. Type **16000** for the Vert field and press ENTER.

11. Press ENTER to select this position.
12. Press F8 (Options).
13. Press TAB three times to move to the Bold field.
14. Select No.
15. Press F10 (Continue) to return to entering text.
16. Type **1.** and press ENTER.

Harvard Graphics suggests a left-aligned position below the "A" in "Advantages."

17. Press ENTER to accept this position.
18. Type **2.** and press ENTER twice to position this text below the 1.
19. Type **3.** and press ENTER twice to align the 3 with the 1, 2, and "A" of "Advantages."
20. Press ESC to return to the Add menu.
21. Select Box.

Harvard Graphics prompts for the first corner of the box.

22. Press F8 (Options) since you want to change how the box will appear.
23. Press TAB five times to move to the Fill field.
24. Select No.
25. Press F8 (Draw) to draw the box.
26. Press F3 (XY position).
27. Type **1500** for the Horiz field and press ENTER. Type **17000** for the Vert field and press ENTER.
28. Press ENTER to select this location.

Harvard Graphics prompts for the opposite corner.

29. Press F3 (XY position).
30. Type **12000** for the Horiz field and press ENTER. Type **10000** for the Vert field and press ENTER.
31. Press ENTER to select this location.

32. Press ESC twice to return to the Draw menu.
33. Select Copy.

Harvard Graphics prompts for the object you want to copy.

34. Move the cross-hairs below and to the right of the box so Harvard Graphics knows you want to select a block of objects.
35. Press ENTER.
36. Press CTRL-HOME to move the cross-hairs above and to the left of the box to include the text and box.
37. Press ENTER twice.

The first time you press ENTER, you are selecting the opposite corner of the box. The second time you press ENTER, you are selecting Choose this. Harvard Graphics prompts for where you want the objects copied.

38. Press F3 (XY position).
39. Type **14000** for the Horiz field and press ENTER. Type **17000** for the Vert field and press ENTER.
40. Press ENTER to select this location.

Harvard Graphics duplicates the box and text. Once you have the second copy, you can make further modifications to each copy.

41. Press ESC since you only want to make one copy.
42. Select Modify and Options.
43. Move the cross-hairs to the new copy of Advantages and press ENTER.
44. Choose Select next since Harvard Graphics selected the box.
45. Select Choose this after Harvard Graphics selects the text.
46. Modify the text to read Disadvantages and press ENTER.
47. Press F10 (Continue) since you are finished modifying the text object.
48. Press F2 (Preview). The chart looks like Figure 9-10.

At this point, you could add the advantages and disadvantages for the option this chart is illustrating. By copying the objects, the boxes have the same vertical position, and the three numbers for the objects are evenly spaced. To finish this chart, you would add a title and modify the numbered objects in each text box to list the advantages and disadvantages.

49. Press ESC twice to return to the Main Menu.

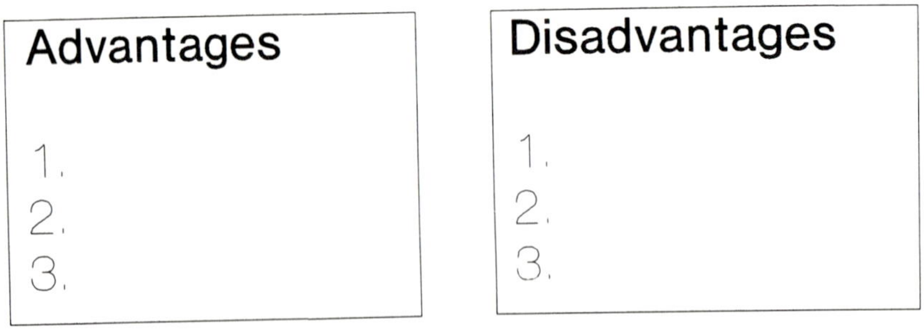

FIGURE 9-10. Chart created by copying objects

50. Press (F3) (Save) to save the chart.
51. Type **COPIES** for the filename and then press (F10) (Continue) to save the file.
52. Press (ESC) to return to the Main Menu.

Adding Symbols

For some of your charts you may be content with using the objects you add through Add in the Draw menu. On the other hand, you may want to add pictures of computers, people, and flowchart symbols to enhance the visual impact of your chart. While you can create these symbols with the objects available through the Add menu, you do not have to. Harvard Graphics provides 500 symbols available in symbol files that you can add to your charts. These symbols are shown in Appendix D, "Symbols Files." In addition, you can also use symbols from Release 2.12 of Harvard Graphics and from Harvard Graphics accessory programs such as Business Symbols or U.S. MapMaker.

You can add a symbol to your chart by following these steps:

1. Press (CTRL-G) to get a chart.
2. Select ACMESALE.CHT from the file list and press (ENTER).

3. Press ESC to remove the chart from the screen and return to the Bar/Line Chart Data form.

You can alternate between editing the chart using Edit/Enter chart and Draw/Annotate. The changes you make after selecting Edit/Enter chart do not affect the objects you create and modify using Draw/Annotate. Conversely, the changes you make after selecting Draw/Annotate do not affect the basic chart data you create by selecting Edit/Enter chart.

4. Press F4 (Draw/Annot) to display the chart in the Draw/Annotate screen.
5. Select Symbol from the Draw menu.

Symbols have their own menu since they have many options available that are unavailable for other objects and because the symbols are stored in separate files.

6. Select Get from the Symbol menu.

Harvard Graphics displays a list of symbol files in the current directory. The symbols found in each of these files are shown in Appendix D. Symbol files have a .SYM extension. If the symbol files are stored in a different directory, press UP ARROW to move to the Directory field and edit the directory that will contain the symbol files.

7. Select ANIPLANT.SYM from the file list.

Harvard Graphics displays all of the symbols in the file. Symbol files have up to 24 symbols.

8. Move the cross-hairs to the deciduous tree, which is the second symbol on the bottom row, and press ENTER.

Pointing to the symbol you want selects it from the symbol file. Once the symbol is selected, Harvard Graphics displays a box representing the object and prompts for the opposite corner of the box that will define the size of the object. Since Harvard Graphics places the symbol in the center of the chart, you may want to move the symbol now or add it in its current position and move it later.

9. Press BACKSPACE.

This removes the starting corner of the box. You can use this key to move the symbol as you add it.

10. Press CTRL-HOME to move to the upper-left corner of the chart.
11. Press ENTER.

Once you lock down one corner of the box, Harvard Graphics prompts you for the opposite box corner to determine the size and position of the symbol.

12. Move the cross-hairs to the same horizontal position as the bottom of "Books" and the same vertical position as the beginning of "Magazines".
13. Press ENTER.

Harvard Graphics draws the object in the box you have selected.

14. Press ESC to return to the Draw menu.

You can change the colors of this symbol so that only a single color is used.

15. Select Modify from the Draw menu.
16. Select Options since you want to change the colors.
17. Point to the tree and press ENTER.
18. Press ENTER to select Choose this.

Since this tree is several objects combined into a group, Harvard Graphics displays the option box for groups.

19. Type **1** for white for the outline color and press ENTER.
20. Type **16** for dark blue, the background color, to use as the Fill color and press ENTER.
21. Type **16** for the color to use for shadows in the object and press ENTER.

Harvard Graphics redraws the symbol using the new color selections. You can usually only select two or three colors for a symbol. With some objects that by default use more than two colors, you may lose detail by changing the colors. Most of the symbols, however, are designed to appear correct when printed with only the outline showing, which you did for the tree by using 1, 16, and 16 as the colors the objects or the symbols use.

22. Press (ESC) three times to return to the Main Menu.
23. Press (CTRL-S) to save the chart.
24. Press (F10) (Continue) to save the file using the same filename and description.
25. Press (CTRL-P) to print the chart.
26. Change any printing settings you want and press (F10) (Continue). Your chart looks like Figure 9-11.

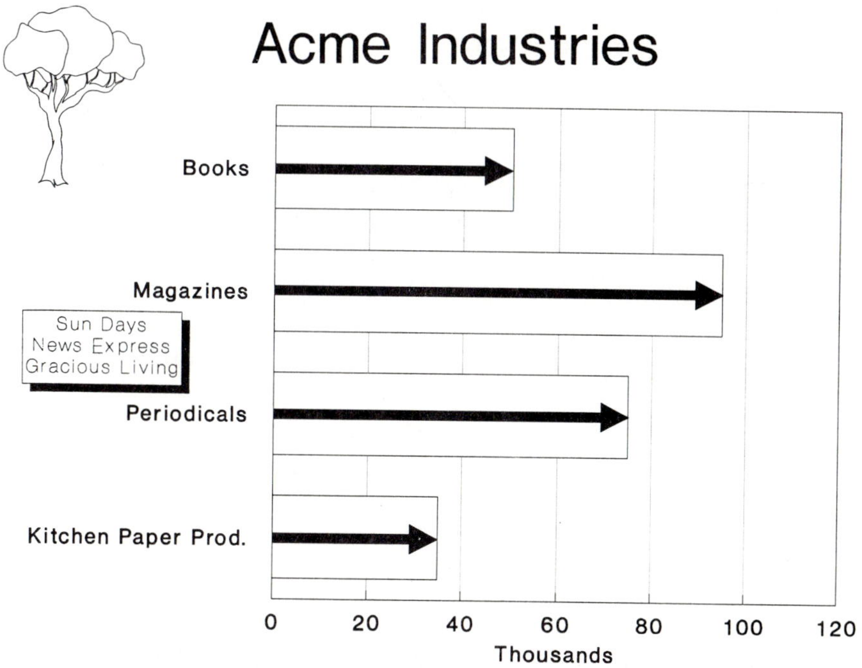

FIGURE 9-11. Final annotated chart

Since a symbol is an object to Harvard Graphics, you can modify the symbol with the same steps you performed to change other objects that you added. Harvard Graphics also has two accessory products, Business Symbols and Military Symbols, that you can use with your charts. These accessories are discussed in Chapter 13. You can also save a chart as a symbol, as discussed in the next section.

SAVING CHARTS AS SYMBOLS Another option for your charts is to save the chart as a symbol. For example, you can save a bar chart as a symbol and use it in a free-form chart. You can change the size and placement of the initial chart within the free-form chart. Figure 9-12 shows a chart created in this way. The two initial bar charts were saved as symbols. Once these charts were created and saved, a free-form chart was created that used these two charts as symbols. Saving the bar charts as symbols allows you to include in the free-form chart any text and symbols that overlay the space the bar chart uses.

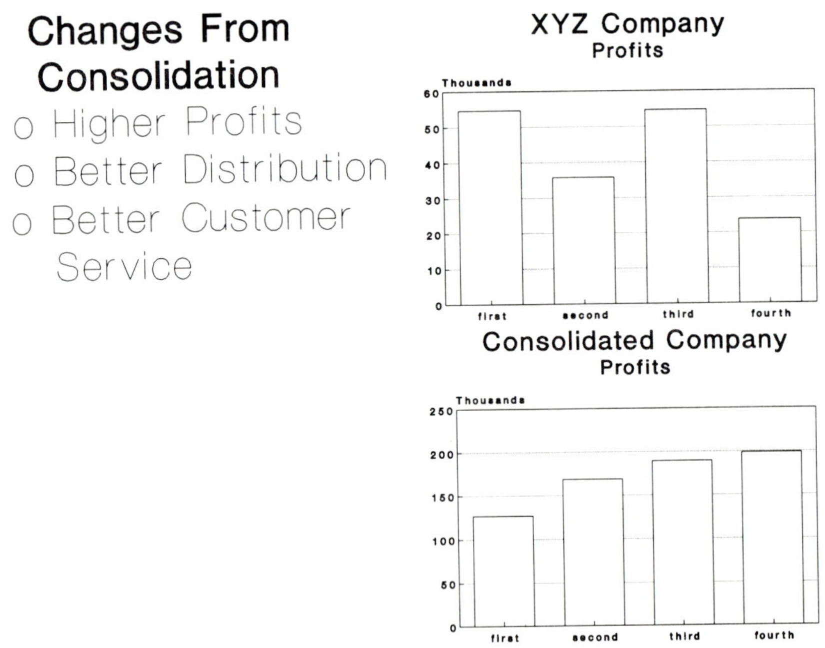

FIGURE 9-12. Chart created by saving bar charts as symbols

You can also use this feature to draw your company logo, save it as a symbol, and use the symbol in other charts. When you save a chart as a symbol, the symbol will not change if the data that originally created the chart changes. For example, if you save a bar chart as a symbol and the data the bar chart uses changes, you must save the chart as a symbol to use it again.

To save a chart as a symbol, follow these steps:

1. Select Get/Save/Remove from the Main Menu.
2. Select Save as symbol.

Harvard Graphics displays the Save Chart As Symbol overlay.

3. Type **MYCHARTS** as the name of the file you want the symbol saved as and press ENTER.

You can save the symbol to a new file or to an existing file. A symbol file can contain up to 24 symbols. You will want each symbol file to contain the same types of symbols so you can find them quickly.

4. If you will be using a plotter to print your charts, select Plotter in the For Device field.

Plotters cannot print well objects that overlay each other. In some cases, if two objects overlap, a plotter fills in the first object and then draws the second one on top. In this case the result may be an indistinguishable silhouette. Appendix B contains additional information about using plotters.

5. Press F10 (Continue) to save the symbol to a file.

If you provided a new filename in step 3, Harvard Graphics displays a New Symbol File overlay.

6. Type **Charts saved as symbols** as the new symbol file's description and then press F10 (Continue).

You only need to enter a file description the first time you save a symbol to a new symbol file. If you entered an existing symbol filename in step 3, the current chart would be added as a symbol to the end of the existing symbol file, and Harvard Graphics would not prompt you for a description. Once a symbol is saved to a file, you can use the symbol in the same way you use the symbols Harvard Graphics provides. Using the chart saved as a symbol in this example, you would enter the Draw/Annotate screen, select Symbol, Get, and MYCHARTS. When Harvard Graphics displays the chart you saved along with any other symbols you added to the file, you would select the symbol you want and then position and size the object just as you would a symbol that came from a symbol file that Harvard Graphics provided.

DRAW PARTNER

As your drawing skills improve, you will want to make changes that you cannot make through Harvard Graphics Draw/Annotate screen. Draw Partner is a Harvard Graphics accessory that comes with Harvard Graphics and can be used within Harvard Graphics. It is automatically installed when you install Harvard Graphics. With Draw Partner, you can perform all of the drawing functions available in the Harvard Graphics Draw/Annotate screen. In addition, you can rotate, flip, and align objects. You can add circular text, arcs, wedges, and freehand drawing. Other options let you zoom on a smaller area of the chart so you can focus on a portion of the chart. The more advanced features of Draw Partner allow you to sweep objects, add points, and group objects. In Draw Partner, you are creating a drawing rather than a chart. You can think of your creation in Draw Partner as a free-form Harvard Graphics chart where you add everything through the Draw/ Annotate or Draw Partner screen.

Using Draw Partner

To use Draw Partner, you can use the Applications menu or the speed key. Using the Applications menu, press F3 (Applications) and select Draw Partner. Using the speed key, press CTRL-D. The initial screen is shown in Figure 9-13. The box on the left contains Draw Partner's main menu. The box that occupies most of the screen is the drawing area where the current drawing will be displayed. The drawing area initially contains the current chart at the time you start Draw Partner.

Several of the menu options that you used in the Draw/ Annotate screen are also here in Draw Partner. For example, Add lets you add text, lines, polylines, polygons, circles, and rectangles. Unlike the Draw/Annotate screen, Move and Size are listed in the Main Menu. Under Modify you will find Options, which is like the same selection available on the Draw/Annotate

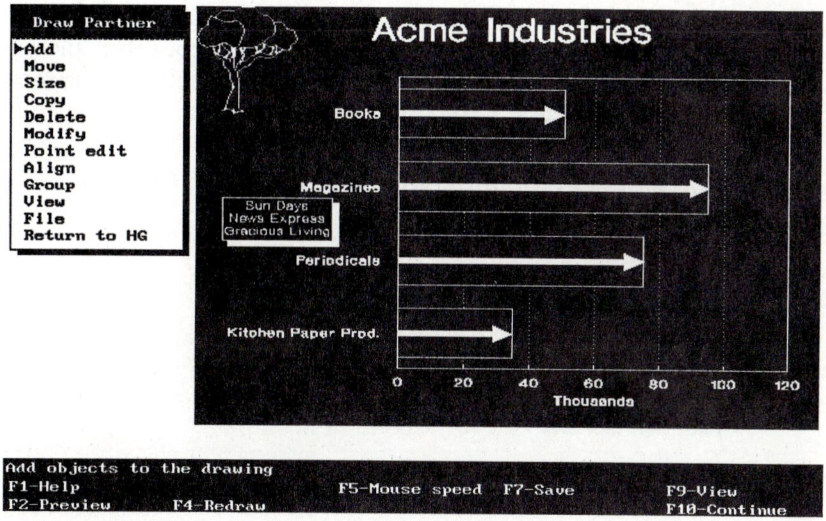

FIGURE 9-13. Initial Draw Partner screen

screen menu. Symbols are listed under File instead of their own menu as in the Draw/Annotate screen. All of the keys you used for the Draw/Annotate screen in Harvard Graphics work the same way in Draw Partner.

With the menu options available through Draw Partner, you can perform the same screen manipulations that you performed in Harvard Graphics. In addition, you can rotate objects, align objects, and zoom the area of the drawing to see it more closely. Other Draw Partner features not covered in this book allow you to edit individual points on existing objects, break and join lines, and group objects.

When you finish using Draw Partner, select Return to HG. After a moment, the screen will display Harvard Graphics with your chart intact. All the changes that you made in Draw Partner are in effect for the current chart.

Adding Objects with Draw Partner

Adding objects with Draw Partner is like adding objects in the Draw/Annotate screen in Harvard Graphics, with two minor differences. One difference is you can select menu items by typing the first letter if the menu item is the only one that starts with that letter. For example, you can select Copy or Size by typing a **C** or **S**. On the other hand, if more than one menu starts with the same letter, typing the first letter highlights the next menu item starting with that letter but does not select the menu item. You can see how easy it is to add objects to an empty drawing area by following these instructions:

1. Select Return to HG to return to Harvard Graphics.
2. Select Create new chart, Text and Free form.

This removes the existing chart from memory.

3. Press CTRL-D to start Draw Partner.
4. Select Add.
5. Select Text.

Instead of a Text Options box, Draw Partner shows a picture of the color, style, and size of the text in the right corner. If you do not like the way the text looks, you can change the text settings.

6. Press F8 (Options) to change the text settings.
7. Press ENTER to change the Size field.
8. Type **10** and press ENTER.
9. Press DOWN ARROW and ENTER to change the Color field.
10. Select White.
11. Press DOWN ARROW and ENTER to move to the Weight field.
12. Select Hollow Bold.
13. Press DOWN ARROW three times and press ENTER once to move to the Drop shadow field.

Draw Partner shows the different locations where you can add a shadow to the text.

14. Select Lower right.
15. Press F8 (Draw) since you have finished making your changes.

Instead of entering the text and positioning it, Draw Partner prompts for where you want the text to start. After you select a location for the text, you will enter the text.

16. Press HOME four times and LEFT ARROW four times to position the text.
17. Press ENTER.
18. Type **Is Your** and press ENTER.
19. Type **Career** and press ENTER.
20. Type **Doing This?** and press ENTER.
21. Press ESC twice since this is the last text you are adding.

The next object this drawing needs is a visual depiction of the career paths of the people this drawing wants to interest. Use a symbol in the ARROWS2 symbol file. Since this arrow is not initially pointing in the direction the drawing needs, you must rotate and flip it later.

22. Press ESC to return to the Draw Partner main menu.
23. Select File.
24. Select Get symbol.

If you need to change the directory containing the symbol files, press F3 (Change dir) and select a new directory before pressing F3 (Files) to list the symbol files.

25. Select ARROWS2.

Draw Partner displays the symbols.

26. Point to the last arrow on the bottom row.

Even though you selected the arrow, the arrow does not appear. The symbols you add through this menu will not appear until you return to the main menu. Since you do not see the symbol, it is tempting to add it again. Once you press ESC, you will see all of the symbols you have added.

27. Press ESC to return to Draw Partner's main menu.

The symbol now appears on top of the text you have added. Even though this is not the position you want nor the size you want, you can manipulate this object so you will have the arrow you want.

28. Select Size.

Draw Partner prompts for the object you want to size. You cannot select a box of objects to move, as you could in the Draw/Annotate screen. While you can assign multiple objects to a group and use the group as a single object, for this example you will change the objects one at a time. Creating groups is beyond the scope of this book.

29. Point to the arrow and press ENTER.

Like Harvard Graphics, Draw Partner puts four dots at the corners of the object. Unlike the Draw/Annotate screen, Draw Partner requires you to confirm your object selection only if there is a potential conflict. Since the arrow overlays the text objects, Draw Partner might think you want to modify the arrow or one of the text objects. If it knows that you can only be selecting one object, you do not have to confirm the object's selection. If the cross-hairs are pointing to a location where more than one object might be selected, Draw Partner displays a confirmation box. Select Next object until Draw Partner selects the correct object. When the correct object is chosen, select This object. When the object you want is chosen, Draw Partner draws a box representing the object and prompts you to change the position of one corner of the box.

30. Press HOME three times to expand the arrow, and then press ENTER.

Since you did not press SHIFT, the height-to-width ratio changes. In this example, the change is intentional.

31. Press ESC since this is the only object you want to change in size. Press F4 (Redraw). Your drawing looks like Figure 9-14.

At this point, you only need to change how the arrow points and its position. You can make these changes by rotating and flipping the arrow and then positioning it.

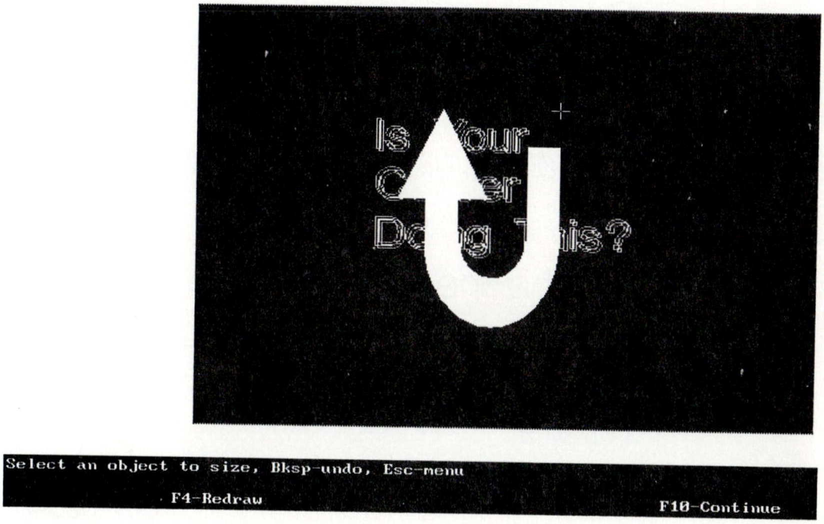

FIGURE 9-14. Initial drawing created with Draw Partner

Rotating and Flipping Objects

One of the deficiencies of the Draw/Annotate screen is its inability to rotate an object. For example, you may want to use the symbol of a hand pointing, but you want the hand pointing to the right instead of the left. Draw Partner has two ways you can change an object's orientation. You can either flip an object or you can rotate it. To visualize the difference, imagine putting your finger on the middle of an object. If you rotate the object, you can spin the object clockwise or counterclockwise, with your finger always remaining on the center point. If you flip the object, imagine a vertical and horizontal line crossing the point where you have your finger. You can flip the object around either line as long as the center point remains in place. Figure 9-15 shows how Draw Partner can rotate an object, in this case a symbol. Figure 9-16 shows how Draw Partner can flip an object.

You can try rotating and flipping an object using the drawing you created in the previous section. To flip and rotate the arrow, follow these directions:

1. Select Modify.

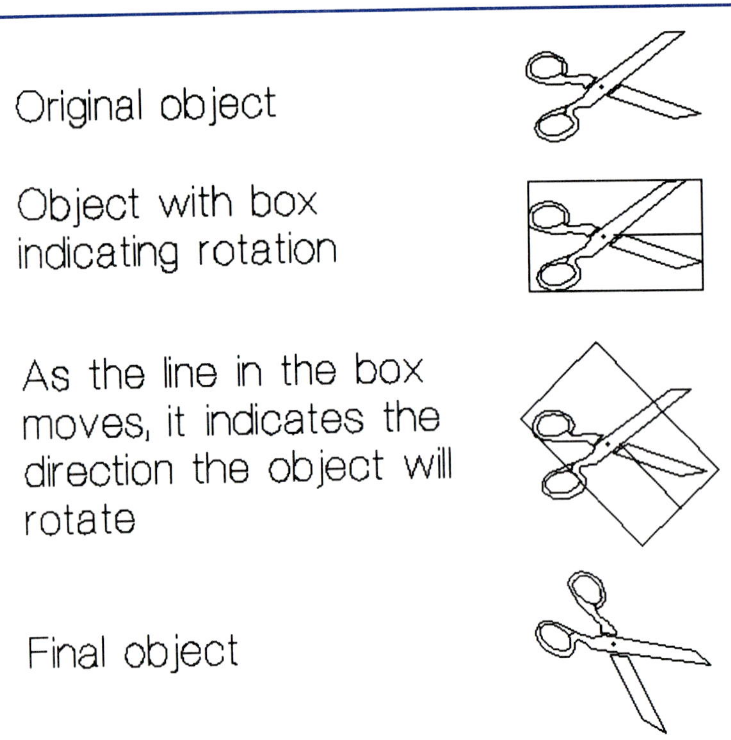

FIGURE 9-15. How Draw Partner rotates an object

Only the Options, Front, and Back selections are the same as the Draw/Annotate screen in Harvard Graphics. When you want to change the text in a text object, use Edit Text rather than Options.

2. Select Flip.

Draw Partner prompts you to select how you want to flip the object.

3. Select Horizontal.

Draw Partner prompts for the object you want to flip. Draw Partner cannot flip text, but it has a feature that converts text into polygons that you can flip. That feature is beyond the scope of this book.

4. Point to the arrow (away from the text) and press ENTER.

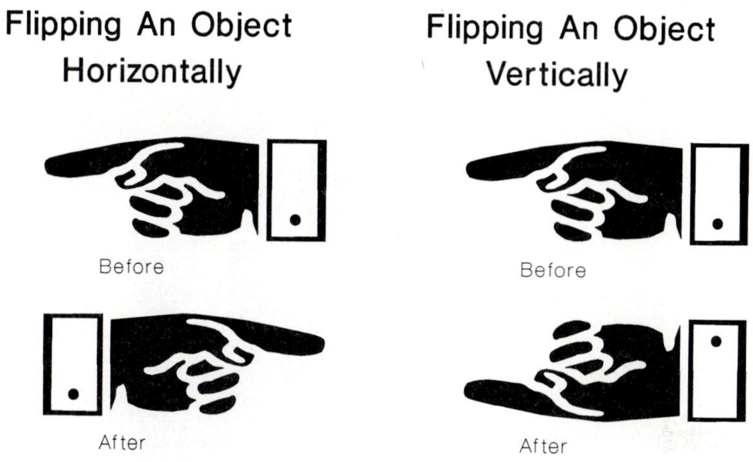

FIGURE 9-16. How Draw Partner flips an object

By pointing to the arrow away from the text, Draw Partner does not need a confirmation on the object you want to flip. Draw Partner flips the object on the screen.

5. Press ENTER again to flip it back to its original position.
6. Press ESC since this is the only object you want to flip.
7. Select Rotate.

Draw Partner prompts for the object you want to rotate.

8. Point to the arrow and press ENTER. The screen looks like Figure 9-17.

Draw Partner draws a box around the object with a line from the center of the box to the edge of the box where the cross-hairs are. At the bottom of the screen is the angle to which Draw Partner will rotate the object. You select the angle by moving the cross-hairs. As you move the cross-hairs, the box and line in the box from the center rotate to indicate the angle that the cross-hairs are selecting.

9. Press F6 (Type angle) to enter the angle of rotation.
10. Type **180** and press ENTER.
11. Press ESC twice to return to Draw Partner's main menu.

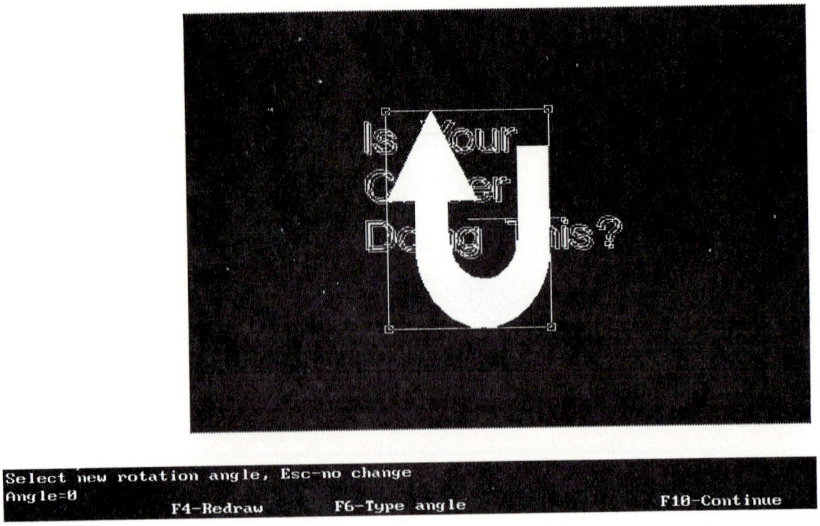

FIGURE 9-17. Rotating an object

Now that the symbol looks the way you want it, you can position the symbol where you want it. Since you can only rotate an object if the corners of the box that represents it do not extend beyond the edge of the drawing, you should rotate objects in the center of the drawing and move them to where you want them later.

12. Select Move.

Draw Partner prompts for the object you want to move. Like sizing an object, you can only move one object at a time.

13. Point to the arrow (away from the text) and press ENTER.

Like Harvard Graphics, Draw Partner draws a box representing the object and prompts you to select the object's position.

14. Move the box up and to the right so that it does not overlay the text and the arrow starts at the end of the third line of text.

15. Press ENTER and F4 (Redraw).

If you do not like the position, press ENTER to select the object again and move the arrow to where you want it. You can continue selecting and positioning the object until it is where you want it.

16. Press ESC since this is the only object you want to move. The drawing looks like Figure 9-18.

Looking Closer at the Drawing

When you are creating a drawing, you may want to look at the drawing more closely. Rather than looking at the computer screen from an inch away, you can expand a portion of the drawing to fill the drawing area. This lets you look at objects closely. Once you zoom the drawing size, you will want to change the drawing area you are viewing. This is called *panning*.

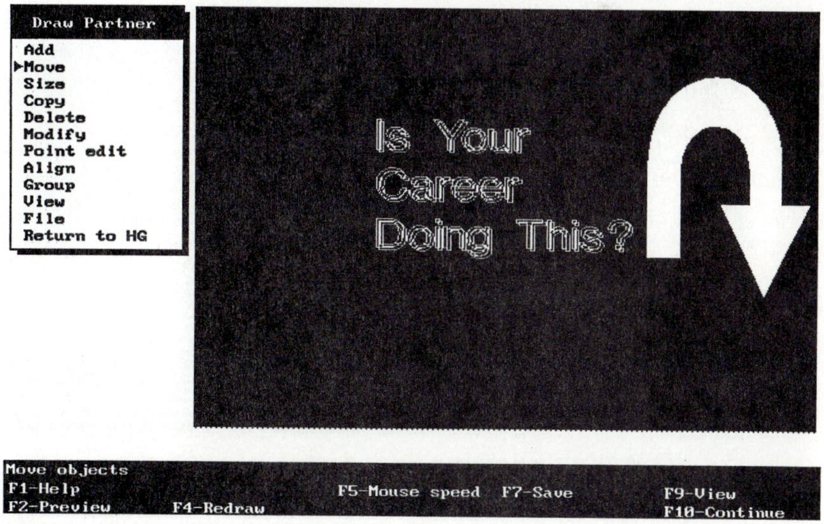

FIGURE 9-18. Drawing after changing object orientation and position

You can try the zooming and panning features of Draw Partner by following these steps:

1. Select View from the main menu or press F9 (View).

2. Select Zoom.

Draw Partner prompts for one corner of a box that will contain the part of the drawing Draw Partner will expand.

3. Move the cross-hairs above and to the left of the "Is Your" text object and press ENTER.

Draw Partner prompts for the other corner of the box. As you move the cross hairs, Draw Partner draws a box showing the current selection.

4. Move the cross-hairs below and to the right of the "Doing This?" text object and press ENTER. The screen looks like Figure 9-19.

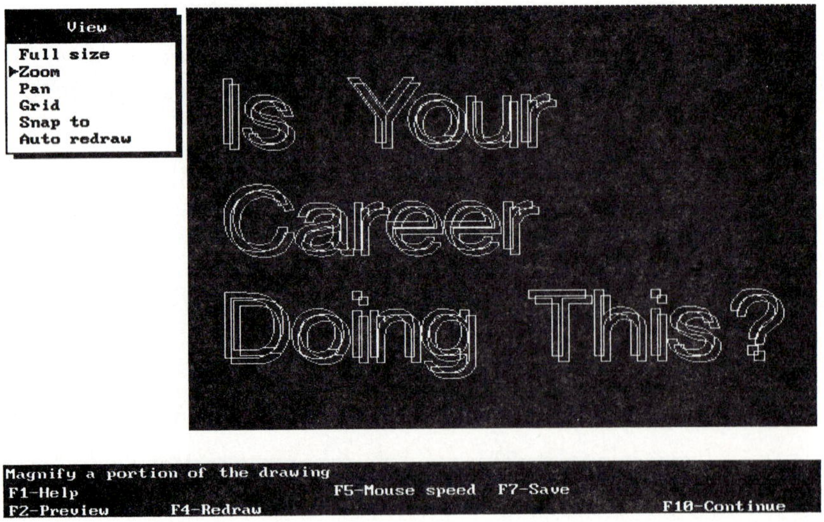

FIGURE 9-19. Zoomed drawing

Draw Partner expands the three text objects so they fill the drawing area. If you press F2 (Preview), you can see that this does not affect the object sizes. Zooming an area allows you to look at a drawing with a magnifying glass and to change the part of the drawing you are viewing in magnification.

5. Select Pan.

Draw Partner prompts for the part of the drawing area to which you want to pan. To pan to a different area, press the arrow keys so that a box representing the area of the drawing overlaps part of the drawing shown in the drawing area and part of the drawing that you want to see.

6. Move the box representing the area to pan the drawing to the right as much as possible and press ENTER.

Draw Partner shifts the area of the drawing shown in the drawing area to the right to show that part of the drawing. When you are looking at a drawing close up, you still have all of the options that were available when the drawing area showed the entire drawing. You can use this zoomed drawing to draw small objects that may be difficult to draw from an unzoomed drawing area. Since you do not want to change the drawing, you will want to return the drawing area to show the entire drawing.

7. Select Full size.

This selection returns the drawing area to show the entire drawing.

8. Press ESC to return to the Main Menu.

Aligning Objects

You have several methods available to align objects that you are adding. You can visually confirm that the objects are aligned and move them into position. In the Draw/Annotate screen, you learned how you can enter the vertical and horizontal position. Another option available in Draw Partner is letting Draw Partner align the objects for you. You can use the alignment features to quickly reposition objects. While alignment is usually thought of for numbers and text, you can use the alignment feature with other types of objects as well. To align objects, you must identify for Draw Partner the object you want to use as the basis for alignment and the other objects you want aligned with the selected object.

You can try these features by horizontally centering the text objects in the drawing shown in Figure 9-18 and vertically centering the arrow with the second text object. To align these objects, follow these steps.

1. Select Align from the Main Menu.

Draw Partner prompts for the object you want to use as the basis for aligning other objects.

2. Point to the "Is Your" text object and press ENTER.

Draw Partner prompts for how you want to align the object you select in relationship to the object you selected in step 1. Figure 9-20 shows how these different objects will appear.

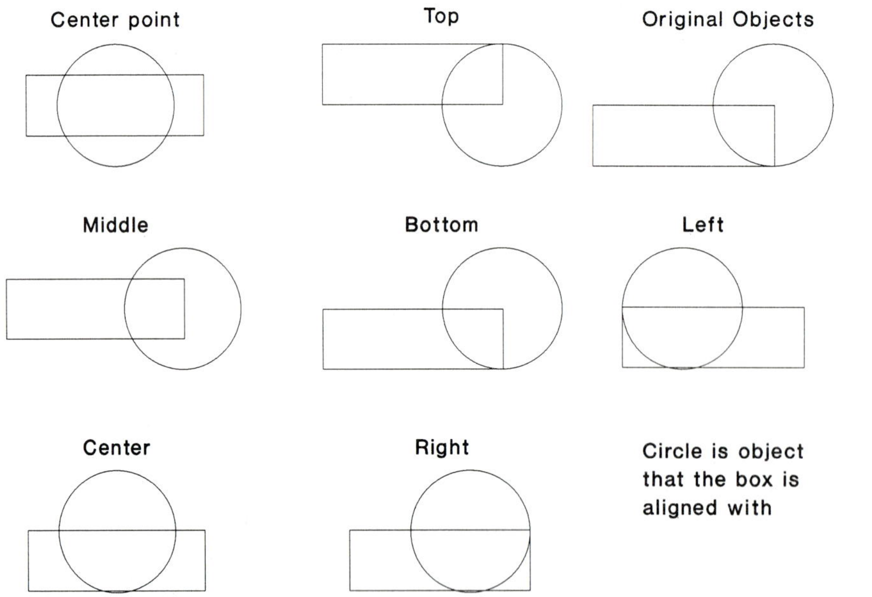

FIGURE 9-20. Different settings for aligning objects

3. Select Center.

Selecting Center changes the horizontal position of the objects so the selected objects are centered with the object selected in step 1. This selection does not change the vertical position. Draw Partner prompts you to select an object you want to align.

4. Point to the "Career" text object and press ENTER.

Draw Partner moves this text object slightly to the right to center it with the one above and then prompts for the next object to align.

5. Point to the "Doing This?" text object and then press ENTER.
6. Press ESC since this is the last object you want to horizontally align with the "Is Your" text object.

Draw Partner prompts for the next object you want to use as the basis for alignment.

7. Point to the "Career" text object and press ENTER.

Draw Partner prompts for how you want to align the object you will select in relationship to this object.

8. Select Middle.

Selecting Middle changes the vertical position of the objects so the selected objects are centered with the object selected in step 7. This selection does not change the horizontal position. Draw Partner prompts you to select an object you want to align.

9. Point to the arrow and press ENTER.

Draw Partner moves this object up so it is vertically centered with the second text object and then prompts for the next object to align.

10. Press ESC twice to return to the main menu since you do not want to align any more objects.
11. Press F2 (Preview) to display the drawing using the full screen. The drawing looks like Figure 9-21.

FIGURE 9-21. Drawing after text

12. Press any key to remove the chart from the screen.

This completes your drawing. Now you are ready to save it.

13. Select Return to HG.
14. Press ESC to return to the Harvard Graphics main menu.
15. Press CTRL-S to save the chart, type **INTROJOB** and press F10 (Continue).
16. Press CTRL-D to return to Draw Partner.

Saving Your Draw Partner Charts

You can save your Draw Partner charts in several file formats. The format you choose will affect what the file includes and how you access the data later. First, you can choose to save the file in Draw Partner's format. This is a good choice when you want to edit the drawing later using Draw Partner. Second, you can save the chart as a symbol which you can use on any other chart you create. Third, you can save the chart as a regular Harvard Graphics chart. When you choose this last approach, the saved chart does not include the chart background information. This means that none of your data or chart options are saved, only the Draw Partner additions to the chart. If you want to save everything as a Harvard Graphics chart, you must return to Harvard Graphics and use the Get/Save/Remove selection to save the chart.

You can try the different ways Draw Partner saves your drawings by following these steps.

1. Select File from Draw Partner's main menu.
2. Select Save drawing.

At this point, Draw Partner lists the Draw Partner drawing files in the current directory, which is the same directory as your Harvard Graphics files. The file list includes the selection New file, which you use to give the current drawing a different name than the ones listed. Above this is the current directory setting. Just as you altered the directory setting to load a symbol into a drawing, you can also alter the directory in which Draw Partner saves the files.

3. Press (ENTER) to select New file.

Draw Partner prompts for the name you want to give to the drawing.

4. Type **CAREER** and press (ENTER).

Draw Partner saves the drawing as a Draw Partner drawing file. If you had selected an existing filename in step 3, you would select Replace when Draw Partner prompted if you wanted the current drawing saved in the drawing file. Another option for saving your drawing is to save it as a Harvard Graphics free-form chart that you can print or use for slide shows.

5. Select Save as chart.

Draw Partner lists the chart files that are in the current directory. At the top is the current directory setting. Draw Partner includes in the chart files list a New file selection, which allows you to use a new name to save the chart.

6. Select New file.

Draw Partner prompts for the name of the chart.

7. Type **CAREER** and press ENTER.

Draw Partner creates a Harvard Graphics chart file containing the drawing you created in Draw Partner. Harvard Graphics considers this chart to be a free-form chart. Since drawing files, chart files, and symbol files use different extensions, you can use the same name for each file. When you save a file in Draw Partner, you are not prompted for a file description as you are in Harvard Graphics.

8. Select Save symbol.

Since the current directory is still the Harvard Graphics directory, you do not need to change the Directory field. Draw Partner lists all of the symbol files in the Harvard Graphics directory.

9. Select MYCHARTS.

Draw Partner adds this symbol to the symbol file you created earlier in the chapter. If you selected New file, you would have created a new symbol file. When you create a new symbol file, you are not prompted for a file description as you are in Harvard Graphics.

10. Press ESC to return to the main menu.
11. Select Return to HG to leave Draw Partner.
12. Press CTRL-G to get a chart.
13. Select CAREER.

Harvard Graphics displays the chart that you created in Draw Partner.

14. Press ESC twice to return to the Main Menu.

From this point you can print the chart, use it in a slide show, or select Draw/Annotate to modify the chart.

The next time you use Draw Partner you may want to edit the CAREER drawing or another drawing you have created with Draw Partner. You can either get the Harvard Graphics chart and then activate Draw Partner or you can activate Draw Partner and get the drawing file. To edit a saved drawing, select File from the main menu and then select Get Drawing. Select the file you want to edit from the list, changing the directory field if necessary. Once you have selected a file and pressed ESC to return to the main menu, the saved drawing will appear on the screen.

chapter 10

CREATING MULTIPLE CHART SCREENS AND SLIDE SHOWS

Getting Started
Creating Multiple Charts
Creating a Slide Show

All your Harvard Graphics activities thus far have focused on one chart at a time. Even the pie chart that showed two pies on the screen was defined as a single chart file. In this chapter you will explore features that allow you to create screens containing multiple charts. These screens display as many as six separate text and analytical charts. A multiple chart is in effect a composite chart created from several individual charts that were previously defined and saved. The completed multiple chart can be saved as a single chart. It can be printed or used in any way you have used single chart files.

A slide show is another way to work with more than one chart. A slide show is a collection of either single or multiple charts, other slide show files, bit-mapped files created with paint programs, and templates. You can also use buttons in a slide show to change the order of the slides presented. You can preview a slide show on your computer screen or you can use it as a way of batching output to a printer, plotter, or film recorder. ScreenShow features can supplement the basic slide show features and allow you to add special effects and timed screen displays. ScreenShow also allows you to create practice cards for your notes or a menu so users can make selections that control the show.

Once you have created your screen shows, you can copy the slide shows to a new location. Harvard Graphics includes a ShowCopy utility to move your slide shows to a new location. Using the ShowCopy utility insures that all of the files used in a slide show are in the new location. This feature is sold as part of a separate ScreenShow accessory but is included in Harvard Graphics 2.3.

In this chapter you will have an opportunity to create multiple charts with chart files from earlier chapters. If you did not create those charts, you can use any chart files on your disk. You will also have an opportunity to organize a slide show of screens and try the special ScreenShow features that can create professional quality output.

GETTING STARTED

In this exercise you first will create a multiple chart from two charts you made in earlier chapters. You then will create a slide show that will print or display each of the charts.

Follow these steps to begin:

1. Select Create new chart from the Main Menu.
2. Select Multiple chart.

Harvard Graphics displays several options that allow you to determine what type of multiple chart you want to create. The standard options use either two, three, or four charts in pre-defined locations, as shown in Figure 10-1. The dots beneath each choice show how the charts will be arranged when printed or displayed. The size and placement of the dots indicate the relative size and placement of the charts.

3. Select Two.

Harvard Graphics displays the Edit Multiple Chart screen, which displays the files in the current directory at the top of the screen. Two positions in

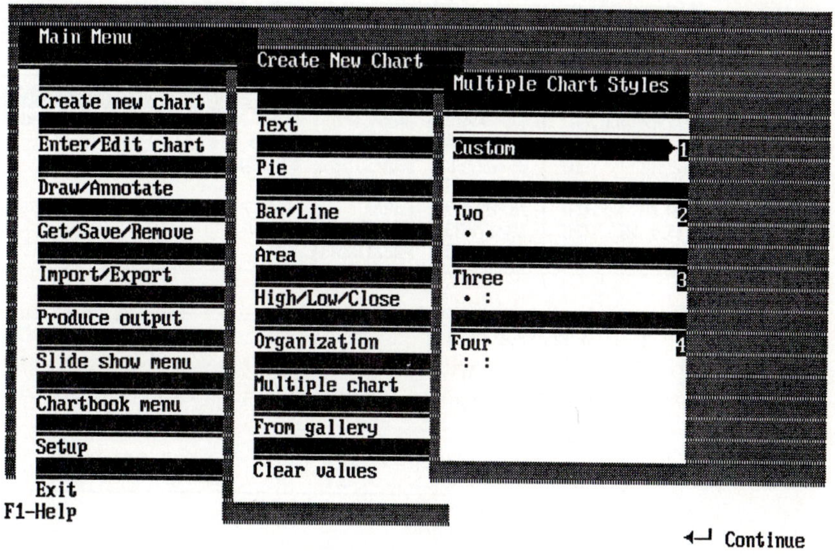

FIGURE 10-1. Multiple chart selections

the middle are used for the filenames of the two charts to be included. You can type names in this area or use the arrow keys to highlight the names of the files you want to include and press (ENTER). Figure 10-2 shows the chart currently highlighted, but you can use the arrow keys to change this entry. Press (ENTER) after making your selection.

4. Press (PGDN) or the (DOWN ARROW) key until the cursor is positioned on the first filename you choose. The filename should have an extension of .CHT. For this example the filename selected will be PIESALE, created in Chapter 4.

5. Press (ENTER) to select the filename.

The cursor moves to the next line for specifying the second chart.

For this example LINE1 created in Chapter 3 will be used as the second chart. You can use any other chart file in the current directory. It is important that you use the same directory because all chart files in a multiple chart must be stored in the same directory.

6. Press (ENTER) to select the second chart you have highlighted.

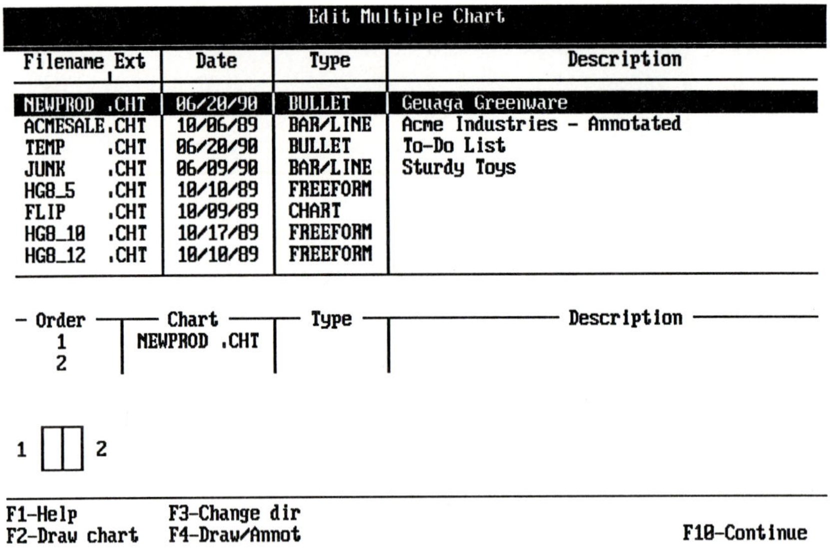

FIGURE 10-2. Highlighting a chart to include in the multiple chart

7. Press (F2) (Draw chart) to display the chart shown in Figure 10-3.
8. Press (ESC) until the Main Menu appears.
9. Choose Get/Save/Remove.
10. Choose Save chart.
11. Type **MULTICHT** and press (ENTER).
12. Type **A few charts** and press (F10) (Continue).

This step saves the multiple chart to disk in a .CHT file, just like the .CHT files created for single files.

Now that you have created a multiple chart, you can print it, use it as part of a slide show, or save it for later reference.

Follow these steps to create a slide show consisting of two screens:

1. Press (ESC) to return to the Main Menu.
2. Select Slide show menu to display the menu shown in Figure 10-4.
3. Select Create slide show.

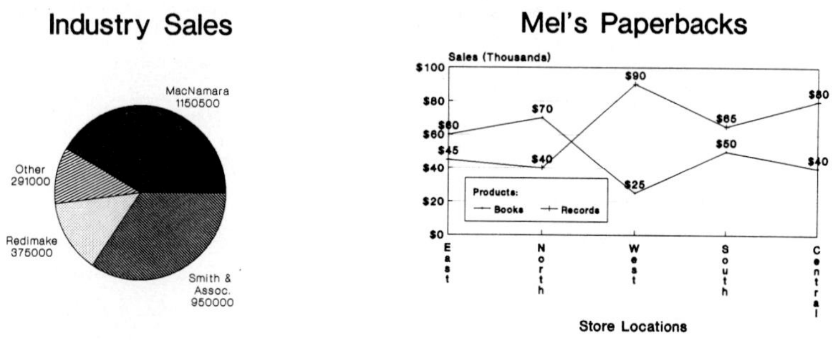

FIGURE 10-3. Multiple chart created from two charts

4. Type **Books** as the name of the file for the slide show, and press ENTER.

You must follow the same naming conventions used for chart files. When Harvard Graphics saves the file it will add .SHW as the filename extension.

5. Type **Book convention presentation** as a description of the slide show contents.

Your entries will look like this:

```
Create Slide Show

Directory: C:\HG

Slide show name: Books

Description: Book convention presentation
```

6. Press F10 (Continue).

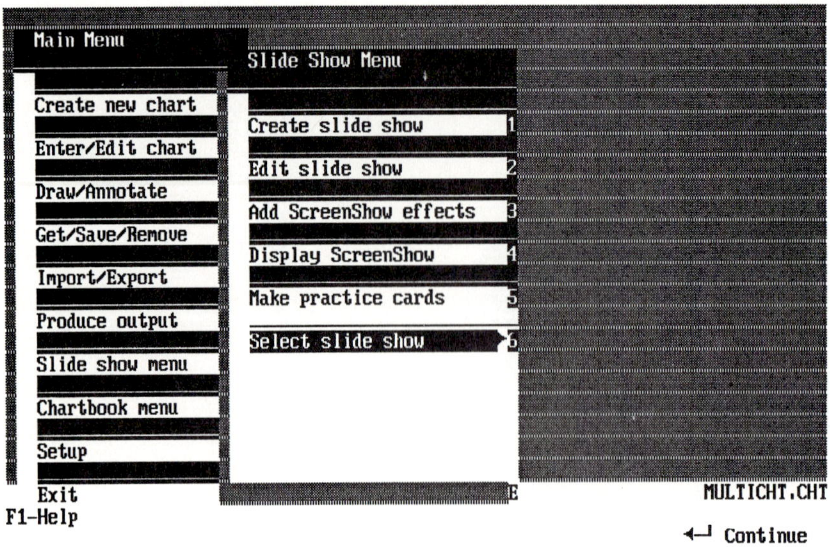

FIGURE 10-4. Slide Show Menu

The Create/Edit Slide Show screen appears for you to use in selecting charts that will be part of the slide show. Your screen will look similar to Figure 10-5, except the filenames will vary depending on the names of the files in your current directory.

7. Press DOWN ARROW or PGDN until PIESALE is highlighted, and then press ENTER.

If you did not create this chart in Chapter 4, you can use any other chart file in your current directory.

8. Use the arrow keys until LINE1 is highlighted, and then press ENTER.

If you did not create this chart in Chapter 3, use any other chart from your current directory.

9. Press ESC until the Slide Show Menu reappears.
10. Select Display ScreenShow, and then press ENTER to advance from slide to slide. You can also use CTRL-E at any time to access the data form for the graph being displayed. You can make changes to the chart data from this form.

Create/Edit Slide Show

Filename Ext	Date	Type	Description
FIG2_G .CHT	09-05-89	BAR/LINE	Sturdy Toys
FIG2_A .CHT	09-05-89	BAR/LINE	Multi-bars
FIG2_B .CHT	09-05-89	BAR/LINE	Multi-bars
FIG2_C .CHT	09-05-89	BAR/LINE	Multi-bars
SLS_90 .CHT	09-06-89	BAR/LINE	1990 sales data for Sturdy Toys
SLSPROJ .CHT	09-06-89	BAR/LINE	Projected sales 1990 - 1993

Show name: BOOKS .SHW

Order	File	Type	Description
1	FIG2_G .CHT		

Show description: Book convention presentation

F1-Help

F10-Continue

FIGURE 10-5. Create/Edit Slide Show form

CREATING MULTIPLE CHARTS

You had an opportunity to take a quick look at multiple charts in the "Getting Started" section of this chapter. There are many other options that you can use to tailor the display on the screen to match your needs. As an example, you can add a text chart to the screen with one or two analytical charts to the right of the text. You also can choose to create a multiple chart with up to six charts on one screen.

Creating a Multiple Chart from Three Charts

You can create a multiple chart with three charts following the same basic steps you used to create a multiple chart with two charts. In this example you will use a text file as one of the charts. You can mix and match text and analytical charts in multiple charts.

Follow these steps to create a three-chart multiple chart:

1. Press (ESC) to return to the Main Menu.
2. Select Create new chart.
3. Select Multiple chart and then select Three.

In the next three steps, you will select three charts. If you do not have these charts on your disk, select any other charts that you might have available.

4. Highlight INTERNAT and press (ENTER) to select the text chart of international representatives you created in Chapter 6.
5. Highlight PIESALE and press (ENTER) to select the pie chart created in the "Getting Started" section of Chapter 4.
6. Highlight LINE1 and press (ENTER) to select one of the line charts you created in Chapter 3. Your Edit Multiple Chart screen looks like Figure 10-6.

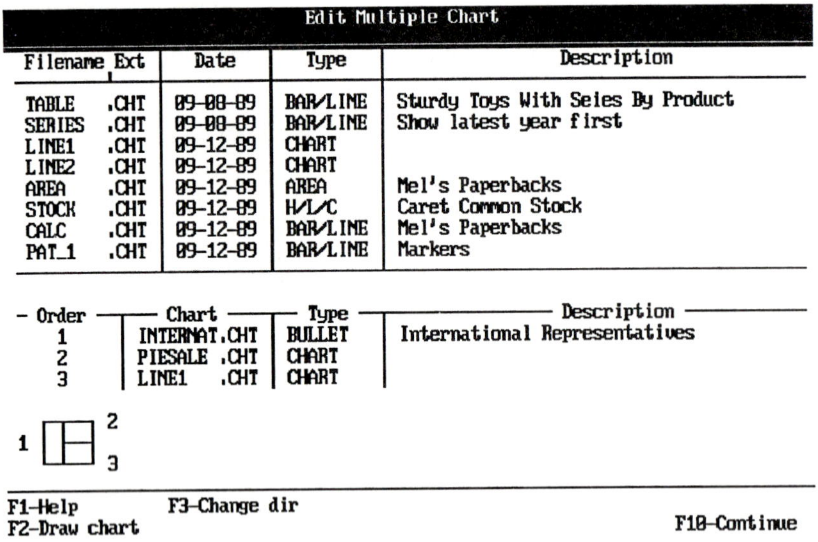

Edit Multiple Chart

Filename	Ext	Date	Type	Description
TABLE	.CHT	09-08-89	BAR/LINE	Sturdy Toys With Seles By Product
SERIES	.CHT	09-08-89	BAR/LINE	Show latest year first
LINE1	.CHT	09-12-89	CHART	
LINE2	.CHT	09-12-89	CHART	
AREA	.CHT	09-12-89	AREA	Mel's Paperbacks
STOCK	.CHT	09-12-89	H/L/C	Caret Common Stock
CALC	.CHT	09-12-89	BAR/LINE	Mel's Paperbacks
PAT_1	.CHT	09-12-89	BAR/LINE	Markers

Order	Chart	Type	Description
1	INTERNAT.CHT	BULLET	International Representatives
2	PIESALE .CHT	CHART	
3	LINE1 .CHT	CHART	

1 2 3

F1-Help F3-Change dir
F2-Draw chart F10-Continue

FIGURE 10-6. Edit Multiple Chart form for a three-chart multiple chart

7. Press (F2) (Draw chart) to view a chart that looks like Figure 10-7.

Notice that chart 1 occupies the left side of the screen and charts 2 and 3 split the right side. All three charts are automatically sized for you to fit within the positions determined for each chart number.

8. Press (ESC) twice to return to the Main Menu.
9. Press (CTRL-S), type **MULT3**, and press (F10) (Continue).

Creating a Custom Multiple Chart

Custom multiple charts offer the most flexibility. You can place up to six charts on one page. Although Harvard Graphics will select an initial position for the charts, you can change the size and placement of these charts yourself. Follow these steps to create a custom multiple chart:

1. Select Create new chart.
2. Select Multiple chart.

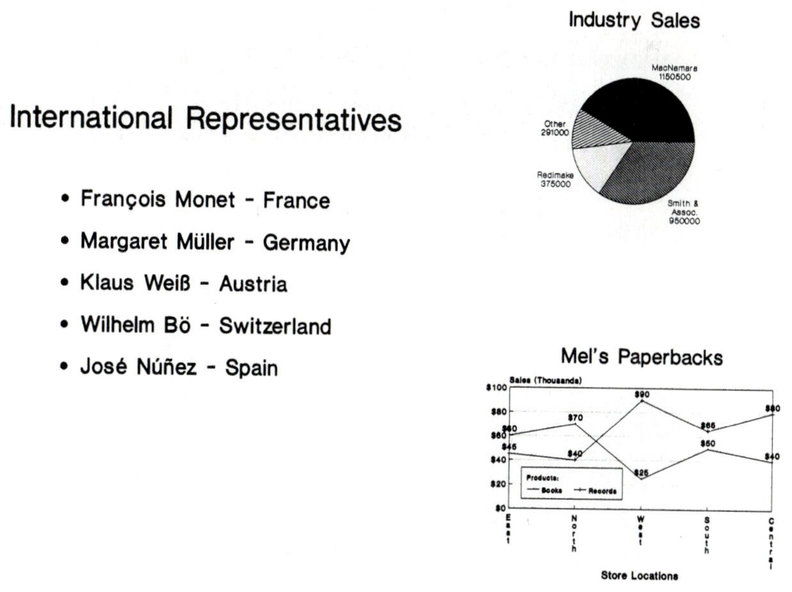

FIGURE 10-7. Multiple chart containing three charts

3. Select Custom. Press the spacebar and (ENTER) to remove the current chart data.

The same Edit Multiple Chart screen that you have used to create other multiple charts appears.

4. Highlight LINE1 and press (ENTER).
5. Highlight PIESALE and press (ENTER).
6. Highlight INTERNAT and press (ENTER).
7. Press (F7) (Size/Place) to reposition and size the charts, and then highlight PIESALE.CHT and press (ENTER) as shown in Figure 10-8.

This screen allows you to select the chart you want to move or resize.

8. Press (CTRL-UP ARROW) once and the (LEFT ARROW) eight times to move the cross-hairs, which represent one corner of the box, up and to the left to define the beginning of a square slightly larger than the current graph.

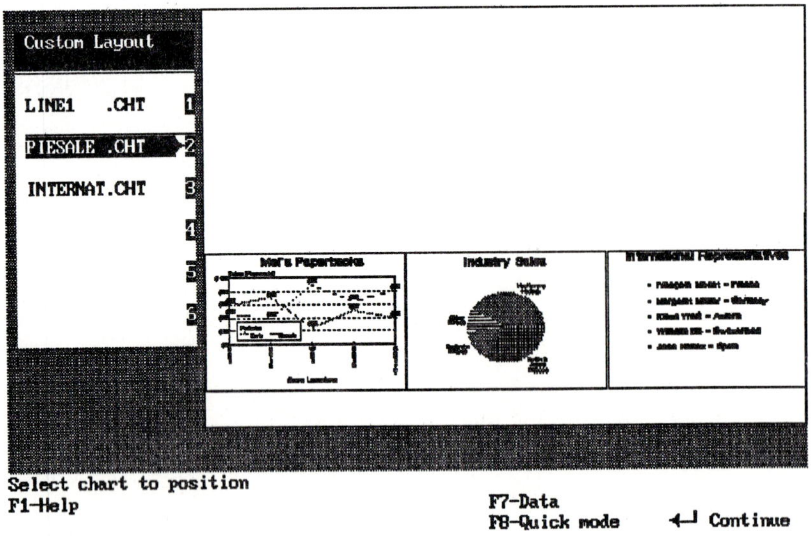

FIGURE 10-8. Sizing and placing charts in a custom multiple chart

9. Press (ENTER) once you have positioned the first corner of the box, and then press (PGDN) twenty times to move the cross-hairs for the lower-right corner, making the box even with the top of the INTERNAT chart but slightly to the right of its leftmost edge. Press (ENTER).

Harvard Graphics moves the chart above the other two, although you may see a few remnants in some cases. These remnants disappear if you escape to the menu and press (F2) (Draw chart) again. If you print the chart, it looks like Figure 10-9.

Printing a Multiple Chart

Printing a multiple chart is no different than printing a single chart. First you must make sure it is the current chart. Next you can select Produce output from the Main Menu. When you choose your output device, the same forms used for single charts appear for your selections. Press (F10) (Continue) to start the actual print operation.

To print the current graph, try these steps:

1. Press (ESC) to return to the Main Menu.

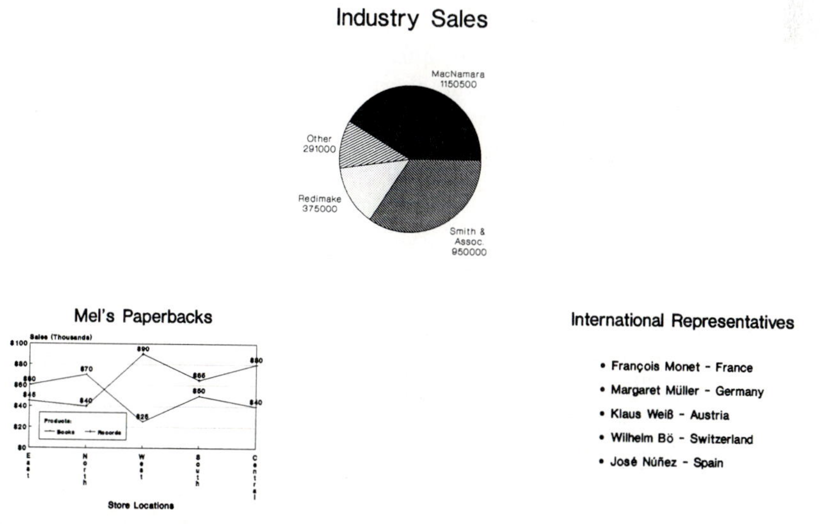

FIGURE 10-9. Custom multiple chart

2. Press CTRL-P to print the chart.
3. Review the current settings, make any required changes, and press F10 (Continue).
4. Press CTRL-S to save the multiple chart.
5. Type **MULTCUST** as the chart name and press ENTER.
6. Type **Customized multiple chart** and press ENTER to save the multiple chart.

CREATING A SLIDE SHOW

In the "Getting Started" section of this chapter, you created a slide show that consisted of two charts. You can add as many as 90 charts to a slide show and use the special ScreenShow effects, which include timing for the image on the screen and methods for drawing and erasing the images placed on the screen. If you have a copy of the ScreenShow Utilities, discussed further in Chapter 13, you can even create .PCX files of screens from other programs which you can add to your screen presentation.

In this section you will learn how to edit a slide show and add special effects. You can use the chart files created in earlier chapters or any other charts or bit-mapped graphic images you have in the directory.

In Harvard Graphics 2.3, you can also add buttons to the chart to select the next slide within a slide show that you will see. This lets you create interactive slide shows and slide shows that you can customize to your presentation. Unlike the charts that you create, Harvard Graphics saves the slide show as you make changes to it. This means that you never have to explicitly save your slide shows. Harvard Graphics saves them when you leave a screen to alter a slide show and return to the Slide Show Menu.

The Basic Creation Process

You are not limited to a single slide show. Each time you want to create a new one, you follow the same basic steps covered in the second section of the "Getting Started" exercise. After you select Slide show menu from the Main Menu, choose Create slide show. Next, enter a slide show name and description before pressing F10 (Continue). You can use the arrow keys to highlight the name of a file that you want to use. You can add files with a .CHT, .TPL, .PIC, or .PCX extension. The last two are graphic image files that are created in other programs. After highlighting a file, press ENTER to add it to the show list. You can continue to select files until you have included all the charts and images you want. When you are ready to work with a different show, you can use Select slide show options from the Slide Show Menu.

Adding Screens to an Existing Slide Show

After you preview a slide show, you may decide that you need to add some additional charts. You can do this with the Edit slide show option in the Slide Show Menu. If there is no active slide show, highlight the name of the slide show you want to edit and press ENTER. If a slide show is active, the Create/Edit Slide Show form is displayed immediately. You can add two additional charts to the slide show you created in "Getting Started" by following these instructions:

1. Select Slide show menu.
2. Select Edit slide show.

The Create/Edit Slide Show form appears on the screen. This screen has several parts, including a list of the files in the current directory at the top of the screen and a list of the slides selected thus far beneath it.

If the slide show you want to use is not active, you must use Select slide show, highlight the show name, and press ENTER before selecting Edit slide show.

3. Check to be sure the highlight displays in both the file list at the top of the screen and the show list beneath it. Any time the highlight does not appear in both places, press TAB until it does.
4. Highlight INTERNAT in the file list and press ENTER.
5. Highlight LINE2 and press ENTER.
6. Press F10 (Continue).
7. Select Add ScreenShow effects from the Slide Show Menu.
8. Press F2 (Preview show) to start the show.
9. Press ENTER to advance from screen to screen in the show until the ScreenShow Effects form displays again. You can also use the

LEFT ARROW and RIGHT ARROW keys to view the preceding or subsequent screen in the slide show.

Deleting Screens from a Slide Show

If you have a file in the show list that you no longer need, you can delete it easily. With the Create/Edit Slide Show form active you can move the highlight to the bottom of the screen. If the highlight displays in both the file list and the show list, press TAB to make the change. The first time you press TAB, Harvard Graphics lets you delete or move charts. By pressing TAB a second time, you can change the slide show file description. Use the arrow keys to move to the filename that you want to delete. Next press CTRL-DELETE to remove the filename. To change the highlight so it also is displayed in the file list at the top of the screen, you can press TAB until it is displayed in both places.

Use these steps to delete the LINE2 chart from the show:

1. Press ESC to return to the Slide Show Menu.
2. Select Edit slide show from the Slide Show Menu.
3. Press TAB to display the highlight only in the show list.
4. Press CTRL-DELETE to remove the slide from the show with the highlight on LINE 2.
5. Press F10 (Continue) when you are finished deleting files.

Outputting the Slide Show

Once you create a slide show, you can display it on your computer screen or output it to another device. When you want to use the screens as part of a presentation, displaying it on a screen can make your presentation easier. If you need a printed copy of the charts, printing the slide show rather than the individual charts allows you to make one request to handle all the printing. This grouping of charts for printing is referred to as *batching* the print output.

DISPLAYING THE SLIDE SHOW ON YOUR SCREEN You can stop the boldfacing, insert a space, and return to the normal font at this point. You can display the charts in the slide show on your screen one by one with the F2 (Preview show) option after selecting Add ScreenShow effects or with Display ScreenShow. When you display a slide show, the first chart in the slide show displays. Without ScreenShow special effects, covered later in the chapter, you must press ENTER to tell Harvard Graphics when to change the chart on the screen. You saw this feature in action in the section on adding charts to a slide show.

OUTPUTTING THE SLIDE SHOW TO A PRINTER If you have a large number of charts to print, printing them one by one can be a slow process. While the printer is printing one chart you cannot work on another chart because the resources of your computer are dedicated to the print process. The length of time is too short to leave the office and proceed with other activities, yet it is too long to sit idly by the printer waiting for one chart to print before you can request another. The solution is in printing a batch of charts together. Although this process does not make any individual chart print more quickly, you can start the process and know that you can leave, attend to other tasks for a half hour or so, and return to the entire batch of charts printed from the one request.

The first step in printing a batch of charts is to define a slide show that contains each of the charts that you want to print. You can follow these steps to print the slide show:

1. Choose Select slide show.
2. Highlight the name of the slide show you want to use and press ENTER. For this example, BOOKS is the name of the slide show that was used.
3. Press ESC to return to the Main Menu and select Produce output.
4. Select Print slide show.

The Print Slide Show Options form appears. You can print with the default settings by pressing F10 (Continue), or you can change one or more options first.

5. Press the spacebar twice to change the quality to High.
6. Press ENTER twice to accept a chart size of Full. The chart will be a full page.

To use one of the other sizes you would use the spacebar to effect the change. Choose one of the other selections to fit more than one chart per page; for example, 1/2 prints two charts on a page.

7. Press ENTER to accept Letter for Paper size.
8. Press ENTER for Printer 1.
9. Press ENTER to accept No for the Color option.
10. Press ENTER to accept No for the Print to disk option.

The default for the next two settings is to print every slide in the slide show.

11. If you do not want to print all the slides, change the From slide and To slide fields.
12. Change the number of copies if you want more than one.
13. If you are printing more than one copy, you can change the default for Collate to No if you want all copies of the first chart printed before printing any copies of the second chart. The Print Slide Show Options form now matches Figure 10-10.

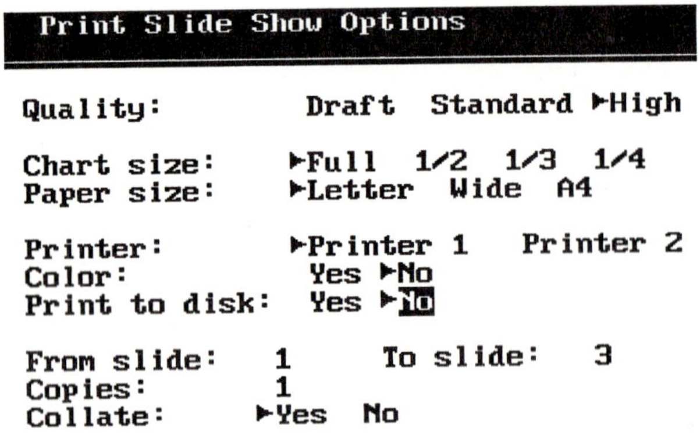

```
Print Slide Show Options

Quality:            Draft  Standard ►High

Chart size:         ►Full  1/2  1/3  1/4
Paper size:         ►Letter  Wide  A4

Printer:            ►Printer 1   Printer 2
Color:               Yes ►No
Print to disk:       Yes ►No

From slide:     1       To slide:    3
Copies:         1
Collate:       ►Yes  No
```

FIGURE 10-10. Print Slide Show Options screen

14. Press F10 (Continue) to begin printing.

Using Practice Cards

Most presenters practice the material in their presentation a few times to develop a level of comfort with the material and format before making their final presentation. Harvard Graphics helps you organize for this task and will allow you to create practice cards containing text or notes for each slide. You can use these while getting ready for a presentation, and you can print a copy to serve as your final notes on the day of the presentation. Even though you will not want to read from them, having a copy handy can help you relax and make a better presentation.

CREATING AND REVISING PRACTICE CARDS You can place statistics, key words, or an outline of your presentation for a slide on a practice card. A separate card is available for each slide in a show and displays key information, like the name of the chart and the slide number and description.

Follow these steps to add a practice card for the PIESALE chart:

1. Select Slide show menu from the Main Menu.
2. Select Make practice cards from the Slide Show Menu.

A blank practice card for the first file in the show list is displayed (see Figure 10-11).

3. Type **Overview of industry sales patterns and the industry domination by several large chains.**

Harvard Graphics automatically handles word wrap at the end of a line, freeing you to concentrate on the contents of your entry.

4. Press TAB twice to move to the Display time field.
5. Type **0:15** to set the display for 15 seconds.

This is one way to set the display time. Another way to set a 15-second display time is to type **15**, and Harvard Graphics assumes your entry is in seconds. You can also use Add ScreenShow effects to set a default time for

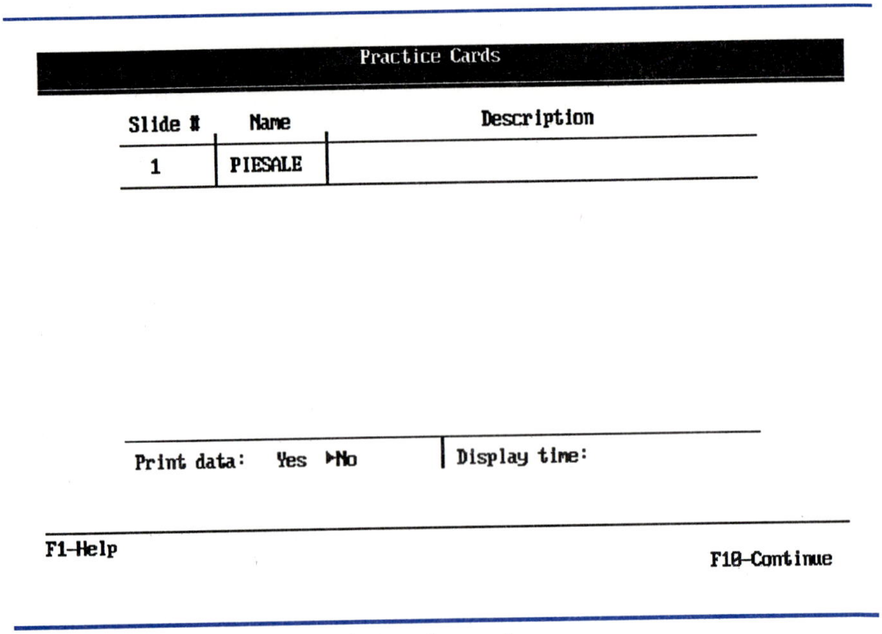

FIGURE 10-11. Blank practice card

all screens or a specific length of time for one screen. You will find that any entry that you make on the Practice Cards form automatically appears on the Add Screenshow Effects form for the screen.

6. Press F10 (Continue) to move to the practice card for the second slide.

The Make practice card option is the same option you will use for revising your notes on existing practice cards. Harvard Graphics always displays the practice card for the first slide, but you can use the keys listed in Table 10-1 to move from card to card, making the required changes.

7. Press ESC to return to the Slide Show Menu.

PRINTING PRACTICE CARDS You can print practice cards and the charts either with or without the data that they describe. The default setting for each card is No, meaning that the associated data does not print unless you change the field. If you change this setting to Yes, the data that the chart uses is printed on a separate page. To print the practice cards for a slide

Key	Function
END	Displays the practice card for the last slide in the show
HOME	Displays the practice card for the first slide in the show
F10 or PGDN	Displays the practice card for the next slide
PGUP	Displays the practice card for the previous slide
TAB	Moves to the Slide # field and allows you to type the slide number for which you want the practice card

TABLE 10-1. Moving Between Practice Cards

show, choose Produce output from the Main Menu and select Print practice cards. Figure 10-12 shows the printout of a practice card for the first slide of a slide show.

Adding ScreenShow Effects

You can create a slide show without the ScreenShow effects, but using them adds a professional quality to your on-screen presentations. The ability to control the timing allows you to relax and focus on your presentation. The ability to add presentation notes with ScreenShow helps you with organizing a large presentation. You can also use ScreenShow to define special effects either as a default or for each individual screen in the show. These effects control the manner and direction for drawing and erasing screens.

SETTING DEFAULTS FOR THE SCREENSHOW The Screenshow Effects form, shown in Figure 10-13, includes a line at the top for default entries. The entries across this line are used when options are not set for individual slides. Entries in the lines for the slides always take precedence over the Default entries.

In Figure 10-13 the only entry in the Default line is in the Draw column, where Replace is the default effect for drawing a new screen. This setting causes the new screen to replace the old screen all at once. You can choose entries for Draw, Draw Direction, Erase, and Erase Direction by using the F6 (Choices) key. All of these are discussed in more detail in the next section, which covers making changes for individual slides. If you want to establish a default display time for slides, you should enter your time in the form *mm:ss,* where *mm* represents the minutes and *ss* represents the seconds.

SETTING OPTIONS FOR INDIVIDUAL SLIDES Any time you want to override the default settings, you can supply an entry on the lines for individual slides. You can change the same settings that are available to set as defaults.

Using Special Effects The special effects provided with ScreenShow allow you to control the drawing and erasing of the screen. As slides are removed and placed on the screen, two distinct processes occur in the transition: the

```
SLIDE #        NAME                        DESCRIPTION
-------    ------------     ----------------------------------------
   1       PIESALE .CHT

Overview of industry sales patterns and the industry
domination by several large chains




                                     DISPLAY TIME:  0:15
```

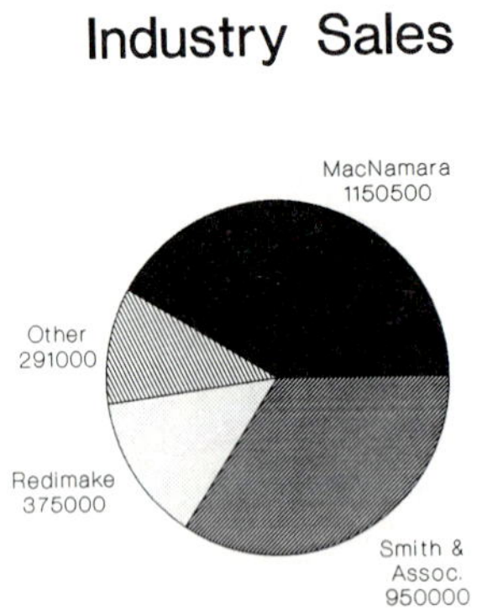

FIGURE 10-12. Printing a practice card with the data

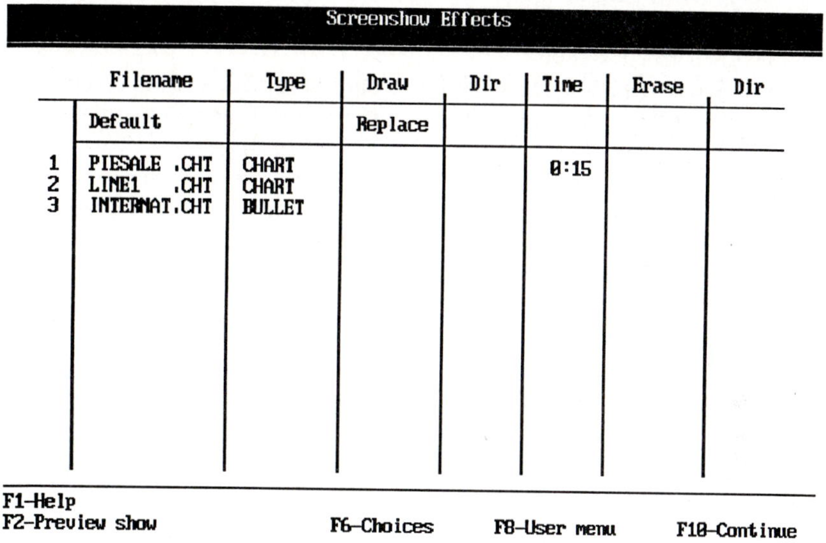

FIGURE 10-13. Form for adding ScreenShow effects

removal of existing information and the addition of new information.

A default setting is established for Draw. The Replace setting causes Harvard Graphics to replace the entire screen at one time as it displays the new image all at once. Many other options for the addition of information on the new chart to the screen are available and are listed in Table 10-2. Some of these options create unique effects: Iris opens like the iris of an eye to reveal more and more of the new image, and Blinds creates the new image with a series of vertical or horizontal strips that expand in size to reveal more of the image until the entire chart is displayed.

There is no default setting established for Erase. Unless you supply a default or a setting for an individual slide the old slide is removed as the new one is added.

Experimentation will help you select attractive options that complement each other. The best options require you to take into consideration the direction with which these special effects are supplied. For example, you may decide to choose Scroll Left to draw a new screen and Scroll Right to erase the old screen.

Setting the Draw and Erase Directions The direction of the draw and erase activities can sometimes improve the results of your slide show. Right, Left,

Up, Down, In, and Out are the direction settings you can select if you press F6 (Choices) with your cursor in either of the Dir columns on the Screenshow Effects screen.

Some special effects are not compatible with setting directions. For example Replace, Overlay, Weave, and Rain do not support setting directions. Fade has a default of Full but supports a change to Down. Iris is the only setting that uses In and Out, and the remaining settings support Up, Down, Right, or Left. Where applicable, the defaults for each effect are also shown in Table 10-2.

Setting the Display Time Once you have practiced your presentation a few times, you will probably know how long you need to display each slide. You can set the display time in Harvard Graphics if you want to automate your presentation. If you are a bit nervous in front of an audience, this may be what you need because it eliminates your worries about forgetting to advance a slide and getting out-of-sync with the display. Adding a display time is also

Setting	Default Direction	Effect
Replace	N/A	Entire screen is replaced at once
Overlay	N/A	Displays charts element by element
Wipe	Right	Erases horizontally or vertically
Scroll	Up	Scrolls the slide on or off the screen
Fade	Full screen	Gradually removes the slide image
Weave	N/A	Weaves in the directions at one time
Open	Down	Opens the screen in a horizontal or vertical line that gradually enlarges
Close	Down	Closes the screen in a horizontal or vertical line
Blinds	Down	Uses horizontal or vertical strips to open a screen
Iris	Out	Opens out from all directions or closes in from all directions
Rain	N/A	Gradually fades on or off with the effect of rain droplets

TABLE 10-2. ScreenShow Effects

a good idea when you are creating a presentation for a trade show or other display where users passing by will stop to look at the screen. Automating the display allows you to reach more users, since they are not required to take an active role in changing the information presented.

You have already seen how you can set the display time from the practice card for a slide. If you want to set different times for all of your slides, you may find it quicker to use the Time column in the Add Screenshow Effects form. As you make your selections, keep in mind that you should allow enough time for everyone viewing the presentation to read a text chart or comprehend the message in a graph. Since there is a great deal of variation in reading speeds you should read the information slowly when you try to determine the appropriate time to use. Naturally multiple charts and charts with a great deal of text require more time than a logo or simple graphic image.

You can use the *mm:ss* format for entering display times. Entering **1:05** displays the chart for one minute, five seconds. If you enter a number by itself without a colon, seconds are assumed; for example, enter **5** to display the slide for five seconds. Enter **0** to display the slide for as short a time as possible.

Trying the Settings Options for an Existing Slide Show You have had a chance to read about all the options that can help you create a professional Screen-Show. Now it's time to try some of these with the slides you have already selected. Follow these steps to add your selections:

1. Select Add ScreenShow effects.
2. Press DOWN ARROW to move to the Draw entry for PIESALE.
3. Press F6 (Choices) to display the special effects list shown in Figure 10-14.
4. Press DOWN ARROW to highlight Iris, and then press ENTER.

Iris uses the default of Out for direction, which starts drawing the chart in the center of the screen and working outward. Another option you may want to try later with the Iris selection is a direction of In, which starts drawing the outside of the chart and works towards the center.

5. Press DOWN ARROW to move to the next line, and then press F6 (Choices).
6. Highlight Rain and press ENTER.

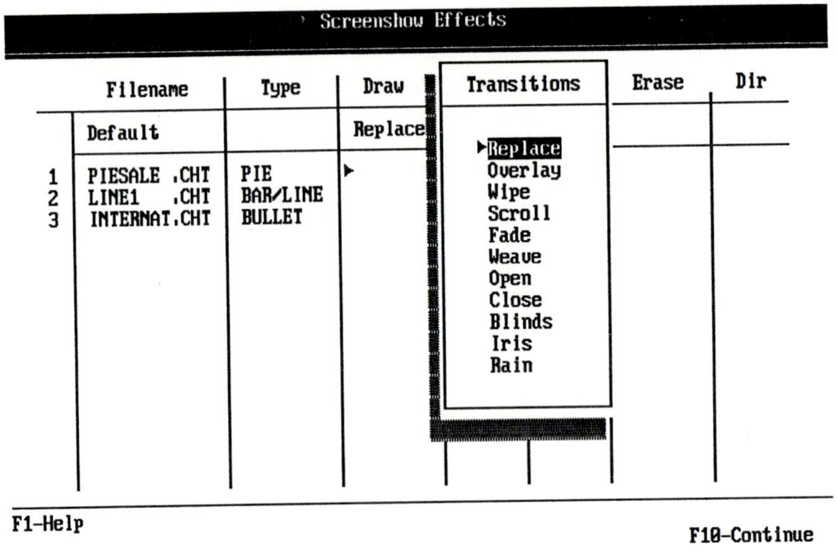

FIGURE 10-14. Choices for special effects displayed

7. Press UP ARROW, and then press TAB to move to the Dir column for PIESALE.
8. Press F6 (Choices) to display the options shown in Figure 10-15, highlight In, and press ENTER.
9. Press TAB followed by DOWN ARROW to move to the Time column for LINE1.
10. Type **10** and press ENTER.
11. Type **20** to allow 20 seconds for INTERNAT.
12. Press UP ARROW two times, and then press TAB to move to the Erase column for PIESALE.
13. Press F6 (Choices) to view the options, and press ESC to leave the Choices display without making a selection.
14. Press HOME to move to the top. You want to position the cursor before starting a preview so it will start on the current slide.

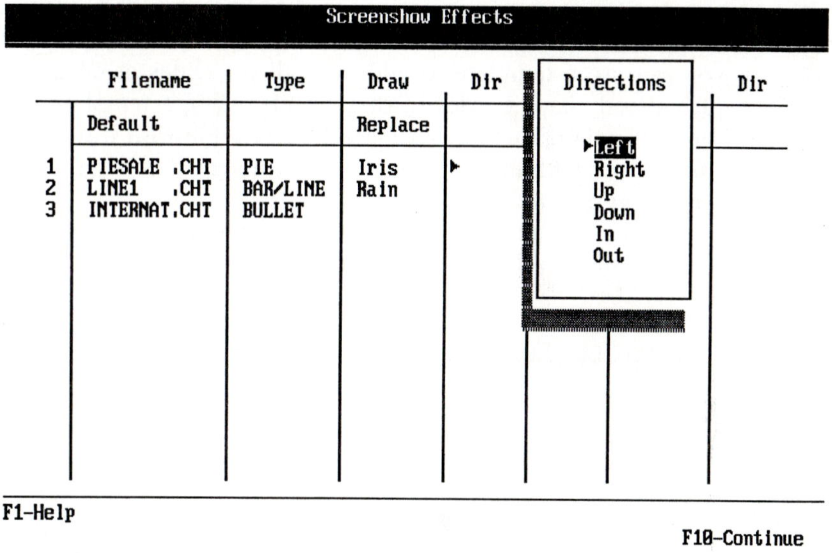

FIGURE 10-15. Choices for directions displayed

15. Press (F2) (Preview show). You do not have to press (ENTER) to make the transition to slide. If you do not supply an entry in the Time column, Harvard Graphics displays the slide until you press a key such as (RIGHT ARROW) or (ENTER).

REORDERING SLIDES You can change the order of the slides in a ScreenShow. To change the location of a slide, you must first highlight the filename in the show list on the Add Screenshow Effects form or Edit Slide Show form. Use (CTRL-UP ARROW) and (CTRL-DOWN ARROW) to relocate the current chart. Follow these steps to change the order of the PIESALE chart and then restore it to its original location.

1. Move the cursor to a row in the PIESALE chart.
2. Press (CTRL-DOWN ARROW) twice to relocate PIESALE.
3. Press (CTRL-UP ARROW) twice to move PIESALE to the top of the list again.
4. Press (ESC) to return to the Slide Show Menu.

USING A TEMPLATE FILE IN A SLIDE SHOW Template files allow you to add a measure of consistency to the slides in a show. If you want to add the same footnote or title to a series of slides without an entry in this field, you can use a template to add it to all the slides at once. If the individual files already have entries in these fields, using a template will not override them. In other words, inserting a template file with a title will not override titles stored with existing chart files, although it will supply a title for chart files where this field is blank.

To create a template that contains a Footnote entry and display it with the ScreenShow charts, follow these steps.

1. Press (ESC) to return to the Main Menu.
2. Select Create new chart.
3. Select Pie. The Pie Chart 1 Data form will appear.

Actually any chart type would be fine for adding a footnote.

4. Press (DOWN ARROW) twice and then type **Gates News Service**, as shown here:

```
                    Pie Chart 1 Data   Page 1 of 2
Title:
Subtitle:
Footnote: Gates News Service
```

5. Press (ESC) to return to the Main Menu.
6. Select Get/Save/Remove.
7. Select Save template to display the form shown in Figure 10-16.
8. Type **FOOTNOTE** for the template name and press (ENTER).
9. Type **Template for the Book Slide Show** for the description.

The setting for Clear values is correct as Yes, and the setting for Import data link is correct as None.

10. Press F10 (Continue) to complete the save operation, and then press ENTER to acknowledge that the chart values are about to be cleared.
11. Press ESC to return to the Main Menu.
12. Select Slide show menu.
13. Select Edit slide show.
14. Highlight **FOOTNOTE.TPL** and press ENTER.
15. Press TAB so the highlight only appears in the show list, and then press CTRL-UP ARROW until the FOOTNOTE file is first in the list.
16. Press F10 (Continue) and select Display ScreenShow.

Notice that each of the individual screens displays the footnote. If you had multiple charts in the slide show, the footnote entry would not be displayed because the individual charts were created before the composite multiple chart was created.

17. Select Edit slide show after the show finishes.
18. Press TAB then move to the FOOTNOTE file.
19. Press CTRL-DELETE to remove it from the show list.

```
Save Template

Directory: D:\HG

Template name:

Description:

Clear values:       ▸Yes  No

Import data link:   ▸None  Lotus  ASCII  Excel
```

FIGURE 10-16. Form for saving a template

BUILDING THE FINAL CHART IN STAGES Because a completed chart can contain more information than your audience can absorb at one time, you can create a building effect by gradually adding more information to the chart. With a text chart this might mean adding one line at a time to the chart. With an analytical chart it might mean adding data series one at a time. In both cases the most efficient way to create the chart is to build the final product and save it. The next step is to strip away one layer at a time, saving each layer. The charts are then presented in reverse order until the final chart is displayed on the screen. Follow these steps to build and display a bullet chart with this effect:

1. Press ESC until the Main Menu is displayed.
2. Select Create new chart, and then select Text followed by Bullet list.

In the following steps you will create the final chart and save it. Then you will begin to eliminate bullet items from the chart, saving each iteration.

3. Type **Keys To Successful Sales** and press ENTER three times.
4. Type **Set goals** and press ENTER twice.
5. Type **Set time frames for achieving goals** and press ENTER twice.
6. Type **Determine cost you will incur to meet goals** and press ENTER twice.
7. Type **Establish a plan** and press ENTER twice.
8. Type **Monitor progress** and press ENTER twice.
9. Press F3 (Save) to save the chart.
10. Type **GOALS5** and press F10 (Continue) to save a chart that looks like Figure 10-17 when printed.
11. Press DOWN ARROW until you move to the last bullet item, then press CTRL-DELETE to remove it.
12. Press F3 (Save) to save the chart.
13. Type **GOALS4** and press F10 (Continue).
14. Press DOWN ARROW until you move to the last bullet item, and then press CTRL-DELETE to remove it.
15. Press F3 (Save) to save the chart.

16. Type **GOALS3** and press F10 (Continue).

17. Press DOWN ARROW until you move to the last bullet item, and then press CTRL-DELETE to remove it.

18. Press F3 (Save) to save the chart.

19. Type **GOALS2** and press F10 (Continue).

20. Press DOWN ARROW until you move to the last bullet item, and then press CTRL-DELETE to remove it.

21. Press F3 (Save) to save the chart.

22. Type **GOALS1** and press F10 (Continue).

23. Press ESC and select Slide show menu.

24. Select Create slide show.

25. Type **SALESGL** and press ENTER.

26. Type **Bullet list of sales tips** and press F10 (Continue).

27. Highlight GOALS1 and press ENTER to select the bullet chart showing the first goal.

28. Highlight GOALS2 and press ENTER.

29. Highlight GOALS3 and press ENTER.

30. Highlight GOALS4 and press ENTER.

31. Highlight GOALS5 and press ENTER.

32. Press ESC to return to the Slide Show Menu.

33. Select Display ScreenShow.

34. Press ENTER to advance through each of the slides until you have returned to the Slide Show Menu.

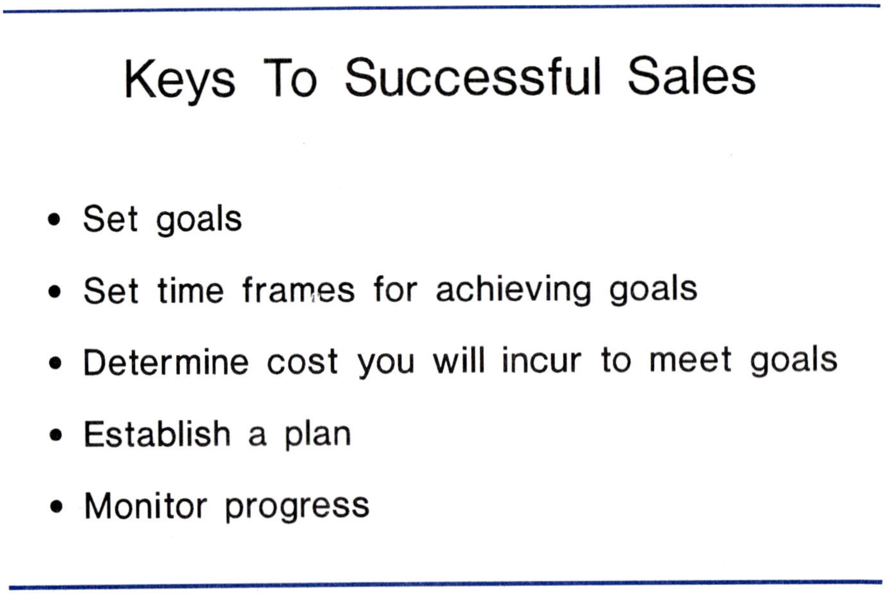

FIGURE 10-17. Complete bullet chart

CREATING A MENU OF USER CHOICES When you create shows about several topics that users will view, you may want to allow them to select the topics they want to see. You can accomplish this by creating a menu on a text chart that lists their options and using the ScreenShow HyperShow feature to display the part of the show that they select.

Building the Special Screens A menu used to guide user selections can be created with a text chart. You may also want to create a text chart to display after the selected screens have displayed. You can use the text chart features you learned in Chapter 6 to build the menu chart shown in Figure 10-18 and the ending chart shown in Figure 10-19. Follow these steps to build the two charts:

1. Press (ESC) to return to the Main Menu.
2. Select Create new chart.
3. Select Text and then select Free form.
4. Using the text in Figure 10-18 as your guide, type **Sample Slide Show Menu** and press (ENTER) six times.

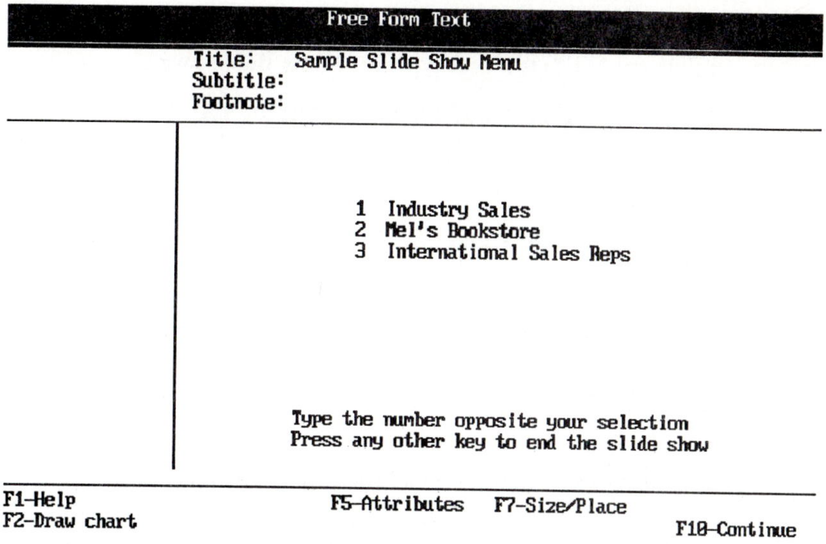

FIGURE 10-18. Creating the beginning screen

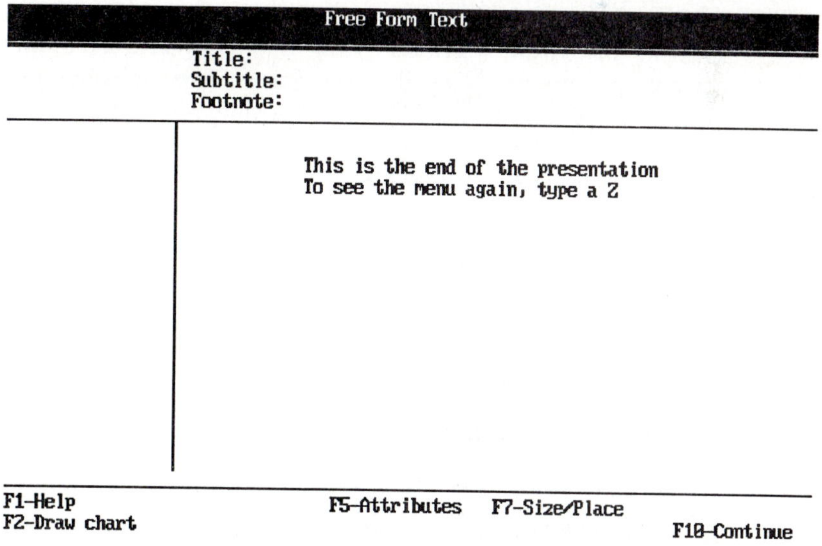

FIGURE 10-19. Creating the closing screen

5. Press the spacebar 16 times to push the menu entry further to the right, and then type **1 Industry Sales.**
6. Press ENTER, and type **2 Mel's Bookstore.**
7. Press ENTER, and type **3 International Sales Reps.**
8. Press ENTER eight times, press the spacebar ten times, and then type **Type the number opposite your selection.**
9. Press ENTER, and type **Press any other key to end the slide show.**
10. Press ESC to return to the Main Menu.
11. Press CTRL-S, type **menu** and then press F10 (Continue).
12. Select Create new chart.
13. Select Text and then select Free form.
14. Using the text in Figure 10-19 as your guide, press ENTER four times and the spacebar ten times and then type **This is the end of the presentation.**
15. Press ENTER and type **To see the menu again, type a Z.**
16. Press ESC to return to the Main Menu.
17. Press CTRL-S, type **LASTSCR**, and press F10 (Continue).

Entering the Menu Selections Now that you have created the two new screens, you are ready to alter the ScreenShow to add user selections for each of these new screens. This means that when either of these two new screens are displayed, the user can influence the next action. Follow these steps to create new entry points into the current slide show presentation:

1. Select Slide show menu.
2. Choose Select slide show.
3. Highlight BOOKS and press ENTER.
4. Select Edit slide show.
5. Highlight MENU and press ENTER to add the screen to the show list.
6. Highlight LASTSCR and press ENTER.
7. Press TAB to make the highlight display only in the show list.
8. Move the highlight down to MENU and then press CTRL-UP ARROW three times to move this screen to the top of the list.

9. Press F10 (Continue).

10. Select Add ScreenShow effects.

11. Press DOWN ARROW to move to the row for MENU.

12. Press F8 (HyperShow) to bring the HyperShow menu to the screen.

You use this box to define the characters a user can type and the slide number that is displayed when the user types the letter. Typing a Go To entry without a Key entry tells Harvard Graphics to display this screen when any other key is pressed.

13. Type **1** and press ENTER to indicate that the user may type **1** to change the order of the slide.

14. Type **2** and press ENTER to indicate that the user may type **2** to change the order of the slide.

15. Type **3** to indicate that the user may type **3** to change the order of the slide.

16. Press UP ARROW twice and then press TAB.

17. Type the following slide numbers, pressing ENTER after each:

    2
    3
    4
    5

These numbers indicate that if the user types **1**, the slide show displays slide 2 next. If the user types **2**, the slide show displays slide 3. If the user types **3**, the slide show displays slide 4. If the user types any other key, the slide show displays slide 5.

18. Press F10 (Continue) to finalize the entries for the MENU screen.

A diamond is added next to MENU, as shown in the display of menu choices in Figure 10-20, which also displays the completed HyperShow menu.

19. Move the highlight to LASTSCR.

20. Press F8 (HyperShow).

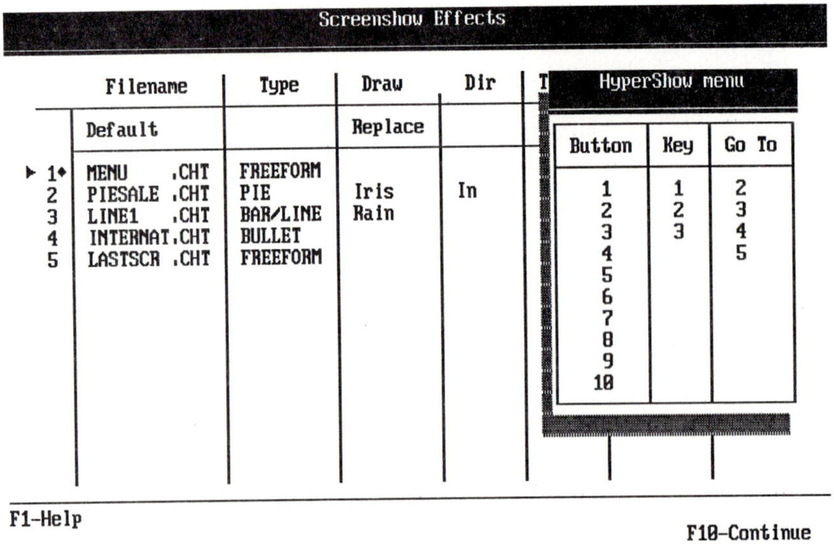

FIGURE 10-20. Adding user menu selections for a screen

21. Type **Z**, press TAB, and then type **1**.
22. Press F10 (Continue).

This allows you to redisplay the menu at the end of the presentation if **Z** is typed.

23. Press ESC to return to the Slide show menu.
24. Select Display ScreenShow.

From the first chart, you can type a number to select which chart you want to see. You can browse through the slide show to display all of the charts and then return to the Slide Show Menu when you are finished.

Using Buttons in a Slide Show

Buttons are areas of a chart that you can click with a mouse and move to the slide assigned to the button. You can use buttons to make HyperShow features that you used before with a mouse. Creating a HyperShow lets you make slide shows interactive. To use buttons, you must add them in the Draw/Annotate or Draw Partner screen. Since using buttons requires several steps, you will want to see how you can use them in the slide show you have used in this chapter. To see how this works, follow these steps:

1. Press ESC to return to the Main Menu.
2. Press CTRL-G to get a chart, select MENU and press ENTER.
3. Press any key to remove the chart and display the Free Form Text form.
4. Press ENTER five times and CTRL-DELETE once.
5. Press the DOWN ARROW and CTRL-INSERT to add a line.
6. Press the DOWN ARROW twice and CTRL-INSERT once to add another line.
7. Press the DOWN ARROW four times and CTRL-DELETE five times to remove some of the blank lines between the middle and bottom lines of text.
8. Press DELETE ten times to remove the spaces before the word "Type."
9. Press the DOWN ARROW. Press DELETE ten times to remove the spaces before the word "Press."
10. Press F7 (Size/Place), press the DOWN ARROW three times, DELETE twice and ENTER to change the size of the text from 3.5 to 5.
11. Press F4 (Draw/Annot) so you can add the buttons.
12. Select Add and Button. Harvard Graphics prompts for a button number.
13. Type **1** and press ENTER.

Harvard Graphics prompts for the first corner of the button. The button is the area on the chart where you can click the mouse and select the function assigned to the button.

14. Press HOME nine times and the RIGHT ARROW three times to move the cross-hairs above and to the left of the 1 in Industry Sales. Press ENTER.

Now Harvard Graphics wants to know the opposite end of the button.

15. Press PGDN four times and the RIGHT ARROW fifteen times to move the cross-hairs below and to the right of 1 Industry Sales. Press ENTER. Harvard Graphics draws a dotted outline representing the button's location. If you want to provide an outline of the button, you

will need to add one by adding a box. After the first button is drawn, Harvard Graphics prompts for another button number for the next button you want to draw.

16. Type **2** and press ENTER.
17. Press ENTER to accept the starting position of the second button.
18. Press END four times and the LEFT ARROW fifteen times to move the cross-hairs below and to the left of 2 Mel's Bookstore. Press ENTER. Harvard Graphics draws a dotted outline representing the second button's location.
19. Type **3** and press ENTER.
20. Press ENTER to accept the starting position of the third button.
21. Press PGDN four times and the RIGHT ARROW twenty four times to move the cross-hairs below and to the right of 3 International Sales Reps. Press ENTER. Harvard Graphics draws a dotted outline representing the third button's location. Now your chart looks like the one in Figure 10-21.
22. Press ESC four times to return to the Main Menu.
23. Press CTRL-S to save the file and press F10 (Continue).

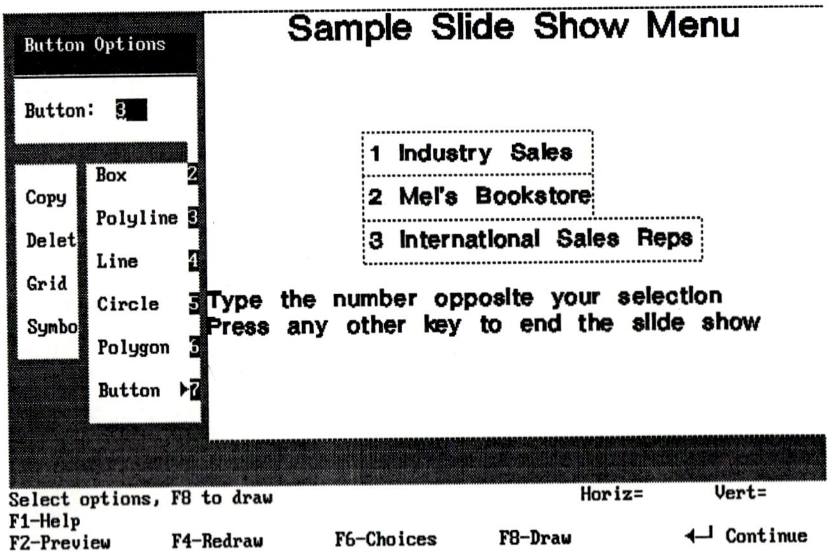

FIGURE 10-21. Adding buttons in a Draw/Annotation screen

Besides using the button numbers 1 through 10, you can also use the special numbers 211 through 217. These numbers are already assigned the function of specific keys. The button numbers, the keys they represent, and the task they perform in a slide show are listed in Table 10-3.

You can add a few of these special buttons as a template so they will appear throughout the slide show. To create a template using some of the special button numbers, follow these steps.

1. Select Create new chart, Text and Free form to remove the existing chart values.
2. Press F4 (Draw/Annot) to display the Draw/Annotate screen.
3. Select Add and Text. Press F8 (Options), type **5.5** (for the text size), and press F8 (Draw).
4. Type **Select** and press ENTER. When Harvard Graphics prompts for a location for the text, press CTRL-END and ENTER to position the text in the lower-left corner of the chart.
5. Type **Quit** and press ENTER. When Harvard Graphics prompts for a location, press the RIGHT ARROW ten times and press ENTER.

Button Number	Key Represented	Task Key Performs in a Slide Show
211	LEFT ARROW	Displays the previous slide
212	RIGHT ARROW	Displays the next slide
213	HOME	Displays the first slide
214	END	Displays the last slide
215	SPACEBAR	Pauses the slide show
216	CTRL-E	Displays the chart data for the currently displayed chart
217	ESC	Returns to the Slide Show Menu

TABLE 10-3. Special Button Numbers and Functions

6. Type **Next** and press ENTER. When Harvard Graphics prompts for a location, press the RIGHT ARROW ten times and press ENTER.
7. Type **or** and press ENTER. When Harvard Graphics prompts for a location, press the RIGHT ARROW ten times and press ENTER.
8. Type **Menu** and press ENTER. Harvard Graphics prompts for a location, press the RIGHT ARROW ten times and press ENTER.
9. Press ESC and select Button.
10. Type **213** and press ENTER to use the button number for the HOME key.
11. Press PGDN and the RIGHT ARROW twice to move the cross-hairs below and to the right of Menu and press ENTER.
12. Press HOME three times and the LEFT ARROW three times to move the cross-hairs above and to the left of Menu. Press ENTER.

The special number buttons look identical to the buttons numbered 1 through 10. The advantage of using them is that you do not have to tell Harvard Graphics the chart to display when a special number button is selected.

13. Type **212** for the next button number and press ENTER.
14. Press the LEFT ARROW fourteen times to move the cross-hairs above and to the right of Next and press ENTER.
15. Press END three times and the LEFT ARROW three times to move the cross-hairs below and to the left of Next. Press ENTER.

Harvard Graphics draws a dotted outline representing the second button's location.

16. Type **217** for the third button and press ENTER.
17. Press the LEFT ARROW four times to move the cross-hairs below and to the right of Quit and press ENTER.
18. Press HOME three times and the LEFT ARROW three times to move the cross-hairs above and to the left of Quit. Press ENTER. Now your chart looks like the one in Figure 10-22.
19. Press ESC four times to return to the Main Menu.
20. Select Get/Save/Remove and Save template.
21. Type MENU and press F10 (Continue).
22. Press ENTER when Harvard Graphics displays the warning that the chart values are about to be cleared.

23. Press ESC to return to the Main Menu.

Now that the buttons are added to the chart and template file, you are ready to add the template to the slide show. To use these buttons you have created, follow these steps:

1. Select Slide show menu and Edit slide show.
2. Highlight MENU.TPL from the list and press ENTER to add the template to the slide show.
3. Press TAB once and CTRL-UP ARROW five times to move MENU.TPL to the top of the slide show and press F10 (Continue).
4. Select Add ScreenShow effects.

In the Screenshow effects screen, you can modify the order of the buttons. You do not need to select an order for the template since the template uses the special button numbers which are already defined.

5. Press the DOWN ARROW twice to move to MENU.CHT in the slide show and press F8 (HyperShow). You can see that the three buttons are already defined. By adding the buttons, you can select which slide you want to display by clicking either the number or the text. Before when no buttons were on the screen, the HyperShow menu selected the keystrokes

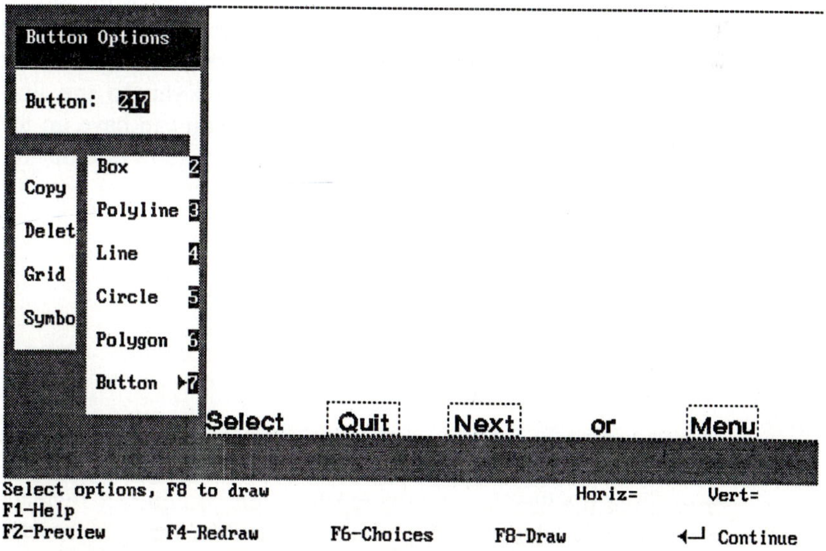

FIGURE 10-22. Using Havard Graphic's predefined buttons

that you could press without providing options for making the same selections with a mouse.

6. Press ESC to remove the HyperShow form.
7. Press the DOWN ARROW to move to PIESALE.CHT and press F8 (HyperShow). Press TAB, type **5**, and press F10 (Continue). This will display LASTSCR.CHT after displaying PIESALE.CHT.
8. Press the DOWN ARROW to move to LINE1.CHT and press F8 (HyperShow). Press TAB, type **5**, and press F10 (Continue). This will display LASTSCR.CHT after displaying LINE1.CHT.
9. Press the DOWN ARROW to move to INTERNAT.CHT and press F8 (HyperShow). Press TAB, type **5**, and press F10 (Continue). This will display LASTSCR.CHT after displaying INTERNAT.CHT.
10. Press F10 (Continue) to return to the Slide Show Menu and select Display ScreenShow.

Now when you view the slide show, you can select the slide you want to see by either typing a 1, 2, or 3, or by using the mouse and clicking 1 Industry Sales, 2 Mel's Bookstore or 3 International Sales Reps. After viewing one of these three, Harvard Graphics displays LASTSCR.CHT. While in any chart of the slide show, you can also select the Quit, Next or Menu buttons with the mouse. Figure 10-23 shows MENU.CHT combined with MENU.TPL. Each has its own buttons but since both are visible, you can select any of the six buttons displayed. The Quit button is equivalent to ESC which returns you to the Slide Show Menu. The Next button is equivalent to the RIGHT ARROW which goes to the next slide. The Menu button is equivalent to HOME which moves you to the first slide in the show. While this slide show has six buttons, you can have up to 20 buttons in your own slide shows. You can also have more than one button assigned the same number.

ShowCopy Utility

Harvard Graphics 2.13 includes a ShowCopy Utility that lets you quickly create, verify and transfer slide shows. You can quickly create a slide show from all of the files in a directory which lets you quickly review all of the files you have in a directory. You can also confirm that you have all of the files that you need to run a slide show. This is important as you are preparing for a presentation. You can also copy all of the slide show files to another location. This feature is used when you are copying the files for a slide show from your hard disk to a floppy and you want to be sure you have all of the files. These three features are used by exiting Harvard Graphics and using the utility from the DOS command prompt.

CREATING ANOTHER COPY OF A SLIDE SHOW When you are preparing for a presentation, you may need your slide show on a different media, such as a floppy disk. The ShowCopy utility can copy the files for you. To copy a slide show, follow these steps:

1. Select Exit to leave Harvard Graphics.
2. Type **SHOWCOPY**, press the SPACEBAR, type the name of the slide show (without the .SHW extension) and the drive and directory where you want the slide show copied. An example of this is **SHOWCOPY C:\HG_FILES\BOOKS A:** to copy the BOOKS slide show and all of its files to drive A. If the slide show is on a different directory, you must supply the drive and directory information of the slide show.
3. Press ENTER.

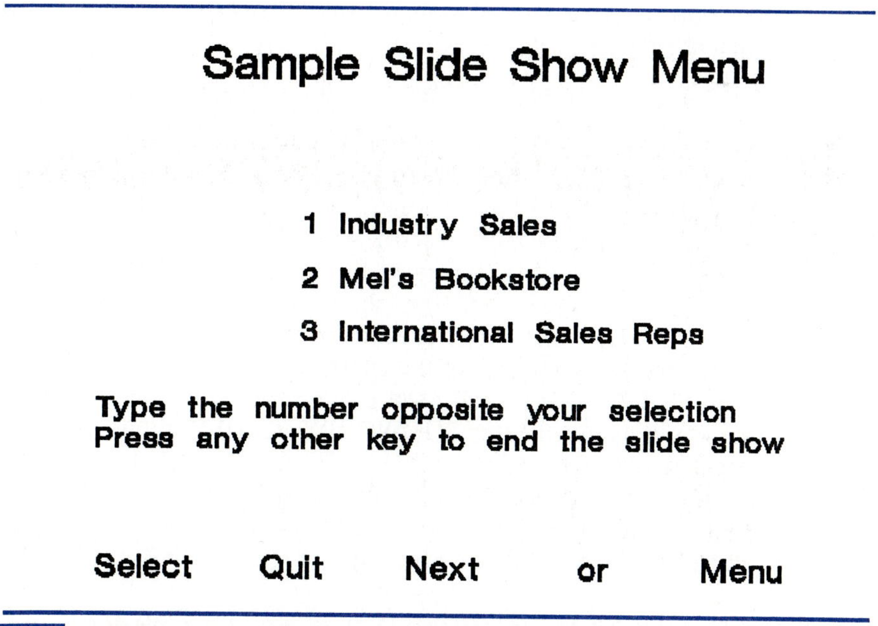

FIGURE 10-23. Using buttons in a slide show

ShowCopy first checks that the destination of the slide show has enough room to contain the slide show. The ShowCopy utility stops and alerts you to this problem if there is not enough room. Next, the ShowCopy utility copies all of the charts, templates, bit-mapped graphics (.PIC and .PCX extensions) and palette files. This assumes that all of the files are stored in the same directory as the slide show file with the .SHW extension. If this is not the case, you must copy the files to the directory containing the slide show file you are copying.

A slide show that you copy with the ShowCopy utility can be run without Harvard Graphics. By adding a space and /a, your copy of the slide show is ready to be used with the ScreenShow Projector. An example of an entry is **SHOWCOPY BOOKS A: /A.** The ScreenShow Projector utility that you need to run a slide show without running Harvard Graphics is available by sending in your registration for Harvard Graphics. The advantage of running a ScreenShow without Harvard Graphics is that you can present a slide show on a machine that has less RAM or disk space than Harvard Graphics requires to run.

The ShowCopy utility has two other parts you may want to add to the command line to copy a slide show. By adding /s at the end, the ShowCopy utility will display a list of the files the utility is copying. By adding /u at the end, the ShowCopy utility updates the description column for the files that you are copying to the destination. You can combine /a, /s, or /u as in **SHOWCOPY BOOKS A: /S /U.**

VERIFYING A SLIDE SHOW Another problem when you are preparing for a presentation, is checking that you have all of the files. This is especially helpful if you have been deleting or moving files. The ShowCopy utility can also check that all of the files in a slide show are available. To verify a slide show, type **SHOWCOPY VERIFY** and press ENTER. If you want to check the slide shows on a different directory, you must supply the drive and directory information of the slide shows as in **SHOWCOPY VERIFY C:\HG_FILES.** ShowCopy checks for each slide show in the directory that the directory contains all of the charts, templates, bit-mapped graphics (.PIC and .PCX extensions) and palette files used by the slide shows. If the slide show is missing a file, the SHOWCOPY VERIFY utility will alert you to this problem.

When you run ShowCopy Verify, you may want to add /s to the command line. By adding /s at the end, the ShowCopy utility displays a list of slide show files the utility is verifying. An example is **SHOWCOPY VERIFY /S.**

CREATING A SLIDE SHOW A third use of the ShowCopy utility is creating slide shows using all of the available charts in a directory. You can use this feature when you want to create a slide show that contains all or most of the charts in a directory. You can also use this when you are not sure what the charts look like and you want to quickly scan them. A third use of creating a quick slide show using all of the charts in a directory is when you want to print all of the charts in a directory. The ShowCopy utility can create a new slide show that uses all of the charts in a directory. To create a new slide show, type **SHOWCOPY CREATE** and press ENTER. If you want to create the slide shows for a different directory, you must supply the drive and directory information of the chart files as in **SHOWCOPY CREATE C:\HG_FILES**. ShowCopy creates a slide show called NEWSHOW.SHW that uses all (or up to the 90 chart limit for slide shows) chart files from the selected directory. Once this slide show is created you can start Harvard Graphics and make changes to the slide show. This slide show does not include templates, bit-mapped graphics (.PIC and .PCX extensions), and palette files.

When you run ShowCopy Create, you may want to add /s to the command line. By adding /s at the end, the ShowCopy utility displays a list of the chart files the utility is adding to the slide show. An example is **SHOWCOPY CREATE /S.**

Adding Animation Effects to Slide Shows

Animation allows you to creating moving effects in a Harvard Graphics 2.3 SlideShow. Just as in movies, animation is achieved with a series of pictures that appear quickly enough that they appear to be moving on the screen.

You can look at the effect of animation in a slide show of animation effects. To see the show, choose Select SlideShow from the SlideShow menu, then select ANIMATOR.SHW and select Display SlideShow. The sample show displays many of the animation effects you can achieve. Each of these effects is stored in a separate chart file.

To use one of the animated effects in your own show, add the chart file to your own slide show. For example, to add the fireworks effect to your show, add the chart FIREWRKZ to your slide show. To customize the chart, use the Draw/Annotate Modify Options command and change the entry "Your Words" to any text you want to use. As you become more proficient with Draw Partner and Draw/Annotate, you can even create your own effects by adding images to charts and replacing them with new images where an image the same color as the background is used to cover the existing image.

chapter 11

CREATING TEMPLATES

Templates are chart definitions that you can use to speed up the production of charts that you create frequently. Templates can also be the ideal solution for users who do not work with Harvard Graphics frequently and want to be able to create a chart immediately after entering their data. If you build a template for these users, they can create their charts month after month without any additional help.

You can save the text and data from a chart that you have defined and recall it whenever you need it. This allows you to use titles, drawings, sizes, locations, labels, settings, and even data repeatedly when you recall the template to create another chart.

Templates can be grouped into chartbooks. For example, you might use a chartbook for the templates you need for weekly sales reports or the annual budget presentation. Another example of template organization is putting all your bullet list or pie chart templates into a chartbook. You can create as many chartbooks as you need to organize all the templates you have saved, with each chartbook containing as many as 90 templates.

In this chapter you will create several templates as well as a chartbook.

GETTING STARTED

To create a template you follow the same procedure as you do for a chart. The differences are in the method used for saving the completed template and in how you can reuse your investment repeatedly. In this section you will create a template that can be used to create a series of bullet charts for the same presentation. The title and footnote entries as well as the font selection are saved in the template, giving a consistent appearance for all the charts created from that template. Follow these steps:

1. Select Create new chart from the Main Menu.
2. Select Text and then select Bullet list.
3. Type **Geauga Greenware** and press ENTER twice.
4. Type **Prepared by Marketing Consultants** and press ENTER.
5. Press ESC to return to the Main Menu and then press F8 (Options).
6. Press TAB twice to move to Font, and then press the spacebar twice to highlight Square Serif.
7. Press F10 (Continue).
8. Press F2 (Draw chart) to view the chart and then press ESC.
9. Select Get/Save/Remove from the Main Menu.
10. Select Save template.
11. Type **GEAUGA** and press ENTER twice to move to the Clear values field.
12. Press the spacebar to change the setting to No.

Without this change the title and footnote entries will not appear on the template when you retrieve it.

13. Press F10 (Continue).

Harvard Graphics will save the template in a file named GEAUGA.TPL. At this point the template is still in memory and could be used to create a chart. To simulate use at a later time, retrieve the saved copy before creating a chart from it.

14. Select Get template from the Get/Save/Remove menu still displayed.
15. Highlight GEAUGA in the list and press ENTER.

Notice the entries already on the chart.

16. Press ENTER and type **New Products** in the Subtitle field.

17. Press ENTER twice to generate the first bullet and type each of the following entries, pressing ENTER twice after each to create bullets:

    Easy-Fire Glaze
    Bisque-Fix
    Disposable Brushes
    High Gloss Greenware Paint

18. Press F2 (Draw chart) to display the chart.

You will see the template entries and square serif font without needing to make the entries. Figure 11-1 presents the chart as it will appear when printed.

19. Press ESC twice to return to the Main Menu.
20. Press CTRL-S to save the chart.
21. Type **NEWPROD** and press F10 (Continue).

The completed chart is not saved as a template but as a chart. Subsequent charts in the presentation will be saved the same way, leaving the original template intact to use with all subsequent bullet charts in the same presentation. If you are creating a Slide Show, another option is to include the template as the first entry and add the charts with the subtitles and bullet entries behind the template.

CREATING TEMPLATES

You have already looked at a quick example of a template that added a title and footnote to make it easy to create a group of charts with some consistency. Other possible template options are altering text placement and sizing, changing text attributes, changing option settings on the Titles &

FIGURE 11-1. Chart created from template

Options form, adding symbols and other enhancements with the Draw feature, changing the font or borders setting, and establishing links to ASCII or worksheet files. Almost anything that can be changed for a chart can be established as a default. The exceptions are print options and the default settings options; the scope of these latter options is not confined to a single chart and cannot be saved with the template settings.

Adding Data to the Template for Testing

Now try creating a bar chart with an overlapping 3D option and sample data for the toy products sold by Unicorn Toys. In this exercise you will not save the data as part of the template, but you will save all of the other options, including a setting for a Gothic font made with F8 (Options). Follow these steps:

1. Select Create new chart.
2. Select Bar/Line and press (F10) (Continue) to accept Name as the X data type.
3. Type **Unicorn Toys** and press (ENTER).
4. Type **Quarterly sales ending 3/31/90** and then press (ENTER).
5. Type **Unit Sales** and press (ENTER).
6. Type the following for the X data values, pressing (ENTER) after each:

   Castle
   Shield
   King & Queen Dolls
   Sword
   Unicorn

7. Complete the entry of the data as shown in Figure 11-2.
8. Press (F8) (Options).
9. Press (TAB) until the cursor is on the legend title for Series 1.

Bar/Line Chart Data

Title: Unicorn Toys
Subtitle: Quarterly sales ending 3/31/90
Footnote: Unit Sales

Pt	X Axis Name	Series 1	Series 2	Series 3	Series 4
1	Castle	500	700	850	
2	Shield	800	900	1100	
3	King & Queen Dolls	600	610	725	
4	Sword	200	225	275	
5	Unicorn	500	700	1300	
6					
7					
8					
9					
10					
11					
12					

F1-Help F3-Save F5-Set X type F9-More series
F2-Draw chart F4-Draw/Annot F6-Calculate F8-Options F10-Continue

FIGURE 11-2. Data entries for testing the bar chart template

10. Type **January**, press DELETE, and press ENTER.
11. Type **February** and press ENTER.
12. Press CTRL-DELETE, type **March**, and press PGDN.
13. Press the spacebar to change the Bar style field to Overlap.
14. Press ENTER and then press the spacebar to change the Bar enhancement field to 3D.
15. Press ESC until the Main Menu appears, then press F8 (Options).
16. Press TAB twice to highlight Font, and then press the spacebar until Gothic is highlighted.
17. Press F10 (Continue) to return to the Main Menu and then select Get/Save/Remove.
18. Select Save template, and the form shown in Figure 11-3 appears on the screen.

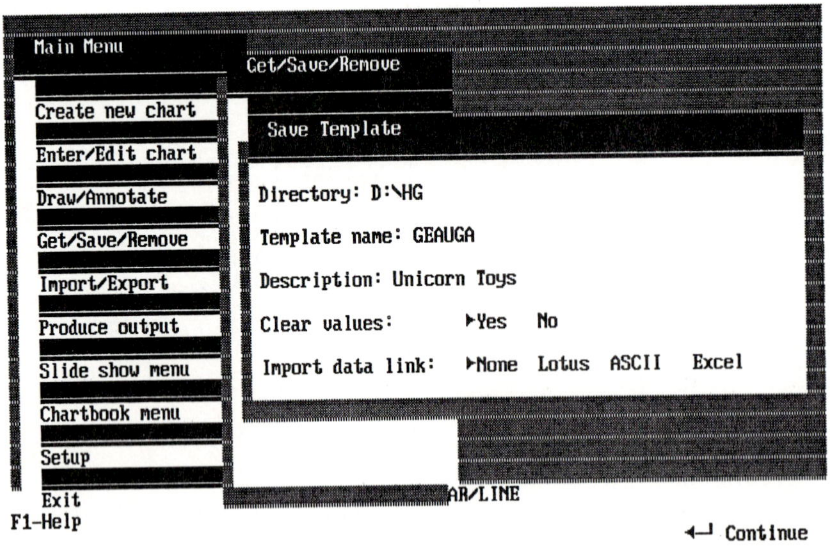

FIGURE 11-3. Save template form

Notice that the name from the previous template is still displayed on the form. If you do not supply a new name, Harvard Graphics will save the new template over the old one.

19. Type **UNICORN** and press (ENTER) twice.
20. Press the spacebar to change the Clear values field to No and then press (F10) (Continue).

All the data is saved in the chart. Although you will need to change the legends and the values each time, the only way to retain the title, subtitle, footnote, and X data names is to retain the existing entries. You must be careful to make all the required updates for the new data, or the chart will display values from the earlier example.

21. Select Get template, type **UNICORN**, and then press (ENTER).
22. Move to the field containing the January numbers for castle sales and begin changing the entries as shown in Figure 11-4.
23. Press (F8) (Options) and then press (TAB) until you move to the legend title for January.

Bar/Line Chart Data

Title: Unicorn Toys
Subtitle: Quarterly sales ending 3/31/90
Footnote: Unit Sales

Pt	X Axis Name	January	February	March	Series 4
1	Castle	900	1005	1025	
2	Shield	1200	1325	1500	
3	King & Queen Dolls	500	800	925	
4	Sword	300	350	375	
5	Unicorn	1200	1500	1800	
6					
7					
8					
9					
10					
11					
12					

F1-Help F3-Save F5-Set X type F9-More series
F2-Draw chart F4-Draw/Annot F6-Calculate F8-Options F10-Continue

FIGURE 11-4. Data entries for the second quarter sales

24. Press CTRL-DELETE, type **April**, and press ENTER.
25. Press CTRL-DELETE, type **May**, and press ENTER.
26. Press CTRL-DELETE and type **June**.
27. Press F2 (Draw chart) to view the chart, which, when printed, looks like the one shown in Figure 11-5. The previewed chart does not display the smaller text using the gothic font, but Harvard Graphics uses the default font for all the text when you print it.
28. Press ESC until the Main Menu appears.
29. Press CTRL-S, type **TOYSQTR2**, and press F10 (Continue) to save the current quarter's data in a chart file.

Adding Symbols to a Template with Draw

Although basic text and analytical charts are easy to create, the draw features require a little more practice for many users. If you want to add a

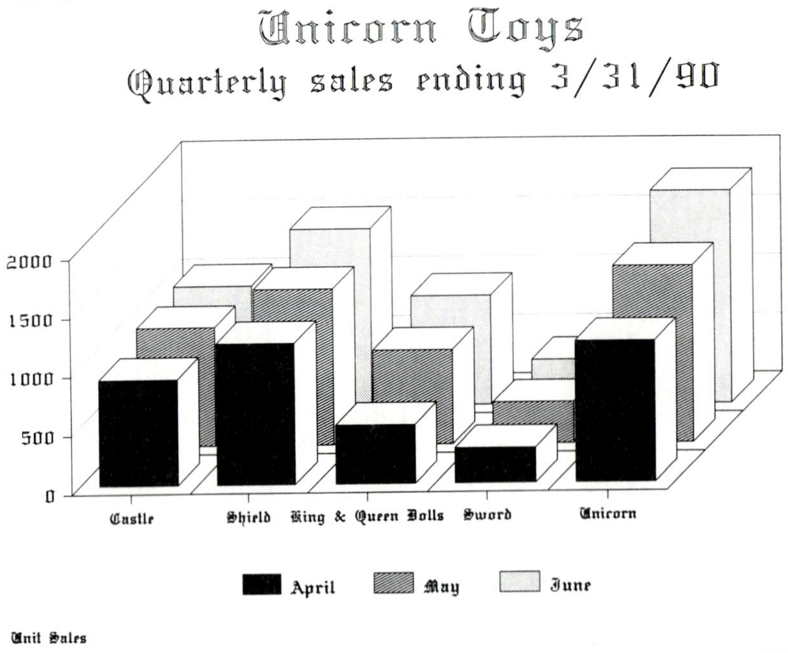

FIGURE 11-5. Bar chart created from template

symbol or drawing like a company logo to a series of charts, you may want to use a template so you only have to do it correctly one time. In the following example, you will create a title and sample entries for a to-do list and then add a symbol to enhance the appearance. When you save the template you will clear the existing values. This means that the template will contain nothing more than the symbol that is needed each time. Follow these steps to create the template:

1. Select Create new chart.
2. Select Text and then select Bullet list.
3. Type **To-Do List** and press ENTER three times.
4. Type **Item 1** after the first bullet and then press ENTER twice.
5. Type **Item 2** after the second bullet and then press ENTER twice.
6. Type **Item 3**.

Although the last four entries will not be saved to the template, placing dummy entries in the chart will help you decide where to locate the drawing.

7. Press F7 (Size/Place) and then press DOWN ARROW three times to move to the size option for the detail bullet entries.
8. Type **4.0** and then press F10 (Continue).

The screen looks like Figure 11-6.

9. Press F4 (Draw/Annot).
10. Select Symbol and then select Get.
11. Press the DOWN ARROW and move the highlight to COMNOBJ2.SYM and press ENTER. If you are using release 2.12, highlight OFFICE .SYM instead.
12. Move the cross-hairs to the clock, which is the last picture in the middle row. With release 2.12, you will find the clock in the second picture from the bottom left.
13. Press ENTER twice to select the clock and the initially suggested position and size.
14. Press ESC and select Modify.
15. Select Move, move to the clock on the screen, and press ENTER.

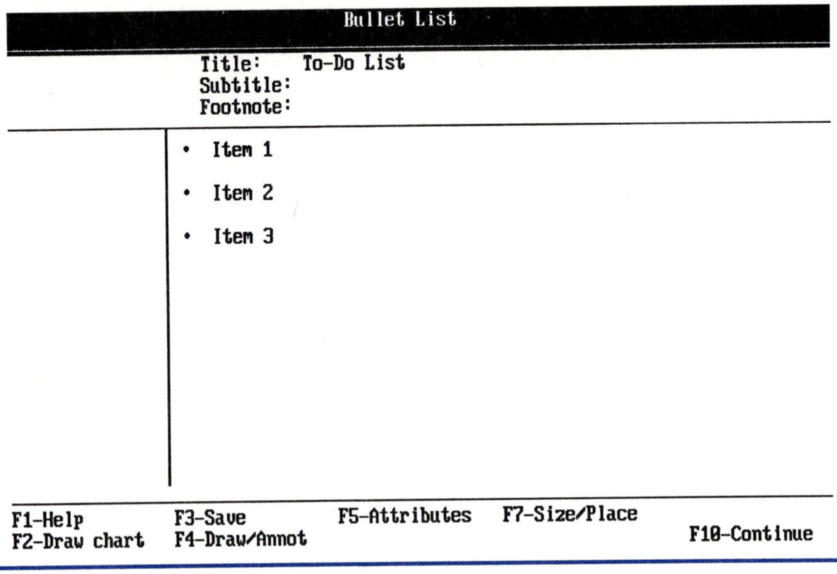

FIGURE 11-6. Entries for bullet list

16. Press ENTER to select Choose this.
17. Press CTRL-PGUP to move to the upper-right corner, and press ENTER to reposition the clock in this location.
18. Select Size, move to the lower-left corner of the clock image, and press ENTER. Press ENTER again to select Choose this.
19. Press SHIFT-UP ARROW a few times to make the clock a little smaller, then press SHIFT-ENTER.
20. Press F4 (Redraw) to redraw the screen and display the text that was covered by the original placement of the clock. Figure 11-7 shows how your screen will look at this time.
21. Press ESC three times to return to the Main Menu and select Get/Save/Remove.
22. Select Save template.
23. Press CTRL-DELETE to remove the existing template name and then type **TODO**.
24. Press F10 (Continue) to accept the defaults, including Clear values, and save the template.

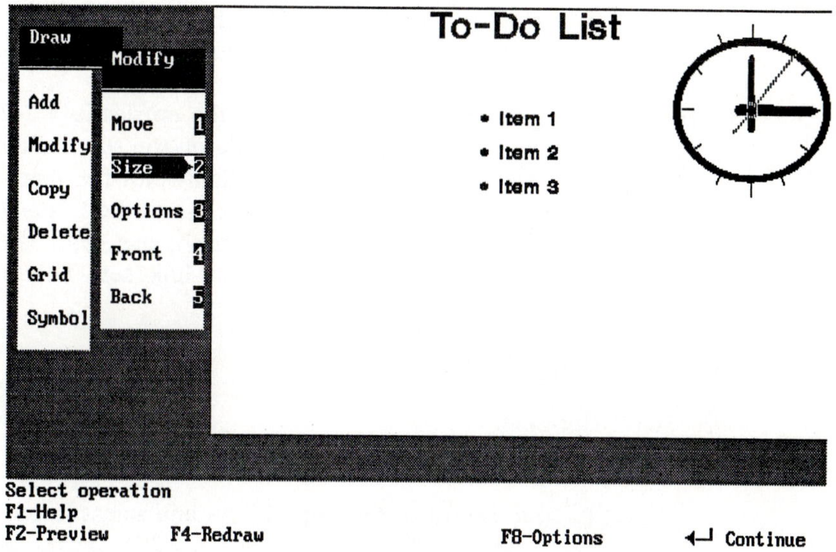

FIGURE 11-7. Adding a clock symbol to the bullet list

25. Press ENTER after reading the warning that the chart values will be cleared.
26. Select Get template.
27. Type **TODO** and press ENTER.

Notice how the chart appears empty. When you press F2 (Draw chart) the clock still displays and continues to do so after you enter your data.

28. Press ESC twice to return to the Main Menu.

Establishing an Import Link

If you are importing Excel, Lotus or ASCII data to create a chart in Harvard Graphics, it is likely to be a recurring need. You might use this capability to graph monthly sales or budget data and will need to process information in the same spreadsheet or word processing files each month. Since specifying the location of the spreadsheet data each time you need a chart can take a few minutes, Harvard Graphics allows you to make the link to the ASCII, Excel, or Lotus data part of the template. Each time you get the template from disk, all the data is automatically brought into the Harvard Graphics chart data form.

In Chapter 5 you created a graph from the entries in a 1-2-3 worksheet named ROYSTON. This file is also available on the supplemental disk. This data showed the actual and projected sales figures for the years 1988 through 1992 for Royston's three top products. You can use the Lotus data originally shown in Figure 5-1 to create another chart. A new chart is created, links defined, and the template is saved with a link set. The detailed steps required are as follows:

1. Select Create new chart.
2. Select Bar/Line.
3. Press **F10** (Continue) to accept an X data type of Name.
4. Press **ESC** to return to the Main Menu and select Import/Export.
5. Select Import Lotus data.
6. Highlight ROYSTON as the name of the file in the current directory that contains the 1-2-3 data you want to import.

If your data is in a different directory, you can press **UP ARROW** and **CTRL-DELETE** to remove the existing drive and directory setting before entering the drive and directory containing the file you want to import.

7. Press **ENTER** to complete the selection.

The Import Lotus Data form that you used in Chapter 5 is displayed.

8. You can specify the title, subtitle, footnote, and series labels with a backslash and a cell address. Harvard Graphics selects them from this address for the first chart, but in the template these addresses are converted to the data they contained when the template was created. Changes in these entries in the spreadsheet do not update the values imported.
9. Ranges are entered next. In the example, data ranges for the X-axis, Series 1, 2, and 3 data are entered. Figure 11-8 shows the entries on the Import Lotus Data form that are used with the Lotus worksheet originally shown in Figure 5-1.
10. Press **F10** (Continue) after completing the Import Lotus Data form.

```
                         Import Lotus Data
      Worksheet name: ROYSTON .WK1

               Title: Royston Company
            Subtitle: 1988 - 1992 Sales
            Footnote:

                       Legend             | Data Range
            ------------------------------+-----------
             X | X axis data              | b4..f4
            ------------------------------+-----------
             1 | Tires                    | b5..f5
             2 | Batteries                | b6..f6
             3 | Chains                   | b7..f7
             4 | Series 4                 |
             5 | Series 5                 |
             6 | Series 6                 |
             7 | Series 7                 |
             8 | Series 8                 |

             Append data:    Yes   ▸No

F1-Help        F3-Select files
               F4-Clear ranges F6-Range names                 F10-Continue
```

FIGURE 11-8. Import Lotus Data form

The data is imported as shown in Figure 11-9.

11. Use (F8) (Options) if you wish to change any of the chart settings.
12. Press (ESC) until the Main Menu appears.
13. Select Get/Save/Remove and then select Save template.
14. Type **LT1** for the template name and press (DELETE).
15. Press (F10) (Continue) to save the template.
16. Press (ENTER) after reading the warning that the chart values will be cleared.
17. Press (ESC) to return to the Main Menu.
18. Select Exit.
19. Start 1-2-3, make some modifications to your worksheet, and save the changes.

In the example, the data for chain sales was altered to 2500, 3500, 4500, 5000, and 6000.

Bar/Line Chart Data

Title: Royston Company
Subtitle: 1988 - 1992 Sales
Footnote:

Pt	X Axis Name	Tires	Batteries	Chains	Series 4
1	1988	2560	3500	4000	
2	1989	2764.8	3815	3500	
3	1990	3200	3900	4000	
4	1991	3456	4251	2100	
5	1992	3732.48	4633.59	1800	
6					
7					
8					
9					
10					
11					
12					

F1-Help F3-Save F5-Set X type F9-More series
F2-Draw chart F4-Draw/Annot F6-Calculate F8-Options F10-Continue

FIGURE 11-9. Imported data

20. Exit from 1-2-3 and restart Harvard Graphics.
21. Select Get/Save/Remove and then select Get template.
22. Type **LT1** and press ENTER.

The new data that you entered in the worksheet cells appears on the Bar/Line Chart Data form after the worksheet data is imported. Figure 11-10 shows the new data automatically imported by the template.

You can use this same feature in a slide show since Harvard Graphics automatically updates each template's data before generating the chart that appears in the slide show. You can combine templates that import data and slide shows to produce a group of charts by selecting Select slide show from the Slide Show Menu and Print Slide Show from the Produce Output menu.

Using Templates in a Slide Show

Besides using templates to create new charts, you can also include templates in slide shows when you want the charts in a slide show to have a consistent appearance. To include a template in a slide show, add the template just as

Bar/Line Chart Data

Title: Royston Company
Subtitle: 1988 - 1992 Sales
Footnote:

Pt	X Axis Name	Tires	Batteries	Chains	Series 4
1	1988	2560	3500	2500	
2	1989	2764.8	3815	3500	
3	1990	3200	3900	4500	
4	1991	3456	4251	5000	
5	1992	3732.48	4633.59	6000	
6					
7					
8					
9					
10					
11					
12					

F1-Help F3-Save F5-Set X type F9-More series
F2-Draw chart F4-Draw/Annot F6-Calculate F8-Options F10-Continue

FIGURE 11-10. Updated data imported into worksheet

you would add a chart or other file to a slide show. When you display or print the slide show, the template affects all charts that are after the template in the slide show. For example, you may have a template that includes a logo in the upper-right corner, just as the TODO template has a clock in the upper-right corner. To include the logo in the other slide show charts, put the template at the beginning of the slide show.

Changing the Default Chart Types

In addition to creating templates for individual projects, you can create standard templates that appear any time you create a specific chart style. You do not need to ask Harvard Graphics to get a template in order for the options stored in this special template to take effect. If you do not like the size or placement of characters on a specific type of chart or would prefer to use a different font on all graphs of a particular type, you can modify the way the initial chart looks. If you always want bar charts to use the Overlay option with 3D, you can make these changes and save them as a special template. Each new bar chart then will be automatically established as a 3D overlay chart. The key to making changes to each of the chart types with a template is to use the names shown in Table 11-1 when saving the template.

You can try this feature by following these steps:

1. Press ESC to return to the Main Menu.
2. Select Create new chart.
3. Select Bar/Line.
4. Press ENTER after reading the warning that the existing data will be removed.
5. Press F10 (Continue) to accept Name as the X data type.
6. Press F8 (Options) to change the settings of the bar chart.
7. Press PGDN to display the second page of Titles & Options.
8. Press the spacebar to change the Bar style field to Overlap.
9. Press TAB to move to the Bar enhancement field.

Chart Type	Default Template Name
Two-column chart	2_COLUMN
Three-column chart	3_COLUMN
Area chart	AREA
Bar or line chart	BARLINE
Bullet list	BULLET
Free-form chart	FREEFORM
High/low/close chart	HLC
Multiple chart	MULTIPLE
Organization chart	ORG
Pie chart	PIE
Simple list	LIST
Title chart	TITLE

TABLE 11-1. Template Names to Create Default Templates

10. Press the spacebar to change the bar enhancement from None to 3D.
11. Press ESC to return to the Main Menu.
12. Select Get/Save/Remove and Save template.
13. Type **BARLINE** and press F10 (Continue) to save the template with the default template name.
14. Press ENTER after reading the warning that the chart values will be cleared.
15. Press ESC to return to the Main Menu.
16. Select Exit to leave Harvard Graphics.
17. Type **HG** to load Harvard Graphics. By exiting and reentering Harvard Graphics, you remove any chart information Harvard Graphics stored.
18. Select Create new chart and Bar/Line.

Harvard Graphics displays the Bar/Line Chart Data form without prompting for the X data type, because the Name data type was selected in the default template.

19. Type **Sales** and press ENTER three times.
20. Type **Widgets** and press ENTER.
21. Type **Gizmos.**
22. Press UP ARROW and TAB to move to the column for the first series values for the first X value.
23. Type **60000** and press ENTER.
24. Type **90000.**
25. Press UP ARROW and TAB to move to the column for the second series values for the first X value.
26. Type **50000** and press ENTER.
27. Type **80000** and press ENTER.
28. Press F2 (Draw chart) to display these values using the template stored in BARLINE.TPL.

You did not have to change the fields in the Titles & Options form to display the bar chart with the overlap bar style and the 3D bar enhancement. If you later decide that you do not want this template, you can delete it by selecting Get/Save/Remove from the Main Menu and then selecting Remove file. When Harvard Graphics displays a list, highlight the file BARLINE.TPL and press ENTER.

CREATING CHARTBOOKS

Chartbooks are collections of templates. You can decide how to organize your templates once you have more than a few and set up chartbooks to contain related templates. Each chartbook you create can contain as many as 90 template files. You can set up chartbooks for specific graph types, or you can set up chartbooks that relate to a project like an annual sales presentation. Organizing all your templates in this manner will make it easier to find the template you want for a particular chart. Harvard Graphics will use the filename you supply and add the extension .CBK for the chartbook file.

To create a new chartbook, follow these steps:

1. Select Chartbook menu from the Main Menu.
2. Select Create chartbook.
3. Type **SAMPLES** and press ENTER to supply a name for the chartbook.

You must follow the same rules as for chart names, limiting your entry to eight characters since a chartbook is a file.

4. Type **Sample charts from Chapter 11** and press F10 (Continue).

The Create/Edit Chartbook form will appear as shown in Figure 11-11.

Adding Templates to a Chartbook

You can use the screen shown in Figure 11-11 to add templates to the chartbook. In this screen, similar to those used for editing screen shows and creating multiple charts, the top of the screen shows all the templates in the current directory that can be added to the chartbook. The lower portion of the screen shows the templates as they are added to the chartbook. Follow these steps to add templates to the current chartbook:

1. Highlight GEAUGA in the list that is at the top of the Create/Edit Chartbook form and press ENTER.

chapter 12

USING MACROS

Macros are stored keystrokes that allow you to repeat a task without all the work. Once you store the keystrokes, only a keystroke or two is needed to repeat the entire task.

If you have worked with other packages like the popular word processors, spreadsheets, and databases, you may have encountered macro capabilities in these programs. Harvard Graphics macros provide similar features and are invoked in a similar fashion. If you are familiar with macro features in any of these other programs you are already halfway to knowing how to use the macro features of Harvard Graphics. Even if you have never tried macro features before, you will find that you can be successful from the start with the easy-to-follow step-by-step directions in the exercises in this chapter.

Harvard Graphics provides macro features through an add-on utility program that comes in the package called MACRO. MACRO requires a hard disk and 512K of free memory to load it. Although it is compatible with other add-on utilities, you may find that you do not have enough room to load both MACRO and other memory-resident utilities with Harvard Graphics. Once you load this utility, it stays resident in your computer's RAM and is ready to record or play back a macro at any time. To be unloaded, MACRO must be the last utility loaded. If it is the last utility loaded, you can prcss ALT-0 (zero) and select Unload MACRO from the menu.

GETTING STARTED

Any task that you execute repeatedly is a good candidate for a macro. Tasks like printing or plotting a copy of the current chart are excellent candidates for a macro because you can use them with any chart.

Follow these steps to create a quick macro for printing:

1. Exit Harvard Graphics if it is still active by typing **E** from the Main Menu.
2. Type **MACRO** and press ENTER to activate the MACRO utility program.

The overlay form shown in Figure 12-1 indicates that the utility is active. As the overlay instructs, you can press ALT-0 to start the utility when you need it. This utility is a TSR (terminate-and-stay-resident) program. It remains in the computer's memory until you unload the utility or restart the computer.

3. Type **HG** and press ENTER to start Harvard Graphics.

```
MACRO 1.1

Press Alt-0 for menu

Copyright 1990 Software Publishing Corporation
```

FIGURE 12-1. Menu box indicating MACRO is loaded

4. Press CTRL-G, and select any chart created in an earlier example.
5. Press ESC twice to return to the Main Menu.
6. Press ALT-O to display the following macro menu:

```
MACRO 1.0
▸Play back a macro
 Record a macro
 Insert delays
 Change macro directory
 Unload MACRO
```

7. Select Record a macro by typing **R** or using the arrow keys to move to your selection and pressing ENTER.

The current macro is designed to work only from the Main Menu. If you want the macro to work regardless of your location within Harvard Graphics menus, you can press ESC four times. Even if you are at the Main Menu, pressing ESC cannot cause a problem since typing **E** is the only way to exit from the menu.

8. Type **PRT** for the macro name and press ENTER.
9. Type **6** to select Produce output.

Rather than using the arrow keys to move to the desired menu option, it is always better to type the option number when you are creating a macro.

10. Type **1** to select Printer.

The Print Chart Options form is displayed.

11. Type **H** to select High for the Quality field.

If you were not recording a macro, you might choose to press the spacebar to make the change, but when you record a selection in a macro it is better to type the letter for the selection. Later when you edit the macro you will find that it is easier to tell what the macro is doing.

12. Press TAB four times to move to the Color field.
13. Type **N** for No.
14. Press F10 (Continue).

Harvard Graphics prints a copy of the current chart, as long as the printer is on.

15. Press ALT-O and select Stop recording macro.

Now that you have created a macro, you should test it to see if it works.

Running a macro stored on disk is referred to as *playing back* the macro. Try these steps to play back PRT:

1. Press ALT-O and select Play back a macro.
2. Type **PRT** and press ENTER to print another copy of the current chart.

As you can see, once the macro is recorded hardly any work is required to complete the task automated by the macro.

RECORDING MACROS

You can record almost any activity that you perform from a Harvard Graphics menu. MACRO will not record mouse selections. You will also not want to use the draw features that have a series of arrow movements, because the drawing created would be dependent on cursor location. Other tasks that you seldom perform do not make good macros since they would not save you much time.

MACRO records macros and plays them back in many situations besides Harvard Graphics. MACRO can be run in accessory packages such as U.S. MapMaker, which is covered in Chapter 13. You can also use MACRO in other products, so that once you become familiar with Harvard Graphics' MACRO utility, you can use it to create macros to perform any repetitive task for you.

When you execute a macro, the macro repeats the keystrokes you have recorded. For example, if you start recording a macro and then press DOWN ARROW three times and ENTER once to select Get/Save/Remove, the macro records pressing DOWN ARROW three times and ENTER once. Therefore, if you execute this macro when the Get/Save/Remove selection is already highlighted, the macro selects Slide show menu from the Main Menu. If you are in the Titles & Options form for one of the chart types, this macro moves you three fields down and presses ENTER on the selected choice. To prevent this from occurring, you want the macro to start from a consistent position, such as the Main Menu. By pressing ESC many times, you ensure that the Main Menu is the active menu. To ensure that the correct menu or field selection is made, use the number of the menu item rather than pointing to the menu selection you want and pressing ENTER. If you start recording a macro and change your mind, you can press ALT-F6 to cancel the recording process.

Entering Data

You can create a macro that supplies data entries on a chart form just as easily as the "Getting Started" macro modified the settings on the Print Chart form. You simply enter the fixed data that will appear every time the macro is run. If you want the data entries to vary each time you run the macro, you must use the variable feature discussed later in this chapter.

You can use MACRO's ability to accept data for entry with the TODO template created in Chapter 11. (If you did not create this template, you can turn back to Chapter 11 and enter the steps required to create it.) When you saved this template, it was not possible to save the chart title because it would have meant saving each of the bullet entries. Follow these steps to create a macro to display and enhance the To-Do list created earlier:

1. Press ALT-O to display the MACRO menu.

You can invoke the macro menu at any point in Harvard Graphics, except when you are viewing a chart or in the Draw/Annotate screen. You can only invoke MACRO outside of Harvard Graphics if the screen is a text-based screen, like Harvard Graphics forms, rather than a graphics screen, like the Draw/Annotate screen.

2. Select Record a macro.

MACRO displays a prompt for the macro name suggesting the current directory to save the macro. You do not need to type a file extension for this filename since Harvard Graphics adds a .MAC extension. Since the macro name is a filename, your entry must follow DOS filename standards. Your entry must be between one and eight characters. You cannot include spaces in the filename, although you can use the underscore (_) to separate words.

3. Type **TODO** to create a macro file called TODO.MAC and press ENTER.

The MACRO menu disappears as you return to Harvard Graphics to record the macro.

4. Press ESC four times to ensure that the macro will always start from the Main Menu.
5. Type **4** to select Get/Save/Remove, and then type **3** to select Get template.
6. Type **TODO** and press ENTER to retrieve the template created in Chapter 11.
7. Type **To-Do List** and press ENTER three times to position for the first bullet entry.
8. Press ALT-O and select Stop recording macro.

You could now type in the specific elements for each bullet item.

Storing Macros in a Different Directory

The macro you created in the previous section was stored in the current directory. On other occasions you may want to store macros in a different directory. For example, if you are using the Harvard Graphics accessory U.S. MapMaker (covered in Chapter 13), you may have it in a different directory than your Harvard Graphics files. You may want to keep all your macro files and Harvard Graphics files in the same directory. The directory you set to store your macros is also the directory MACRO looks at when you select a macro to play back.

To set the directory, press ALT-O to display the MACRO menu. Select Change macro directory. MACRO displays the current directory setting. You can edit this setting to be the directory you want. Once you enter the directory you want and press ENTER to finalize it, the drive and directory is used whenever you record or play back a macro. The exception is if you enter directory information when you enter the name of the macro you are creating or playing back.

Naming Macros

You have two options for recording macros. You can provide a name like TODO, which is descriptive of the task the macro performs. This option gives you eight characters to describe the macro. Another option is to give the macro a name that lets you perform the macro by pressing (ALT) and a letter or number. These are one-key macros. This option provides 36 different macro names, although the macro name is not descriptive like the longer macro names. To make a macro a one-key macro, name the macro with one letter or number. To execute the macro later, press (ALT) and the letter or number of the macro name. For example, if the macro is named P.MAC, you can execute this macro by pressing (ALT-P).

Displaying Messages

When a macro is executing, you want to let the user know what is happening. For example, if the macro is saving the chart to a floppy disk, you may want to tell the user that the macro is saving a file and the user should not touch the disk in the drive until the light goes out. When the macro is performing a task that takes time, a message tells the user the machine is not locked up. Messages can also be used when your macro has variables and you want to tell the macro user what they should enter.

You can create a macro that uses a message to warn the user that the macro is saving a file and will take several minutes. To create this macro, follow these instructions:

1. Press (ESC) to return to the Main Menu.
2. Press (ALT-O) to display the MACRO menu.
3. Select Record a macro.

MACRO displays a prompt for the macro name and suggests the directory to save the macro to. If you wanted to save the macro to a different directory, you would modify the directory setting before you entered the filename.

4. Type **SAVEWAIT** for the macro name and press (ENTER).

The MACRO menu disappears as you return to Harvard Graphics to record the macro.

5. Press (ESC) four times to ensure that the macro will always start from the Main Menu.
6. Press (CTRL-F10) to tell MACRO that you want to display a message.

MACRO displays an overlay box. You can type a message of up to 78 characters.

7. Type **Go get a cup of coffee. Saving the file will take a few minutes.** and press ENTER.
8. Type **5** to select Import/Export, and then type **8** to select Export picture.
9. Type **PICTOUT** for the Picture name field and press ENTER.
10. Type **H** to select High for the Picture quality field and press ENTER.
11. Type **H** to select HPGL for the Format field, and press F10 (Continue) to save the file in this format.
12. Press ESC to return to the Main Menu.
13. Press ALT-O and select Stop recording macro.

Now every time you need the current chart saved in HPGL format you can execute the SAVEWAIT macro. This macro assumes that there is no file named PICTOUT. After executing the macro, you must rename the PICTOUT file to another name. When you execute this macro, it displays the message as shown in Figure 12-2. The user knows that after they press

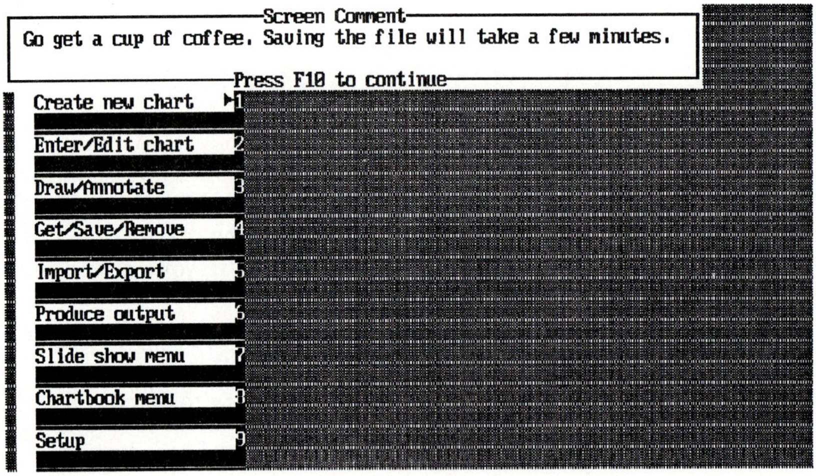

FIGURE 12-2. Macro displaying a message

F10 they can work on another task, since Harvard Graphics will be busy saving the file for the next few minutes. Harvard Graphics has another feature that lets you display a message using up to 22 lines, but this feature is beyond the scope of this book.

Documenting a Macro

Harvard Graphics does not allow you to edit macro code directly from the macro program. You can use utilities like EDLIN or a word processor to make changes to your entries, as you will see in a later section. The problem is that it is often difficult to remember exactly what each step you recorded was trying to accomplish when some time has elapsed between the macro recording and your review.

Harvard Graphics allows you to add comments anywhere within a macro file. Although you cannot see the comments with MACRO or Harvard Graphics, they are incorporated into the macro code if you ever need to make changes.

You can add up to 78 characters of documentation on a line of a macro from within the MACRO utility. At the point where you want to add the documentation, all you need to do is press ALT-F10. If you choose to add documentation from within an editor or a word processor, as described later, you can add up to 255 characters of documentation at any location in a macro.

Follow these steps to create a documented macro that displays and then saves the current chart:

1. Press ALT-O to display the MACRO menu.
2. Select Record a macro.

MACRO displays a prompt for the macro name, and suggests the directory to save the macro to. If you want to save the macro to a different directory, modify the directory setting before you enter the filename.

3. Type S for the macro name and press ENTER.

This macro will be a one-key macro that you can execute by pressing ALT-S.

4. Press ESC four times to ensure that the macro always returns to the main menu.
5. Press F2 (Draw chart) since you want the macro to display the current chart.
6. Press ESC to remove the chart from the screen.

When you display a chart in a macro, you should use ESC to return to the current chart.

7. Type **4** to select Get/Save/Remove, and then type **2** to select Save Chart.
8. Press ALT-F10 to start entering a comment.
9. Type **This macro lets the user enter the file name and description** and press ENTER.
10. Press ALT-O and select Stop recording macro.

When you look at the macro, this comment will appear as:

<*This macro lets the user enter the file name and description>

11. Press ESC twice to return to the Main Menu.

MODIFYING MACROS

The only way to change a macro from within Harvard Graphics is to reenter it. If the macro has any length, this could be a problem. The solution is to use a word processor or line editor to make the change. Most word processors support ASCII files, which are used by MACRO for its macro files. All you need to remember is to tell your word processor that you want to work with an ASCII file and you want to use the Harvard Graphics directory when attempting to find the macro file. You can also use the DOS editor EDLIN to edit the file. To look at the file, you can use a word processor, or you can print the file. You also can view the file by using the DOS TYPE command. Issue the DOS TYPE command by entering **TYPE** followed by a space and the filename, including the .MAC extension, and then press ENTER. Figure 12-3 shows the text stored in a macro file.

```
D>type savewait.mac

<CMD>T0<CMD>

<CMD>P40<CMD>
<ESC><ESC><ESC><ESC><CMD><*Go get a cup of coffee. Saving the file will take a f
ew minutes.><CMD>
50pictout<ENTER>h<ENTER>h<F10><ESC>
D>
```

FIGURE 12-3. Macro file

Key Equivalents

If you plan to modify existing macros or enter new ones with an editor or word processor, you must be familiar with acceptable entries for keys. Harvard Graphics is particular about both spelling and capitalization for all the key-equivalent entries. If you do not make entries that represent the keystrokes you want, the macro is unlikely to perform the task you need. The keystrokes that a macro recognizes and the representation of the keystrokes that MACRO stores in the macro file are shown in Table 12-1.

Other macro commands and the tasks they perform are shown in Table 12-2. Most of these commands are for the more advanced macros features.

The first two commands in the macro file are required. The first command controls the timing delay, or the time between executing commands. Often this is set at 0 so the macro executes quickly. The second command controls the polling delay, or the time between keystrokes. This is initially 40, but you may need to increase it if your macro contains keystrokes that it is not performing. An executing macro will "lose keystrokes" when MACRO supplies the keystrokes too fast for Harvard Graphics to process. This problem is solved by increasing the polling delay. After these two commands are the commands that the macro performs.

Making Corrections

When you execute a macro that does not perform as you expected, you have two solutions. First, you can record the macro again. This is an ideal solution

Keystroke	**Macro Representation**
function key	<F1> through <F10>
letter	A through Z
number	0 through 9
symbols (except + − and >)	` ! @ # $ % ^ & *()_ =[ ]{ };:'"?,./
ALT-*number*	<Alt0> through <Alt9>
ALT-*letter*	<AltA> through <AltZ>
ALT-*function key*	<AltF1> through <AltF10>
ALT-−	<Alt−>
ALT-=	<Alt=>
BACKSPACE	<BKS>
CTRL-*letter*	<CtrlA> through <CtrlZ>
CTRL-*function key*	<CtrlF1> through <CtrlF10>
CTRL-DELETE	<CtrlDEL>
CTRL-DOWN ARROW	<CtrlDN>
CTRL-END	<CtrlEND>
CTRL-HOME	<CtrlHOME>
CTRL-INSERT	<CtrlINS>
CTRL-LEFT ARROW	<CtrlLFT>
CTRL-RIGHT ARROW	<CtrlRGT>
CTRL-PGUP	<CtrlPGUP>
CTRL-PGDN	<CtrlPGDN>
CTRL-UP ARROW	<CtrlUP>
DELETE	<DEL>
DOWN ARROW	<DN>
END	<END>
ENTER	<ENTER>
ESC	<ESC>

TABLE 12-1. Keystrokes and Macro Representation (*continued on next page*)

Keystroke	Macro Representation
HOME	<HOME>
INSERT	<INS>
LEFT ARROW	<LFT>
PGDN	<PGDN>
PGUP	<PGUP>
RIGHT ARROW	<RGT>
SHIFT-*function key*	<ShftF1> through <ShftF10>
SHIFT-TAB	<ShftTAB>
TAB	<TAB>
UP ARROW	<UP>
– (minus or hyphen sign)	<MIN>
+ (plus sign)	<PLS>
<	<<

TABLE 12-1. (*continued*) Keystrokes and Macro Representation

if you want to replace a macro with different instructions or if the macro is very short. To replace a macro with new instructions, start recording the new macro and provide the existing name as the name of the macro you want to record. MACRO prompts you if you want the new macro to overwrite the old. Select Yes and press ENTER to replace the old macro with the new instructions. Then record the new macro instructions as you would a new macro.

The second possibility is to edit the macro to correct mistakes or to add new macro instructions. When you edit the macro using a word processor or another type of editor, you should check that all of your entries match the representations for keystrokes. You also want to check for extra spaces, which in a macro are treated like other characters since the macro types the space just as if you did. End each line with a carriage return. Once you edit the macro, you will want to test it to ensure that it performs as expected.

Try editing a macro using EDLIN to add comments to the macro file SAVEWAIT.MAC that will explain the "H" for High and the "H" for HPGL. While the following instructions are for EDLIN, you can use any text editor. To modify this macro file, follow these steps:

1. Exit Harvard Graphics if it is still active by typing **E** from the Main Menu.
2. Type **EDLIN SAVEWAIT.MAC** and press ENTER.

EDLIN is a text editor accompanying DOS. If your DOS files are in a different directory, such as DOS, you may need to precede this command with the directory name and backslash as in \DOS\EDLIN SAVEWAIT.MAC. Once EDLIN is loaded, End of input file and the command prompt (an asterisk) appear.

3. Type **L** and press ENTER.

Macro Command	Action
<**text*>	Comment that documents a macro
<AUTO>	Starts executing the same macro from the beginning
<CMD> <**text*> <CMD>	Displays the text as an on-screen message
<CMD>F[*path*]filename <CMD>	Executes the macro specified by the path and filename
<CMD>P*number*<CMD>	Sets the polling delay
<CMD>R*hh:mm:ss:nn*<CMD>	Delays macro execution for the amount of time set by *hh:mm:ss:nn*, where *hh* is hours, *mm* is minutes, *ss* is seconds, and *nn* is milliseconds
<CMD>T*number*<CMD>	Sets the timing delay
<CMD>W*hh:mm*<CMD>	Delays macro execution until the time set by *hh:mm*, where *hh* is hours and *mm* is minutes
<STOP>	Stops macro execution and unloads MACRO from memory if possible
<VFLD> <VFLD>	Inserts a variable field

TABLE 12-2. Macro Commands

L is the EDLIN command to list the file. You can see the file contents. When EDLIN displays lines in a file, it marks the current one with an asterisk to the right of the line number and colon. This asterisk does not affect the file and can be ignored.

4. Type **6** and press ENTER to edit the sixth line.

EDLIN displays line 6 and prompts for your new entry.

5. Press the RIGHT ARROW 17 times so the first "H" appears.

As you press the RIGHT ARROW, EDLIN displays the next character in the line. This is quicker than retyping the entire line.

6. Type **<*High quality>**.

This comment describes the first "H." The asterisk without a <CMD> macro command instructs MACRO that this command is a comment, and will be ignored when MACRO executes this macro.

7. Type **<ENTER>h**.

When you type macro keystroke representations such as **<ENTER>**, you must be sure to use the correct spelling and capitalization and include both brackets.

8. Type **<*HPGL format>**.

This comment describes the second "H."

9. Type **<F10><ESC>** and press ENTER.

By pressing ENTER you are telling EDLIN you are finished with the line. The asterisk command prompt returns as EDLIN prompts for the next command.

10. Type **L** and press ENTER to list the macro, which looks like Figure 12-4.
11. Type **E** and press ENTER to save the file and end EDLIN.

12. Type **HG** and press ENTER to load Harvard Graphics.

PLAYBACK PROCEDURES

Once you have a macro recorded, you can execute it by pressing ALT-O and selecting Play back a macro. At the MACRO prompt type the macro name. If the macro is not stored in the directory you expect, edit the drive and directory so it is the one that contains the macro you want. Once the filename, drive, and directory are entered, press ENTER to start executing the macro. The macro executes the keystrokes you entered when you recorded the macro. If you display a chart by pressing F2, the chart remains visible for 30 seconds unless you tell MACRO to continue with the keystrokes by pressing CTRL-RIGHT SHIFT. If Harvard Graphics displays a chart after getting a file, MACRO immediately performs the next instruction. If you need to stop macro execution, press ALT-END.

If you named the macro using a single letter or number, you have another alternative for executing the macro: press ALT and the letter or number that is the macro name.

Once you execute a macro, MACRO remembers the macro name. The next time you press ALT-O and select Play back a macro, MACRO suggests the last executed macro as the macro you want. You can press CTRL-DELETE to remove this and enter a new name, or press ENTER to accept this macro name.

If your macro does not perform as you expected, you have several options. You can edit the macro file if you know where the mistake occurred. For some mistakes, like misspelling a keystroke representation, MACRO tells

```
*l
        1:
        2:*<CMD>T0<CMD>
        3:
        4: <CMD>P40<CMD>
        5: <ESC><ESC><ESC><ESC><CMD><*Go get a cup of coffee. Saving the file wi
ll take a few minutes.><CMD>
        6: 50pictout<ENTER>h<*High quality><ENTER>h<*HPGL format><F10><ESC>
*
```

FIGURE 12-4. Macro file after editing

you that a comment command is missing the asterisk. Another option for finding where an error occurred in a macro is to execute the macro a step at a time.

Executing a Macro Step-by-Step

When a macro contains an error, it may be difficult to find where the error occurred because the macro executed too quickly for you to follow along. You can slow the macro's execution so you can follow the steps the macro performs. Executing a macro one step at a time also lets you see and understand the steps the macro is performing. Before you execute a macro step-by-step, print the macro so you have a copy of the macro instructions that you can follow as MACRO performs the instructions.

Execute the SAVEWAIT macro step-by-step by following these instructions:

1. Press ALT-O to display the MACRO menu and select Play back a macro.

MACRO prompts for the macro you want to execute.

2. If a macro name is displayed, press BACKSPACE until the displayed macro name is removed.
3. Type **SAVEWAIT** and press ENTER.

MACRO starts executing the keystrokes stored in the SAVEWAIT macro. As the first step, the macro displays the message box.

4. Press F10 to remove the message box.
5. Press CTRL-ALT to display this menu:

```
                 | Pause |
▸Single-step playback                  No
 Pause playback for       keys         No
 Resume macro playback          Yes
```

This menu lets you change how the macro is played back.

6. Select Single-step playback.

This changes the No to Yes.

7. Press ESC to remove the Pause menu and to return to Harvard Graphics.
8. Press any key.

MACRO now enters the next macro instruction. To continue entering the next macro instruction, continue pressing any key. You can keep doing this until the macro is completed, but if the macro is long you may want to follow only part of the macro one step at a time and the rest of the macro at normal speed.

9. Press CTRL-ALT to display the Pause menu.
10. Select Single-step playback to change the Yes to No.
11. Press ESC to remove the Pause menu and to return to Harvard Graphics.

The macro continues at its initial speed until the macro is finished or you change the macro speed again by pressing CTRL-ALT and selecting Single-Step Playback.

UNLOADING MACRO

When you have finished using Harvard Graphics and are ready to use another software program, you must remove MACRO from the computer's memory. MACRO remains in memory until you unload the program or you restart the computer. You will want to unload MACRO when you are finished using it; that way the memory space MACRO used is made available for other programs. Also, to use another program that uses ALT-O, such as Professional Write, you must unload MACRO. To unload MACRO, leave Harvard Graphics; press ALT-O and select Unload. Assuming you can remove MACRO from memory, you will be prompted to press ENTER to confirm that you want to unload MACRO. Once you press ENTER, the MACRO menu disappears. You also might see the message "Cannot Unload Macro" if MACRO was not the last loaded TSR (terminate-and-stay-resident) program. In this case, you must first unload the TSR's that you loaded after MACRO before you can unload MACRO. You also unload MACRO when you restart the system.

USING ADVANCED FEATURES

In addition to the basic features you have learned so far, MACRO has advanced features that you will find useful as you develop your own macros. With more advanced features of MACRO, you can create macros that use variables. This lets you enter unique information each time the macro is run, run one macro in another (which is called *nesting*), and add delays to the macro to change when MACRO performs the next instruction.

Using Variables

The macros you have created so far all perform the same task every time you execute the macro. Another type of application would be a macro that prompts you to enter information and uses that information in the chart or as the chart's filename. When you are recording a macro, you must tell MACRO that you want to accept user input. The user input is a variable that you must add to the macro. Examples of a variable are the data a chart uses and the filename used to save a file.

To add a variable, press CTRL-– (CTRL and the hyphen or minus key). MACRO stops recording your keystrokes since you are entering the variable information you want to use as you record the keystrokes that will be stored in the macro. When you have finished entering the keystrokes for the variable information and are ready to enter the remaining keystrokes you want recorded in the macro, press ALT-0. The remaining keystrokes you press will be recorded.

If you look at a macro file with a variable, you will see <VFLD> <VFLD>, which represents where the macro will pause so you can enter the variable keystrokes. When you run the macro, MACRO performs the execution up until the <VFLD><VFLD> instruction. Then MACRO displays a message. Press F10 to continue and enter the variable keystrokes. When you have finished entering any variable keystrokes you want to enter, press ALT-0 and MACRO will continue to execute the remaining instructions. When you are entering the variable information, MACRO does not recognize CTRL-DELETE, CTRL-INSERT, CTRL-UP ARROW, and CTRL-DOWN ARROW. You do not want to create situations that require the user to press these keystrokes, such as rearranging the order of data values. Also, before you enter a variable, you should display a message indicating the information the user should enter.

You can try creating a macro using variable information by following these keystrokes:

1. Press ALT-O to display the MACRO menu.
2. Select Record a macro.

MACRO prompts for the macro name and directory to save the macro to.

3. Type **PIE** for the macro name and press ENTER.
4. Press ESC four times to ensure that the macro always returns to the Main Menu.
5. Type **1** to select Create new chart and type **2** to select Pie.
6. Type **Sales Distribution Between Products** and press ENTER three times to move to where the label for the first slice should be entered.
7. Press CTRL-F10 since you want to display a message.
8. Type **Enter the products to list in the pie chart** and press ENTER.
9. Press CTRL-– to start entering variable information. The screen will not change.
10. Type **Toys** and press ENTER.
11. Type **Games** and press ENTER.
12. Type **Stuffed Animals.**
13. Press ALT-O to start recording the macro key-strokes again.

Once again, the screen will not change. If you see the MACRO menu, you did not press CTRL-– You will want to select Stop recording macro, press ESC and try again.

14. Press HOME once and TAB four times to move to where the value for the first pie slice will be entered.
15. Press CTRL-F10 since you want to display a message.
16. Type **Enter the values for the products to list in the pie chart** and press ENTER.

17. Press CTRL-— to start entering variable information.
18. Type **110000** and press ENTER.
19. Type **200000** and press ENTER.
20. Type **150000** and press ENTER.
21. Press ALT-O to start recording the macro keystrokes again.
22. Press F2 (Draw chart) to display the chart made with this data.
23. Press ESC twice to return to the Main Menu.
24. Press CTRL-S to save the chart.
25. Press CTRL-F10 since you want to display a message.
26. Type **Enter the filename for the chart** and press ENTER.
27. Press CTRL-— to start entering variable information.
28. Type **PIEMAKE** and press ENTER.
29. Press ALT-O to start recording the macro keystrokes again.
30. Press F10 (Continue) to save the chart.
31. Press ALT-O and select Stop recording macro.

Now that you have created the macro, try executing it.

1. Press ALT-O to display the MACRO menu.
2. Select Play back a macro.

MACRO prompts for the macro name and directory. It displays the last macro executed.

3. Press BACKSPACE until the previous macro name is removed.
4. Type **PIE** for the macro name and press ENTER.

MACRO starts executing the macro until it reaches the variable. Before it reaches the variable, it displays a message in the box to enter the products to list in the pie chart.

5. Press F10 to remove the message box and display this message:

```
——————Variable Field——————————
Press F10 to start typing in the variable
field. When you're done, press Alt-0 to
resume playback.
—————Press F10 to continue—————
```

6. Press F10 to remove the second message box and start entering variable information.
7. Type **Engines** and press ENTER.
8. Type **Motors** and press ENTER.
9. Type **Cans** and press ENTER.
10. Type **Aluminum Foil.**

This macro does not care how many labels and values you enter for pie slices.

11. Press ALT-O to execute the remaining macro instructions. MACRO continues executing the macro until it reaches the next variable. Before it halts execution again, it displays a message in the box to enter the values for the products.
12. Press F10 twice to remove the message boxes and start entering variable information.
13. Type **600000** and press ENTER.
14. Type **800000** and press ENTER.
15. Type **420000** and press ENTER.
16. Type **350000** and press ENTER.
17. Press ALT-O to start executing the remaining macro instructions.

MACRO executes the rest of the macro until it reaches the last variable. The chart remains on the screen for 30 seconds. The last message box prompts you to enter the filename to use to save the chart.

18. Press F10 twice to remove the message box and enter the filename.
19. Type **PIEMETAL** and press ALT-O to execute the rest of the macro.

The macro executes the last macro instructions. In this macro, you have only entered the information that changes each time you use the macro. The macro only performs the keystrokes for the pie chart that remains the same.

Nesting

When you create several macros, you may want to combine them. For example, if you create a macro to save a chart and another to print the chart, you could combine these two macros into one. When one macro calls another, it is called *nesting*. When you use a macro in another, you do not have to reenter the macro instructions to perform the same task. It also reduces errors, since you are using a macro that you know works as you expect. To use a macro in another macro that you are recording, press ALT-O when you are at the point where you want the other macro executed. Select Play back a macro and enter the macro name you want to play back. The macro you selected will execute. When the macro finishes, continue recording the rest of the macro. Nesting macros in this way adds another level to the original macro. You can have up to 12 levels in a macro.

You can try nesting macros by creating a macro that saves a chart and combining it with a macro that prints a chart.

1. Press ALT-O to display the MACRO menu and select Record a macro.
2. Type **SAVEPRNT** for the macro's name and press ENTER.
3. Press ESC four times so the macro moves to the Main Menu.
4. Press CTRL-S to save the chart.
5. Press F10 (Continue) to save the chart with the same settings that it was saved with the last time.

You may remember from the "Getting Started" section that you did not start the PRT macro by pressing ESC several times. To use the PRT macro, you must be in the Main Menu.

6. Press ALT-O and select Play back a macro.
7. Press BACKSPACE until any previous macro name is removed.
8. Type **PRT** and press ENTER to print another copy of the current chart.

Harvard Graphics prints the current chart with the Quality field set to High and the Color field set to No. When MACRO finishes executing the macro, you can enter any additional keystrokes you want to record. Since there are no more keystrokes for this macro, you can finish recording the macro.

9. Press ALT-O to display the MACRO menu and select Stop recording macro.

The SAVEPRNT macro now contains the instructions to execute the PRT macro after saving the current chart. This macro assumes that the chart has been saved before you execute this macro. If you look at the macro file, you will see <CMD>FC:\HG\PRT.MAC<CMD>, which tells the SAVEPRNT macro to execute the PRT macro.

Adding Delays

MACRO performs the keystrokes in a macro as fast as possible, but in some cases you may not want the macro executed this way. For example, if you have a group of charts to print, you may want to delay printing them until lunch time so the printing will not disturb others. MACRO has four time delays that you can add to macros. Two of them, timing delays and polling delays, have already been mentioned because they always appear at the beginning of the macro file. You also can add two other types, real-time and wait-until delays. You can add multiple delays to a macro as well.

A real-time delay postpones the macro execution for a defined period of time. A real-time delay also changes the length of time a chart appears if the delay is added just before you press F2. You can use real-time delays to show a screen or to wait until the user has performed an action, such as putting a disk into drive A. A wait-until delay postpones the execution of a macro instruction until the time set by DOS. This time delay requires that the time stored by the computer be correct. If the time DOS displays when you enter TIME is incorrect, you must enter a new time in the format the command suggests. The real-time and wait-until delays only affect the macro instruction after the delay. After the macro waits for the time set by the delay, the macro continues the macro execution as before. To add a delay to a macro, record the macro until you reach a point where you want to add a delay. Press ALT-O to display the MACRO menu and select Insert delays. Then select the type of delay you want. MACRO prompts for the length of the delay. For a timing delay, you must type a number between 0 and 999. An increment of 1 is equal to 18 seconds. For the polling delay, you must enter a number between 0 and 9999. Although the default is 40, you want to change it only if the macro is losing keystrokes. For a real-time delay, enter a number between 0 and 32767 that represents the number of seconds the macro should wait before executing the remaining instructions. For a wait-until delay, you must type the entry in *hh:mm* format where *hh* represents hours and *mm* represents minutes. Type the number or time and press **ENTER**. Press **ESC** twice to return to the MACRO menu, and then remove the MACRO menu from the screen.

Follow these instructions to create a macro that uses these delays and changes the settings of the current pie chart:

1. Press **ALT-O** to display the MACRO menu and select Record a macro.
2. Type **CHANGPIE** and press **ENTER** for the macro name.
3. Type **2** to select Enter/Edit chart.
4. Press **F8** (Options) to display the first page of the Pie Titles & Options form.
5. Press **F7** (Size/Place), type **7**, and press **F10** (Continue) to reduce the size of the text.
6. Press **TAB** five times to move to the 3D effect field and type **Y**.
7. Press **TAB** three times to move to the Fill style field and type a **B** for Both.
8. Press **PGDN** to move to the second page of the Pie Charts Titles & Options form.
9. Press **END** to move to the Percent format field for Pie 2.
10. Press **SHIFT-TAB** five times to move to the Show percent field for Pie 1, and type a **Y** for Yes.
11. Press **ALT-O** and then select Insert delays to display this menu:

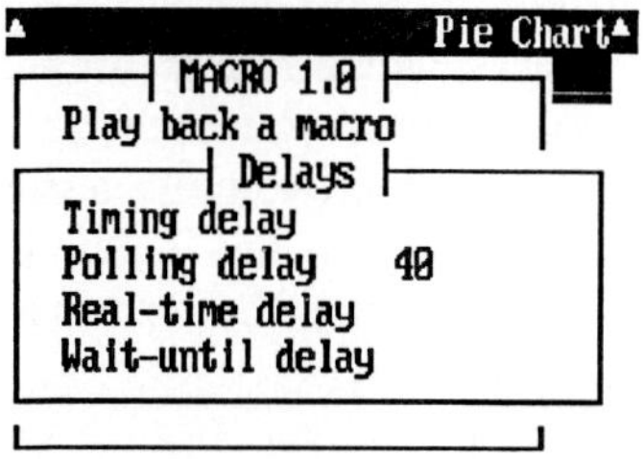

12. Select Real-time delay.

MACRO prompts for the number of seconds that you want to delay the macro.

13. Type **15** and press ENTER.
14. Press ESC twice to remove the MACRO menu from the screen.
15. Press F2 (Draw chart) to view the chart.
16. Press ESC twice to return to the Harvard Graphics Main Menu.
17. Press CTRL-S to save the chart.
18. Press F10 (Continue) to save the chart with the same settings that it was saved with the last time.
19. Press ALT-O to display the MACRO menu and select Stop recording macro.

Now that you have created the macro you will want to try executing it:

1. Press ALT-O to display the MACRO menu.
2. Select Play back a macro.

MACRO prompts for the macro name and directory. It displays the last macro executed.

3. Press BACKSPACE until the previous macro name is removed.
4. Type **CHANGPIE** for the macro name and then press ENTER.

MACRO executes the macro and waits 15 seconds before it displays the chart. After the chart is displayed, the macro continues executing the remaining instructions at MACRO's normal speed. The real-time delay only affects the command after the delay is inserted. Like the SAVEPRNT macro you created earlier, this macro assumes that you have saved the current chart before you execute this macro. If you look at the CHANGPIE macro file, you will notice <CMD>R*0:0:15:0*<CMD>, which represents the real-time delay. MACRO converts the number of seconds you enter into the time representation used in the macro command. When you run a macro with a real-time or wait-until delay, you can cut short the delay by pressing CTRL-RIGHT SHIFT to immediately start executing the next macro instruction after the delay.

chapter 13

USING OTHER APPLICATIONS AND ACCESSORY PRODUCTS

Harvard Graphics 2.3 includes the features of some accessories marketed by Software Publishing to enhance the features of earlier releases of the product. Draw Partner, which was originally marketed as an accessory, is now included with every copy of Harvard Graphics 2.3. The features of Designer Galleries are now included as chart galleries any time you choose to create a chart. Some of the ScreenShow Utilities features are now also included with the product. Other accessories such as Business Symbols, Military Symbols, Quick-Charts, and U.S. MapMaker still add significant value to the product.

Some of the accessories provide symbols and charts that are used by copying the files to the directories you are using with Harvard Graphics. Other accessories are programs that are run outside of Harvard Graphics. These accessory programs can be attached as applications that are executable without leaving Harvard Graphics. Draw Partner is automatically attached as an application with a permanent link. You can attach as many as seven other applications including Lotus 1-2-3 or DOS.

If you have some of these accessories from earlier releases of Harvard Graphics, you can continue to use the accessory with Harvard Graphics 2.3. Even those that can be attached as applications can still be run separately if you choose, although you will find the ability to use the accessory without leaving Harvard Graphics to be a desirable enhancement.

In this chapter you will learn how to attach applications to Harvard Graphics 2.3. You will also learn how to execute applications that have been attached. You will also have the opportunity to review some of the capabilities that accessories add to the product. Draw Partner, since it is included with the product, is covered separately in more detail in Chapter 9.

WORKING WITH OTHER APPLICATIONS

Like many other popular business software packages, Harvard Graphics 2.3 has added a feature to allow you to use another program without exiting from Harvard Graphics. Your current chart will remain in memory while you execute another program. When you return to Harvard Graphics you will be able to continue to work with the current chart.

Draw Partner and a slide service application are attached when you install Harvard Graphics. Although you cannot remove the application link to Draw Partner, you can use the other seven options, including the one for the AGX Slide Service, to attach the other applications. Once set up you will be able to invoke the application from a menu and return to Harvard Graphics whenever you are ready.

Setting Up Applications

You can use the seven slots to set up applications that will be useful in many ways. You might choose to set up DOS to allow you to exit to DOS without leaving Harvard Graphics. You might choose to set up an accessory for Harvard Graphics like U.S. MapMaker to allow you to create a map chart. You might set up another application such as Lotus 1-2-3 or WordStar to allow you to access a different type of data without removing Harvard Graphics from memory.

Setting up a new application is easy, all you need to do is follow these steps:

1. Select Setup from the Main Menu.
2. Select Applications from the Setup menu.

An applications screen like the one shown in Figure 13-1 will appear. Figure 13-1 already shows two additional applications that have been added since installation.

3. Press **TAB** to move to the next empty Menu Item field.
4. Type a descriptive name or the actual name for your application.
5. Press **TAB**, then type a maximum size for your application in K if you know the correct number of bytes. If not, leave the Maximum size (K) field blank. Harvard Graphics switches to programs less than 640K faster if it knows the program size.
6. Press **TAB** to move to the Command field.
7. Type the command you would enter from the Harvard Graphics directory to start the program, then press **F10** (Continue) unless you want to add additional applications.

Your entry might include the name of a drive or directory of the .BAT, .COM, or .EXE file that you wish to execute if it is not in the Harvard Graphics directory or is not accessible through a path statement in your AUTOEXEC.BAT file. Including the directory of the program in the path statement allows you to run the program from any directory. For example, to execute Lotus 1-2-3 when this program is stored in a directory called 123, you can modify your path statement to include 123 as in:

```
PATH C:\123;
```

If you make this modification you can enter **123** as the Command field entry when accessing this program through Harvard Graphics. Without the path entry for 1-2-3, you need to enter **C:\123\123** as the Command field.

```
                              Applications

Menu item 1: Draw Partner            Menu item 5:
Maximum size (K):                    Maximum size (K):
Command: HGDP.EXE                    Command:

Menu item 2: AGX Slide Service       Menu item 6:
Maximum size (K):                    Maximum size (K):
Command: toagx                       Command:

Menu item 3: DOS                     Menu item 7:
Maximum size (K):                    Maximum size (K):
Command: c:\command.com              Command:

Menu item 4: 1-2-3 Release 2.2       Menu item 8:
Maximum size (K):                    Maximum size (K):
Command: 123                         Command:

F1-Help
                                     F8-Options          F10-Continue
```

FIGURE 13-1. Applications screen additions

To add DOS as an application you need to invoke the DOS command processor, COMMAND.COM. Your command entry would be **COMMAND.COM**, **C:\DOS\COMMAND.COM**, or **C:\COMMAND.COM** depending upon the location of COMMAND.COM and whether or not this location is part of the path statement in your AUTOEXEC.BAT file. If you feel uncertain of the entry to make for a particular program, try executing the program from your Harvard Graphics directory. Whatever entry works from this location will start the program if you type this entry in the Command field.

To add additional applications, repeat steps 3 through 7 in the next empty application slot. If you want to change or remove a current application, you must change or delete the entries on the Applications form shown in Figure 13-1. When you are finished, press F10 (Continue) to return to the Setup menu, then ESC to return to the Main Menu.

Executing an Application

You can start Draw Partner or another installed application by pressing F3 (Applications) from the Main Menu. The Applications menu shown in Figure 13-2 will appear.

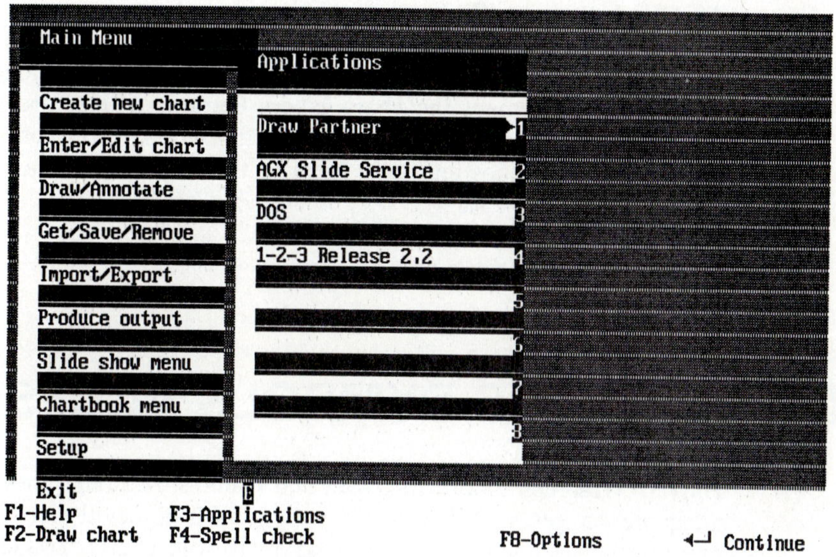

FIGURE 13-2. Applications menu

To start the application, highlight your choice and press ENTER or type the number associated with the desired selection.

Returning to Harvard Graphics

Once you are finished using your application, you will want to return to Harvard Graphics. You should save any data entered in your application before returning or it will be lost when you exit the program. Exit your program in the normal way and you will be back in Harvard Graphics at the Main Menu with your current chart still in memory. If you exited to DOS, you will need to type **EXIT** and press ENTER to return to Harvard Graphics.

USING ACCESSORIES

The four accessories covered in this chapter are Business Symbols, Quick-Charts, U.S. Mapmaker, and Military Symbols. The two symbol accessories supplement the symbols that are part of the package. Once you install these accessories you can work with the symbols they provide just as you do with the ones included with the package. You use the same menu commands to add, move, and change the colors on these symbols as you do for the ones included in Harvard Graphics. Quick-Charts provides additional predefined charts that supplement the chart gallery features of Harvard Graphics 2.3. U.S. Mapmaker is a stand-alone package that allows you to create additional city and country maps and save them in the format of a Harvard Graphics chart.

THE BUSINESS SYMBOLS ACCESSORY

Harvard Graphics 2.3 provides over 500 symbols. Although these symbols are adequate to get you started, if you publish a newsletter or give many presentations you will want to add variety to your charts. You can purchase a copy of the Business Symbols accessory to add hundreds of additional symbols including computers and peripheral equipment, math symbols, furniture, chemical symbols, and symbols that represent different industries. Figure 13-3 shows several charts that use symbols from the Business Symbols accessory. Adding one of these symbols requires the same steps for adding symbols that you learned in Chapter 9.

Installing Business Symbols

To install the Business Symbols accessory, place the 5 1/4-inch Business Symbols Disk 1 or the 3 1/2-inch Business Symbols disk into drive A and type **COPY A:*.* C:\HG\SYMBOLS**. If your Harvard Graphics symbols are not stored in the HG\SYMBOLS directory on drive C, substitute the correct drive and directory information in place of C:\HG\SYMBOLS. If you are using the 5 1/4-inch disks, replace Business Symbols Disk 1 with Business Symbols Disk 2 when the symbols files from the first disk are copied. Then press F3 to repeat the DOS command and press ENTER. This copies the second disk of symbol files to your hard disk.

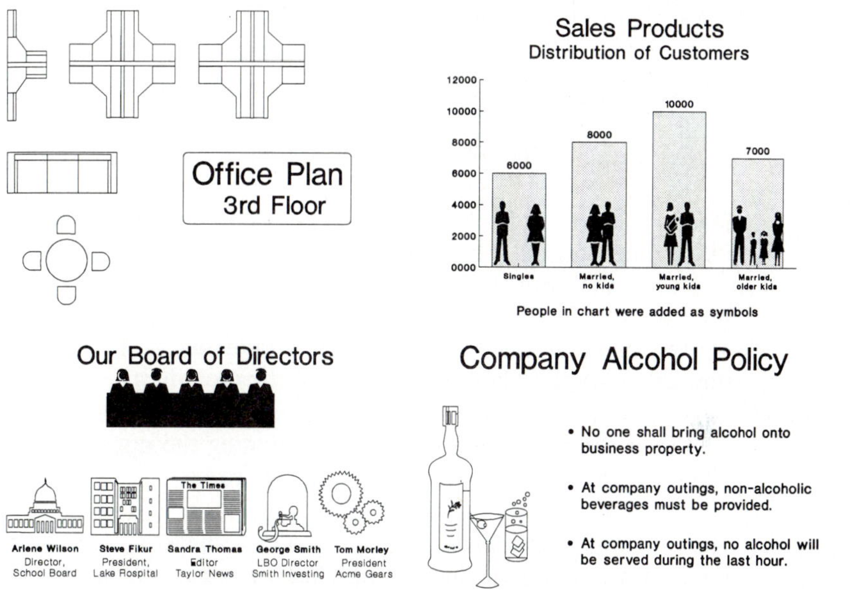

FIGURE 13-3. Charts using symbols from the Business Symbols accessory

Once the symbol files are on your hard disk, you can use the symbols. To add one of the symbols provided with the Business Symbols accessory, follow these steps:

1. Look in the booklet that comes with the Business Symbols accessory for the symbol you want and the file that it is in.
2. Select Draw/Annotate from the Main Menu of Harvard Graphics.
3. Select Symbol from the Draw menu.
4. Select Get from the Symbol menu.

Harvard Graphics displays a list of the symbol files. If the symbol files for the Business Symbols accessory are in a different drive or directory, press UP ARROW so the cursor is on the Directory field and press CTRL-DELETE. Then type the drive and directory containing the Business Symbols files.

5. From the list of files displayed, select the symbol file that contains the symbol you want to use.

Harvard Graphics displays the symbols contained in the file.

6. Select the symbol that you want to use.

Harvard Graphics displays an initial position and size. If you want to change its starting position, press BACKSPACE and position the cross-hairs where you want the symbol to start and press ENTER. Then Harvard Graphics prompts you for the opposite box corner. As you position the box, you can always maintain the height-to-width proportion of the symbol by holding down the SHIFT key as you position the cross-hairs.

7. Select the size of the image by positioning the upper-right corner so the box is the size that you want the image to be.

Harvard Graphics draws the symbol using the size and position selected. Once this object is added to the chart, you can modify it using the other menu options in the Draw/Annotate screen.

Creating a Chart Containing Business Symbols

You can follow these steps to create the chart in Figure 13-4, which uses symbols to show the industries one business represents.

1. Select Draw/Annotate from the Main Menu.

If you already have a chart in memory, you must remove it by selecting Create new chart, Text, and Free form, and then pressing ESC to return to the Main Menu.

2. Select Add from the Draw menu.
3. Select Text from the Add menu.
4. Press F8 (Options) to change the size of the text you will enter.
5. Press CTRL-DELETE, type **8**, and then press F10 (Continue).
6. Type **Acme's Industries** and press ENTER.

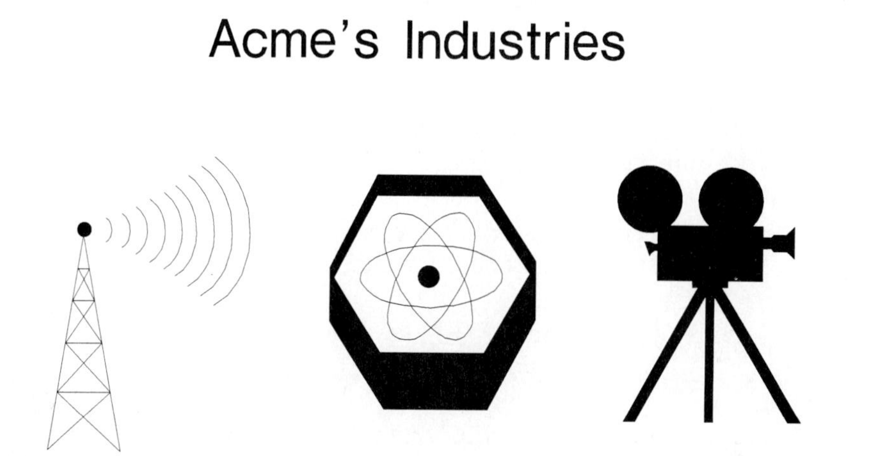

FIGURE 13-4. Chart created with symbols from the Business Symbols accessory

Harvard Graphics prompts for the location of the text.

7. Press UP ARROW to position the box so the vertical position is between 18000 and 19000. Press ENTER.
8. Press ESC twice to return to the Draw menu.
9. Select Symbol from the Draw menu.
10. Select Get from the Symbol menu.

If the symbol files for the Business Symbols accessory are in a different drive or directory, press UP ARROW so the cursor is on the Directory field, then press CTRL-DELETE. Type the drive and directory containing the Business Symbols files.

11. Select BUILD2.SYM as the symbol file you want to use.

Harvard Graphics displays the symbols contained in the BUILD2.SYM file.

12. Select the transmitter symbol (the first one on the third row).

Harvard Graphics displays an initial position and size.

13. Press BACKSPACE to choose a new starting position for the object.

Harvard Graphics prompts for the first box corner.

14. Press F3 (XY position), type **2000**, press ENTER, type **6000**, and press ENTER twice.

This selects the lower-left corner of the box that will contain the object. Harvard Graphics prompts for the opposite box corner.

15. Hold down the SHIFT key and press PGUP 15 times. Press ENTER while holding down the SHIFT key.

This makes the transmitter retain the shape it has in the symbol file.

16. Select Get from the Symbol menu.
17. Select CHEMICAL.SYM.

Harvard Graphics displays the symbols contained in the CHEMICAL.SYM file.

18. Select the atomic symbol (middle one on the last row).

Harvard Graphics displays an initial position and size.

19. Press BACKSPACE to choose a new starting position for the object.

Harvard Graphics prompts for the first box corner.

20. Press F3 (XY position), type **10000**, press ENTER, type **6000**, and press ENTER twice.

By positioning the object with F3 (XY position), you are ensuring that the objects have the same vertical position.

21. Hold down the SHIFT key and press PGUP 15 times. Press ENTER while holding down the SHIFT key.

Harvard Graphics adds the atomic symbol in the same shape as the original symbol.

22. Select Get from the Symbol menu.
23. Select COMMUNIC.SYM.

Harvard Graphics displays the symbols contained in the COMMUNIC.SYM file.

24. Select the movie camera symbol (third one on the last row).

Harvard Graphics displays an initial position and size.

25. Press BACKSPACE to choose a new starting position for the movie camera.
26. Press F3 (XY position), type **18000**, press ENTER, type **6000**, and press ENTER twice to select the first box corner.
27. Hold down the SHIFT key and press PGUP 15 times. Press ENTER while holding down the SHIFT key. Press ESC to return to the Draw menu.

Harvard Graphics adds the movie camera in the same shape as the original symbol. In each of the three symbol cases, if you did not press SHIFT as you selected the size for the object, the width of the object would have been stretched.

28. Press F2 (Draw chart) to display the chart using the full screen. Your chart looks like Figure 13-4.
29. Press ESC twice to return to the Main Menu.
30. Select Get/Save/Remove.
31. Select Save chart.
32. Type **BUS_SYM** as the filename and press F10 (Continue).
33. Press ESC to return to the Main Menu.

THE QUICK-CHARTS ACCESSORY

In Chapter 11 you learned how to create your own templates. You also used the chart galleries in Chapter 9 to create a chart quickly. If you are short on time or do not feel very creative, you can look to the Quick-Charts accessory as another source of templates. Quick-Charts gives you 125 templates to choose from. In addition Quick-Charts also has a slide show that lets you visually select the template you want to use. The Quick-Charts accessory provides the template files, charts that use the template files, a slide show to display the templates included, and chartbook files organized according to chart type.

Installing Quick-Charts

To install the Quick-Charts accessory from DOS, make drive A current by typing **A:** and pressing ENTER. Place the Quick-Charts Disk 1 into drive A and close the drive door, if any. If you are using the 3 1/2-inch disk, place it in drive A. Type **INSTALL** followed by the drive and directory in which you want the Quick-Chart templates stored, and then press ENTER. If you do not supply a drive and directory, the installation program uses C:\QCHARTS. If the directory does not exist, the installation program creates it. You may want to store the template files in a different directory so they do not interfere with your other chart files. If you are using the 5 1/4-inch disks, the installation program prompts you to place the Quick-Charts Disk 2 in drive A. Replace Quick-Charts Disk 1 with Quick-Charts Disk 2 and close the drive door, if any. When the installation program has finished copying the files, it displays a message telling you that the templates are ready to use. You can use the Quick-Charts templates from a 3 1/2-inch disk or a high-density 5 1/4-inch disk if you copy the files from the original disk(s) to the 3 1/2-inch or 5 1/4-inch disk you want to use.

Using One of the Quick-Charts Templates

Once the templates are on your hard disk or on a floppy disk, you can use the templates. You can quickly find the template you want by looking through the accessory's manual or by using the Preview Gallery. To use one of the templates provided with the Quick-Charts accessory, follow these steps:

1. Select Get/Save/Remove from the Main Menu.
2. Select Get template.
3. Press UP ARROW to move to the Directory field.
4. Modify the Directory field to include the drive and directory for the template files and press ENTER.

For example, if you used the default of QCHARTS to hold the Quick-Chart templates, you would modify the directory to C:\QCHARTS. Harvard Graphics lists all of the template files provided with Quick-Charts.

5. From the list, select the template file that contains the template you want to use.
6. Make the additional changes you want for the chart.

Entering Data to Create a Sales Forecast with a Quick-Charts Template

By following these steps you can use a template to create the chart in Figure 13-5 that shows forecast sales for two divisions.

1. Select Get/Save/Remove from the Main Menu.
2. Select Get template.
3. Press UP ARROW to move to the Directory field.
4. Modify the Directory field to include the drive and directory for the template files and press ENTER.
5. Select the BY220.TPL template file from the list since this file contains the template you want to use.

Harvard Graphics displays the Bar/Line Chart Data form. In this form, you need to enter only the data you want to graph and the text the chart will use.

6. Type **Sales Projections** and press ENTER for the chart title.
7. Type **For Years 1990-1994** and press ENTER twice for the chart subtitle and to move to the X data column.
8. Type **1990** and press ENTER.
9. Type **1991** and press ENTER.
10. Type **1992** and press ENTER.
11. Type **1993** and press ENTER.

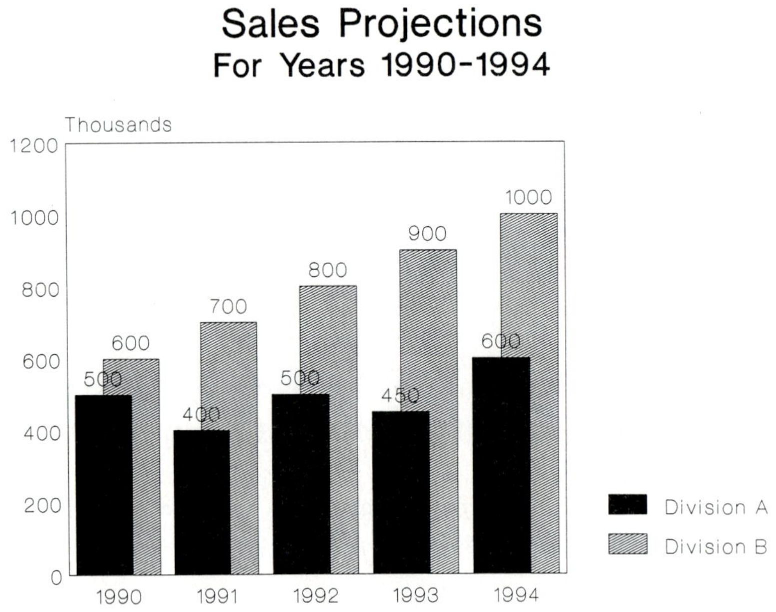

FIGURE 13-5. Chart created with template from the Quick-Charts accessory

12. Type **1994** and press ENTER.
13. Press HOME and TAB to move to the first row in the first series.
14. Press F6 (Calculate), type **Division A** for the legend title, and then press F10 (Continue).

Since you did not enter a calculation, Harvard Graphics does not perform one. This step lets you quickly change the legend text.

15. Type **500000** and press ENTER.
16. Type **400000** and press ENTER.
17. Type **500000** and press ENTER.
18. Type **450000** and press ENTER.
19. Type **600000** and press ENTER.

20. Press HOME and TAB twice to move to the first row in the second series.
21. Press F6 (Calculate), type **Division B** for the legend title, and then press F10 (Continue).
22. Type **600000** and press ENTER.
23. Type **700000** and press ENTER.
24. Type **800000** and press ENTER.
25. Type **900000** and press ENTER.
26. Type **1000000** and press ENTER.
27. Press F2 (Draw chart) to display the chart shown in Figure 13-5.

Since you used the template, many of the changes you would have entered after pressing F8 (Options) are already performed for you.

28. Press any key to remove the chart from the screen.
29. Press ESC to return to the Main Menu.
30. Press CTRL-S to save the chart.
31. Press SHIFT-TAB and modify the Directory field to store the chart in the directory containing your chart files. Press ENTER to move to the next field.
32. Type a new filename such as **SALEPROJ** and press ENTER.

You do not want to use the template filename since template filenames are not descriptive of the data stored in the chart.

33. Press CTRL-DELETE, type a file description, and press ENTER.

A file created with a Quick-Charts template uses the description of the template until you replace it with another description.

Using the Preview Gallery

While Quick-Charts provides many templates, you may not remember all of the chart templates available. You can browse through the booklet to find the template you want. Another option is the Preview Gallery, which lets you display the templates available. The Preview Gallery is a slide show that is interactive. By making selections, you choose which charts in the slide show you want to see. All of the Quick-Charts templates are displayed in the slide show, grouped according to the chart type and, for some chart types, whether the chart displays labels.

To view the Preview Gallery, follow these steps:

1. Select Slide show menu from the Main Menu.
2. Choose Select slide show.
3. Press UP ARROW to move to the Directory field.
4. Modify the Directory field to include the drive and directory for the Quick-Charts template files.

For example, if you used the default of QCHARTS to hold the Quick-Chart templates, you would modify the directory to C:\QCHARTS. Harvard Graphics lists all of the slide show files provided with Quick-Charts.

5. Select QCHARTS.SHW as the slide show file that you want to use.
6. Select Display screenshow from the Slide Show Menu.

After an opening screen, the initial screen shown in Figure 13-6 displays graphs of the different chart types.

7. Type the number representing the chart type you want.

The slide show displays either another selection, such as different chart options, or starts showing the templates available for the selected chart type. When the slide show displays more selections, type the number for the selection you want or type **G** to return to the previous gallery. When the slide show displays the template selections available for the chart type selected, you can type **N** to display the next template of the selected chart type or **P** to display the previous template of the selected chart type. As you find the templates you want, write the filenames that appear as the chart's subtitle. When you have finished viewing the templates, press ESC to return to the Slide Show Menu. You can also press CTRL-E to edit the

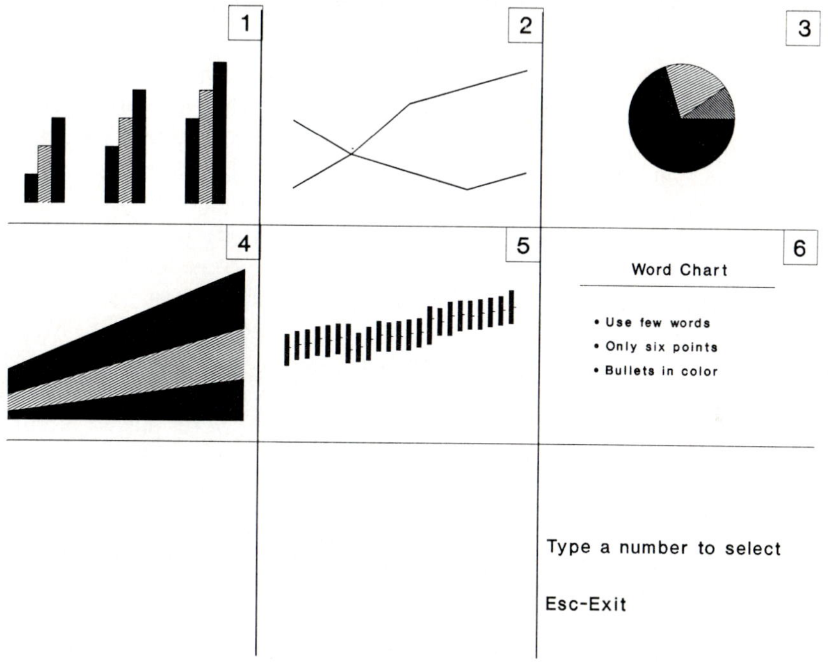

FIGURE 13-6. Screen in Quick-Charts Preview Gallery

chart displayed for the template. Pressing CTRL-E is the same as returning to the Main Menu and selecting Get/Save/Remove and Get template.

Using Templates with a Chartbook

Another option for selecting the template you want to use is to select the template through a chartbook. To select a template through a chartbook, select Chartbook menu from the Main Menu and then choose Select chartbook. After changing the directory to the one containing the Quick-Charts files, select the chart type from the list. Quick-Charts has a chartbook for each chart type listed. Next, select Create chart. When Harvard Graphics lists all of the templates in the chartbook you selected, highlight the one you want from the list and press ENTER. Harvard Graphics displays an empty form for entering data for the chart type.

THE U.S. MAPMAKER ACCESSORY

Although Harvard Graphics 2.3 provides symbols for cities and country maps, you may want more detailed charts that let you select the states and cities. You can use the U.S. MapMaker accessory to create detailed maps of the United States and choose from 32,000 cities and towns. If you need to show geographic information in your sales meetings, you will find this product to be truly amazing. Using it for a single presentation can completely offset the cost of the product when you consider how expensive it is to produce comparable-quality materials in other ways.

You select the states and cities you want and the U.S. MapMaker accessory puts them in the correct place. Even villages and small towns are a part of this database. As a test, I entered Gates Mills, OH, and Glenn, MI, as two of the smallest towns I know, and both were placed accurately on the respective state maps.

U.S. MapMaker also has several other features that are not covered here but you will learn as you increase your skills with this accessory. With the U.S. MapMaker, you can create color-coded maps based on numerical data. You can import these numbers if they are stored in ASCII files, so you do not have to reenter them. You can use these features to emphasize where your customer base is located or how the states are divided into sales regions.

Installing U.S. MapMaker

To install the U.S. MapMaker accessory, go to your Harvard Graphics directory. Type **MD MAP** and press ENTER. This creates a subdirectory under the HG subdirectory called MAP. Type **CD MAP.** This DOS command makes the MAP subdirectory the current directory. Place U.S. MapMaker Disk 1 into drive A and close the drive door, if any. If you are using a 3 1/2-inch disk, all files are on that one disk. Type **A:INSTALL** and press ENTER. After the files from the first disk are copied, the installation program prompts you to type **1** if your monitor displays colors or **2** if your monitor does not, and then press ENTER. If you are using 5 1/4-inch disks, you are prompted to enter U.S. MapMaker Disk 2. Replace U.S. MapMaker Disk 1 with U.S. MapMaker Disk 2 and close the drive door, if any. Once the accessory is installed, the installation program displays a message.

Starting U.S. MapMaker

After the accessory is installed, you can run the U.S. MapMaker accessory by typing **usmap** and pressing ENTER. From the Main Menu, you can build a map by selecting the states and cities you want to appear in the map. While you are building a map, you can view it by pressing F2 (Preview). You can get help by pressing F1 (Help). You can start a new map by selecting Clear Work from the Main Menu. You can exit the U.S. MapMaker by selecting Exit from the Main Menu.

Adding States

Add a state to a map by following these simple steps:

1. Select Add/Edit states.

Any states currently in the map are listed in alphabetical order. To add a new one to an existing map, press INSERT When you press INSERT in a new map, the U.S. MapMaker accessory lists the states you can add. As you type the name of the state, the highlight is moved to the state that matches the keystrokes you have typed.

2. Highlight the state you want and press ENTER. This displays a box like this:

```
            Alabama
 --------------------------------
 Inside color              Blue
 Border color        Royal blue
```

You can change the color of the border or the interior color of the state by selecting the option and pressing ENTER. You can select a color from the list by highlighting it and pressing ENTER.

3. Press F10 (Continue) to add the state to the current map.

When you view the map, the states appear using the colors selected for the border and fill color. Each state appears in the relative position that it appears in a complete map of the United States, with the entire map filling the screen. To edit a state, highlight the state you want to change and press ENTER. From the displayed box, you can change the colors used for the state. If you want to delete a state, highlight the state and press DELETE. You will be prompted to confirm that you want to delete the state. You can confirm your action by highlighting Yes and pressing ENTER or cancel the action by highlighting No and pressing ENTER. When you have finished adding states, press ESC to return to the Main Menu.

Adding Cities

Adding a city to a map uses the same steps as adding a state to a map. If you try to add a city from a state that is not already on the map, U.S. MapMaker adds the state and the city. To add a city, follow these steps:

1. Select Add/Edit cities.

Any cities currently in the map are listed in alphabetical order. To add a new one to an existing map, press INSERT. When you press INSERT in a new map, the U.S. Map-Maker accessory prompts for the name of the city. You do not have to type the entire name, but you must type at least the first two letters.

2. Type at least two letters of the city you want and press ENTER.

Once you have typed at least two letters of the city name and press ENTER, a box appears listing all of the cities in its database that start with the letters that you provide. You can use PGUP and PGDN to scroll through lists that take more than one screen. From this box, highlight the city you want and press ENTER. Another option is to enter the entire city name followed by a comma and the state. Once the city and its state are selected, the following box appears:

Pinellas Park, FL	
Text	Pinellas Park
Text color	White
Symbol type	Dot
Symbol color	Gold

You can change the text identifying the city, the color of the text identifying the city, the symbol marking the city, and the color of the symbol marking the city. When you highlight an option and press ENTER, a selection box is displayed. You can choose a selection from the list and press ENTER.

3. Press F10 (Continue) to add the city to the current map.

When you press F2 (Preview), the cities appear using the options you have selected. U.S. MapMaker knows the position of 32,000 cities. Each city appears in the relative position that it appears in a complete map of the state.

To edit the settings for a city, highlight the city you want to change and press ENTER. From the displayed box, you can change any of the selections. If you want to delete a city, highlight the city and press DELETE. You are prompted to confirm that you want to delete the city. Confirm your action by highlighting Yes and pressing ENTER, or cancel the action by highlighting No and pressing ENTER. Figure 13-7 shows a map using the

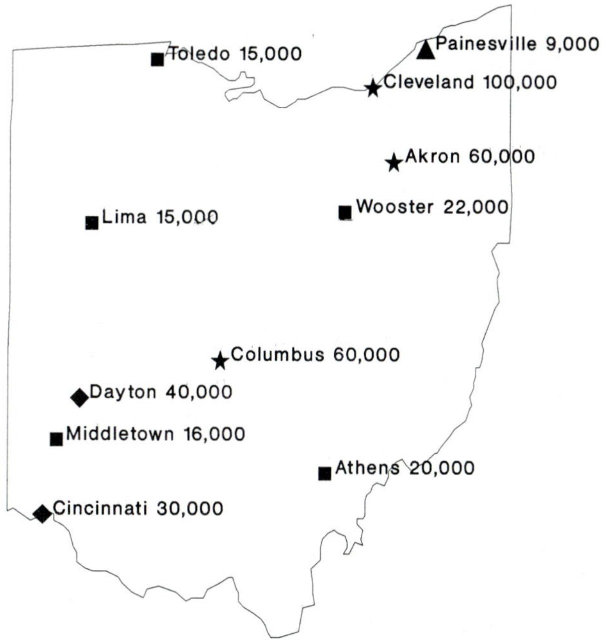

FIGURE 13-7. Map using city options

different options for cities, including modifying the text that appears next to each city and using different symbols to classify the cities into different groups. When you have finished adding cities, press ESC to return to the Main Menu.

Adding Groups

While you can add all of the cities and states you want, your map will progress slowly if you have many cities and states to enter. A quicker approach is to add a group of states or cities. Adding a group to a map is similar to adding a single city or state. Follow these steps:

1. Select Add a group.

The U.S. MapMaker accessory prompts for a group listing the available selections. From the selections you can see that you can add groups of states or a state and the major cities in the state. You can use PGUP and PGDN to browse through the selections.

2. Highlight your choice and press ENTER.

Once you have selected the group, the box appears allowing you to change the border color of the states, the inside color of the states, the color of the text identifying the city, the symbols marking the cities, and the color of the symbols marking the cities. When you highlight an option and press ENTER, a selection box is displayed. You can choose a selection from the list and press ENTER.

3. Press F10 (Continue) to add the city to the current map.

When you view the map, the group of states and cities you have added all use the options you have selected. When you select Add/Edit States or Add/Edit Cities, the cities and states added as a group appear in the list just as if you added them individually. To change the settings for a group, you must edit them using Add/Edit states or Add/Edit cities from the Main Menu. Figure 13-8 shows a map that was created by adding the group New England States, adding the groups of major cities for each state, and then adding individual cities by selecting Add/Edit cities from the Main Menu.

FIGURE 13-8. Map created by adding a group of states and major cities, and then adding individual cities

Saving Maps

U.S. MapMaker offers three ways to save a map. You can save the map as U.S. MapMaker uses it. Save a map this way if you plan to edit the map later. Save the map as a chart if you plan to use the map as a Harvard Graphics chart. You also can save the map as a symbol that you can use with other charts. To save a map, select Get/Save Work. Select Save map if you want to edit the map later. Select Create HG symbol if you want to save the map as a Harvard Graphics symbol. Select Create HG chart if you want to save the map as a Harvard Graphics chart. When U.S. MapMaker prompts for a filename, type the filename, editing the drive and directory if you want. After you enter the filename, press (ENTER).

Later, if you want to return to a map you have saved with the Save Map option, select Get/Save Work and Get map. When U.S. MapMaker prompts for a filename, press (ENTER) when the drive and directory are the one you want. The accessory lists the map files in the selected drive and directory. Highlight the map you want and press ENTER.

Once a map is saved as a Harvard Graphics chart or symbol, you can treat the file just as you would treat other Harvard Graphics charts or symbols. You can incorporate them into slide shows, annotate the charts, and bring the symbols into other charts. Figure 13-9 shows a map created with U.S. MapMaker saved as a Harvard Graphics symbol and brought into another chart.

THE MILITARY SYMBOLS ACCESSORY

The Military Symbols accessory provides symbols not available from the Business Symbols accessory. This accessory provides over 200 military sym-

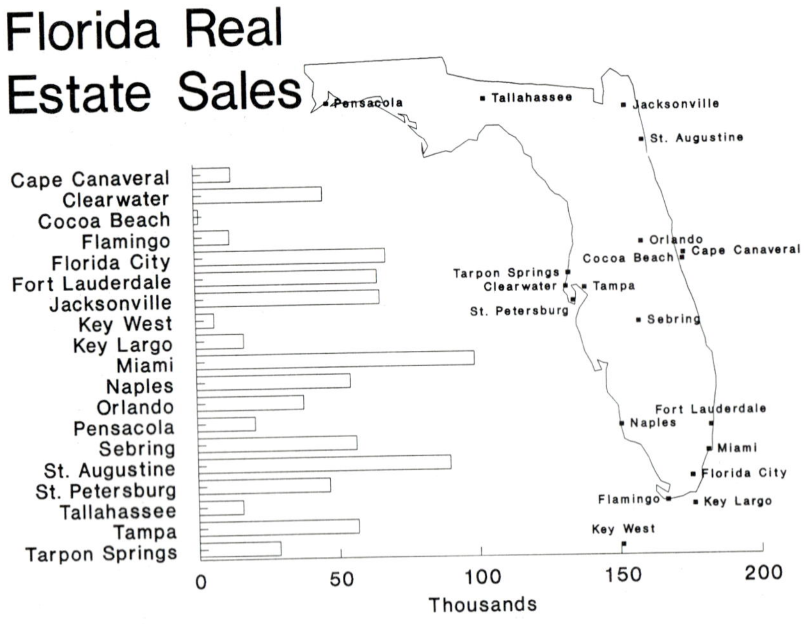

FIGURE 13-9. Chart with map added as a symbol

bols, including planes, ships, artillery, insignia, soldiers, and other miscellaneous symbols. Figure 13-10 shows several charts that use symbols from the Military Symbols accessory. Adding one of these symbols requires the same steps for adding symbols that you learned in Chapter 9.

Installing Military Symbols

To install the Military Symbols accessory, place the first 5 1/4- or 3 1/2-inch Military Symbols disk into drive A. Type **COPY A:*.* C:\HG\SYMBOLS** and press ENTER. If Harvard Graphics is not stored in the HG\SYMBOLS directory on drive C, substitute the correct drive and directory information. After copying the files from the first disk, replace the first disk with the second, press F3 to repeat the DOS command, and press ENTER. If you are using 5 1/4-inch disks, repeat these steps for the third and fourth Military Symbols disks.

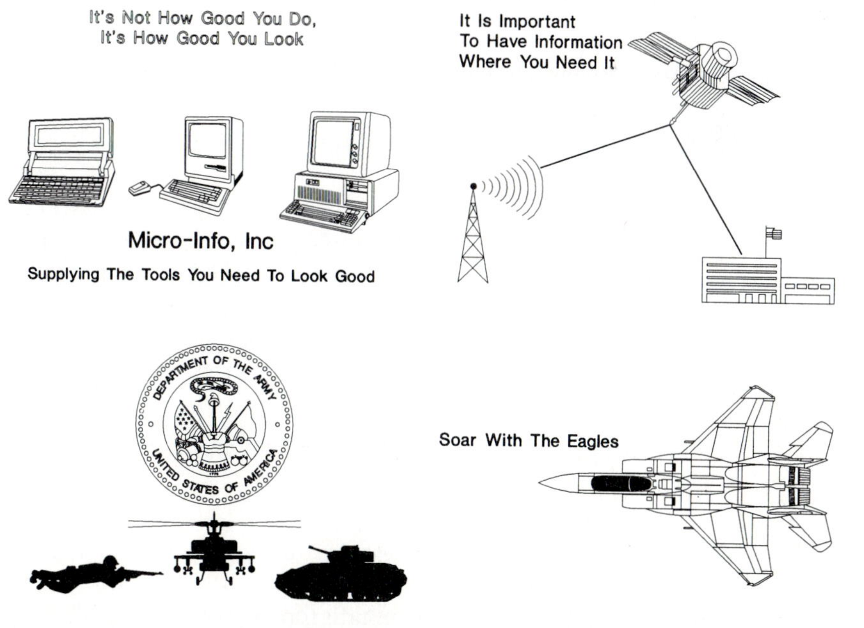

FIGURE 13-10. Charts using symbols from the Military Symbols accessory

Once the symbol files are on your hard disk, you can use the symbols. To add one of the symbols provided with the Military Symbols accessory, follow these steps:

1. Look in the booklet that comes with the Military Symbols accessory for the symbol you want and the file that it is in.
2. Select Draw/Annotate from the Main Menu of Harvard Graphics.
3. Select Symbol from the Draw menu.
4. Select Get from the Symbol menu.

Harvard Graphics displays a list of the symbol files. If the symbol files for the Military Symbols accessory are in a different drive or directory, press UP ARROW so that the cursor is on the Directory field, and then press CTRL-DELETE. Then type the drive and directory containing the Military Symbols files.

5. Select the symbol filename from the list of files displayed that contains the symbol you want to use.

Harvard Graphics displays the symbols contained in the file.

6. Select the symbol from the group that you want to use.

Harvard Graphics displays an initial position and size. If you want to change its starting position, press BACKSPACE, position the cross-hairs where you want the symbol to start, and press ENTER. Then Harvard Graphics prompts you for the opposite box corner. As you position the box, you can always maintain the height-to-width proportion of the symbol by holding down the SHIFT key as you position the cross-hairs.

7. Select the size of the image by positioning the upper-right corner so the box is the size that you want the image.

Harvard Graphics draws the symbol using the size and position selected. Once this object is added to the chart, you can modify it using the other menu options in the Draw/Annotate screen. You can combine symbols in the Military Symbols accessory with the symbols that accompany either Harvard Graphics or the Business Symbols accessory.

Creating a Chart Containing Military Symbols

You can try creating the chart in Figure 13-11, which can be an introductory chart to a slide show that illustrates a new marketing strategy, by following these steps.

1. Select Draw/Annotate from the Main Menu.

If you already have a chart in memory, you will want to remove it by selecting Create new chart, Text, and Free form, and then pressing ESC to return to the Main Menu.

2. Select Symbol from the Draw menu.
3. Select Get from the Symbol menu.

If the symbol files for the Military Symbols accessory are in a different drive or directory, press UP ARROW so the cursor is on the Directory field and press CTRL-DELETE. Then type the drive and directory containing the Military Symbols files.

4. Select WEAPON.SYM as the symbol filename that you want to use.

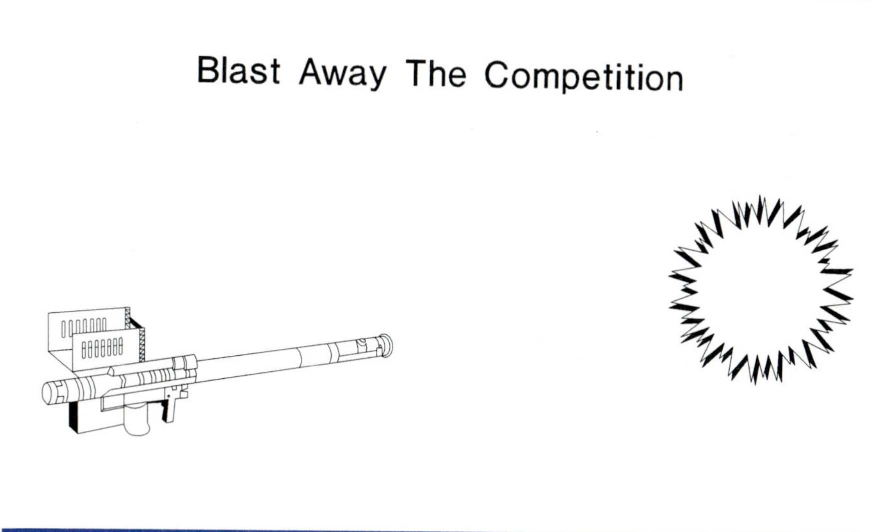

FIGURE 13-11. Chart created with symbols from the Military Symbols accessory

Harvard Graphics displays the symbols contained in the WEAPON.SYM file.

5. Select the stinger symbol (fourth one on the first row).

Harvard Graphics displays an initial position and size.

6. Hold down the SHIFT key and press END five times. Press ENTER while holding down the SHIFT key.

This makes the stinger retain the shape it has in the symbol file, although your symbol is smaller than the originally suggested size.

7. Select Get from the Symbol menu.
8. Select STARS1.SYM as the symbol filename that you want.

Harvard Graphics displays the symbols contained in the STARS1.SYM file. You can also select the STARS.SYM file if you have the symbol files from Harvard Graphics 2.12.

9. Select the round starburst (second one in the bottom row). In the STARS.SYM file, the round starburst is the first one in the second row.

Harvard Graphics displays an initial position and size.

10. Press ENTER to accept the size and position.
11. Press ESC to return to the Draw menu.
12. Select Modify and Move.

Harvard Graphics prompts for the object to move.

13. Press ENTER twice to select the starburst to move.
14. Press CTRL-RIGHT ARROW to quickly move to the right side.
15. Press ENTER to accept the new position.
16. Press ESC to return to the Draw menu.
17. Select Add from the Draw menu.
18. Select Text from the Add menu.
19. Type **Blast Away The Competition** and press ENTER.

Harvard Graphics prompts for the location of the text.

20. Press F3 (XY Position), type **13000**, press ENTER, type **15000** and press ENTER twice.
21. Press ESC three times to return to the Main Menu.
22. Press CTRL-P to print the chart.

If you want to change the settings Harvard Graphics will use to print the chart, make these changes now.

23. Press F10 (Continue). Your chart looks like Figure 13-11.
24. Press CTRL-S to save the chart.
25. Type **BLOWAWAY** as the filename and press F10 (Continue).

appendix A

INSTALLING HARVARD GRAPHICS

Installing Harvard Graphics
Setting Up Harvard Graphics
Installing VDI

This appendix describes the steps you will perform to install Harvard Graphics and the equipment you might use. This appendix also covers how you may want to change the settings. If you need to use a VDI device driver, this appendix also gives the installation instructions.

INSTALLING HARVARD GRAPHICS

Installing Harvard Graphics is a simple process. Since Harvard Graphics has several hardware requirements, you should check that your computer meets the requirements. Once you know you have the correct equipment, you can install Harvard Graphics. The steps you perform for installing depend on whether you are using 3 1/2- or 5 1/4-inch disks.

Requirements for Harvard Graphics

Harvard Graphics has a few requirements that your computer must meet in order to run. It requires at least 512K of RAM, which is the memory your computer uses to temporarily store programs as your computer executes them. You can find out how much RAM your computer has by entering **CHKDSK** and pressing ENTER. The output displays information such as the number of files on a disk, the number of hidden files, and the amount of space left on the disk. The next to last number, total memory, is the amount of RAM your computer has. While Harvard Graphics requires 512K of RAM, computers can have more than this. If your computer has 640K of RAM, you can use a VDI device to export a picture in a Metafile format (see Chapter 5), run Harvard Graphics on a network, use the MACRO program (see Chapter 12), or use another TSR program such as the Screen-Show utility (see Chapter 13).

Your computer also must have a hard drive with a minimum of 2.4 MB of space (preferably 6 MB of space). The computer must also have an 80-column monitor. The number of columns is determined by how many characters fit across the screen. The computer also needs a graphics adapter, such as CGA, EGA, or VGA, that creates graphics screens Harvard Graphics uses to draw charts. Finally, you will want an output device to print, plot, or create slides from your charts.

Backing Up Your Disks

Your Harvard Graphics disks represent an investment you have made. Since you want your investment protected, you should make a second copy of the Harvard Graphics disks so you can use them in place of your originals if they are damaged. Since making additional copies is an infringement of the copyright law, you only want to make a copy for archival purposes which is specifically allowed by the software license. Since Harvard Graphics can use 3 1/2- or 5 1/4-inch disks, the instructions for backing up each size of disks are given separately.

BACKING UP 3 1/2-INCH DISKS Harvard Graphics comes with five 3 1/2-inch disks. To back up these disks, follow these steps:

1. Format five blank 3 1/2-inch disks by inserting a disk in drive A, typing **FORMAT A:**, and pressing ENTER. You must format each disk separately.

2. Put the Harvard Graphics Program disk in drive A and an unformatted disk in drive B.
3. Type **COPY A:*.* B:** and press ENTER.

This copies all of the files in drive A to drive B. Since the Harvard Graphics disks are write protected, you cannot accidentally overwrite the files.

4. Repeat steps 2 and 3 for the four remaining disks.

If you do not have two 3 1/2-inch disk drives, you must create a temporary subdirectory on your hard disk, copy the Harvard Graphics disks to the temporary subdirectory, and then copy the files in the temporary directory to formatted disks.

Once the backups are made, label the disks and place the original disks in a safe location.

BACKING UP 5 1/4-INCH DISKS Harvard Graphics 2.3 comes with ten 5 1/4-inch disks. To back these disks up, follow these steps:

1. Format ten blank 5 1/4-inch disks by inserting a disk in drive A, typing **FORMAT A:**, and pressing ENTER. You must format each disk separately.
2. Put the Harvard Graphics Program Disk 1 in drive A and an unformatted disk in drive B.
3. Type **COPY A:*.* B:** and press ENTER.

This copies all of the files in drive A to drive B.

4. Repeat steps 2 and 3 for the remaining nine disks.

After you copy files to the formatted disks, label the disks so you know which disk contains the different types of files. Once the backups are made, place the original disks in a safe location.

Installing Harvard Graphics on Your Hard Disk

Once you have the backup copy made, you are ready to install Harvard Graphics on your hard disk. Follow these steps:

1. Put Disk 1 in drive A.
2. Type **A:** and press ENTER.
3. Type **INSTALL** and press ENTER.

INSTALL is a utility program created to copy the Harvard Graphics files to your hard disk. Since the files on the disks are in a compressed format and the INSTALL program uncompresses them, you must use the INSTALL program to copy the files to your hard disk. The INSTALL program prompts for the drive that you want to contain Harvard Graphics. Harvard Graphics lists the hard drives that you can select from.

4. Highlight the drive where you want to install Harvard Graphics.

Harvard Graphics prompts for the directory in the drive where you want to install Harvard Graphics. The INSTALL program initially suggests HG but you can change it to any valid directory name. This book assumes that you install Harvard Graphics to C:\HG.

5. Accept the directory information or alter the directory information and then press ENTER.

The INSTALL program displays the Harvard Graphics Install menu. You can select which files are copied to the selected directory. Unless you are short of disk space, you should select All files except VDI devices. This installs the Harvard Graphics program files, the palette files that select the colors used by the charts, the symbol files, the files for the Harvard Graphics tutorial, and the sample files so you can quickly use Harvard Graphics chart files. You can select one of the other selections to install only the types of files described.

If you provide an existing drive and directory that contain Harvard Graphics files, the INSTALL program will prompt to ask if you want to install the new Harvard Graphics files over the previous version. To do so, select Yes. If you select No, the INSTALL program returns to step 4.

6. Highlight the type of files you want to install and press ENTER.

The INSTALL program prompts for your country. Selecting the country chooses the date, time, number and currency formats to match the customs of the selected country. If your country is not listed, select another country that uses the same date, time, number and currency formats.

7. Highlight a country and press ENTER.

The INSTALL program copies the files from the disks to your hard disk. If the directory does not exist, the INSTALL program creates it. After the INSTALL program copies all of the files it needs from the current disk, it then displays a message to insert the next disk. As the INSTALL program copies the files, it lists the files it is copying on the screen.

8. Remove the current disk from drive A and insert the disk that the INSTALL program prompts for. Press ENTER.
9. Repeat step 7 until the INSTALL program copies all of the files from all disks and then displays a message that Harvard Graphics is installed.

If you selected All files except VDI devices, the INSTALL program copies most of the files to your Harvard Graphics directory. The only files that you have not copied are the files you need if you are printing to a VDI device. The instructions for copying the files for a VDI device are at the end of this appendix. If you plan to use Draw Partner with a CGA or Hercules monitor, you must load the GRAPTABL utility that is included with DOS before you run Harvard Graphics. Once these steps are complete, you are ready to select your printer and screen as discussed later in the chapter. You can start Harvard Graphics by typing **HG** and pressing ENTER.

SETTING UP HARVARD GRAPHICS

Once Harvard Graphics is installed, you will want to make some changes to it so it knows the type of equipment you are using. For example, you should tell Harvard Graphics the printer or plotter you are using. Also you may want to tell it the type of screen you are using so your charts can be optimally displayed. To make these changes, select Setup from the Harvard Graphics Main Menu. You only need to change the settings for the output devices you will use. For example, if you use only one printer to print your charts, you do not need to select a second printer or a plotter. When you have finished making the changes, press ESC to return to the Main Menu and then type **E** to exit Harvard Graphics.

Selecting a Printer

You must select a printer before you print a chart so that Harvard Graphics knows the format in which it must send information to the printer. If you do not select the printer or you select a wrong one, your chart will not print as expected. To select a printer, select Printer 1 from the Setup menu. Harvard Graphics lists the printers that can be used to print your charts. Select your printer from the list and press ENTER. Harvard Graphics displays an overlay box. From this box you can select how the printer is attached to your computer. LPT1, LPT2, LPT3, COM1, and COM2 are the possible selections. If you select COM1 or COM2, you also must select the baud rate, the data bits, the stop bit, and the parity setting. To learn the correct selections, check your printer manual or consult the person who set up the computer and printer for you. When you have selected LPT1, LPT2, LPT3, or the parity setting for COM1 or COM2, Harvard Graphics returns you to the Setup menu. You then can select Printer 2 and perform the same steps to select a second printer that you plan to use to print charts.

Selecting a Plotter

Just as you must select a printer before you print a chart, you must also select a plotter before you can plot a chart. If you do not select a plotter or select the wrong one, your chart will not print as expected. To select a plotter, select Plotter from the Setup menu. Harvard Graphics lists the plotters that it can use to plot your charts. Select your plotter from the list and press ENTER. If you want to use B-size paper in the plotter, select the plotter name followed by B-size. Harvard Graphics displays an overlay box to select how the printer is attached to your computer. You can choose LPT1, LPT2, LPT3, COM1, or COM2. If you select COM1 or COM2, you must also select the baud rate, the data bits, the stop bit, and your parity setting. You can find the correct settings by checking the printer manual. When you have selected LPT1, LPT2, LPT3, or the parity setting for COM1 or COM2, Harvard Graphics returns you to the Setup menu.

Selecting a Film Recorder

If you are using a film recorder to create slides from your charts, you must tell Harvard Graphics about the film recorder so the correct information is sent to the file that will be converted to a slide. Select Film recorder from the Setup menu. Harvard Graphics lists the film recorders that it supports. Select the film recorder you will use and press ENTER.

Next, if you selected the Lasergraphics PFR or LFR, PTI Montage, Matrix, or Videoshow film recorder, enter the drive and directory where you want the files stored and press ENTER. If you want the files stored in the current directory, leave this blank by pressing ENTER without making an entry. If you selected a Polaroid film recorder or the PTI ImageMaker, you must select the film type you plan to use. If you selected a Bell & Howell recorder, Lasergraphics PFR or LFR, Videoshow, or PTI ImageMaker or Montage, select whether the charts will use the film recorder's hardware fonts. Hardware fonts may look nicer than the same Harvard Graphics fonts and take less time to record, but the available sizes are more limited. When the last selection is made, press F10 (Continue) to save these settings and return to the Setup menu.

If you have selected the PTI ImageMaker or a Polaroid film recorder, you must select the port to which the film maker is connected (LPT1, LPT2, LPT3, COM1, or COM2). For the two serial ports, you must also select the baud rate, parity, data bits, and stop bits.

Selecting a Screen

For most screens, Harvard Graphics checks the graphics adapter and selects the correct way to display the charts. For some types of computers and monitors, when a computer has two graphics adapters, or when the monitor is monochrome, you may want to change the setting for the screen. To select the screen setting, select Screen from the Setup menu. Harvard Graphics lists the graphics adapters. The Default screen selection lets Harvard Graphics determine the display adapter to use on the basis of the display adapter it finds. Select your display adapter from the list and press ENTER. Harvard Graphics then returns you to the Setup menu.

INSTALLING VDI

When you installed Harvard Graphics, you did not install the Virtual Device Interface (VDI) files. VDI is software written by Graphics Software Systems that converts the output of one program or device to the input of another program or device. For example, when you send a chart to a printer, Harvard Graphics converts the data in the chart into a format that the printer understands. For output devices that Harvard Graphics does not directly support, it uses VDI to make the conversion. You do not have to install the VDI files unless you will be using a device that uses VDI. Examples of uses of VDI are exporting a chart to a Metafile format and using a graphics adapter, printer, plotter, or film recorder that Harvard Graphics does not directly support. Examples of these printers and film recorders are AST TurboLaser, CalComp ColorMaster, Matrix TT200, PTI Montage, Bell & Howell CDI IV or Quintar 1080, Lasergraphics PFR or LFR, and Matrix PCR or QCR.

To install the VDI files, follow these steps:

1. Insert Disk 1 in drive A.
2. Type **A:** and press ENTER.

This entry makes drive A the current drive.

3. Type **INSTALL** and press ENTER.

Harvard Graphics lists the hard drives that you can select from.

4. Highlight the drive where you want to install Harvard Graphics.

Harvard Graphics prompts for the directory in the drive where you want to install Harvard Graphics. This is the same drive where you installed the Harvard Graphics program files.

5. Accept the directory information or alter the directory information and then press ENTER.
6. Select VDI device files from the Harvard Graphics Install menu.

The INSTALL program lists the VDI devices that you might use with Harvard Graphics.

7. Highlight the printer, film recorder, or other device you are using VDI with and press ENTER.

The INSTALL program prompts you to insert another disk.

8. Insert the disk the INSTALL program is prompting for and press ENTER.

The INSTALL program copies the VDI files for the selected device to your hard disk. If the directory does not exist, the INSTALL program creates it.

When the INSTALL program copies all of the files it needs from the current disk, the INSTALL program displays a message telling you to press ENTER to return to the Main Menu.

9. Press ENTER to return to the Install Harvard Graphics menu.
10. Insert Disk 1 into drive A and press ENTER.

At this point you can return to step 6 to add the files for other VDI devices or select Exit to leave the INSTALL program.

The INSTALL program creates a VDI subdirectory on your hard disk and copies the appropriate VDI files to this directory. Since each device has its own files and this batch file only copies the files for the device you selected, you must perform steps 6 through 10 for each VDI device you plan to use.

Changing CONFIG.SYS

Once the files are copied, you must edit your CONFIG.SYS file so Harvard Graphics knows where to look for the VDI files and DOS knows which device drivers you will use. You need to add one line for each VDI device you will use and another line that is used by all VDI device drivers. To add these lines, use a word processor, EDLIN, or the COPY command. To use the DOS COPY command, type **CD** and press ENTER to change to the root directory. Then type **COPY CONFIG.SYS+CON CONFIG.SYS** and press ENTER. Once you type the lines you want to add, press CTRL-Z and ENTER to add these lines to the existing CONFIG.SYS file.

The line you must add for each device is shown here:

Device	**Line to Add**
AST TurboLaser	device=C:\vdi\LL.sys
Bell & Howell Color Digital Imager IV	device=C:\vdi\bellhowl.sys
Bell & Howell Quintar 1080	device=C:\vdi\bellhowl.sys
CalComp ColorMaster	device=C:\vdi\clrmstr.sys
Lasergraphics PFR, LFR, PTI Montage	device=C:\vdi\LL.sys
Matrix PCR, QCR, and TT200	device=C:\vdi\mtxscodl.sys
Metafiles	device=C:\vdi\meta.sys

After you add the lines for the VDI devices, you must add the line

device=C:\vdi\gsscgi.sys. Before your computer will use the changes you have made to the CONFIG.SYS file, you must restart your computer. This is usually done by pressing CTRL-ALT-DELETE.

If you are in a network, you may need to ask the network administrator to make the changes to the CONFIG.SYS file for you.

Telling Harvard Graphics to Use VDI

Once you have copied the files and made the changes to the CONFIG.SYS file, you can use Harvard Graphics with VDI. The steps you must perform to tell Harvard Graphics that you want to use a VDI for output varies depending on the output device you are using VDI for. For each device listed here, perform the given steps before entering Harvard Graphics:

- *AST TurboLaser* Switch to the Harvard Graphics directory by typing **CD\HG** and pressing ENTER. Then type **TURBO** and press ENTER. Select Setup from the Harvard Graphics Main Menu, Printer 1 or Printer 2, and AST TurboLaser.
- *Bell & Howell Color Digital Imager IV and Quintar 1080* Switch to the Harvard Graphics directory by typing **CD \HG** and pressing ENTER. Then type **INITBH** and press ENTER. Select Setup from the Harvard Graphics Main Menu, Film recorder, and CDI IV, 1080.
- *CalComp ColorMaster* Switch to the Harvard Graphics directory by typing **CD \HG** and pressing ENTER. Then type **CLRMSTR** followed by COM1, COM2, or LPT1, which represents how the printer is connected to your computer. Press ENTER. Then select ColorMaster after selecting Printer 1 or Printer 2 from the Setup menu.
- *Lasergraphics PFR or LFR and PTI Montage* Switch to the Harvard Graphics directory by typing **CD \HG** and pressing ENTER. Then type **LLFR** and press ENTER. Select Setup from the Harvard Graphics Main Menu, Film recorder, and RASCOL II/PFR, LL Compatible, or Montage.
- *Matrix PCR, QCR, and TT200* Switch to the Harvard Graphics directory by typing **CD \HG** and pressing ENTER. Next, type **INITMVP** and press ENTER. Select Setup from the Harvard Graphics Main Menu, Film recorder, and MVP SCODL (MATRIX fonts) to use the Matrix software fonts or MVP SCODL (HG fonts) to use Harvard Graphics fonts.
- *Metafiles* VDI is ready to use as described in Chapter 5.

- *Other* This is for the VDI device drivers for other products that are not supplied with the package. For these selections, you may need to make entries from the DOS prompt perform the same commands as the commands stored in the batch files for the other VDI device drivers. The exact instructions are found in the manual that accompanies the output device. After entering the DOS commands, select Setup from the Harvard Graphics Main Menu; Printer 1, Printer 2, Plotter, or Film recorder; and then VDI.

appendix B

OUTPUT OPTIONS

Using a Second Printer
Using a Plotter
Using a Film Recorder

All the examples in this book have printed the charts to a printer, but Harvard Graphics has other options with which you can output your charts: a second printer, a plotter, and a film recorder. The option that best meets your needs depends on what you plan to do with the charts. With these different output options, you can create printed charts, transparencies, and slides. Appendix A discussed how you can tell Harvard Graphics which printers, plotter, and film recorder you will use. You must tell Harvard Graphics the devices you will use before you use them so it sends the chart to the output device in a format that the printer, plotter, or film recorder can understand. The other options for producing output are easy to use, and this appendix contains the information you will need to use any of them.

USING A SECOND PRINTER

Harvard Graphics lets you select two printers at a time that you can use to print your charts. The advantage of having two printers selected is that you can quickly select which printer you will use by changing the Printer field in the Print Chart Options overlay box that appears when you select Produce output and then Printer from Harvard Graphics' Main Menu or when you press CTRL-P. Then Harvard Graphics uses the printer you selected by choosing Setup from the Main Menu and Printer 2. Other than changing the Printer field, printing to Printer 2 is identical to printing to Printer 1.

USING A PLOTTER

A *plotter* is an output device that draws its output. If you think of a printer as a typewriter that puts dots in the correct places, you would consider a plotter as someone drawing an image with a pen. When a printer draws a chart, it does so from top to bottom. A plotter draws each part of an image before drawing the next part. For instance, the plotter draws a bar chart title, then the subtitle, then the chart axes, and so on until it completes the entire chart. Plotters are frequently used for drawing charts, especially transparencies.

Since a plotter draws one part of the image at a time, you want to avoid overlapping objects in the charts you create. This is usually not a problem when you use the forms available from the Create new chart option in the Main Menu. Overlapping objects becomes an issue when you add objects to a chart using the Draw/Annotate screen. For example, assume you have a chart that contains the combination of objects shown here:

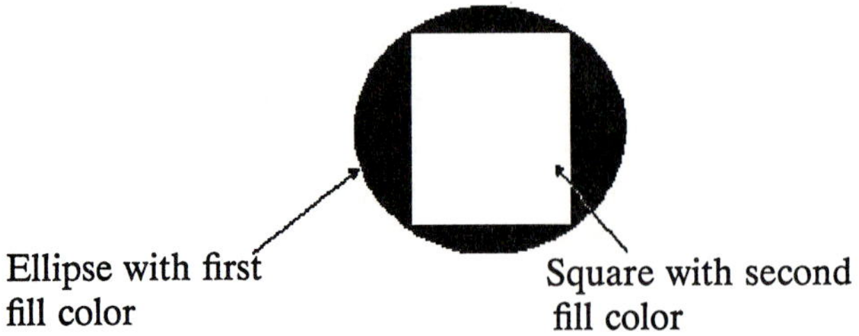

The text and arrows are not part of the chart but are added to illustrate the objects in the chart. When Harvard Graphics prints the chart to a printer, it analyzes the chart like this:

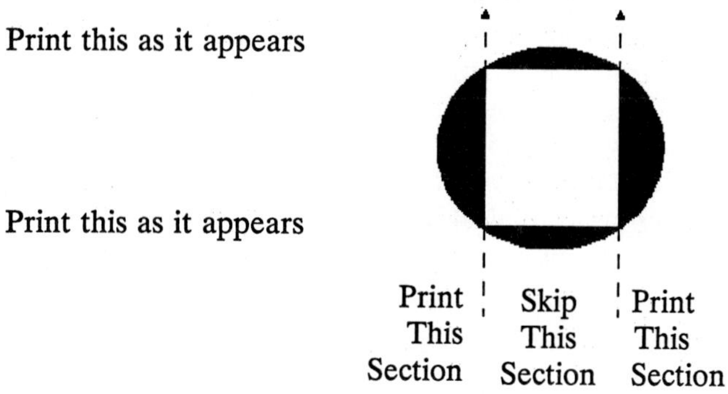

This analysis prints the chart correctly. When Harvard Graphics prints the chart to a plotter, it prints one object and then another, so the combined objects looks as follows:

Overlapping also causes problems in plotting some symbols. If this problem occurs, change the symbol you are using.

To print a chart to the plotter instead of the printer, select Plotter from the Produce output menu. Then change the following fields to reflect how you want your output to appear:

- *Quality* Like printing, this field controls the sharpness of the chart. The higher the quality the longer the plotter takes to draw your chart. If you choose Draft, the text uses the hardware default font, each letter takes the same amount of space, solid colors appear as patterns, and text that changes colors within a line is ignored as well as text characteristics such as boldface and italics. If you choose Standard, text is proportionally spaced (like the text in this book), filled areas in pie slices and bars are filled, text colors are the ones you set, and text characteristics such as boldface and italics are ignored. If you choose High, the chart uses the Harvard Graphics fonts, characters as well as bars and slices are filled in, the text uses the colors you select, and boldface and italics appear as you selected.

- *A-size paper format* Select Letter if you are using 8 1/2- by 11-inch paper. Select A4 if you are using the special-sized paper called A4 size.
- *Transparency* If you are plotting on a transparency, select Yes; otherwise select No. When Harvard Graphics prints to a plotter on a transparency, the plotter draws slower so the lines do not smear and the lines appear thicker. Also pie slices and columns are slightly separated so the colors do not run. When you print to a transparency, be sure to use transparency pens since the ink in pens designed for paper does not adhere to the transparency. Also, do not touch the ink on the transparency for at least 15 minutes so the ink can dry completely.
- *Pause for Pen* Select Yes if your chart uses more colors than your plotter has pen holders; Harvard Graphics pauses for you to change pens when necessary. Select No if you only have the pens in the pen holder and you want Harvard Graphics to use those. When Harvard Graphics pauses the plotter, replace the pen in the second pen holder position with the next pen color. The colors in the on-screen chart are different from the colors of the output since the colors of the output depend on which color you place in the pen holders.
- *Number of Copies* Enter the number of copies of the chart you want. Unless your plotter has continuous-feed paper, Harvard Graphics and the plotter pause every time you need to insert the next page or transparency.

The Plot Slide Show Options overlay box contains From slide, To slide, and Collate fields in addition to the fields that appear in the Plot Chart Options overlay box. These additional fields perform the same tasks they perform for printing a slide show.

USING A FILM RECORDER

Another option for displaying charts is slides. Several film recorders can display and record screens that you can convert to slides. Some film recorders store the screens in a file and expose the film at a later time. To output a chart to a film recorder, you must first install the film recorder according to the directions provided with it. If you are using a film recorder other than Polaroid Palette, Polaroid PalettePlus, or PTI ImageMaker, you will need to install a VDI device driver as described at the end of Appendix A. To direct output to a film recorder, select Film recorder from the Produce Output Menu. Harvard Graphics displays the Record Chart Options overlay in which you enter the number of copies you want, and then press ENTER. Harvard Graphics advances the film after it is exposed. If you selected 669 film type for the Polaroid Palette or PalettePlus, Harvard Graphics prompts you to replace the film after making each copy. After replacing the film in the camera, press ENTER to expose the next chart. If the film recorder is the Lasergraphics PFR or Matrix PCR or QCR, Harvard Graphics stores the charts in files in the directory you entered for the Slide file directory field when you selected the film recorder.

You can also use a film recorder to record a slide show. To record a slide show, select Produce output and Record slide show. The Record Show Options overlay displays the From slide, To slide, and Collate options that are available when you print a slide show to a printer.

appendix C

CHART SAMPLER

Harvard Graphics offers eight different chart types with text, pie, bar, line, area, high/low/close, organization, and multiple as the main options. Each of these major choices have numerous variations, making hundreds of possibilities. In these next few pages you will find examples of the major chart types along with a few of the variations you can add. Unless noted otherwise, the other options retain their default settings. Most of these charts are included on the supplemental disks.

Text Title Chart using the default settings

Text Title Chart after using F7 (Size/Place) to set the size to 8 for each level and setting the Top entry to Left, the Middle entry to Center, and the Bottom entry to Right

Creative Computers

Better computer service

Free software support

Free computer classes

Text Simple List with Title Size set to 9 and Detail Size set to 7. Placement was also changed to Left using F7 (Size/Place)

Creative Computers

 Better computer service

 Free software support

 Free computer classes

Text Simple List with a symbol added from the COMPUTR3.SYM file and copied

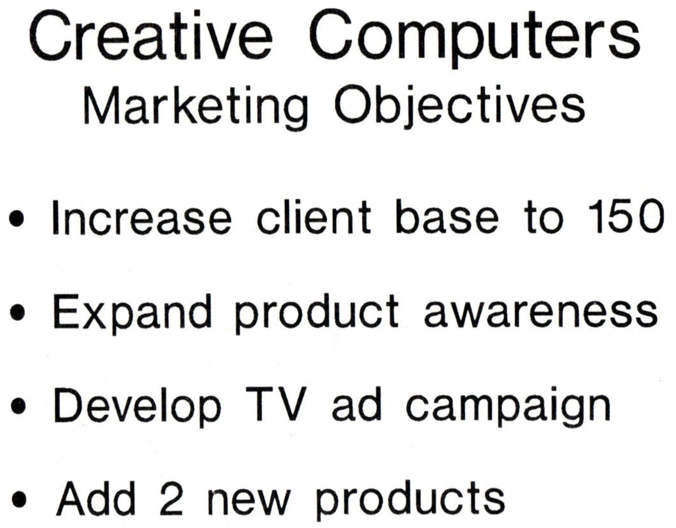

Text Bullet List using the defaults

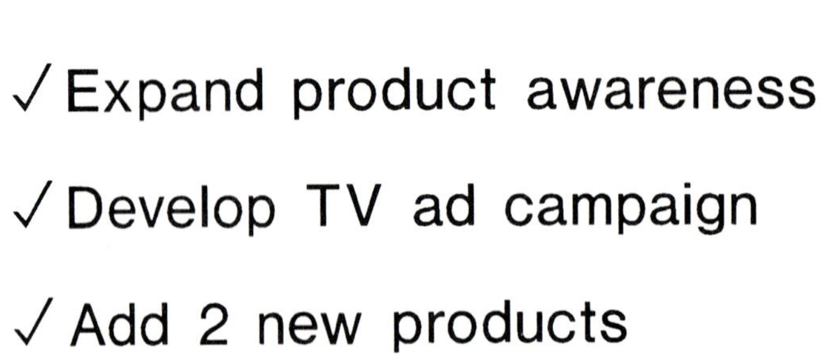

Text Bullet List using F7 (Size/Place) with bullet shape changed to check

Choosing The Right Condo

Lake View	Garden City
3 parking spaces per unit	2 parking spaces per unit
24 Hour security	Resident controlled entrances
Private patios	Community gardens
Private docks	Boat ramps

Text Two column with size 4 used for Detail entries

Finding the Right Condo

Lake View	Garden City
3 parking spaces per unit	2 parking spaces per unit
24 Hour security	Resident controlled entrances
Private patios	Community gardens
Private docks	Boat ramps

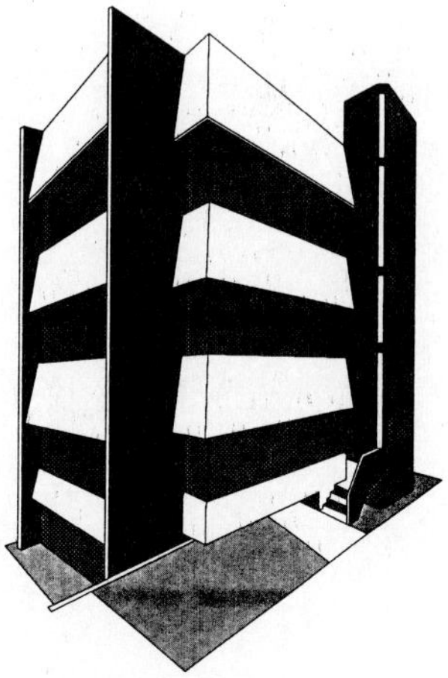

Text Two Column with title deleted, chart saved as symbol, symbol added from BUILD3.SYM to new chart, and then added chart saved as symbol

Stevens Company

Product Sales

	1989	1990
Product A	1,250	1,575
Product B	2,345	3,214
Product C	4,500	5,415
Product D	2,500	2,890

Text Three Column using defaults

Stevens Company

Product Sales

	1989	1990
Product A	1,250	1,575
Product B	2,345	3,214
Product C	4,500	5,415
Product D	2,500	2,890

Text Three Column using F8 (Options) from Main Menu to select Gothic font

Stevens Company
Product Sales

	1989	1990
Product A	1,250	1,575
Product B	2,345	3,214
Product C	4,500	5,415
Product D	2,500	2,890

Text Three Column using SHIFT-F5 (Attributes) to turn off Fill for title and subtitle

---

Steinway Parts Leads in Sales

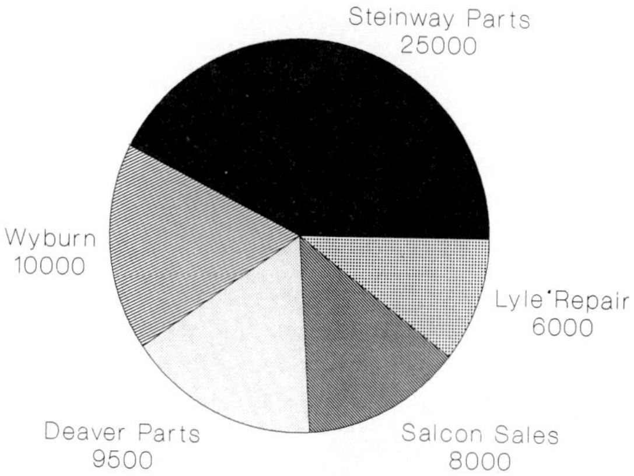

Pie chart using defaults

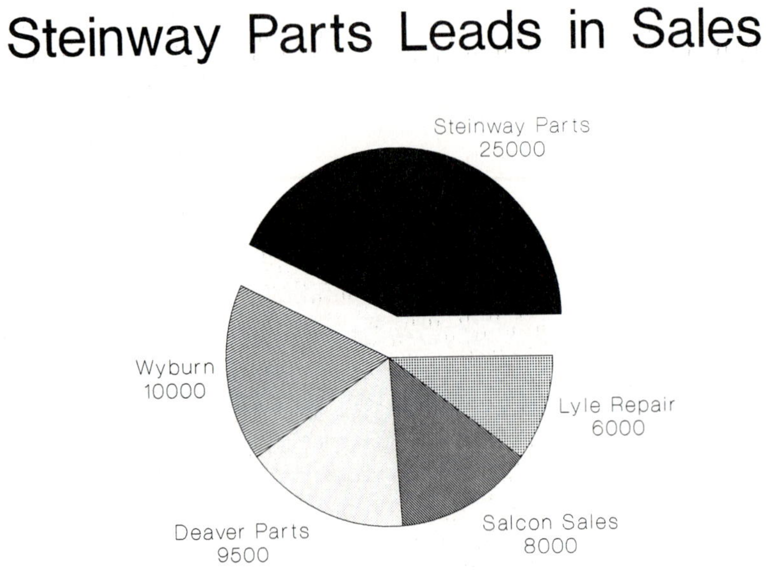

Pie Cut Slice Yes for Steinway

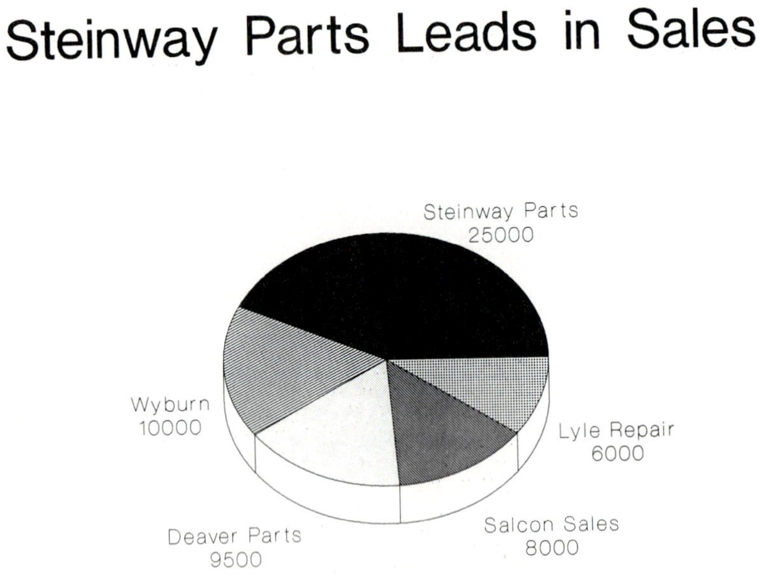

3D Pie

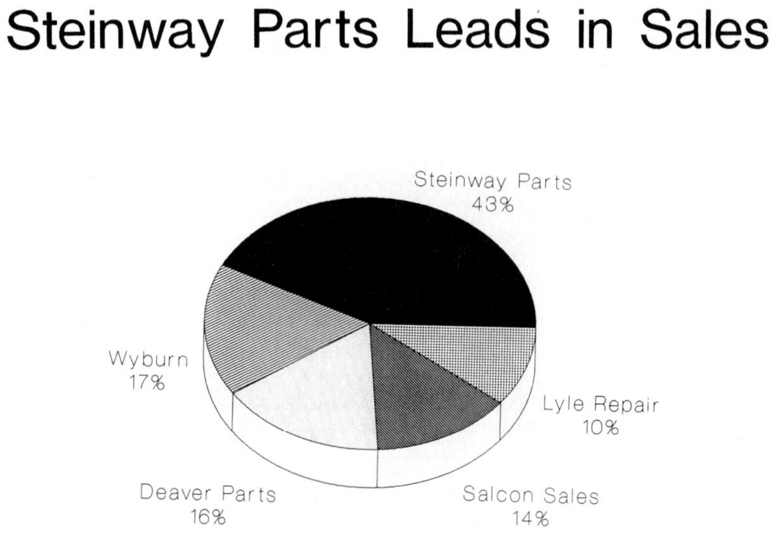

3D Pie with Show Percent Yes and Show Value No

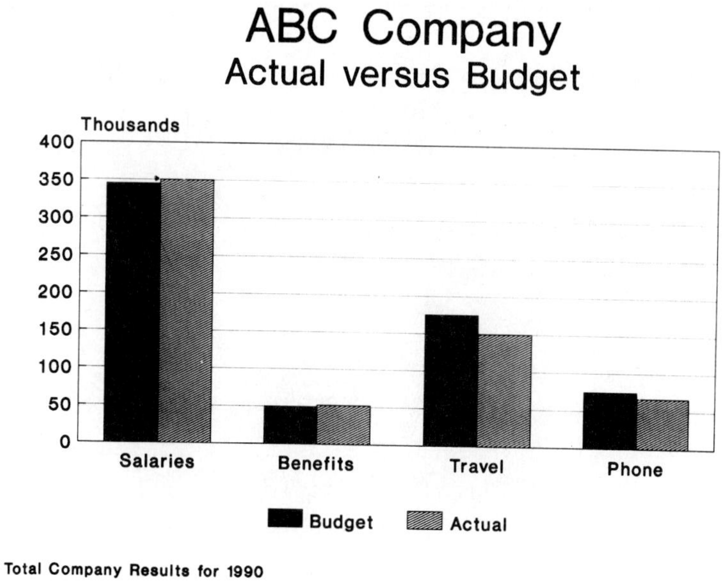

Bar chart using defaults

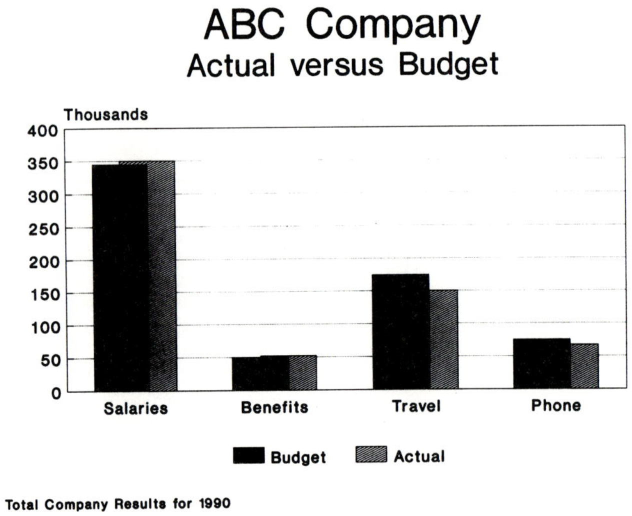

Bar chart with Overlap

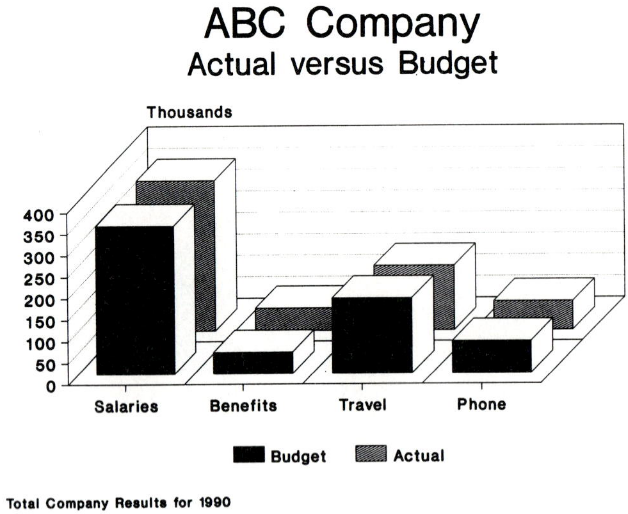

3D Bar chart with Overlap

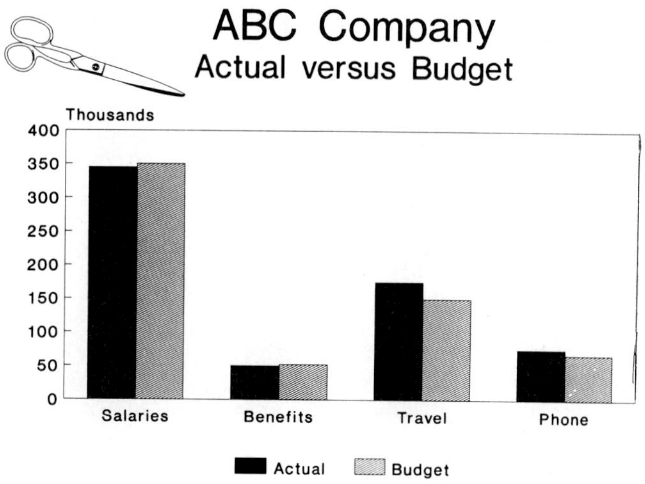

Bar chart with symbol for budget-cutting scissors added with Draw/Annotate from COMNOBJ2.SYM

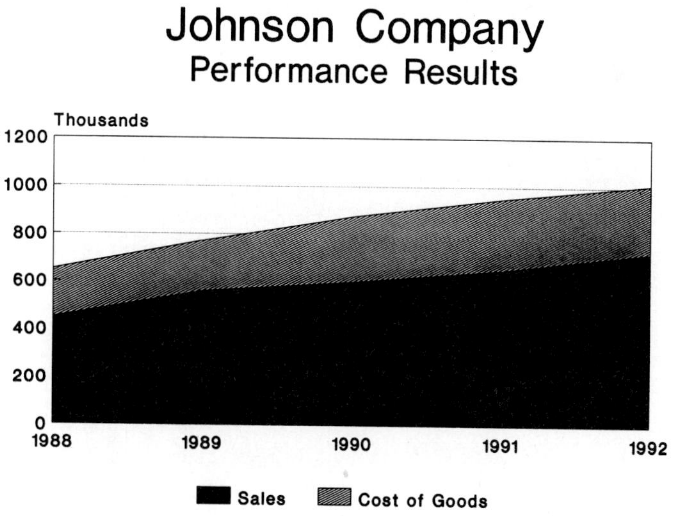

Area chart with defaults

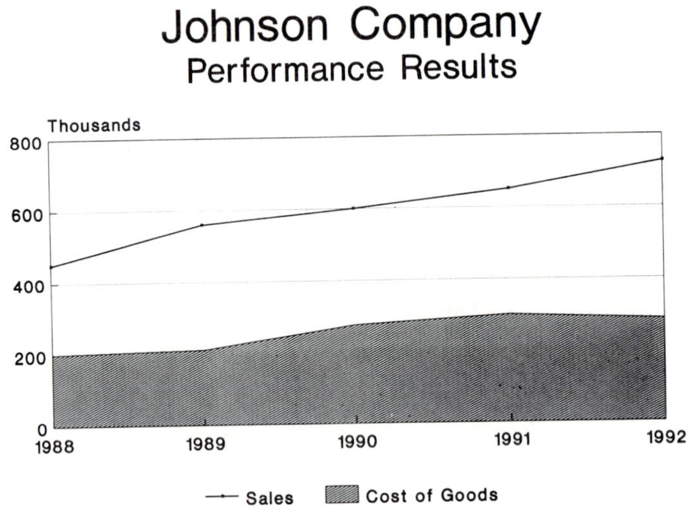

Area chart with first series shown as a line using Line Style 2 and Pattern 2 for series 2

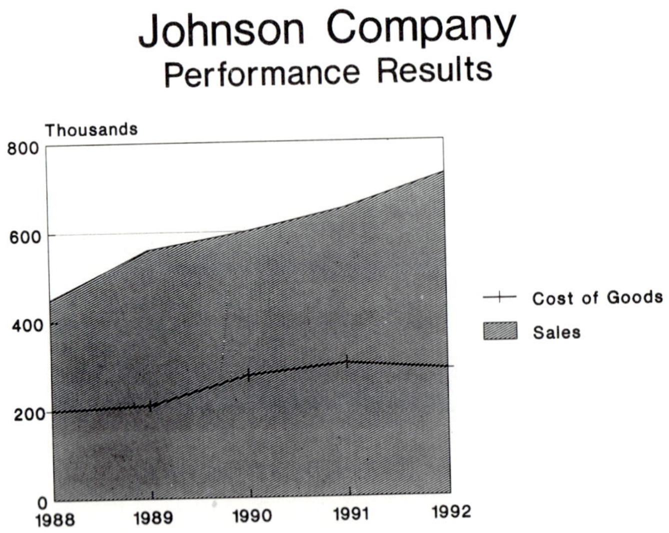

Area chart with first series shown as an area chart and second series shown as a line. Option 2 selected for both line and pattern styles. Legend moved to the right.

appendix D

SYMBOLS FILES

Harvard Graphics provides a number of symbols files that you can use to add interest to any chart. Each file contains a number of different symbols that you can select after choosing the file. This appendix provides a look at each of the symbols in these files to allow you to easily select the file you want (see Figures D-1 through D-35).

The only difference between these symbols and the ones on your screen is that some of the symbol patterns were changed slightly to provide the necessary contrast for black and white. The position of each symbol on the page mimics its position on your screen when you retrieve the file. You must move a cross-hair to the desired symbol with the keyboard or a mouse and press **ENTER** to make a selection.

FIGURE D-1. The ANIMALS.SYM file

FIGURE D-2. The ANIPLANT.SYM file

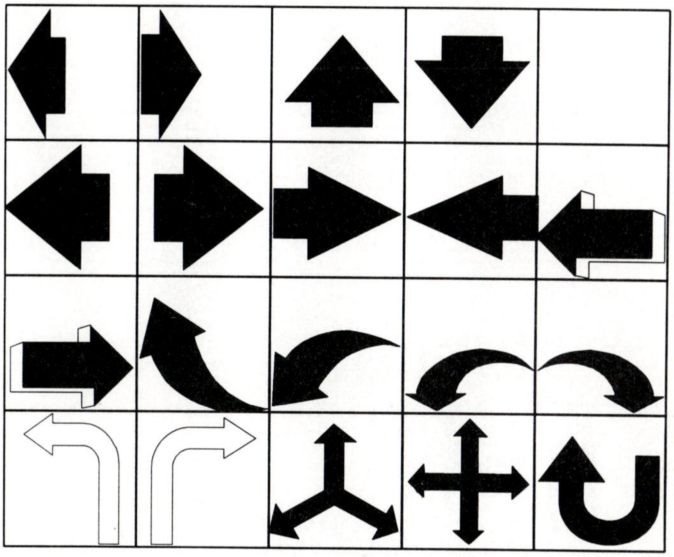

FIGURE D-3. The ARROWS2.SYM file

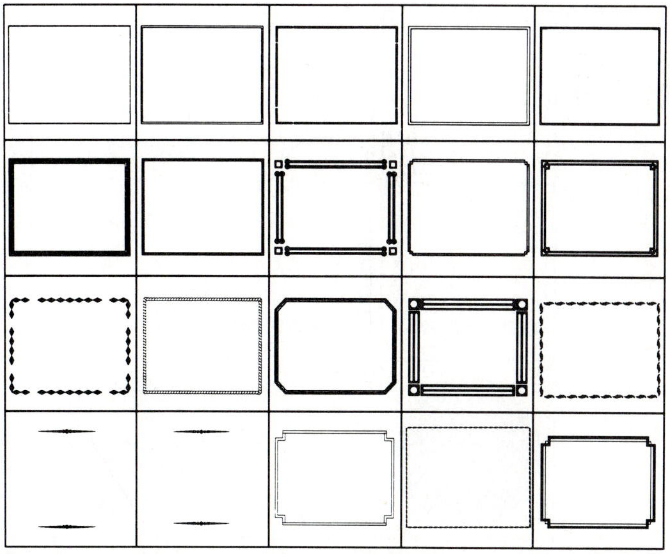

FIGURE D-4. The BORDERS.SYM file

FIGURE D-5. The BUILD3.SYM file

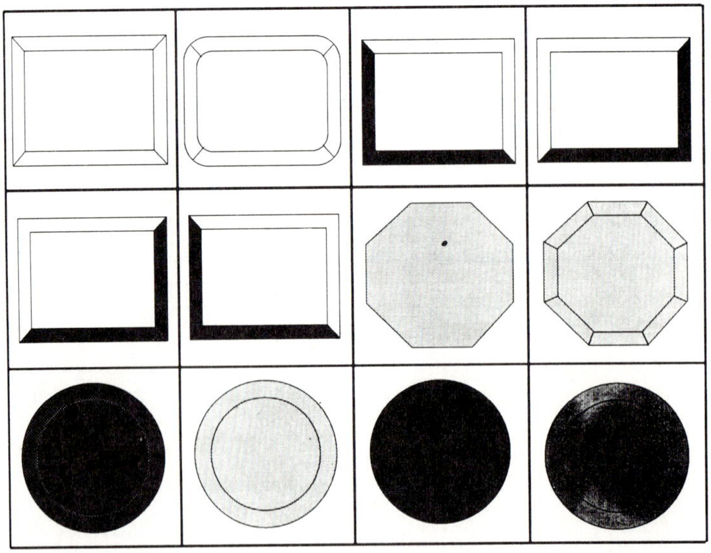

FIGURE D-6. The BUTTONS1.SYM file

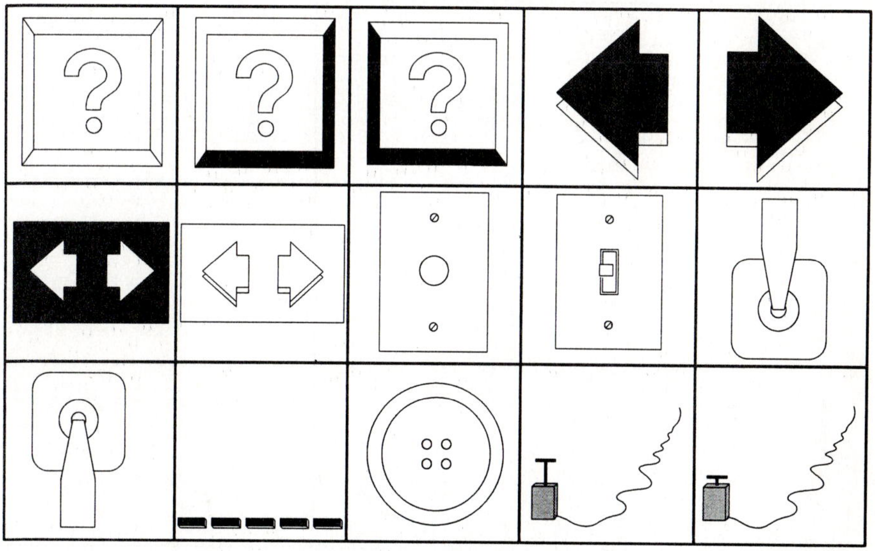

FIGURE D-7. The BUTTONS2.SYM file

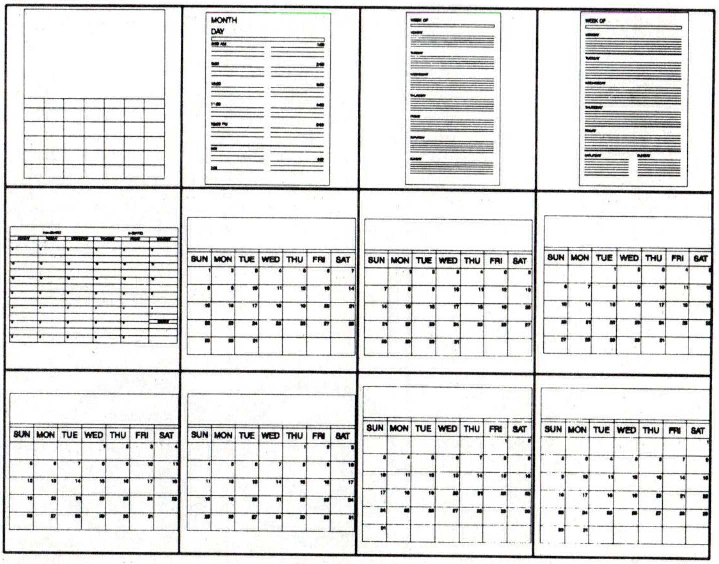

FIGURE D-8. The CALENDAR.SYM file

FIGURE D-9. The COMNOBJ1.SYM file

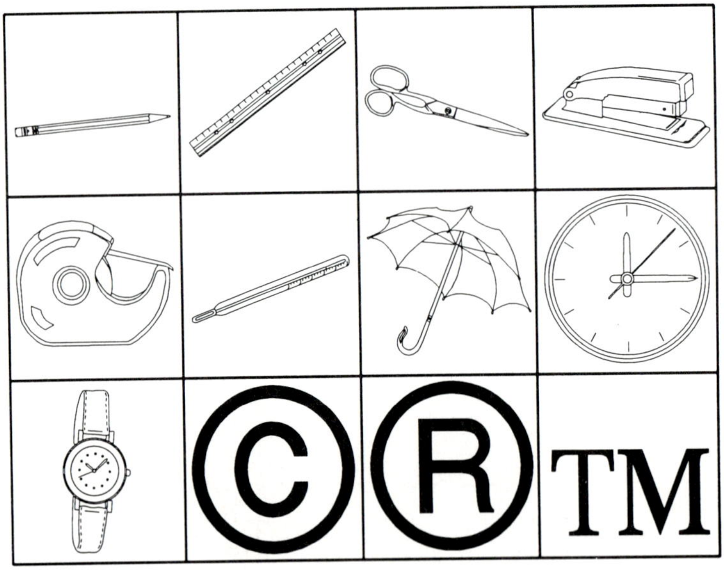

FIGURE D-10. The COMNOBJ2.SYM file

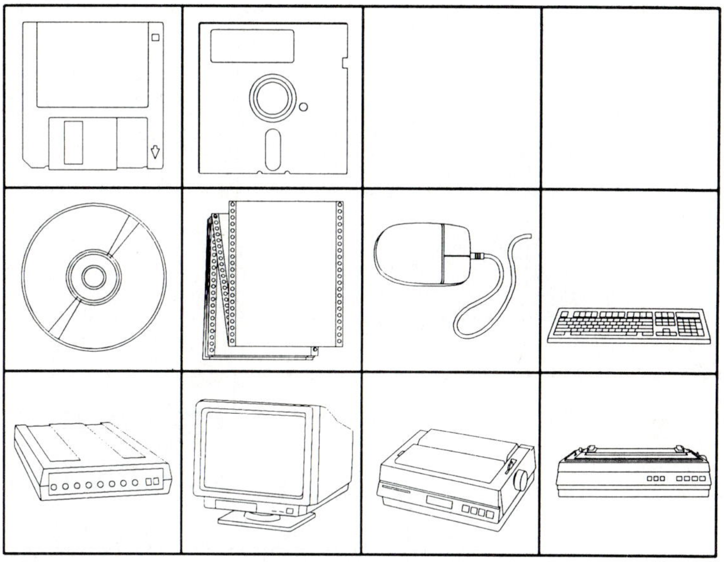

FIGURE D-11. The COMPUTR2.SYM file

FIGURE D-12. The COMPUTR3.SYM file

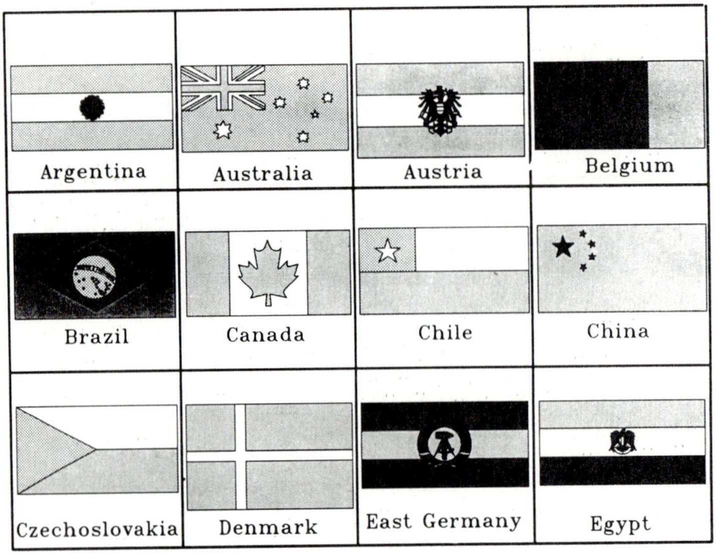

FIGURE D-13. The FLAGS1.SYM file

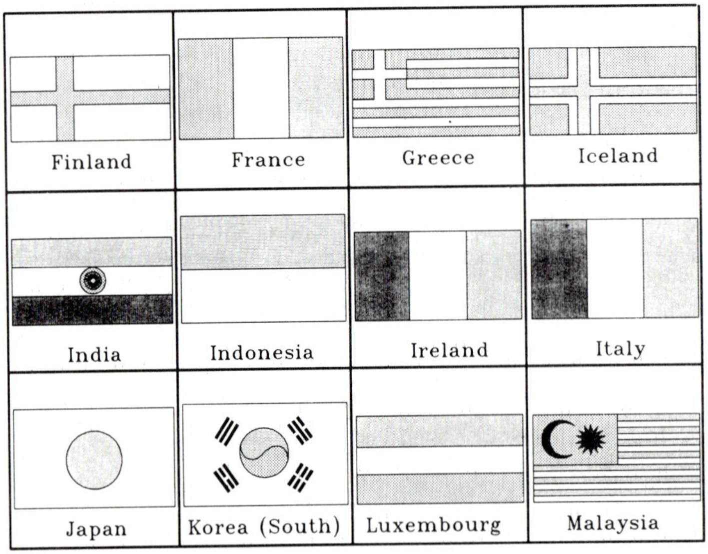

FIGURE D-14. The FLAGS2.SYM file

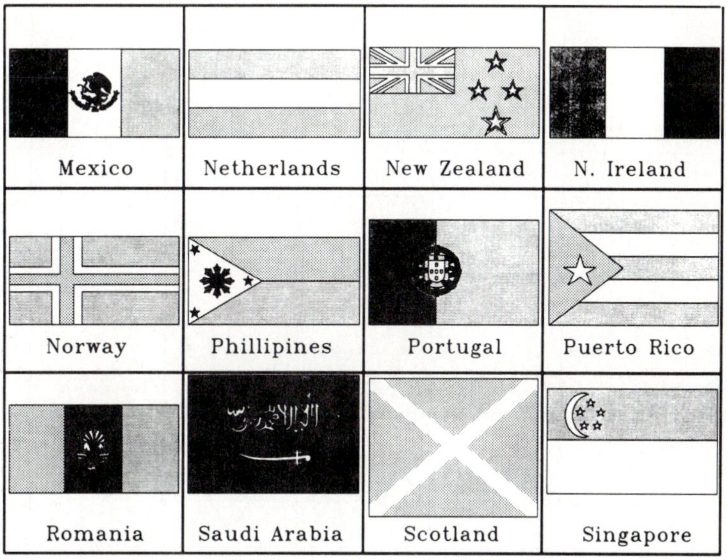

FIGURE D-15. The FLAGS3.SYM file

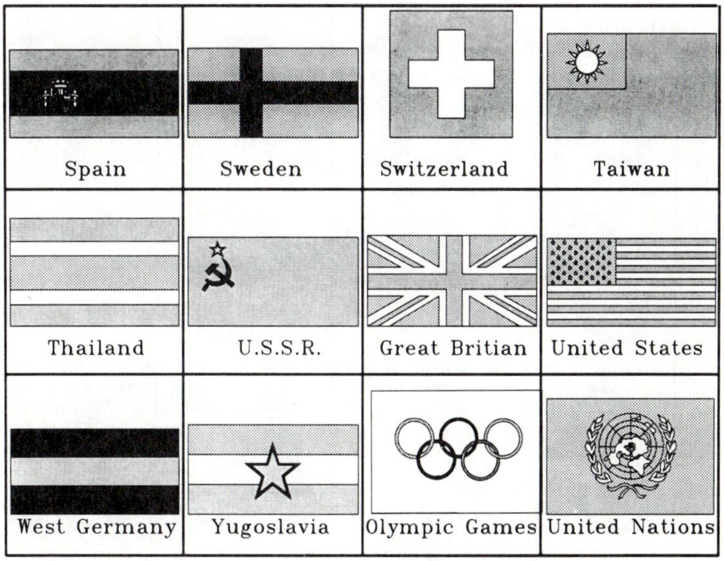

FIGURE D-16. The FLAGS4.SYM file

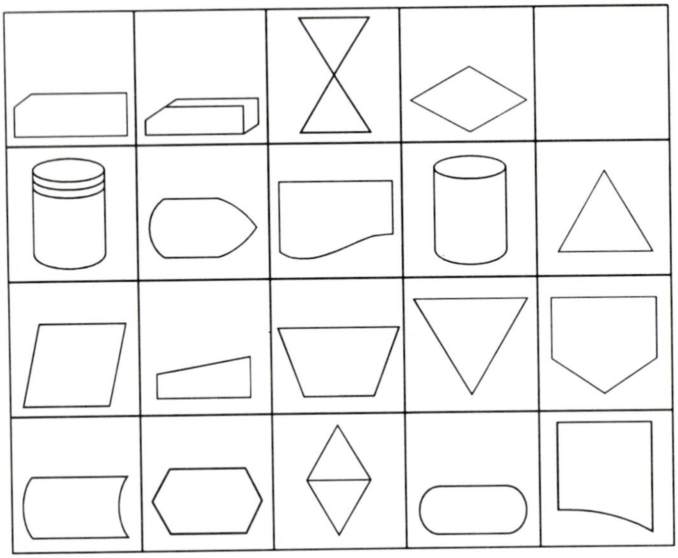

FIGURE D-17. The FLOWCHT.SYM file

FIGURE D-18. The GREEKLC1.SYM file

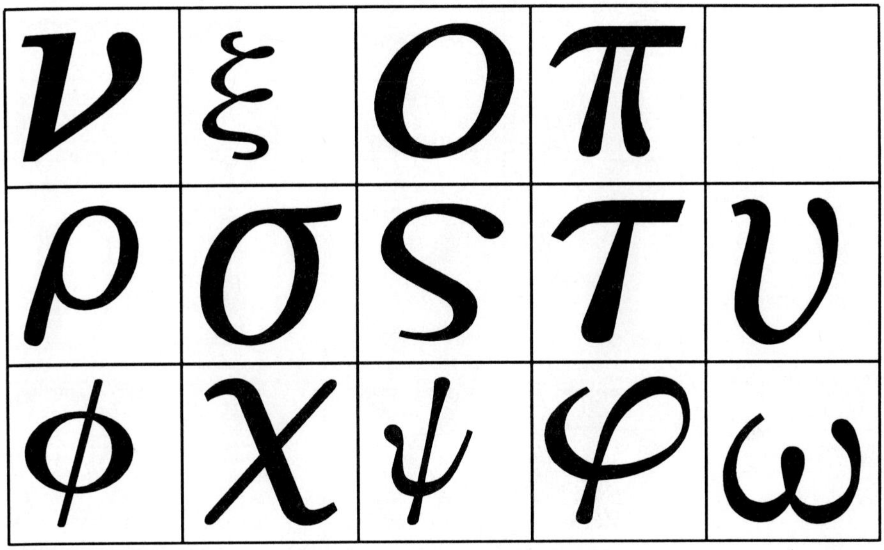

FIGURE D-19. The GREEKLC2.SYM file

FIGURE D-20. The GREEKUC1.SYM file

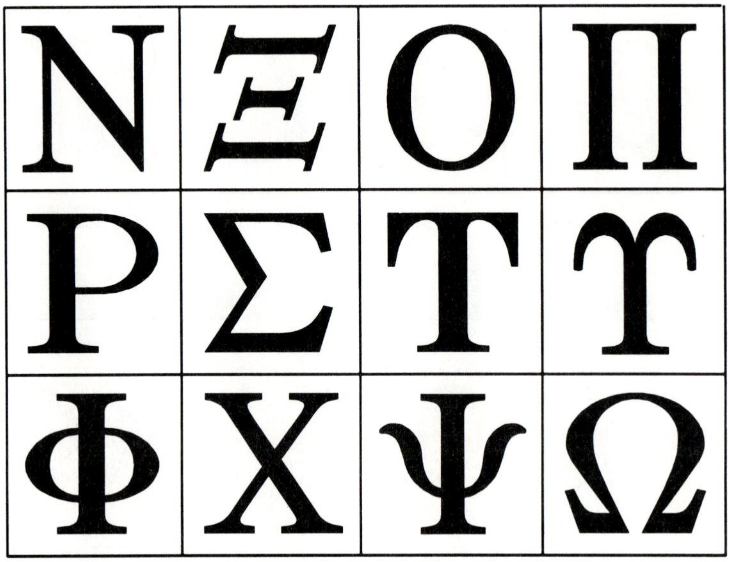

FIGURE D-21. The GREEKUC2.SYM file

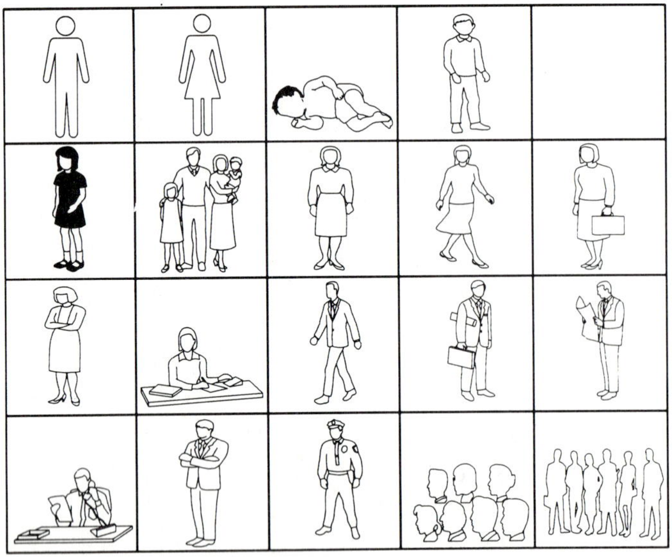

FIGURE D-22. The HUMANS4.SYM file

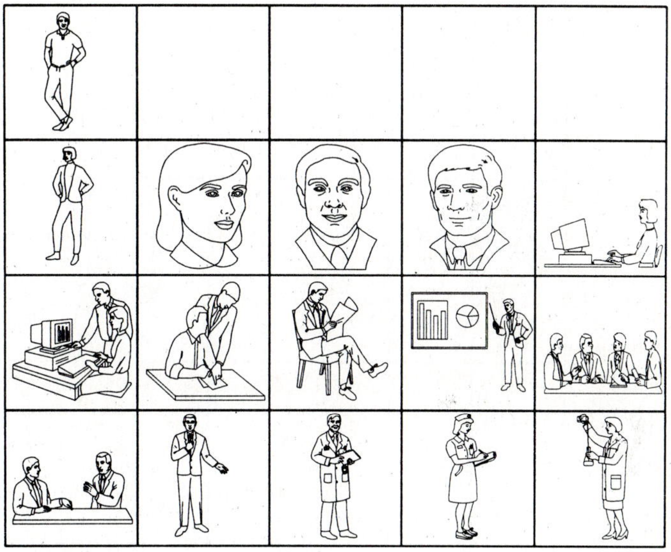

FIGURE D-23. The HUMANS5.SYM file

FIGURE D-24. The INDSTRY1.SYM file

FIGURE D-25. The INDSTRY2.SYM file

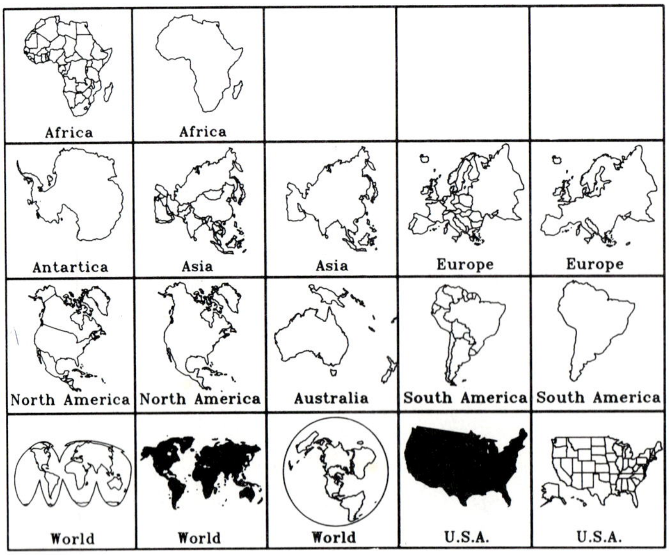

FIGURE D-26. The MAPS1.SYM file

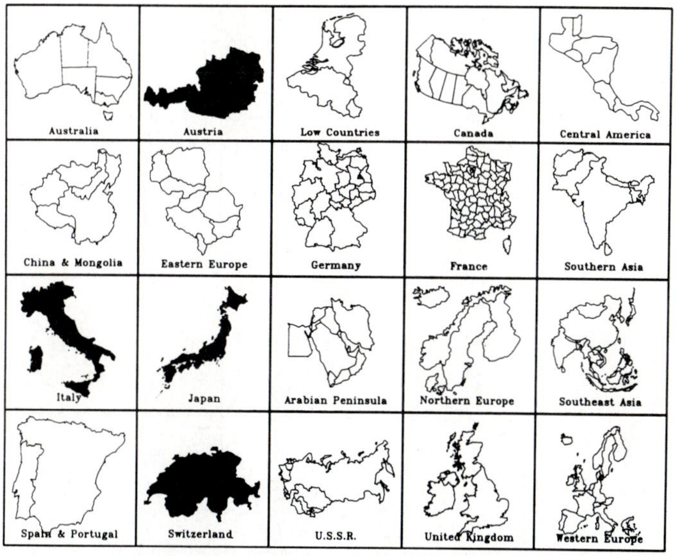

FIGURE D-27. The MAPS2.SYM file

FIGURE D-28. The MONEY.SYM file

FIGURE D-29. The OFFICE4.SYM file

FIGURE D-30. The PRESENT2.SYM file

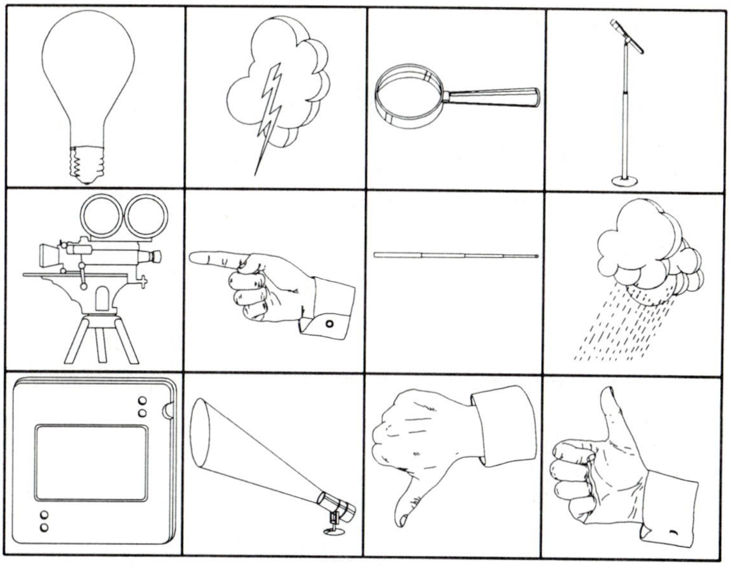

FIGURE D-31. The PRESENT3.SYM file

FIGURE D-32. The SIGNS.SYM file

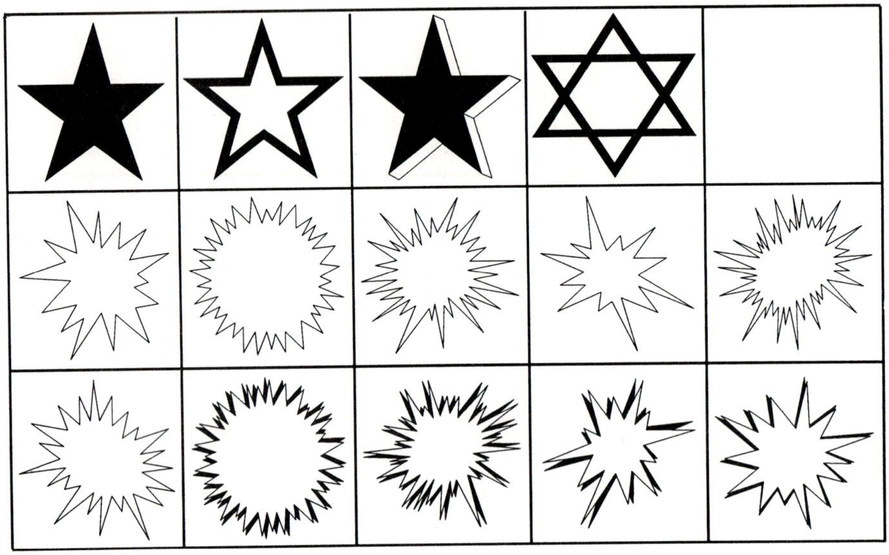

FIGURE D-33. The STARS1.SYM file

FIGURE D-34. The TRANSPT1.SYM file

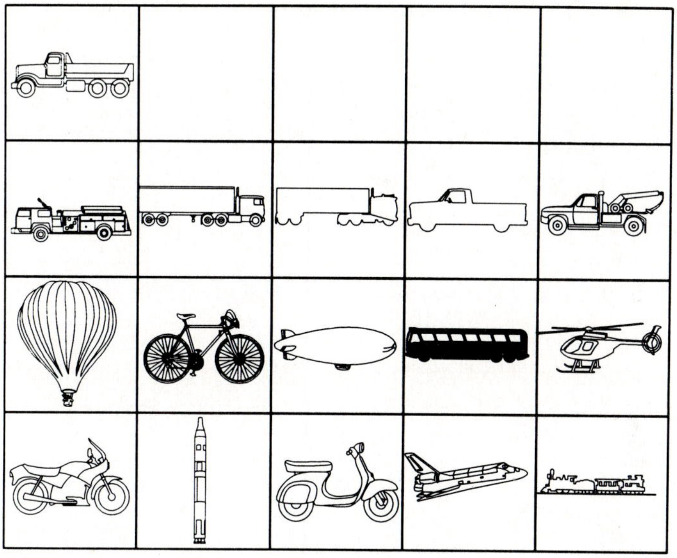

FIGURE D-35. The TRANSPT2.SYM file

INDEX

A

C

D

E

F

G

H

I

K

L

M

P

T

U

V

W

X

Y

Z

The manuscript for this book was prepared and submitted to Osborne/McGraw-Hill in electronic form. The acquisitions editor for this project was Elizabeth Fisher and the project editor was Janis Paris.

Text design by Judy Wohlfrom and Pamela Webster, using Times Roman for text body and Swiss Boldface for display.

Cover art Bay Graphics Design, Inc. Color separation by Phoenix Color Corporation. Screens produced with InSet from Inset Systems, Inc. Book printed and bound by R.R. Donnelley & Sons Company, Crawfordsville, Indiana.

Harvard Graphics 2.3 Command Card

MAIN MENU FUNCTION KEYS

Command Keys	Main Menu Options	Function
1	Create new chart	Creates a new text or analytical chart
2	Enter/Edit chart	Enters or changes chart data or other chart options
3	Draw/Annotate	Adds drawings, symbols, or text any place on a chart
4	Get/Save/Remove	Gets, saves, or removes a chart or template, or converts a chart or template file
5	Import/Export	Transfers files between programs
6	Produce output	Creates output on a printer, plotter, or film recorder
7	Slide show menu	Creates, displays, or modifies a slide show
8	Chartbook menu	Creates or edits a chartbook
9	Setup	Changes default options
E	Exit	Exits to DOS
F1	Help	Help
F2	Draw chart	Draws current chart
F3	Applications	Lists applications accessible from Harvard Graphics
F4	Spell check	Checks spelling in current chart
F7	Size/Place	Sizes and places chart on screen
F8	Options	Sets current chart options for orientation, borders, font, and palette

Harvard Graphics 2.3 Command Card

CREATING NEW CHARTS

Command Keys	Function
1 1	Creates a Text chart
1 2	Creates a Pie chart
1 3	Creates a Bar/Line chart
1 4	Creates an Area chart
1 5	Creates a High/Low/Close chart
1 6	Creates an Organization chart
1 7	Creates a Multiple chart
1 8	Creates a chart from a template by selecting a model graph in the gallery
1 9	Creates a chart by deleting data in the current chart

SETUP MENU

Command Keys	Function
9 1	Establishes default settings
9 2	Selects printer 1 from a list
9 3	Selects printer 2 from a list
9 4	Selects plotter from a list
9 5	Selects film recorder from a list
9 6	Sets screen option
9 7	Sets color palette options
9 8	Adds other programs or Harvard Graphics accessories used within Harvard Graphics

Harvard Graphics 2.3 Command Card

IMPORT/EXPORT

Command Keys	Function
5 1	Imports Lotus graph
5 2	Imports Lotus data
5 3	Imports ASCII data
5 4	Imports delimited ASCII data
5 5	Imports Excel chart
5 6	Imports Excel data
5 7	Imports CGM metafile
5 8	Exports current chart as a picture file in Professional Write, HPGL, or encapsulated PostScript format
5 9	Exports CGM metafile

PRODUCING CHART OUTPUT

6 1	Prints current chart
6 2	Plots current chart on plotter
6 3	Sends current chart to film recorder
6 4	Prints the data for current chart
6 5	Prints slides in current slide show
6 6	Plots charts in current slide show
6 7	Records charts in current slide show on a film recorder

Harvard Graphics 2.3 Command Card

PRODUCING CHART OUTPUT (cont.)

Command Keys	Function
6 8	Prints practice cards you create for slide show notes
6 9	Prints list of charts in a slide show

SLIDE SHOW MENU

Command Keys	Function
7 1	Creates new slide show
7 2	Edits existing slide show
7 3	Adds ScreenShow effects for transitions
7 4	Displays ScreenShow
7 5	Creates practice cards for notes
7 6	Makes slide show active

CHARTBOOK MENU

Command Keys	Function
8 1	Creates new chartbook
8 2	Edits existing chartbook
8 3	Makes chartbook active
8 4	Creates a chart from template in a chartbook

Harvard Graphics 2.3 Command Card

DRAW FEATURES

Command Keys	Function
3 1	Adds boxes, lines, text, circles, polygons, polylines and buttons to the chart
3 2	Moves or changes size or characteristics of objects on chart
3 3	Copies objects to other parts of chart
3 4	Deletes one or more objects on chart
3 5	Displays alignment grid on screen for laying out objects
3 6	Adds a predrawn symbol to screen from one of Harvard Graphics' symbol libraries or from your own files
F2	Previews chart with drawing additions
F4	Redraws chart
F8	Displays options

GET/SAVE/REMOVE

Command Keys	Function
4 1	Gets chart file
4 2	Saves chart in a file
4 3	Gets template file
4 4	Saves current chart as a template file
4 5	Removes file from disk
4 6	Saves chart as a symbol
F3	Changes the current directory

Harvard Graphics 2.3 Command Card

EDITING CHARTS

After selecting [2], Enter/Edit chart, there are no further menu options although there are a number of function keys to help with your task.

[F1]	Help	Displays help for current options
[F2]	Draw chart	Draws chart on screen
[F3]	Save	Saves chart
[F4]	Draw/Annot	Displays chart in Draw/Annotate screen
[F2]	Attributes	Displays attributes for graph text
[F6]	Colors	Displays choices for color or other options
[F7]	Size/Place	Displays overlay to select text size and alignment
[F8]	Options	Displays an options screen or redisplays data after invoking options
[F9]	More series	Displays additional series when one of the data forms is displayed
[F10]	Continue	Saves current settings and continues

Science You Can't See

by Suzanna Loper

SEEDS OF SCIENCE ROOTS OF READING®

Published and Distributed by
Delta Education
...because children learn by doing.®
A member of School Specialty Science

Published and Distributed by

Delta Education
...because children learn by doing.®

A member of School Specialty Science

These materials are based upon work partially supported by the National Science Foundation under grant numbers ESI-0242733 and ESI-0628272. The Federal Government has certain rights in this material. Any opinions, findings, and conclusions or recommendations expressed in this material are those of the author(s) and do not necessarily reflect the views of the National Science Foundation.

Developed at Lawrence Hall of Science and the Graduate School of Education at the University of California at Berkeley

Seeds of Science/Roots of Reading® is a collaboration of a science team led by Jacqueline Barber and a literacy team led by P. David Pearson and Gina Cervetti.

Delta Education LLC
PO Box 3000
Nashua, NH 03061
1-800-258-1302
www.deltaeducation.com

Science You Can't See
594-0075
ISBN: 978-1-59821-549-6
Printing 2 – 7/2011
Standard Printing Company, Canton, OH

Contents

Out of Sight

Many scientists gather evidence by observing with their own eyes.

They may study mice, moons, or **molecules**, but all scientists are alike in one way. They all use **evidence** to answer questions. Scientists don't just guess what the answer might be. They find evidence and figure out an answer that fits the evidence.

One good way to find evidence about something is to **observe** it directly—for example, by touching it or looking at it.

But what about scientists who study things that *can't* be seen or touched? These things may be too small or too hard to reach or too far away to observe directly. These scientists still need evidence to answer their questions. How is it possible to find evidence about something you can't see?

To study things they can't observe directly, scientists make **inferences**. An inference is something you figure out based on evidence. For example, picture yourself opening your lunch bag and taking out an apple. A hunk of the apple is missing. There are scrapes on the apple that look as if they were made by teeth. You could make the inference that someone opened your lunch bag and took a bite of your apple. You didn't directly observe anyone biting the apple, but you have plenty of evidence to show that it happened.

What inference could you make about what happened to this apple?

We Can't See a *Tyrannosaurus rex*

You may have watched movies about *Tyrannosaurus rex* dinosaurs or seen pictures of them in books. But nobody has seen a live *T. rex* walking around because they have all been dead for millions of years. Still, scientists would like to know more about these dinosaurs. What did they look like? How and what did they eat? What was the world around them like?

An artist created this picture to show how a *Tyrannosaurus rex* may have hunted.

These are fossil bones of a *Tyrannosaurus rex*.

Scientists can't watch a *T. rex* hunting for food or eating. How can scientists answer their questions about *T. rex* when they can't observe these dinosaurs? Scientists use **fossils** to try to answer questions about dinosaurs. Everyone knows about fossil bones, but fossils can also be formed from leaves, footprints, and other things left behind by animals and plants. Fossils are evidence about what living things were like long ago.

Karen Chin studies dinosaurs.

Karen Chin is a scientist who asks: How and what did dinosaurs eat? She studies **coprolites**, which are fossil droppings. The dinosaurs may be gone, but they left their droppings behind. Inside the droppings were bits of the plants and animals that dinosaurs ate. Some of these bits remain inside coprolites today. By observing coprolites, Chin can find evidence about what dinosaurs ate and what the world around them was like.

This is a fossil dinosaur dropping.

Chin studied a huge coprolite found in Canada. She measured the size of the coprolite and cut it open to find out what was inside. She observed that the coprolite contained the crushed bones of a young dinosaur. Because the coprolite was so big, and because it contained dinosaur bones, Chin was able to **infer** that it must have come from a *T. rex*, the only large meat-eating dinosaur known to have lived in that area of Canada. By observing the coprolite, Chin got evidence about what the *T. rex* ate and how it chewed and digested its food.

Every piece of dinosaur evidence is part of the puzzle.

Even though Chin will never see a live *T. rex*, she can make inferences about what these dinosaurs were like, based on the evidence she finds. Other scientists find evidence about dinosaurs and make inferences, too. The members of the **scientific community** share their inferences with one another and work together to find out all they can.

"It's like putting together a huge puzzle," says Chin. "Bones are big pieces of the puzzle, but coprolites give us more key evidence. We'll never finish the puzzle, but as we keep fitting in more and more pieces, our picture of dinosaurs gets better and better."

We Can't See the Deep Ocean Floor

Scientists know more about the surface of the planet Mars than they do about some parts of the Earth's ocean floor! In most parts of the ocean, the water is so deep that you can't see the ocean floor from a boat on the surface. Many parts of the ocean floor are too deep for scientists to visit, even in a submarine. But knowing about the ocean floor is important for understanding life in the ocean. How can scientists get evidence about the ocean floor when it is so hard to observe directly?

Edward Saade (SAHD-ee) is a scientist who studies the ocean floor. Saade asks questions like these: How deep is the ocean floor in different places? Is it sandy or rocky? Where in the ocean are fish and other animals most likely to live?

Edward Saade studies the deep ocean floor.

Saade used a tool called an **echo sounder** to make maps of a big area of the ocean floor near the coast of California. He traveled across the surface of the ocean in a boat. The echo sounder sent out sound waves as the boat moved along. The sound waves traveled through the water and bounced off the ocean floor.

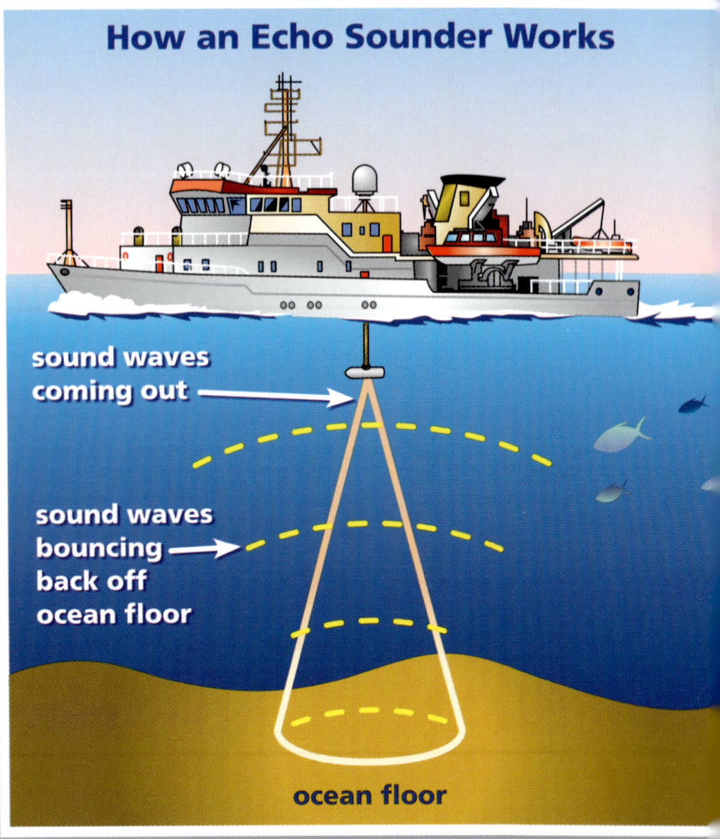

Saade's echo sounder measured how long it took for the sound waves to bounce back to the boat. The longer the sound waves took, the farther away the ocean floor was. Based on this evidence, Saade was able to infer how deep the ocean was in different places. He made maps that showed his inferences about what the ocean floor was like.

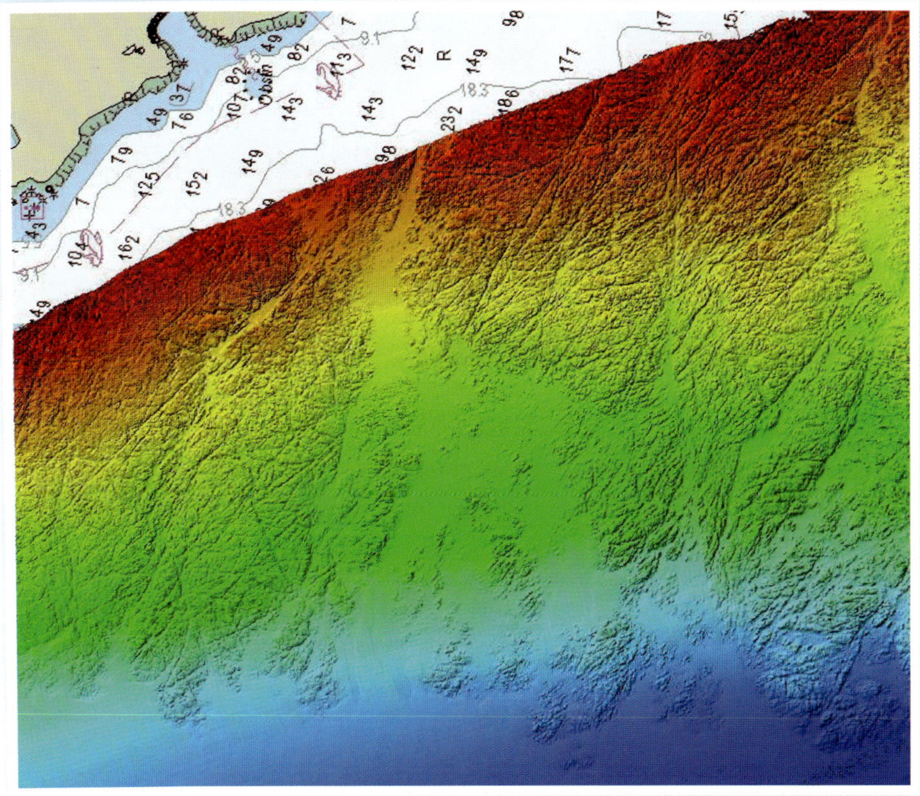

The colorful part of the map shows the inferences that Saade made about the depth of the ocean floor. Each color stands for a different depth. The dark blue part is the deepest, and the red part is the shallowest.

Saade doesn't work alone—he is part of the scientific community. Saade worked with scientists who collected other evidence about the ocean, such as the **temperature** of the ocean in different places. Saade and the other scientists put the different kinds of evidence together into a computer **model**. The computer model used all this evidence about the ocean to make predictions about where fish might live.

These animals live on the ocean floor. Different parts of the ocean floor are home to very different fish and other living things.

Scientists checked these predictions by going diving in a few places and directly observing the fish living there. These **observations** helped the scientists **evaluate** their computer model. When the scientists' observations of fish living near the ocean floor matched the model for those places, the scientists knew their computer model was **accurate**.

Saade's maps of the ocean floor help the scientific community learn more about life in the ocean. Saade enjoys studying the hidden secrets of the ocean floor. He says, "You get to discover parts of the world that nobody knew about before."

We Can't See Atoms and Molecules

Atoms and molecules are so tiny that scientists can't observe them directly. How did scientists figure out that atoms and molecules existed if they couldn't see them?

More than 200 years ago, scientists began to find evidence that the world was made of atoms and molecules. For example, scientists discovered that water could be changed into hydrogen **gas** and oxygen gas. This evidence helped the scientific community figure out that water is made of molecules that are formed of hydrogen atoms and oxygen atoms.

Antoine-Laurent Lavoisier was a scientist in the 1700s. He split water molecules into hydrogen atoms and oxygen atoms.

This is a model of a water molecule. The red ball represents an oxygen atom, and the white balls represent hydrogen atoms. The sticks represent how the atoms are joined together.

Over time, the scientific community found more and more evidence of atoms and molecules. Based on this evidence, scientists made models of atoms and molecules. The scientists evaluated their models carefully. Whenever they found new evidence about atoms and molecules, they would check to see if their models matched the new evidence. If the models didn't match the evidence, they changed the models.

Farid El Gabaly studies atoms. The machine next to him is a special microscope.

It's still impossible to see atoms and molecules, but scientists have many ways to find evidence about them. Farid El Gabaly (fah-REED el gah-bah-LEE) is a scientist who studies atoms. He is interested in **magnetic** atoms. One of El Gabaly's questions is this: What **patterns** do magnetic atoms form in very, very small pieces of metal?

El Gabaly uses a special kind of **microscope** that sends out beams of **electrons**, which are even tinier than atoms. The electrons bounce off magnetic atoms and bounce back to a computer. The electrons won't bounce off atoms that are not magnetic. Based on what bounces back, the computer makes a picture showing how the magnetic atoms are arranged.

These are pieces of cobalt. The ones that El Gabaly uses are much, much tinier than these.

El Gabaly used his microscope to study a metal called cobalt. He knew that cobalt was magnetic, but he didn't know how the magnetic atoms were arranged. He used his microscope to find out.

The microscope sent beams of electrons at a tiny piece of cobalt. The electrons bounced back to a computer, which made the picture below. The white spots show areas where electrons bounced off cobalt atoms, and the gray spots show areas where electrons didn't bounce back.

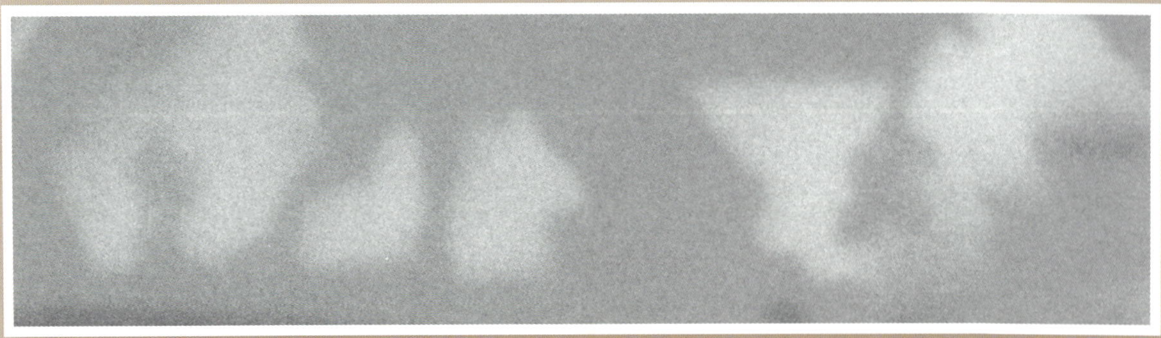

Farid El Gabaly made this image with a special microscope. The picture shows patterns of atoms in a very tiny piece of metal.

El Gabaly knew that the electrons only bounced back from places where the cobalt atoms were magnetic. Based on his evidence, he inferred that magnetic atoms in cobalt form a pattern where they clump together in groups.

Knowing more about the patterns that magnetic atoms form could help scientists make tiny computer parts. With these parts, people could make smaller, faster, and better computers.

El Gabaly says it is very exciting to make images of something that is too small to see. For scientists, atoms are like tiny new worlds to discover!

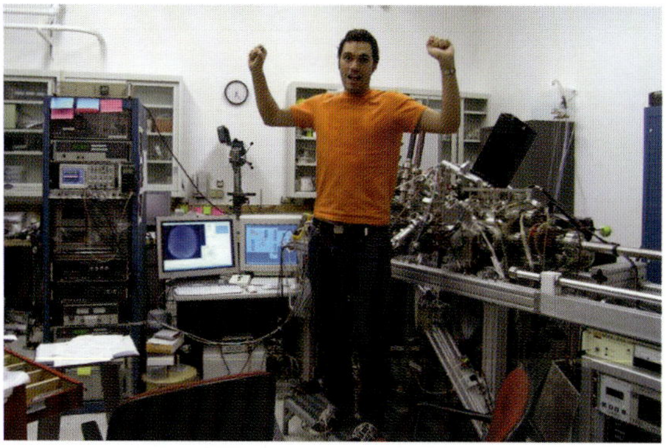

Some scientists study things that are too deep, too hot, too far, too old, too fast, or too small to look at or measure. But these scientists don't just guess what the things they're studying might be like. They need evidence! These scientists all find ways to get evidence about things they will never see or touch directly.

Space scientists have to make lots of inferences about stars, planets, and galaxies that are too far away to observe directly.

Glossary

accurate: correct or right

atom: a tiny piece of matter that is too small to see

coprolite: a fossil animal dropping

echo sounder: a tool that bounces sound waves off the ocean floor to help scientists figure out how deep the ocean floor is

electron: a tiny piece of matter that is even smaller than an atom

evaluate: to judge how useful or accurate something is

evidence: clues that help explain something or answer a question

fossil: evidence of life from the past, such as fossil bones, footprints, or leaf prints

gas: matter that doesn't hold its shape, spreads out in all directions, and is usually invisible

infer: to figure something out based on evidence

inference: something you figure out based on evidence

magnetic: having to do with the push or pull between two magnets or the pull of a magnet on some kinds of metal

microscope: a tool that helps people see very small things or make images of very small things

model: an object, a diagram, or a computer program that helps us understand something by making it simpler or easier to see

molecule: a group of atoms joined together in a particular way

observation: information that you gather with any of your five senses

observe: to use any of the five senses to gather information about something

pattern: something that repeats or happens in a predictable way

scientific community: scientists around the world who share ways of thinking

temperature: how hot or cold something is